THE
INTERNATIONA
ecotourisi
SOCIETY

SUSTAINABLE TOURISM & THE MILLENNIUM DEVELOPMENT GOALS

Effecting Positive Change

Edited by

Dr. Kelly S. Bricker
Associate Professor, Department of Parks, Recreation, and Tourism
University of Utah
Salt Lake City, Utah
United States of America

Dr. Rosemary Black
Senior Lecturer, School of Environmental Sciences
Charles Sturt University
Albury, New South Wales
Australia

Dr. Stuart Cottrell
Associate Professor, Human Dimensions of Natural Resources
Colorado State University
Fort Collins, Colorado
United States of America

JONES & BARTLETT
LEARNING

World Headquarters
Jones & Bartlett Learning
5 Wall Street
Burlington, MA 01803
978-443-5000
info@jblearning.com
www.jblearning.com

Jones & Bartlett Learning books and products are available through most bookstores and online booksellers. To contact Jones & Bartlett Learning directly, call 800-832-0034, fax 978-443-8000, or visit our website, www.jblearning.com.

Production Credits
Publisher: Cathleen Sether
Executive Editor: Shoshanna Goldberg
Associate Acquisitions Editor: Megan R. Turner
Editorial Assistant: Agnes Burt
Production Editor: Jessica Steele Newfell
Senior Marketing Manager: Jennifer Stiles
VP, Manufacturing and Inventory Control: Therese Connell
Composition: CAE Solutions Corp.
Cover and Title Page Design: Kristin E. Parker
Rights & Photo Research Associate: Amy Rathburn
Rights & Photo Research Assistant: Joseph Veiga
Cover Image: © worradirek/ShutterStock, Inc.
Printing and Binding: Edwards Brothers Malloy
Cover Printing: Edwards Brothers Malloy

Library of Congress Cataloging-in-Publication Data
Sustainable tourism and the millennium development goals : effecting positive change / edited by
    Kelly S. Bricker, Rosemary Black, Stuart Cottrell.
      p. cm.
    Includes bibliographical references and index.
    ISBN 978-1-4496-2823-9 (pbk. : alk. paper)
    1. Sustainable tourism. 2. Ecotourism. I. Bricker, Kelly S. II. Black, Rosemary. III. Cottrell, Stuart.
    G156.5.S87S88 2012
    338.4'791—dc23   2012010368

6048

Printed in the United States of America
16 15 14 13 12   10 9 8 7 6 5 4 3 2 1

To my parents, Charles and Annette Aschenbrenner, who set the example to help others in need, value diversity, play fair, and explore wild places, and for instilling an intense appreciation for our planet's amazing biodiversity; and to my husband, Nathan, for his love and for continuing to inspire a life filled with wonderful adventure.

—Kelly Bricker

To my parents, John and Dorothy Black, for instilling in me a strong sense of social justice, fairness, and compassion for all.

—Rosemary Black

To my parents, Richard and June Cottrell, who helped me appreciate the beauty and wonders of the environment in my own backyards; and to my wife, Jana Raadik-Cottrell, who has instilled in me the sense to enjoy the simple pleasures of each and every day.

—Stuart Cottrell

BRIEF CONTENTS

CONTENTS

SECTION I — Introduction to Ecotourism, Sustainable Tourism, and the Millennium Development Goals

SECTION VI   Developing Partnerships

SECTION VII Conclusions

Ecotourism: From Small Beginnings to Global Influence

David Western, African Conservation Centre, Nairobi, Kenya

The modern traveler has spawned a multi-trillion-dollar industry with a global reach and impact that can lift entire nations out of poverty or cause social and environmental havoc. The global travel industry emerged during the 20th century; rising wealth and disposable incomes in the West and the abundance of cheap oil heralded long-haul flights and mass tourism. The wholesaling of culture and nature saw cruise ships and minibus safaris invade remote places, disrupt cultures, and despoil the wilds. Despite its downside, global tourism was viewed as an economic boon to poor nations and a boost to natural heritage and nature conservation.

Even as tourism grew to the largest economic transfer of wealth from north to south, the World Bank and many donors took tourism off their development agendas in the 1980s because of its crass image and poor record in bringing equitable and sustainable development. The withdrawal coincided with a counter-trend in tourism, driven by discriminating and concerned tourists bent on avoiding crowds, doing well by the local communities, and preserving the wilds. This new sensibility was driven in part by environmental and political protest movements of the 1960s and by the growing ranks of young travelers. The nascent niche market for the concerned traveler had no clear philosophy to distinguish it from mass market travel. Ecotourism was still an ideal about leaving the people and places better off and feeling good about doing so. It had no name, no forum, and no agenda for improving the image and impact of tourism.

What gave voice and reason to ecotourism was the growing global consensus over the state of the planet, unsustainable development, and disappearing nature, leading to the World Commission on Environment and Development in 1984 and the Earth Summit of 1992. The two summits put sustainable development and biodiversity based on justice and security firmly on the global agenda. Global tourism came under scrutiny for its lack of social and environmental good.

Megan Epler Wood was a filmmaker and traveler deeply concerned about the global impact of tourism. In 1990 she came to Amboseli to interview me for a television documentary on the community-based conservation approach we were developing for wildlife tourism in Kenya. We were out filming a throng of minibuses churning up the friable dust around a herd of elephants in the morning. In the afternoon we talked to Maasai pastoralists about a new tourist campsite they had set up outside the park for the more discerning visitors. Side by side were the two faces of Kenya's tourism, one cutting up Amboseli, harassing cheetahs, and excluding the traditional occupants from their prime lands in the interest of wildlife and tourism, the other easy on the environment and beneficial to the Maasai.

Megan asked if I thought these tentative steps towards ecologically and socially responsible tourism in Amboseli would succeed against cheap minibus safaris bent on the Big Five and a pit stop at a cultural village. I told Megan that I was hopeful, but we needed to have a strong case to convince the industry and the government. That evening, off camera, Megan broached another question. Would I help her launch the Ecotourism Society as the board president? I was surprised at her request and dubious that we could pull it off, but I hadn't reckoned with Megan's fervor or the caliber of the board members.

The atmosphere at the first board meeting in Washington, DC, was infectious. We sensed that tourism was at a watershed, up against the behemoth of globalization but with the rising winds of environmentalism, democratization, and community-based conservation blowing at our backs. Shortly afterwards, at an Airlie House retreat in Virginia, we laid out the first charter of the Ecotourism Society (now The International Ecotourism Society, or TIES).

The hardest challenge facing TIES was to give ecotourism a clear and succinct definition. We came up with several versions, but eventually settled on "responsible travel to natural areas that conserves the environment and improves the well-being of local people." Foremost, the definition captured the traveler's concern for the places and peoples visited. Well-being was chosen carefully to avoid the mass market's preoccupation with income to the exclusion of social and environmental values. Communities should decide for themselves what was in their interests.

The Achilles heel of ecotourism at its inception was its misplaced hope that a good conscience and sound science could save nature by bringing benefits to local communities. Ecotourists were far too few to save a patch of forest from loggers and ranchers, let alone the Amazon. And in reality, a few well-meaning visitors could do more harm on foot by transmitting a virus to a mountain gorilla than could an indifferent hoard of minibus tourists crowded around a lion. Ecotourism fees were a pittance compared to mass tourism—far too small to alleviate poverty, build schools and health clinics, and tackle political marginalization. Mass tourism had far more potential than ecotourism to change the world for the better—if it adopted the ideals and standards that ecotourism stood for.

TIES made a small but important beginning with its *Handbook of Ecotourism*, laying out a road map by illustrating good practices and the positive impact of ecotourism. The handbook targeted governments, donors, global bodies, and industry. Another task TIES set itself was to promote national and regional bodies and support them in hosting workshops and conferences. We had in mind that ecotourism, built from the bottom up, would flourish as a movement and complement top-down changes.

One of the first examples of TIES's local partnership was the Ecotourism Society of Kenya (ESOK, now Ecotourism Kenya), launched in 1993. TIES, in collaboration with the Kenya Wildlife Service and ESOK, convened the Tourism at a Crossroads conference in Nairobi in 1997. The conference drew participants from around the world, including Africa's future ecotourism champions Namibia, Botswana, and South Africa. Kenya was highlighted as including both the worst of mass tourism and the best of ecotourism. The conference launched the Kenya Tourism Federation to improve the image and practices of the industry and boost the Kenyan ecotourism market. Coinciding with Kenya Wildlife Service's Parks Beyond Parks campaign, Kenya's ecotourism lodges and local wildlife conservancies burgeoned even as beach and minibus safaris dropped sharply in the wake of political unrest in 1997, then again post-9/11.

Today, Kenya has over 50 community wildlife sanctuaries, a welter of new ecotourism lodges, and hundreds of local enterprises coordinated by the Federation of Community Tourism Organizations. Private and community conservancies account for more wildlife than all of Kenya's parks and reserves combined, protected by thousands of community scouts.

Efforts similar to Kenya's sprang up around the world, most notably in Australia, Costa Rica, and the Seychelles. Such national initiatives have set new benchmarks, standards, and performance indicators for the tourism industry, and upgraded global tourism for the better.

Big operators with high turnover rates and thin margins have resisted the new standards. Yet others have launched their own green labels to burnish their image and take advantage of conscientious clients. Governments in developing countries were loath to rock the boat and upset the large tourist companies with deep pockets and tireless lobbyists. For them, mass tourism earns hard currency needed to pay for imports and national debts, so visitor numbers counted and ecotourism was easy to dismiss as elitist and paltry.

Despite formidable opposition, ecotourism made steady progress in illustrating good and bad practices, raising awareness among travelers, governments, industry, communities, and the media. The persistent and consistent message of ecotourism over the last two decades has shown the dark side of tourism in trampling habitats and ignoring human rights and dignity. The spread of democracy after the collapse of the Berlin Wall has also given a fillip and a voice to communities muted by the global tourism juggernaut.

The United Nations International Year of Ecotourism in 2002 was a turning point in the global recognition of tourism as a stimulus to sustainable development. The World Bank and donor nations have put tourism back on the development agenda, this time aligned with the Millennium Development Goals, aimed at reducing poverty, improving education and health, addressing inequality and inequity, and sustaining the environment.

The bottom-up stimulus ecotourism has given communities, and the top- down influence it has had on governments, is influencing tourism for the better, even though there is a long way to go. Many tour operators and hoteliers take advantage of ill-prepared communities ignorant of businesses and fair trade practices. The impact on communities measured by the Millennium Development Goals is still far too weak. Ill-conceived donor and NGO funding feeds greed, corruption, and nepotism and undermines a community's traditional governance capacity.

The missing ingredient in tourism's movement towards sustainable development is all too often a failure to rebuild the very thing that tourism breaks down on first contact, a sense of community and governance structures. Once broken, the institutions that bind a community together and create the awareness, skills, and capacity to engage its members for common benefit and progress are hard to replace. Even harder to restore is the traditional knowledge and skill for using the environment sustainably. But be replaced they must and can be, if tourism is to bring sustainable development. The following example will show the need for good governance.

In the early 1990s, Kenya had no legally constituted wildlife associations through which local communities could exert their views on wildlife policies. Good-willed visitors and a few tour operators spent years struggling against local suspicions, tussles, and jealousies, trying to develop tourism on community lands. Local leaders filched money and gave jobs to relatives. Tourist revenues became a source of conflict and corruption.

Legalizing these associations gave communities a voice and representation. The associations raised conservation and development funds, set up conservancies, and trained members in business and conservation skills. These new skills spurred collaboration, openness, and accountability among communities and their development partners.

Tourism was the trigger for wildlife associations, and ecotourism the stimulus to better practices. Once the communities showed tangible results, a growing number of visitors gave money and supplies for education, health, water projects, and other developments.

The positive effects of better governance among wildlife associations are, like so much else in ecotourism, often invisible and always hard to measure. They begin with a change in attitude, then behavior, and by incremental steps, lead to more sustainable and equitable development and conservation.

Ecotourism has followed much the same route as community-based conservation. Starting from small beginnings, ecotourism has become a global movement. The movement has highlighted best practices and set principles and standards that have raised the bar of the world travel industry. Voluntary initiatives among travelers, tour operators, conservationists, and communities bent on bettering their lives and their environment began the change in attitudes and behavior. Policy and regulation followed and encouraged good practices, not the other way around. Tourism has far to go in meeting the goals of sustainable development and the conservation of natural diversity, but ecotourism has given it a cause and direction.

The International Ecotourism Society: A Brief History

Ayako Ezaki, Director of Communications
Dr. Kelly S. Bricker, Chair of the Board of Directors

In the 1980s, ecotourism became a conservation strategy that helped transform people's interest and excitement in regions of high biodiversity. The concept of ecotourism began taking shape, and destinations around the world embraced this concept as a way of strengthening the roles of parks and protected areas as effective tools for conservation, while at the same time offering tangible—and sustainable—economic opportunities (The International Ecotourism Society [TIES], 2010).

In 1990, the Ecotourism Society (later renamed The International Ecotourism Society, or TIES) was launched by a team organized by Megan Epler Wood as the world's first international nonprofit association dedicated to ecotourism—defined as "responsible travel to natural areas that conserves the environment and improves the well-being of local people" (TIES, 1990)—as a tool for conservation and sustainable development. The early years of TIES saw a significant growth of community projects and business initiatives that put into practice the key idea, viewing ecotourism as a tool to fund local conservation and fuel economic development as well as an increasing awareness among consumers and industry stakeholders of the important potentials of ecotourism.

Global Spotlight on Ecotourism

In 2002, the United Nations put ecotourism in a global spotlight by declaring that year the International Year of Ecotourism (IYE), highlighting "the need for international cooperation in promoting tourism within the framework of sustainable development" (United Nations Economic and Social Council, 1998). In 2001 and 2002, TIES organized regional meetings in Belize, India, Kenya, Peru, Thailand, the Seychelles, and Sweden, in preparation for the World Ecotourism Summit in Quebec City, Canada, in May 2002.

These local, national, and international gatherings highlighted the continuing growth and development of ecotourism as a tool for conservation and sustainable community development. They solidified the idea that tourism, when handled properly, can provide tangible opportunities to promote, and perhaps more importantly, to finance the global goals of sustainable development, poverty alleviation, and the protection of the earth's natural and cultural heritage.

In 2006, the *New York Times* Travel section selected "eco-tourism" as the Buzzword of the Year, noting:

> Eco-tourism—travel that preserves the environment and promotes the welfare of local people—continues to gain momentum. Impressed by the success of countries like Costa Rica and Ecuador, which have lured flocks of travelers for mountain treks and jungle safaris, a growing number of regions across the globe are turning to eco-tourism as a strategy for economic growth. (Higgins, 2006)

The popularity of ecotourism, as confirmed by the *New York Times*, one of the world's most influential newspapers, was both a blessing and a curse. On one hand, the greater awareness of the concept helped strengthen the movement to support responsible tourism practices contributing to conservation and the well-being of communities; on the other hand, the buzzword status of ecotourism brought with it the potential for misleading messages and gave rise to what is to this date "the mortal enemy" of ecotourism: greenwashing,[1] or marketing and public relations approaches that deceptively portray a company or product as environmentally friendly, without actions to substantiate the claim.

Fighting Green-Washing and Empowering Consumers

With the growing awareness of issues such as climate change, deforestation, and loss of natural resources, more and more travelers have started to seek ways to minimize their footprint and maximize their positive impact. Their expectations of authentic sustainability performance by destinations and businesses are ever higher.

One of the ways for TIES to respond to this emerging consumer trend and to actively work against greenwashing was investing in efforts to educate travelers. Thus, "Your Travel Choice

---

[1] It is worth noting that the term *greenwashing* is said to have been coined by New York environmentalist Jay Westervelt in a 1986 essay describing the hotel industry's practice to recommend guests reuse their towels to "save the environment" (Swan, 2011).

Makes a Difference"—the slogan for TIES's ongoing awareness-building initiatives—was born. Since 2006, through consumer campaigns and educational outreach, TIES and its partners (including Rainforest Alliance, United Nations Foundation, and UNESCO World Heritage Centre) have been promoting the roles of travelers in achieving the tourism industry's sustainability goals.

In order to provide convenient access to many of the lessons, ideas, and best practice stories that have been identified through the "Your Travel Choice Makes a Difference" initiatives, and to continue providing new insights, TIES created Your Travel Choice Blog (http://www.yourtravelchoice.org), an interactive platform to engage, educate, and inspire everyone to make travel choices that make a difference. Initiatives like these highlight the roles of travelers—consumers whose financial contributions make tourism possible—as critical stakeholders in the tourism industry, and their contributions to making tourism more sustainable.

State of the Industry: Challenges and Opportunities

Marking the fifth anniversary of the IYE, TIES and its partners convened the Global Ecotourism Conference (GEC) in May 2007 in Oslo, Norway. The Oslo Statement on Ecotourism was produced by TIES to summarize the results of the GEC and to assist in the efforts to improve sustainability practices by the tourism industry. It included the following key recommendations:

- Recognize the valuable role that ecotourism plays in local sustainable development.
- Maximize the potential of well-managed ecotourism as a key economic force for the conservation of tangible and intangible natural and cultural heritage.
- Support the viability and performance of ecotourism enterprises and activities through effective marketing, education, and training.
- Address some of the critical issues facing ecotourism in strengthening its sustainability.

These recommendations served as the framework of TIES's work in the following 5 years; some of its notable achievements included:

- Establishing partnerships with destination organizations to assist in the development of ecotourism, both at the grassroots and national levels, through training programs focusing on product development, business strategies, and marketing approaches
- Strengthening relationships with leaders in the field of biodiversity conservation and environmental stewardship, and seeking new ways of implementing the principles of ecotourism to support community-based conservation efforts
- Creating new platforms, such as ecoDestinations (http://www.ecotourism.org/ecodestinations), to connect travelers with inspiring ecotourism stories and opportunities, through educational programs and advocacy initiatives
- Playing a leading role in advancing knowledge of sustainability practices in the tourism industry by implementing research projects on various topics, including climate change and volunteer travel

Mainstreaming Sustainability in the Tourism Industry

Ecotourism has matured over the years, and now, this sector, which was once considered a niche for "nerdy" conservationists, has provided a strong impetus to promote sustainability in the mainstream tourism industry. For example, most major hotel chains today are investing in some form of sustainability practices (e.g., energy conservation, waste and water management, community volunteer projects), and many are taking steps to authenticate their efforts by following certification requirements and standards set by the Global Sustainable Tourism Criteria.[2]

Addressing new challenges and opportunities related to these developments, TIES now organizes the annual Ecotourism and Sustainable Tourism Conference (ESTC), a leading international industry conference focused on practical solutions to advance sustainability goals for the tourism industry. Supporting TIES's mission to engage and educate the ecotourism community, as well as to promote awareness among various stakeholder groups, the ESTC provides learning and networking opportunities with the ultimate goal of reinforcing the roles of tourism in building a sustainable future (Ecotourism and Sustainable Tourism Conference, n.d.).

As noted in the Oslo Statement on Ecotourism, the role of tourism in supporting sustainable development and the achievement of the Millennium Development Goals, notably the alleviation of poverty, has become recognized as a critical industry responsibility. Through the ESTC and various partnership efforts, TIES continues to strengthen these important roles that the global tourism industry plays and to empower tourism stakeholders to effectively address today's social, environmental, and economic challenges.

Ecotourism Today and Development Goals for Tomorrow

The definition, meaning, principles, and application of the term *ecotourism* continue to be an often-debated topic in the industry. The nuances of how the term is used will no doubt continue to motivate discussions among tourism practitioners, conservation professionals, and community stakeholders. The principles, guidelines, and tenets of ecotourism will continue to evolve, reflecting the ever-changing realities and needs of the global tourism industry as well as opportunities driving support for sustainability practices in the industry.

Despite these changes in perceptions and expectations, the fundamentals of ecotourism—that it contributes to conservation and benefits communities—have remained a vital source of inspiration for destinations, businesses, and communities around the world, and are particularly relevant to the sustainability issues facing the tourism industry today and the roles of tourism in addressing those issues.

---

[2] The GSTC Criteria, established by the Global Sustainable Tourism Council, are guiding principles representing the minimum changes necessary for travel and tourism businesses to adopt to protect the world's natural and cultural resources while supporting conservation and poverty alleviation (http://www.gstcouncil.org).

Just as international conservation and development organizations have had to recognize the importance of tackling poverty concerns in order to achieve long-term conservation success, the tourism industry must continue to look for creative strategies to support the economic–environmental balance and focus on harmonizing economic gains and conservation priorities. The global development priorities and targets set forth by MDGs, healthy communities, thriving ecosystems, and socially and politically fair systems are key to the long-term well-being of the tourism industry. All tourism stakeholders, therefore, have an inherent interest in promoting progress in these global development fronts.

By continuing to educate the tourism industry and the traveling public about the intricate relationship between the health of our planet and the future of tourism, TIES seeks to utilize the collective knowledge of its network, representing stakeholders from over 120 countries, to strengthen the industry's contributions to international development goals.

This publication is a dedication to all those who work tirelessly to utilize tourism as a means for positive change in society. From community-based tourism efforts to the international collaboration of United Nations groups and NGOs—the power of tourism is sought after as a development and conservation tool. These are exciting and challenging times, and although we showcase some of the efforts towards positive change, we also note there are many untold stories yet to be shared and many challenges yet to be overcome. Since 1990, TIES has supported and will continue to support all efforts that protect and nourish conservation of biodiversity, quality of life for all humanity, and sustainable economic development.

References

Ecotourism and Sustainable Tourism Conference (ESTC). (n.d.). About the ESTC. Retrieved June 14, 2012, from http://www.ecotourismconference.org/about-estc

Higgins, M. (2006). Buzzword of the year: Eco-tourism. *New York Times.* Retrieved June 14, 2012, from http://travel2.nytimes.com/2006/01/22/travel/22ecotourism.html

International Ecotourism Society. (1990). What is ecotourism? Retrieved June 14, 2012, from http://www.ecotourism.org/what-is-ecotourism

International Ecotourism Society. (2010). Ecotourism now and then. Retrieved June 14, 2012, from http://www.ecotourism.org/ecotourism-then-and-now

Swan, G. (2011). On the alert for misleading ads. *New York Times.* Retrieved June 14, 2012, from http://green.blogs.nytimes.com/2011/11/16/on-the-alert-for-misleading-ads

United Nations Economic and Social Council. (1998). Resolution 1998/40—Declaring the year 2002 as the international year of ecotourism. Retrieved June 14, 2012, from http://www.un.org/documents/ecosoc/res/1998/eres1998-40.htm

When embarking on this project, we realized we are indeed optimists—that ecotourism and sustainable tourism development can be utilized to create positive change. Yet, each of us has directly experienced the result of tourism done poorly, not only to the environment but also to local economies and communities. We therefore come to *Sustainable Tourism & The Millennium Development Goals: Effecting Positive Change* with realistic expectations, while trying to unite the economic potential of tourism with the need to address the concrete social and environmental challenges our planet faces today.

Tourism remains a key source of foreign exchange for one-third of developing countries and one-half of less developed countries and has significant potential as a driver for growth in the world economy. Furthermore, ecotourism and sustainable tourism, commonly referred to as "green tourism," carry the potential to increase employment directly; reduce poverty at the community level; improve efficiencies of water, energy, food supply, and waste systems; and create locally produced goods and services through cultural heritage and environmental conservation efforts (United Nations Environment Programme, 2011).

The commitment put forward by the United Nations Millennium Development Goals called for the international community to rally around an expanded vision of poverty reduction and pro-poor growth that situates human development at the center of social and economic progress. It also recognizes the critical role biodiversity conservation plays in supporting these concepts, particularly the dependence of poor people on natural resources. A connection was needed between a strong economic driver on one hand (tourism) and the need to find practical ways to attain economic development, but not at the expense of environmental sustainability. We set out to create the connection and provide examples of both success stories and inherent associated challenges when utilizing the potential of sustainable tourism to confront some of the significant social and environmental issues we face today.

We do not believe sustainable tourism is the panacea to all the challenges we face as a global society; however, we do believe it has the potential to support the health and well-being of residents, biodiversity conservation efforts, and cultural heritage preservation, while creating a mechanism for education, equal opportunities for women, and human rights. In the following chapters, we consider the possibility of sustainable tourism in all of its manifestations to address the Millennium Development Goals.

As we ventured down this path, it seemed clear to us that although the potential clearly exists, to date we have not fully realized sustainable tourism's potential. We hope *Sustainable Tourism & The Millennium Development Goals: Effecting Positive Change* begins to raise questions about tourism's contribution to the Millennium Development Goals and even creates a stronger critique of its potential; if so, we will have done our work well. We hope this text raises as many questions as it potentially answers, and continues to inspire ideas, solutions, research, creativity, and the ingenuity needed for sustainable tourism to become a development tool to create positive change.

References

United Nations Environment Programme. (2011). Tourism: Investing in energy and resource efficiency. In: *Towards a green economy: Pathways to sustainable development and poverty eradication* (pp. 410–447). Paris, France: Author.

Editors

Dr. Kelly S. Bricker, Associate Professor, Department of Parks, Recreation, and Tourism, University of Utah, Salt Lake City, Utah, United States

Dr. Bricker, an Associate Professor at the University of Utah in the Department of Parks, Recreation, and Tourism, works on sustainable tourism management, with research/teaching experience in ecotourism, sense of place, natural resource management, environmental and social impacts of tourism, certification, and tourism and quality of life. She is chair of the board of The International Ecotourism Society and the Global Sustainable Tourism Council. She also works on recreation and environment issues with HDR Engineering in Sacramento, California. Dr. Bricker earned her PhD at The Pennsylvania State University, where she specialized in sustainable tourism/natural resource management. Since 1998, Dr. Bricker continues to work with her husband and partners on a rural highlands ecotourism project called Rivers Fiji. She is a qualified diver, sailor, and wilderness travel leader; enjoys sea kayaking; and maintains a lifelong passion for ecotourism.

Dr. Rosemary Black, Senior Lecturer, School of Environmental Sciences, Charles Sturt University, Albury, New South Wales, Australia

Dr. Black works as a Senior Lecturer at Charles Sturt University, teaching and undertaking research in the fields of ecotourism, tour guiding, heritage interpretation, sustainable behaviors, and adventure tourism. She has over 30 years of experience in the tourism industry and academia. She has authored 3 books and over 30 publications. Dr. Black undertakes applied research with industry partners including protected area management agencies, tourism agencies, and community-based organizations.

Dr. Stuart Cottrell, Associate Professor, Human Dimensions of Natural Resources, Colorado State University, Fort Collins, Colorado, United States

Dr. Cottrell, an Associate Professor in the Department of Human Dimensions of Natural Resources at Colorado State University (CSU), focuses his research and teaching on sustainable tourism development and protected area management in EU protected areas. Dr. Cottrell completed his PhD at The Pennsylvania State University and taught at Wageningen University in the Netherlands for 6 years prior to coming to CSU in 2004. He is an avid sailor, diver, and outdoor recreation enthusiast.

Contributors

Dr. Sylvie Blangy, Researcher, Centre d'Ecologie Fonctionnelle et Evolutive, Centre National de la Recherche Scientifique (CEFE-CNRS), Département Interactions, Ecologie et Sociétés, Montpellier, France

Dr. Blangy is a researcher at the French National Research Center (CNRS, CEFE) in Montpellier, France. She works in the Arctic and sub-Arctic regions in collaboration with the Cree, Inuit, and Saami communities, developing community-designed and -led participatory action research projects, tools, and methodologies adapted to aboriginal contexts. These are aimed at addressing these communities' concerns, such as the social and cultural impacts of industrial development, tourism, and climate change on their culture, language, and lifestyles.

Nathan Bricker, MS, Department of Parks, Recreation, and Tourism, University of Utah, Salt Lake City, Utah, United States

Nathan is the Coordinator of the Natural Resources Learning Program within the Department of Parks, Recreation, and Tourism at the University of Utah; he has more than 25 years of experience in adventure travel and outdoor education. Prior to his position at the University of Utah, he was the General Manager for O.A.R.S., Inc. In 1998, with his partners, Nate created Rivers Fiji, an ecotourism program that operates in the highlands and remote coastal areas of Viti Levu, Fiji Islands. With the Mataqali of the rural highlands and his partners at O.A.R.S. and Sotar, Nate established the Upper Navua Conservation Area (UNCA), now Fiji's first and only Ramsar site and Fiji's first-ever lease for conservation.

Marieloz Bonilla Moya, MSc, Directora de Proyectos, ISOECO-Turismo Sostenible, Costa Rica

Marieloz graduated with a BA in Tourism Business and Management. She also holds a Master of Science in Leisure and Environments from the University of Wageningen. Marieloz is a university professor, senior consultant, and educator with over 20 years of experience in sustainable development issues and organizations. She is a pioneer professional on community-based tourism with emphasis on community autonomy and capacity-building programs in Costa Rica and Central America. Marieloz has diverse and in-depth experience in the facilitation of educational trips programs for Canadian universities and secondary schools.

Dr. Christine Buzinde, Assistant Professor, Department of Recreation, Park, and Tourism Management, The Pennsylvania State University, University Park, Pennsylvania, United States

Dr. Buzinde's research area focuses on sociocultural aspects of the tourism industry, with a particular emphasis on the politics of representation within heritage tourism sites and endogenous community tourism development. Her research occurs in the Mexican Mayan Riviera and in the Ngorongoro National Park in Tanzania.

Dr. Jack Carlsen, Professor of Sustainable Tourism, Curtin University, Western Australia

Dr. Carlsen is currently Professor of Sustainable Tourism at Curtin University, Western Australia, as well as founder and co-director of the Curtin Sustainable Tourism Centre. He has an extensive research track record and has produced more than 150 scholarly publications on various topics related to tourism planning, development, monitoring, and evaluation.

Dr. Carl Cater, Lecturer, Tourism Program, School of Management and Business, Aberystwyth University, Aberystwyth, United Kingdom

Dr. Cater is a lecturer in tourism at Aberystwyth University, Wales. His research centers on experiential tourism, and he maintains an interest in both the practice and pursuit of sustainable outdoor tourism activity. He is a fellow of the Royal Geographical Society and a qualified pilot, diver, lifesaver, and mountain and tropical forest leader. Dr. Cater is a co-author (with Dr. Erlet Cater) of *Marine Ecotourism* (CABI, 2007) and is an editorial board member of *Tourism Geographies, Journal of Ecotourism*, and *Tourism in Marine Environments*.

Joseph M. Cheer, Associate Director, Australia International Tourism Research Unit (AITRU) and PhD Scholar, National Centre for Australian Studies (NCAS) School of Journalism, Australian and Indigenous Studies (JAIS) Faculty of Arts, Monash University, Caulfield East Victoria, Australia

Joseph is currently teaching in the Graduate Tourism program at the National Centre for Australian Studies, School of Journalism, Australian and Indigenous Studies, Faculty of Arts. His current research focuses on the emerging area of pro-poor tourism, with particular attention to tourism and sustainable livelihoods in the South Pacific region. Prior to joining Monash University, Joseph worked in the international development field in the South Pacific as part of a tourism industry capacity-building and training project funded by AusAID.

Lucky Chhetri, Director, 3 Sisters Adventure Trekking, Nepal, and Founder, Empowering Women of Nepal

Lucky is the co-founder of Empowering Women of Nepal (EWN) and 3 Sisters Adventure Trekking Company, both based in Pokhara, Nepal. EWN and 3 Sisters work in partnership to promote and empower women through adventure tourism. Their goal is to encourage "fellow Nepali sisters to become self-supportive, independent, decision-making women." Lucky and her sisters' work has been awarded several international prizes including the Geotourism Challenge, sponsored by Ashoka Changemakers and *National Geographic*.

Dr. Rachel Dodds, PhD, Associate Professor, Ryerson University, Ted Rogers School of Hospitality and Tourism Management, Toronto, Ontario, Canada

Dr. Dodds is currently an Associate Professor at the Ted Rogers School of Hospitality and Tourism Management at Ryerson University. She also is the director of Sustaining Tourism, a boutique consultancy that examines sustainable tourism, community-based tourism, and tourism research and development. She has over 20 years of experience in the tourism industry and has travelled to over 70 countries.

Dr. Holly Donohoe, PhD, Assistant Professor, Department of Tourism, Recreation and Sport Management, College of Health and Human Performance, University of Florida, Gainesville, Florida, United States

Dr. Donohoe has collaborated on research projects and provided consultant support to many organizations and agencies, including the World Leisure Organization, the Canadian Parks and Recreation Association, and the Canadian Index of Wellbeing. Her general research interests include the geography of tourism, with specific focuses on Indigenous tourism, sustainable and ecotourism, heritage tourism marketing, outdoor recreation management, e-tourism, and e-leisure.

Dr. Daniel L. Dustin, PhD, Professor, Department of Parks, Recreation, and Tourism, University of Utah, Salt Lake City, Utah, United States

Dr. Dustin is Professor and Chair of the Department of Parks, Recreation, and Tourism in the College of Health at the University of Utah. Dr. Dustin's academic interests center on environmental stewardship and the moral and ethical bases for leisure and recreation activity preferences and behaviors.

Dr. Paul F. J. Eagles, Professor, Department of Recreation and Leisure Studies, University of Waterloo, Waterloo, Ontario, Canada

Dr. Eagles is a Professor at the University of Waterloo. He has 35 years of planning experience and over 360 publications to his name. His research has involved over 25 countries, with strong emphasis on eastern and southern Africa, Central America, and Australia/New Zealand. For 15 years he was the chair of the Task Force on Tourism and Protected Areas for the World Commission on Protected Areas, one of the commissions of the International Union for Conservation of Nature.

Emily Eddins, PhD Candidate, Human Dimensions of Natural Resources, Colorado State University, Fort Collins, Colorado, United States

In her research, Emily takes a sustainable livelihoods approach to understanding the roles volunteer tourism can play in collaborative conservation efforts and to promoting and enhancing collaboration among multi-scale volunteer tourism partnerships to better identify, implement, and manage projects that maximize benefits for the daily lives of people in host communities and their surrounding ecological systems.

Richard G. Edwards, Founder, ecoism

As founder of ecoism, Richard is committed to helping companies and destinations benefit from taking a more practical and cost-effective approach to marketing, while working to develop and promote a socially and environmentally responsible approach to travel. *Condé Nast Traveler* cites Richard as a Top Travel Specialist for his ability to bring results-oriented travel marketing and great product together with sustainability to build award-winning trips for upscale adventure travelers.

Ayako Ezaki, Director of Communications, The International Ecotourism Society, Washington, DC, United States

Ayako's roles include member communications, social media, content development, and leading the TIES editorial team. Ayako graduated from the College of Social Studies at Wesleyan University. Through her academic career, she developed a keen interest in the corporate social responsibility movement and nonfiction writing. She is originally from Japan and has traveled extensively throughout Europe and Asia.

Kelly Galaski, Program and Operations Manager, Planeterra Foundation, Toronto, Canada

Kelly is responsible for Planeterra's community development projects throughout Latin America and has worked in tourism for 15 years. Alongside in-country project coordinators and "Planeterra Ambassadors," she identifies local partners for the development of projects in important destinations for travel industry partners, helping to link local community initiatives and small businesses to the tourism economy. She holds a Bachelor of Commerce degree and a Masters in Environmental Studies degree with a focus on community tourism development.

Erika Harms, Executive Director, Global Sustainable Tourism Council, Washington, DC, United States

Erika is the Executive Director of the Global Sustainable Tourism Council. She manages and oversees the implementation of activities under the framework of the GSTC, an initiative that provides a clear set of standards, protocols, processes, and measurements for how businesses can better the planet and practice sustainable tourism. In 2008, *Condé Nast Traveler* recognized her as a "Trail Blazer" in Sustainable Tourism, and in 2010 she received the Hospitality Sales and Marketing Association International award for Top 25 Most Extraordinary Minds in Sales and Marketing.

Svitlana Iarmenko, PhD Candidate, Department of Recreation, Park, and Tourism Management, The Pennsylvania State University, University Park, Pennsylvania, United States

Svitlana completed a master's degree at East Carolina University and is currently working on her doctorate at the Pennsylvania State University. Her research focuses on émigrés and examines issues of acculturation, migrant reflections on adaptation to a host country, and manifestations of diaspora identity.

Dr. Deborah L. Kerstetter, PhD, Professor, Department of Recreation, Park, and Tourism Management, The Pennsylvania State University, University Park, Pennsylvania, United States

Dr. Kerstetter is a Professor in Recreation, Park, and Tourism Management at The Pennsylvania State University, where she primarily teaches marketing, tourism behavior, and research methods. Her research focuses on understanding and explaining the nature of tourists' decision-making behavior as well as the impact their behavior has on the host's culture and environment. Working with her graduate students and colleagues, she also has explored residents' perspective of tourists and tourism development.

Wendy Brewer Lama, MES, Ecotourism Specialist/Consultant and Director, KarmaQuest Ecotourism and Adventure Travel, Half Moon Bay, California, United States

Wendy is an Ecotourism Specialist, working throughout the Himalayas and Central and South Asia with international organizations including UNESCO, USAID, WWF, and the Mountain Institute. Wendy has helped shape ecotourism livelihoods and policy development at community to national levels. Wendy co-owns and operates KarmaQuest Ecotourism and Adventure Travel, an award-winning company that specializes in educational, adventure, eco-, and cultural trips throughout Asia. She also teaches an ecotourism course for the University of Puget Sound.

Hitesh Mehta, FASLA, President, HM Design, Fort Lauderdale, Florida, United States

Mr. Mehta is one of the world's leading authorities, practitioners, and researchers on sustainable tourism and ecotourism physical planning. He has been interviewed, featured, or mentioned in over 110 international magazines, newspapers, books, and blogs. In July 2006, *National Geographic* identified Mr. Mehta as one of five Sustainable Tourism Pioneers in the world. Mr. Mehta, an adjunct professor, has authored three books. His firm, HM Design, is currently working on environmentally and socially friendly projects in Kenya, China, and Dominica.

Brad Nahill, Marketing Director and Co-Founder, SEE Turtles, Portland, Oregon, United States

Brad launched SEEtheWILD to build the market for wildlife conservation tourism. He has worked in sea turtle conservation, ecotourism, and environmental education for 12 years with organizations including Ocean Conservancy, Rare, and Asociacion ANAI (Costa Rica). He has also consulted for several ecotourism companies and nonprofits. Brad has a BS in Environmental Economics from The Pennsylvania State University and teaches a class on ecotourism at Mount Hood Community College.

Steve Noakes, Senior Lecturer, School of Management and Marketing, Central Queensland University, Australia

Steve is Senior Lecturer (Tourism) at Central Queensland University, School of Management and Marketing; founding Chair of the international project management company, Pacific Asia

Tourism Pty. Ltd; director of Ecolodges Indonesia; and board member of the Global Sustainable Tourism Council. He has contributed to the World Bank–supported Global Tiger Initiative and a range of philanthropic sustainable tourism projects throughout Asia and the Pacific for more than three decades. He also works as Promoter of the Save the Tiger Fund and was the inaugural winner (2008) of the Ecotourism Australia Ecotourism Medal for extensive contributions to environmentally sensitive tourism development.

Chris Pesenti, RED Sustainable Travel, La Paz, Mexico

Chris launched RED Sustainable Tourism out of his decade-long efforts building up grassroots conservation organizations throughout northwest Mexico. Chris also co-founded Pro Peninsula in 2001 in an effort to strengthen the conservation movement throughout the Baja California peninsula. He has a BA in International Affairs from the University of Colorado and a master's degree in Pacific International Affairs from UCSD's Graduate School of International Relations and Pacific Studies.

Dr. Jana Raadik-Cottrell, PhD, Human Dimensions of Natural Resources, Colorado State University, Fort Collins, Colorado, United States

Dr. Raadik-Cottrell, tourism lecturer/researcher at Kuresaare College of Tallinn University of Technology, is a nature-based tourism specialist/lecturer with expertise on island community development via sustainable tourism on Saaremaa Island, Estonia. Dr. Raadik-Cottrell completed her PhD in Human Dimensions of Natural Resources (HDNR) at Colorado State University and her MS degree at Wageningen University in the Netherlands. She is currently an adjunct faculty member with HDNR.

Jeremy Schultz, PhD Candidate, Department of Parks, Recreation, and Tourism, University of Utah, Salt Lake City, Utah, United States

Jeremy is currently completing his final year of doctoral studies at the University of Utah in the Department of Parks, Recreation, and Tourism. His current research efforts include ecotourism projects in Fiji's rural highlands, sustainable recreation perceptions and the U.S. Forest Service, and sustainable tourism certification programs in the United States. In addition to his research, Jeremy works on curriculum development and instruction in sustainable tourism at the University of Utah.

Dr. Keri A. Schwab, PhD, Assistant Professor, Department of Parks, Recreation, and Tourism, University of Utah, Salt Lake City, Utah, United States

Dr. Schwab completed her PhD and master's degrees at the University of Utah in the Department of Parks, Recreation, and Tourism, with a focus on experiential education and a research focus on leisure in the family context. Dr. Schwab's current research interests include understanding family leisure and looking at youth experiences in after-school recreation programs.

Sue Snyman, Environmental Policy Research Unit, University of Cape Town; and Wilderness Safaris

Sue has a Master of Business Science (Economics) from the University of Cape Town, South Africa, and is currently working towards a PhD (Economics) at the same university. Her PhD research focus is on the socioeconomic impact of high-end ecotourism in remote, rural communities adjacent to protected areas, based on over 1,800 community surveys in six southern African countries. Sue has 14 years' experience in the luxury ecotourism industry in southern Africa.

Dr. Anna Spenceley, Research Affiliate, School of Tourism and Hospitality, Faculty of Management, University of Johannesburg, South Africa

Dr. Spenceley is a tourism specialist based in South Africa, and a Research Affiliate of the School of Tourism and Hospitality at the University of Johannesburg. She is the founder of Spenceley Tourism and Development cc (STAND), Chair of the IUCN World Commission on Protected Areas (WCPA) Tourism and Protected Areas Specialist Group, and vice chair of the board of the Global Sustainable Tourism Council. Her recent works include "Responsible Tourism: Critical Issues for Conservation and Development," published by Earthscan. See http://www.anna.spenceley.co.uk.

Ferry Van de Mosselaer, Wageningen University, Cultural Geography Group, Wageningen, The Netherlands

Ferry is Junior Researcher at Wageningen University, the Netherlands. He completed his MSc in Leisure, Tourism and Environment at Wageningen University with a minor in International Development Studies. Currently he is co-director at Atelier on Tourism Development, a multidisciplinary platform for knowledge dissemination and solutions in sustainable tourism development.

Professor V. R. (René) Van der Duim, Special Professor of Tourism and Sustainable Development, Wageningen University Cultural Geography Group, Wageningen, The Netherlands

Dr. Van der Duim is a Special Professor of Tourism and Sustainable Development at Wageningen University, the Netherlands. He completed his PhD at Wageningen University, studying tourism from an actor-network perspective. His current research focuses on sustainable tourism development and on the relations among tourism, conservation, and development in sub-Saharan Africa. He co-edited the books *Landscape, Leisure and Tourism*; *ANT and Tourism*; and *New Alliances for Tourism, Conservation and Development in Eastern and Southern Africa*.

Dr. Wolfgang Strasdas, PhD, Eberswalde University for Sustainable Development, Germany

Dr. Strasdas is a professor for sustainable tourism at Eberswalde University for Sustainable Development (Germany) and an advisory board member of TIES. He studied environmental planning in Germany and the United States and holds a PhD in Ecotourism in Developing Countries.

Dr. Strasdas has worked as a tourism consultant throughout the world, particularly in Africa and Latin America. His current research focuses on tourism and climate change as well as on certification for tour operators.

Dr. David Western, African Conservation Centre, Nairobi, Kenya

Dr. Western is the founding executive director of African Conservation Centre. Raised in Tanzania and now a Kenyan citizen, he has spent over 37 years engaged in research in Kenya, studying the interactions among livestock, wildlife, and humans, with the aim of developing conservation strategies applicable at an ecosystem scale. As former director of the Kenya Wildlife Service and conservation director for Wildlife Conservation Society, Dr. Western has been active in many areas of conservation, including community-based conservation, international programs, conservation planning, ecotourism, training, directing governmental and nongovernmental organizations, and public education. He and his wife, Dr. Shirley Strum, spend several months each year in California, where Dr. Strum is professor of anthropology at the University of California at San Diego. Their daughter, Carissa, just completed her undergraduate degree at University of California at San Diego, and their son, Guy, is currently studying at University of California at Santa Barbara.

Lijun Xu, PhD Candidate, Department of Recreation, Park, and Tourism Management, The Pennsylvania State University, University Park, Pennsylvania, United States

Having received an MS in Geographical Information System from the Chinese Academy of Sciences, Lijun works to integrate GIS tools into her research on tourism and outdoor recreation. Lijun has a profound interest in tourism and global environmental change and hopeful tourism as well as crowding and conflicts within tourism and outdoor recreation settings.

ACKNOWLEDGMENTS

We would like to acknowledge the support we received from many individuals and organizations without whom this text would not have been completed. First and foremost, we would like to thank the contributors for writing, revising, and submitting their chapters for inclusion in this volume. Their support and faith in us as editors are welcomed and greatly appreciated.

Our sincerest thanks go to the reviewers, who generously gave their time and expertise to provide feedback and comments for the authors and who have enhanced the quality of the chapters. All of our contributors to this project also reviewed chapters, and we certainly appreciate the time and effort of each author. We also were fortunate to secure external reviewers and appreciate their work: Trisia Farrelly, Harold Goodwin, Jerusha Greenwood, Kevin Markwell, Callie Spencer, Louise Twining-Ward, and Heather Zeppel.

We would like to thank the founder of The International Ecotourism Society (TIES), Megan Epler Wood, and the first president, Dr. David Western—together, their vision and effort to start the organization and in moving the principles of ecotourism into communities worldwide are very much appreciated by an innumerable community of ecotourism stakeholders. We also thank the numerous people who have dedicated their time and efforts to support TIES since 1990 and our current staff, Ayako Ezaki and Ferdinand Wepps, whose years of dedication have made this and many other initiatives possible, as well as our Board of Directors, whose volunteer contributions help the organization's global impact.

We would also like to thank Dr. David Western for his Foreword—we feel very fortunate to have the first president of TIES contribute to this text.

The support of the University of Utah, Charles Sturt University, and Colorado State University, where Kelly, Rosemary, and Stuart, respectively, work as academics, is greatly appreciated.

Finally, we would like to express our sincere thanks for the support of the Health Science team at our publisher, Jones & Bartlett Learning. They have been a delight to work with and helped make all of this possible.

Introduction to Ecotourism, Sustainable Tourism, and the Millennium Development Goals

An Introduction to Tourism and the Millennium Development Goals

Kelly S. Bricker, Stuart Cottrell, and Rosemary Black

World tourism has grown significantly in the past 50 years; it is now recognized as the world's largest industry, with sizeable economic benefits—upwards of US$6 trillion in 2011 (World Travel and Tourism Council [WTTC], 2011). In addition, world tourism is the world's largest employer, generating 260 million jobs, or nearly 1 out of every 12 jobs globally (WTTC, 2011). Originally promoted as a "smokeless" industry, the impact of over 900 million travellers (WTTC, 2011) roaming the globe at the start of the new millennium has forced governments, nongovernment organizations (NGOs), communities, and the tourism industry to recognize the importance of sustaining the environments upon which communities and tourism depend.

Sustainable tourism requires an intricate balance of social, environmental, and economic efforts to support positive change from a very local to a very global perspective. In contemplating the principles of ecotourism (see **Box 1.1**) and the effort behind the establishment of the Global Sustainable Tourism Criteria (Global Sustainable Tourism Council [GSTC], 2012), note there is unprecedented movement toward and strong support of tourism as a global engine, which can support the UN Millennium Campaign to achieve the Millennium Development Goals (MDGs) by 2015.

Box 1.1   The International Ecotourism Society's Principles of Ecotourism

Ecotourism is about uniting conservation, communities, and sustainable travel. This means that those who implement and participate in ecotourism activities should follow the following ecotourism principles:

- Minimize impact.
- Build environmental and cultural awareness and respect.
- Provide positive experiences for both visitors and hosts.
- Provide direct financial benefits for conservation.
- Provide financial benefits and empowerment for local people.
- Raise sensitivity to host countries' political, environmental, and social climate.

Source: From The International Ecotourism Society. (2012). What Is Ecotourism? Retrieved March 27, 2012, from http://www.ecotourism.org/what-is-ecotourism

---

The MDGs express the unprecedented commitment of global leaders to address key development priorities through a set of specific goals and targets, which include the following (United Nations [UN], 2011):

- MDG 1: Eradicate Extreme Poverty and Hunger

   Target: Halve the proportion of people living on less than a dollar a day and those suffering from hunger.

- MDG 2: Achieve Universal Primary Education

   Target: Ensure that all boys and girls complete primary school.

- MDG 3: Promote Gender Equality

   Target: Eliminate gender disparities in primary and secondary education by 2005 and in all levels by 2015.

- MDG 4: Reduce Child Mortality

   Target: Reduce by two-thirds the mortality rate among children under 5.

- MDG 5: Improve Maternal Mortality

   Target: Reduce by three-quarters the ration of women dying during childbirth.

- MDG 6: Combat HIV/AIDS, Malaria, and Other Diseases

   Target: Halt and begin to reverse the spread of HIV/AIDS and the incidence of malaria and other major diseases.

- MDG 7: Ensure Environmental Sustainability

   Targets: (1) Integrate the principles of sustainable development into country policies and programs and reverse the loss of environmental resources; (2) reduce by half the proportion of people without access to safe drinking water; and (3) achieve significant improvement in the lives of at least 100 million slum dwellers.

- MDG 8: Global Partnership for Development

   Targets: (1) Develop further an open trading and financial system that includes a commitment to good governance, development, and poverty reduction—nationally and internationally; (2) address the least developed countries' special needs and the special needs of landlocked and small island developing states; (3) deal comprehensively with developing countries' debt problems; (4) develop decent and productive work for youth; (5) in cooperation with pharmaceutical companies, provide access to affordable essential drugs in developing countries; and (6) in cooperation with the private sector, make available the benefits of new technologies—especially information and communication technologies.

These MDGs form the basis for this text, with two primary goals in mind: first, the goal of bringing increased awareness to the MDGs, and second, to inspire the tourism industry toward significant and practical contributions in realizing the targets of the MDGs. To this end, our book is organized around the work and targets outlined by the MDGs. This text is meant as an introduction to a complex journey that employs the power of sustainable tourism to address environmental and societal ills.

We begin with examples of how various MDGs are addressed generally in Xel-Há, Mexico, and provide a case study from the South Pacific. We then move to addressing each of the MDGs through case studies and research. An overview of the challenges and successes associated with tourism and poverty reduction is provided in Chapter 3. Case studies of both indigenous tourism and the connection between wild tiger conservation and poverty reduction provide examples of the challenges and complex connections between communities and conservation. The section on education, empowerment, and building community capacity explores research from Africa, and case studies from Fiji and Costa Rica address MDGs 2 and 3. In Section IV, the relationship between the tourism industry and disease prevention is discussed. Chapter 5 presents recommendations for action by the industry, and Chapter 6 explores tourism's contribution to community well-being for several communities in the Yasawa Islands, Fiji. We then address MDG 7 with Chapter 7, which focuses on ecotourism's contribution to preserving natural areas and biodiversity, and with Chapter 8, which explores ecotourism's role in ensuring environmental sustainability in marine environments. Chapter 9 explores vulnerabilities, responsibilities, and mitigation strategies with respect to ecotourism and climate change, and Case Study 7 provides a specific example in which species protection and tourism merge as a partnership. Case Study 8 illustrates the role of tourism planning for the environment in the Turks and Caicos.

Lastly, this text addresses MDG 8 by exploring partnerships within the tourism industry, from the role of volunteer tourism in Chapter 10, supported by clear examples of partnerships in action, to Case Study 9, which addresses the supply chain and community benefits. Chapter 11 addresses partnerships in certification and accreditation, ecotourism, and sustainable tourism programs. Chapter 12 provides examples of partnership development within PAN Parks, with Case Study 10 providing the background and progress of the Global Sustainable Tourism Criteria as a means for worldwide partnership development. Chapter 13 brings everything together by considering what we have learned from the case studies and how tourism might continue to forge a path to positive change.

We are confident in the continuing growth of tourism, and forever optimistic in the hope for a more sustainable development of tourism, which could be attained by addressing the targets of the MDGs.

References

Global Sustainable Tourism Council (GSTC). (2012). Global Sustainable Tourism Criteria for Hotels and Tour Operators. Retrieved March 27, 2012, from http://new.gstcouncil.org/resource-center/gstc-criteria

The International Ecotourism Society. (2012). What Is Ecotourism? Retrieved March 27, 2012, from http://www.ecotourism.org/what-is-ecotourism

United Nations (UN). (2011). Millennium Development Goals. Retrieved from http://www.un.org/millenniumgoals

World Travel and Tourism Council (WTTC). (2011). *Travel & Tourism 2011*. Retrieved March 27, 2012, from http://www.wttc.org/site_media/uploads/downloads/traveltourism2011.pdf

Corporate Social Responsibility and the Millennium Development Goals: The Case of Xel-Há, Mexico

Christine Buzinde, Lijun Xu, and Svitlana Iarmenko

LEARNING OBJECTIVES

- To recognize the link among the Millennium Development Goals (MDGs), sustainable tourism, and corporate social responsibility (CSR)
- To learn how efforts undertaken by tourism businesses employing CSR can contribute to the achievement of the MDGs
- To recognize the challenges of adopting a "business model," which is aligned with social welfare

The MDGs were developed primarily to focus on less economically developed (LED) countries in regions such as northern and sub-Saharan Africa; East, Southeast, South, and West Asia; Oceania; Latin America; and the Caribbean. Interestingly, these regions are not only some of the world's most impoverished geopolitical locales but also, in many cases, established or growing tourism destinations that are dependent on revenue generated through tourism. For many LED nations, tourism often is the sole source of foreign exchange funds (Brohman, 1996; Yunis, 2004). According to Hawkins and Mann (2007), "80% of the 56 countries with poverty reduction strategies cite tourism as one option for economic growth, employment, and poverty reduction. Several (Ethiopia, Tanzania, Uganda, Ghana, Nigeria, Mozambique, Kenya, Cambodia, and Honduras) give it equal weight with agriculture and manufacturing" (p. 353).

As shown in **Figure 2.1**, the international tourism receipts earned by LED nations amounted to US$11.6 billion in 2009 (Trading Economics, 2011). Furthermore, tourism represents up to 45% of the exports of services offered by LED nations, and it is often one of the few industries that offers job opportunities in these countries (United Nations World Tourism Organization [UNWTO], 2010b). Accordingly, tourism can be viewed as "integral to the [capitalistic] system that drives the global economy" (Kalisch, 2010, p. 85), and, in fact, the United Nations (UN), specifically the World Tourism Organization (UNWTO) branch, has pointed to tourism as a viable vehicle through which the MDGs can be accomplished. Such an endorsement ought to be viewed with caution because scholars have long argued that tourism within LED nations often is associated with high levels of leakage (i.e., money leaving the nation) (Boo, 1990;

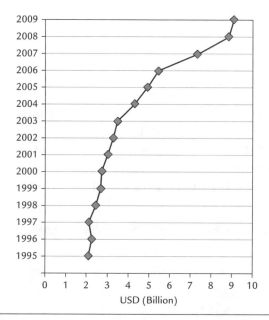

Figure 2.1   International tourism receipts for least developed countries (from 1967 to 2012).
Source: Data from Trading Economics. (2012). International tourism; receipts (US dollar) in least developed countries UN classification. Retrieved March 14, 2012, from http://www.tradingeconomics.com/least-developed-countries-un-classification/international-tourism-receipts-us-dollar-wb-data.html

Britton, 1996; Cater, 1987; Konadu-Agyemang, 2001; Meyer, 2010). According to McCulloch, Winters, and Cirera (2001), it is estimated that "between 55% and 75% of tourism spending" (p. 248) occurring within LED nations leaks out to more economically developed countries (MEDCs). As a result, economic benefits for LED nations often are minimal. Furthermore, revenue generated through tourism is often unequally distributed among residents of LED nations, resulting in a wider gap between the rich and the poor (Britton, 2004; Kiss, 2004). Although the lowest income households benefit, they do so at a lower degree in comparison to their higher income counterparts (Blake, Arbache, Sinclair, & Teles, 2008). In light of these issues, the UN recommends the adoption of *sustainable tourism* as the most suitable form of tourism (given its focus on environmental, economic, and social aspects) through which the MDGs can be met (UNWTO, 2010a).

According to Redclift (2005), the concept of *sustainability* is generally viewed as the foundation on which to base planning initiatives, hence its adoption by UNWTO in relation to the MDGs development paradigm. This liaison has to be carefully examined on a number of different fronts. On the one hand, the move beyond neoliberal policies, which have traditionally characterized initiatives proposed by multilateral organizations like the International Monetary Fund (IMF), has to be celebrated. On the other hand, linking social welfare and the improvement of peoples' livelihoods to *sustainable tourism*, a term/practice that many argue is ill-defined and often misunderstood, is problematic to say the least (see Butler, 1999). The UNWTO defines sustainable tourism as "tourism which leads to management of all resources in such a way that economic, social and aesthetic needs can be fulfilled while maintaining cultural integrity, essential ecological processes, biological diversity and life support systems" (UNWTO, 1997). However, despite the aforementioned definition, scholars have encountered difficulty as they attempt to operationalize the concept of sustainability (Butler, 1999). Nonetheless, from a theoretical perspective, it can be argued that sustainable tourism can offer a foundation on which to build the MDGs.

Perhaps in recognition of some of the aforementioned issues, the UN (2004) proposed other avenues through which the MDGs can be met, such as corporate social responsibility (CSR). As a concept/practice, CSR has been around since the 1950s and has been adopted in a variety of contexts, including tourism (Sheldon & Park, 2011). Various definitions for the concept exist, but a commonly referenced definition is one proposed by the World Business Council for Sustainable Development (WBCSD), which states that CSR is the "continuing commitment by business to behave ethically and contribute to economic development while improving the quality of life of the workforce and their families as well as of the local community and society at large" (WBCSD, 1999, p. 6). Arguably, CSR exhibits operational ambiguities similar to those scholars have associated with sustainable tourism, and it is yet another neoliberal approach to public well-being; however, the UN continues to endorse it, in part perhaps due to its wide use in the business sector. Within the UN system, "[t]he idea of linking for-profit business [through CSR interventions] with the broad concerns of governments for economic and social development, and achievement of the Millennium Development Goals (MDGs), is becoming increasingly" important (UN, 2004, p. 3). Social welfare interventions vis-à-vis CSR practices are viewed by the UN as "conducive to . . . rural development" in LED nations and the achievement of the MDGs (2004, p. 3). The UN "builds upon the CSR model [to] promote partnerships of willing government, business and other stakeholders" (p. 1) within LED nations; these multistakeholder partnerships "can be seen as attractive and cost-effective means to enhance rural development strategies in settings of limited regulatory capacity" (p. 4).

CSR practices have become mainstream aspects of the business sector over the years (Marsden, 2006), but, unfortunately, tourism research on the matter has remained scarce, as is stated by Sheldon and Park (2011). As a result, relatively little is known about CSR initiatives aimed at improving social welfare or the various ways in which such efforts are aligned with the MDGs. In an effort to remedy this gap in tourism scholarship, this chapter focuses on CSR practices undertaken by a tourism organization within an LED nation in order to understand business interventions implemented to improve social welfare, particularly as it relates to some of the MDGs. This chapter draws on research on Xel-Há, a tourism enterprise located in Mexico that uses CSR practices.

Within LED nations, private businesses such as Xel-Há sometimes help to solve local and global issues, particularly in instances when the governments in question have failed to take on the duty of social welfare (Marsden, 2006; Sheldon & Park, 2011). It is important to investigate how tourism businesses embrace social welfare in order to understand "the distribution of benefits and dis-benefits resulting from tourism activities" (Hall & Brown, 2010, p. 143). The subsequent section presents a discussion on tourism scholarship and MDGs-related issues. This is followed by a discussion on the efforts undertaken by Xel-Há. The chapter concludes with a critical discussion of the problems entailed in linking social welfare to private industry.

Tourism Scholarship on Issues Related to the MDGs

Over the last few decades, a number of organizations and scholars have dedicated attention to examining "how the tourism industry could be harnessed more effectively for poverty re-duction," environmental sustainability, and overall societal well-being (Meyer, 2010, p. 167). Numerous studies have focused on poverty alleviation, and indeed this is a key area in tour-ism scholarship that can be linked to MDG 1 (Ball, 2009; Britton, 1982; Manyara, Jones, & Botterill, 2006; Zhao & Ritchie, 2007). Through this line of research, various forms of alternative tourism have been proposed, all of which focus on generating net economic, social, environmental, or cultural benefits for the poor by maximizing the distribution of benefits (Ashley, Boyd, & Goodwin, 2000; Ashley, Roe, & Goodwin, 2001; Roe & Urquhart, 2001; Sandbrook, 2008).

These forms of alternative tourism can facilitate the involvement of the local community in tourism endeavors and hence alleviate extreme poverty (Gurung & Coursey, 1994; Harrison & Schipani, 2007; Manyara & Jones, 2007; Mitchell & Ashley, 2007; Neto, 2003; UNWTO, 2010a; Wunder, 2000, 2001). For instance, according to Christine and Sharma (2008), when tourism is undertaken through a community-based approach, it can reduce poverty by supporting small enterprises, reducing leakage, enhancing educational opportunities, and promoting construction of infrastructure as well as conservation of natural resources.

In terms of generating employment, the UNWTO states that the economic benefits accrued by those employed in the tourism industry trickle down to approximately 4 to 10 family members, who in turn contribute to the local economy through the purchase of goods (UNWTO, 2006). Arguably, workforce exploitation can occur, leakage can take place, and, in many instances, "employment . . . does not reach the poorest segments of society because of generally low skills base and the lack of foreign languages" (Meyer, 2010, p. 174). Linking tourism to social welfare, particularly the MDGs, Marafa (2007) states that it

> can be a major avenue of generating income, empowerment and poverty alleviation that are in line with . . . MDG 1. The successes achieved in MDG 1 can reverberate in positive indices in pursuing other MDGs with discernible impacts in MDGs 3, 4 and 5. Where alternative tourism or new wave tourism is promoted with relevant input from local communities, MDGs 7 and 8 can be achieved. (p. 2)

As related to gender equality, data produced by the International Labor Organization (ILO) indicate that 46% of the tourism workforce is represented by women, resulting in rapid shifts in family structure, employment status, and lifestyle (Hong, 1985; Levy & Lerch, 1991; Monk & Alexander, 1986; Smaoui, 1979). Although women have long been gainfully employed within the tourism industry (a contribution to MDG 3), they continue to experience horizontal and vertical gender segregation, "sex-role stereotyping and gendered structures of work and related pay differences between men and women in tourism" (Aitchison, 2005, p. 212; Scheyvens, 2002). Within LED nations, women, on average, are paid less than men and they are often overloaded with senior management responsibility for middle management salaries (Aitchison, Jordan, & Brackenridge, 1999). Furthermore, tourism often fuels the sex industry, exacerbating the exploitation, trafficking, and abuse of women and young children and resulting in the violation of human rights and gender equality (Graburn, 1983; Jeffreys, 1999; Petterman, 1998).

The disempowerment and exploitation of women is more prevalent and pervasive in situations wherein women and their children (particularly girls) have no access to basic education. Although the provision of education is not often viewed as a primary objective for tourism enterprises, it is argued that income earned from tourism allows parents in tourism-dependent LED nations to pay education costs, consequently augmenting primary gross enrollment ratios in the long-term. Additionally, awareness that good jobs require a certain level of education could be a probable stimulus for primary school completion. Tourism could also boost the professional and entrepreneurial training within the local community. Linking certain forms of tourism development to education, it can be argued that the former has the potential of increasing foreign exchange earnings, creating employment, and generating tax-based revenue, all of which can be geared towards the provision of public infrastructure, such as primary and secondary schools (Cater, 1987); this is one way through which MDG 2 can be achieved.

As relates to efforts to combat HIV/AIDS, tourism scholarship on the prevention of such severe communicable diseases is scarce. Forsyth (1999) argues that tourism is well placed to implement HIV/AIDS prevention campaigns precisely because as an industry it is significantly affected by HIV/AIDS. The author states that the tourist industry is at particular risk from the pandemic because of the mobility of the workforce, the presence of sex tourists, and the heavy reliance of many countries upon tourism revenues. Some people have speculated that potential tourists' fear of AIDS could discourage them from visiting certain countries; others have even suggested that tourism should be discouraged because the industry contributes to the spread of HIV/AIDS. When traveling, tourists often take risks that they would not take at home. They tend to drink more, use drugs more, and generally be more adventurous while on vacation. Such adventures often include taking sexual risks. When tourists have sex with prostitutes, hotel staff, and others in the local population, a bridge can be created for HIV to cross back and forth between the tourist's home country and the tourist destination (Forsyth, 1999, p. 278). As a result, there is certainly a need to focus on and to implement HIV/AIDS awareness strategies targeted to tourists and locals, as articulated by MDG 6 (Forsyth, 1999; Romero-Daza & Freidus, 2008). Given the link between tourism and HIV/AIDS, any prevention campaigns would be beneficial to the host community and the tourism industry.

Focusing on the link between human dimensions and the environment, scholars have augmented knowledge on sustainable tourism, arguing that if practiced in ways that take into account asymmetric power relations, it could improve social welfare as well as assist in the achievement of the MDGs. In 2002, the UN World Summit on Sustainable Tourism (WSSD), held in Johannesburg, spurred discussions on the notion of development aimed at eradicating poverty while protecting the environment. During the summit a plan of implementation was developed that informs sustainable tourism initiatives (UN, 2004). Similarly, the Global Sustainable Tourism Council (GSTC) has developed global sustainable tourism criteria that help guide the tourism industry onto a path to sustainability (GSTC, n.d.).

Many tourism organizations have adopted certain sustainability approaches, at times in lieu of or in addition to CSR practices (Amponsah-Tawiah & Dartey-Baah, 2011). In fact, many organizations are contributing indirectly to poverty reduction and environmental protection through CSR practices, particularly in LED nations when government representatives are absent and/or unwilling to tend to public welfare (Sheldon & Park, 2011). The subsequent section presents the research on Xel-Há to illustrate the company's attempts to contribute to social welfare through CSR practices.

Xel-Há, Mexico

This section describes the efforts undertaken by Xel-Há through its sustainable tourism and CSR programs, and illustrates the links between these efforts and the MDGs. The information provided is derived from public reports (written in Spanish and/or English) issued by Xel-Há, which describe the initiatives undertaken by the company. Xel-Há is a marine park located in Mexico's Mayan Riviera, a few miles south of the city of Cancún (see **Figure 2.2**).

The park is strategically situated in an area that enables it to tap into the international tourist market (Manuel-Navarrete, Pelling, & Redclift, 2011).

Xel-Há showcases a plethora of local flora and fauna as well as local Mayan culture. The park opened in 1994 and is owned by El Grupo Xcaret (Xcaret Group), a company that also owns other parks such as Xcaret and Garrafón. As a collective the parks employ approximately 2,300 employees (Abreu, 2009). Within its tourism promotional material, Xel-Há informs tourists that it offers a "wide range of fun attractions that allow for contact with nature in a safe and environmentally friendly" locale. The park receives over 2 million domestic and international tourists per year (Xel-Há, 2011).

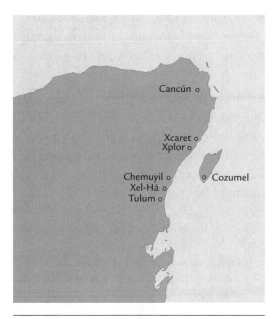

Figure 2.2 Map of the Mayan Riviera: Xel-Há and Chemuyil.

Poverty Alleviation

The management team at Xel-Há has established a number of initiatives that contribute to poverty alleviation. One initiative has been to contribute economically by employing locally and purchasing local products, which in essence increases the multiplier effect within the surrounding communities. Reports produced by Xel-Há state that "almost 100% of [its] suppliers are Mexican due to selection criteria that take into consideration the geographical location and manufacturing site of their products" (Xel-Há, 2011). Online tabulated data produced by Xel-Há indicate that the park had 1,635 suppliers from the Quintana Roo region (the state in which the park is located), resulting in approximately US$194 million for the region; 1,853 suppliers from the Yucatan Peninsula (municipal region), which yielded approximately US$220 million dollars for the area; and 2,747 suppliers from other Mexican regions, which resulted in approximately US$278 million for those locales. Business undertaken with suppliers located in the surrounding region of the Yucatan peninsula "amounts to 67% while contributions to the nation amount to 33% of Xel-Há's expenditures on supplies" (Xel-Há, 2011).

Based on these data, Xel-Há can be viewed as an important economic generator, particularly given that it is located in a tourist region full of foreign corporations that contribute more to leakage than to long-term investments in the local community. Locally owned large-scale tourism organizations are indeed scarce within this region (Wilson, 2008). Certainly, one can argue that even the foreign-owned tourism corporations contribute economically through job provision; however, a counterargument is that often employees are not well compensated for the duties rendered. By contrast, Xel-Há offers monetary compensation for employment at levels higher than foreign-owned tourism corporations located in the region.[1] Given the aforementioned economic issues, it can be argued that the park is in a position to contribute to the accomplishment of MDG 1.

Community Development

The park has been instrumental in the establishment and maintenance of Chemuyil, a nearby community in which most tourism employees working in the region reside. The town of Chemuyil was founded as a support center for the tourism industry about 15 years ago. Over the past 13 years, Xel-Há has embarked on a number of community development initiatives in Chemuyil. The park also implemented a number of community-led initiatives relating to health, education, public service, housing, and recreation activities, as well as environmental protection and education programs. In an online report, park officials state that

> unlike many other towns in the Quintana Roo region, where growth introduces many social contrasts, Chemuyil is a model community in the Riviera Maya: a clean and orderly town with close to zero illiteracy rate and very low crime index, where children and young people grow up healthy and have real opportunities to succeed within contemporary society. (Xel-Há, 2011)

Since 2009, Xel-Há has aided the community through maintenance of the town's roads, roundabouts, sidewalks, landscaping, garbage collection, and recycling initiatives (Xel-Há, 2011). The park also has worked on improving the local baseball field, named Samuel Mukul May (Xel-Há, 2011).

In addition to these initiatives, Xel-Há also created a community development center called La Ceiba. Initially the center was established as a local library, but it has since evolved into a site at which technology-based classes are conducted, medical and legal clinics are held, Alcoholics Anonymous (AA) members congregate, and local sports organizations are headquartered (Xel-Há, 2011). Initiatives such as the legal clinic offer residents the opportunity to gain knowledge on the procedures required to obtain "a low interest home loan, marital separation and child custody" (Xel-Há, 2011). In an effort to prevent the "ghettoization" of Chemuyil and to transform it into a community that is aesthetically pleasing, Xel-Há created a Paint Your House contest (Xel-Há, 2011). The park establishes the contest guidelines and also donates paint to local families who choose to participate in the contest. Cash prizes are awarded to families with the best paint façade. The community development efforts undertaken by the park are a strong foundation on which to create further initiatives that enable the park to contribute to MDG 8, which deals with addressing the needs of LED nations through global partnerships. The park has identified some needs that can be further addressed, monitored, and evaluated through targeted partnerships for development. Additionally, the efforts undertaken to improve the living standard of Chemuyil residents

---

[1] This information is based on personal communication with Xel-Há employees and personnel from several other businesses in the area, 2010.

are a foundation for meeting MDG 8, particularly as it relates to improving the lives of marginalized groups.

Education

Most organizations have a vested interest in ensuring their employees have the opportunity to participate in education programs, particularly if the knowledge attained translates into improved productivity. Xel-Há extends educational opportunities to any "adult residents of Chemuyil . . . to complete/pursue primary or secondary education" but also provides them the chance to undertake postsecondary education (Xel-Há, 2011). This community educational initiative is facilitated by an agreement within El Instituto Estatal de la Educación de los Adultos (equivalent to a continuing education institute) as well as a partnership with an online educational institute, Edusat (Abreu, 2009). Undoubtedly, these efforts are well aligned with MDG 2, which promotes the achievement of universal education (UNWTO, 2010a). As mentioned earlier, the park was instrumental in "creating and sustaining a local library, La Ceiba," which also houses the community's technological training center (Xel-Há, 2011). An online report produced by Xel-Há indicates that "approximately 7,900 people used La Ceiba Library" and "over 400 workshops sessions" were held at the location; additionally, "in 2008 a total of 40 diplomas were awarded" to locals who had participated in "workshops on basic computer skills" while "in 2009 a total of 53 diplomas were conferred" (Xel-Há, 2011).

On an organizational level, Xel-Há ensures its employees and their children are constantly afforded opportunities to pursue the education programs of their choice. For instance, the Zero Education Backlog program offers scholarships to the children of Xel-Há employees (Xel-Há, 2011). In coordination with the National Institute for Adult Education (INEA), the park offered grade school, junior high school, and high school adult education programs during working hours, in addition to offering bonuses to individuals who had completed their studies. In 2009, 26 staff members completed their education under the auspices of the Zero Education Backlog program, and 322 scholarships were given to employees' children (Xel-Há, 2011).

Given its environmental ethic, park officials are also heavily investing in educating the local communities, particularly the youth, about their collective roles and responsibilities in preserving and conserving the environment. The park "has developed environmental programs at different schools in Quintana Roo" (Xel-Há, 2011). Through the Free Environmental Education program, which primarily focuses on "youth residing in the Quintana Roo school district," the park delivered workshops aimed at instilling a culture of preserving and caring for the environment to more than 6,000 youth (Xel-Há, 2011). These ongoing efforts, which have been in place for the last 10 years, occur in collaboration with the Quintana Roo State Ministry of Education (SEQ). Other youth-focused initiatives include donations to the Save the Children Foundation, which operates a recreational library for young boys and girls; at this location, youth learn about cultural values, engage in theatrical endeavors, and learn about proper nutrition and hygiene (Xel-Há, 2011). Last but not least, the park also has been involved in working with local indigenous groups, with the goal of preserving local, regional, and national cultural traditions (Xel-Há, 2011). The park specifically collaborates with "the Indigenous Peoples Institute and the Felipe Carrillo Puerto and Tulum Mayan Culture Centers to organize free folkloric ballet, singing and theater productions for the community" (Xel-Há, 2011).

Gender Equity

For each of the past "five years, the park has received the Model of Gender Equality Award (Modelo de Equiad de Género) granted by the National Women's Institute (Instituto Nacional de la Mujeres)" (Xel-Há, 2011). This award is granted after a detailed audit, and it certifies that the company offers equal opportunities for advancement to women as compared to their male counterparts. These efforts may seem trivial to some Western readers, but it is important to mention that within nations where machismo is pronounced, women's rights often are ignored. Thus, efforts to instill values of gender equality, albeit at the organizational level, are a step in the right direction for many local women whose voices continue to be silenced in various forms.

Health

In collaboration with local government officials, the park aided in the construction of the Chemuyil Medical Care Unit, which was built in 2007 (Xel-Há, 2011). Through partnerships with the Ministry of Health (SESA), the National Integral Family Development System (DIF) and the National Human Rights Commission (CNDH), the park has provided "mobile clinics for Chemuyil residents" that offer "programs on preventative medicine, immunization, dental and optical treatments" (Xel-Há, 2011). There are six recurrent workshops topically centered on issues of "sex education, prevention of sexually transmitted diseases, teenage pregnancy, prevention of psycho-social problem," and motivational talks that inspire youth to take charge of their lives in meaningful ways regardless of their circumstances (Xel-Há, 2011). Although these health-related initiatives are not directly related to combating malaria or HIV/AIDS, they do indirectly contribute to MDG 6 through prevention programs as well as to MDGs 4 and 5 through educational programs geared toward teenage mothers.

The Environment

As a nature-based tourism park, Xel-Há engages in a number of environment-related endeavors. Xel-Há conserves original vegetation and through its technical teams it has "developed successful rescue methods, transplanting, cultivation and propagation of shrubs and trees, unique" to the area as well as reforestation of disturbed areas (Xel-Há, 2011). In 2009, the park was engaged in "the reforestation of 65,000 regional and other endangered species of plants (specifically *Trinax radiata*)"; it also is actively working to "prevent the introduction of non-native forests" (Xel-Há, 2011). This initiative is a foundation on which further efforts can be implemented in order to contribute to MDG 8, which promotes efforts toward sustainability, particularly reduction of biodiversity loss.

The park was awarded the Green Globe International Certification for Sustainable Tourism due to its well-established "environmental management system," which incorporates "specific programs directed towards caring for and preserving the environment, recycling and environmental education" (Xel-Há, 2011). Interestingly, the criteria for this award also recognize efforts undertaken to offer educational opportunities and health services as well as measures taken to ensure gender equity.

In 2008, the park won the "National Recycling Contest (under the auspices of SEMARNAT, the Ministry of the Environment and Natural Resources, and COPARMEX, the Businessmen's Chamber of Commerce)" for its exemplary waste management and recycling programs, which have been implemented in the park as well as in Chemuyil (Xel-Há, 2011). Environmental programming as directly related to tourists has entailed prohibiting the use of nonbiodegradable sunblock lotion; tourists' bags are searched upon entry, nonbiodegradable products are confiscated, and free samples of the appropriate products are distributed (Xel-Há, 2011). Also exemplary of the environmental initiatives implemented by the park is a volunteer program designed to clean up local beaches that often are awash with nonrecyclable trash (Xel-Há, 2011). The park also has developed industry outreach programs that entail meetings within industry stakeholders such as "local hotels, condominium associations and civic organizations" to discuss ways in which the local environment can be protected; drawing on its own experiences and best practices, park officials disseminate necessary knowledge to industry players (Xel-Há, 2011).

A Business Approach to Social Welfare: Problems and Prospects

Tourism has been heralded as an avenue through which the MDGs can be achieved because it "is often one of the only viable sources of growth and/or export earnings in many LEDCs" (Meyer, 2010, p. 165). The UN has identified CSR-based interventions as an avenue through which social welfare in LED nations can be improved. However, some problems emerge as one critically examines the association among tourism, CSR-prompted practices, and the MDGs.

First and foremost, the direct involvement of tourism enterprises in social welfare endorses an approach wherein "market forces are left to determine economic dynamics and social systems" (Kalisch, 2010, p. 87). This approach is problematic when one takes into consideration the fact that the international tourism industry is "dominated by transnational corporations, mainly based in developed countries . . . and these organizations have substantial power . . . and potentially create unequal exchanges" (Hall & Brown, 2010, p. 149). Furthermore, within a climate of economic uncertainty and/or political instability, transnational tourism corporations, as transient foreign entities, might choose to curtail or completely abandon extant social responsibility commitments. Such circumstances might offer the perfect scapegoat, particularly given that the adoption of responsible practices has "traditionally received a predictably low priority" from business enterprises (Miller, 2001, p. 590). Thus, one wonders how uncertain economic or sociopolitical circumstances influence business commitments to social welfare initiatives (see Henderson, 2007). It would be remiss to overlook the fact that some private businesses such as Xel-Há that operate within LED nations often choose to take on the role of social welfare, particularly in instances where the local government has failed to act. But caution is needed because, as long as the approach to social welfare "remains locked within an ethos based on profit generating, industry expanding intentions," few strides towards long-term social welfare will be attained (Hall & Brown, 2010, p. 143). Furthermore, such approaches will result in the concretization of neoliberal approaches to public services and social welfare.

Second, placing social welfare within a business paradigm is problematic because there are neither specific guidelines nor requirements that determine how businesses implement social welfare programs. For instance, in the case of CSR, business approaches can range from superficial initiatives that focus on the organization to meaningful commitments to change aimed at remedying societal problems. Elaborating on the various approaches to CSR, Hall and Brown (2010) state that businesses can adopt one of the following: a minimalist approach (e.g., focus is on human resource issues), a philanthropic approach (e.g., focus is on donations/gifts related to company projects), an encompassing approach (e.g., focus is on the broader community with the aim of leading the cause of change), or a social activist approach (e.g., the business is designed and executed to affect change). Based on this CSR typology, Xel-Há can be viewed as an enterprise that adopts a philanthropic approach because its initiatives are designed principally to improve the livelihoods of its labor force; it benefits from a healthy, educated, and proximal labor force. Thus, if LED nations want to encourage industry approaches to social welfare, they have to find ways to provide incentives for businesses that move beyond company-centered foci and adopt in-depth and grounded (encompassing or social activist) approaches to improving societal well-being. Furthermore, in the absence of neutral assessment and supervision of the actual outcomes of CSR, companies like Xel-Há are left to *define* social welfare as they see fit and to *self-report* only that which makes marketing sense. There have been calls within the CSR literature to examine ways in which companies could assess the effectiveness of their programs, but the reality is that private actors lack incentives to critically assess the design and actual outcomes of their CSR activities (see Fougère & Solitander, 2009).

Third, the focus on industry also is problematic because it further cripples LED governments and prevents them from initiating and/or maintaining social welfare programs. For instance, the liaison between MDG and CSR, in many ways, further places the onus on businesses to enact a role typically allocated to governments. Could dependency on transnational tourism corporations to implement social welfare programs be equated with reliance on foreign aid programs (i.e., IMF programs that cripple rather than heal LED economies), and can both be viewed as events that can undermine the power and agency of LED governments? Some scholars argue that tourism might not be an effective avenue through which to improve social welfare because it promotes dependency on TNCs (Meyer, 2010; Scheyvens, 2009). According to Hall and Brown (2010), a profit-generating ethos to public welfare creates a

> "hollowing out" of the state and dispersal of power to a multiplicity of unelected . . . business interests involved in the often fragmented governance of regions resulting in a "democratic deficit." This means that governments are less able to protect their citizens from exploitation. This raises important questions concerning the ethical underpinnings of tourism processes and location of responsibilities for stakeholder welfare. (p. 149)

The "democratic deficit" can perhaps be remedied through the development of policies devised by LED nations that focus on issues of equity and democracy (Kalisch, 2010). Such an assertion assumes that LED nations are accountable, have the necessary resources, and are immune to corruption. Yet reality reveals that "corruption and the levels of intensity to which it is practiced" is an imminent problem that plagues both LED nations and transnational corporations (Wheeler, 2005, p. 267) and is linked to global issues of inequality. Indeed, it can be argued a "significant commitment to directly address[ing] the structural causes of global inequity" is a necessary foundation on which to build social welfare goals for LED nations (Hall & Brown, 2010, p. 150). Thus, a micro- and macro-level approach is necessary to better understand tourism's role in exacerbating inequalities as well as its potential contribution to improving social welfare (Meyer, 2010).

Conclusion

In this chapter, we have discussed research on Xel-Há and have argued that although this tourism enterprise's CSR practices showcase a strong foundation on which to respond to social welfare programs such as the MDGs, there are nonetheless a few problems with adopting a business ethos to societal well-being. Unless these problems are addressed, and in the absence of neutral assessment and supervision of CSR outcomes, society will continue to find itself in a predicament wherein neoliberal approaches continue to exacerbate global inequities.

References

Abreu, J. L. (2009). Situación actual de la RSE en el sector turístico Mexicano. *International Journal of Good Conscience, 4(2), 160–173.*

Aitchison, C. C. (2005). Feminist and gender perspectives in tourism studies: The social-cultural nexus of critical and cultural theories. *Tourist Studies, 5*(3), 207–224.

Aitchison, C. C., Jordan, F., & Brackenridge, C. (1999). Women in leisure management: A survey of gender equity. *Women in Management Review, 14*(4), 121–127.

Amponsah-Tawiah, K., & Dartey-Baah, K. (2011). Corporate social responsibility in Ghana. *International Journal of Business and Social Science, 2*(17), 107–112.

Ashley, C., Boyd, C., & Goodwin, H. (2000). Pro-poor tourism: Putting poverty at the heart of the tourism agenda. Retrieved May 10, 2011, from http://www.odi.org.uk/resources/download/2096.pdf

Ashley, C., Roe, D., & Goodwin, H. (2001). *Pro-poor tourism strategies, making tourism work for the poor. A review of experience.* Nottingham, England: Pro-Poor Tourism Partnership.

Ball, M. (2009). Tourism and poverty alleviation. *Travel and Tourism Analyst, 1*, 1–38.

Blake, A., Arbache, J., Sinclair, T., & Teles, V. (2008). Tourism and poverty relief. *Annals of Tourism Research, 35*(1), 107–126.

Boo, E. (1990). *Ecotourism: The potentials and pitfalls.* Washington, DC: World Wildlife Fund.

Britton, S. G. (1982). The political economy of tourism in the third world. *Annals of Tourism Research, 9*(3), 331–358.

Britton, S. G. (1996). Tourism, dependency and development: A mode of analysis. In Y. Apostolopoulos, S. Leivadi, & A. Yiannakis (Eds.), *The sociology of tourism: Theoretical and empirical investigations* (pp. 155–172). New York: Routledge Press.

Britton, S. G. (2004). Tourism, dependency and development: A mode of analysis. In S. Williams (Ed.), *Tourism: Critical concepts in the social sciences* (Vol. III, pp. 29–48). London: Routledge.

Brohman, J. (1996). New directions in tourism for third world development. *Annals of Tourism Research, 23*(1), 48–70.

Butler, R. W. (1999). Sustainable tourism: A state of the art review. *Tourism Geographies, 1*(1), 7–25.

Cater, E. (1987). Tourism in the least developed countries. *Annals of Tourism Research, 9*(3), 331–358.

Christine, I. T., & Sharma, A. (2008). Millennium Development Goals: What is tourism's place? *Tourism Economics, 14*(2), 427–430.

Forsyth, S. (1999). HIV/AIDS and tourism. *AIDS Analysis Africa, 9*(6), 4–6.

Fougère, M., & Solitander, N. (2009). Against corporate social responsibility: Critical reflections on thinking, practice, content and consequences. *Corporate Social Responsibility and Environmental Management, 16*, 217–227.

Global Sustainable Tourism Council (GSTC). (n.d.). Adopt the Global Sustainable Tourism (GST) Criteria. Retrieved November 3, 2011, from http://new.gstcouncil.org/page/adopt-the-criteria

Graburn, N. H. H. (1983). Tourism and prostitution. *Annals of Tourism Research, 10*, 437–442.

Gurung, C. P., & Coursey, M. D. (1994, August). Nepal, pioneering sustainable tourism. The Annapurna conservation area project: An applied experiment in integrated conservation and development. *Rural Extension Bulletin, 5*.

Hall, D., & Brown, F. (2010). Tourism and welfare: Ethics, responsibility and wellbeing. In S. Cole & N. Morgan (Eds.), *Tourism and inequality: Problems and prospects* (pp. 143–163). Cambridge, MA: CABI.

Harrison, D., & Schipani, S. (2007). Lao tourism and poverty alleviation: Community-based tourism and the private sector. *Current Issues in Tourism, 10*(2), 194–230.

Hawkins, D. E., & Mann, S. (2007). The World Bank's role in tourism development. *Annals of Tourism Research, 34*(2), 348–363.

Henderson, J. C. (2007). Hotel companies in Phuket, Thailand, after the Indian Ocean tsunami. *Hospitality Management, 26*, 228–239.

Hong, E. (1985). *See the Third World while it lasts: The social and environmental impact of tourism with special reference to Malaysia.* Penang, Malaysia: Penang's Consumer Association.

Jeffreys, S. (1999). Globalizing sexual exploitation: Sex tourism and the traffic in women. *Leisure Studies, 18*(3), 179–196.

Kalisch, A. (2010). Fair trade in tourism: a marketing tool for social transformation? In S. Cole & N. Morgan (Eds.), *Tourism and inequalities: Problems and prospect* (pp. 85–105). Cambridge, MA: CABI.

Kiss, A. (2004). Is community-based ecotourism a good use of biodiversity conservation funds? *Trends in Ecology and Evolution, 19*(5), 232–237.

Konadu-Agyemang, K. (2001). Structural adjustment programs and the international tourism trade in Ghana, 1983–1999: Some socio-spatial implications. *Tourism Geographies, 3*, 187–206.

Levy, D. E., & Lerch, P. B. (1991). Tourism as a factor in development: Implications for gender and work in Barbados. *Gender & Society, 5*, 67–85.

Manuel-Navarrete, D., Pelling, M., & Redclift, M. (2011). Critical adaptation to hurricanes in the Mexican Caribbean: Development visions, governance structures, and coping strategies. *Global Environmental Change, 21*, 249–258.

Manyara, G., & Jones, E. (2007). Community-based tourism enterprises development in Kenya: An exploration of their potential as avenues of poverty reduction. *Journal of Sustainable Tourism, 15*(6), 628–644.

Manyara, G., Jones, E., & Botterill, D. (2006). Tourism and poverty alleviation: The case for indigenous enterprise development in Kenya. *Tourism Culture and Communication, 7*(1), 19–37.

Marafa, L. M. (2007). Tourism leisure and the MDGs: The relevance to Africa's development. Retrieved May 3, 2011, from http://www.iipt.org/africa2007/PDFs/Tourism%20Leisure%20and%20the%20MDGs_IIPT2007_Marafa.pdf

Marsden, C. (2006). In defense of corporate responsibility in corporate social responsibility. In A. Kakabadse & M. Morsing (Eds.), *Corporate social responsibility: Reconciling aspiration with application* (pp. 400–412). New York: Palgrave Macmillan.

McCulloch, N., Winters, L., & Cirera, X. (2001). *Trade liberalization and poverty: A handbook.* London: Center for Economic Policy Research.

Meyer, D. (2010). Pro-poor tourism: Can tourism contribute to poverty reduction in less economically developed countries? In S. Cole & N. Morgan (Eds.), *Tourism and inequality: Problems and prospects* (pp. 164–182). Cambridge, MA: CABI.

Miller, G. (2001). Corporate responsibility in the UK tourism industry. *Tourism Management, 22,* 589–598.

Mitchell, J., & Ashley, C. (2007). Can tourism offer pro-poor pathways to prosperity? Examining evidence on the impact of tourism on poverty. Retrieved February 2, 2011, from http://www.cabdirect.org.ezaccess.libraries.psu.edu/abstracts/20083139160.html

Monk, J., & Alexander, C. S. (1986). Free Port fallout: Gender, employment, and migration on Margarita Island. *Annals of Tourism Research, 13,* 393–413.

Neto, F. (2003). A new approach to sustainable tourism development: Moving beyond environmental protection. *Natural Resources Forum, 27,* 212–222.

Petterman, J. J. (1998). Sex, money and morality: Prostitution and tourism in South-East Asia. *Asian Women, 6,* 183–190.

Redclift, M. (Ed.). (2005). *Sustainability: Critical concepts in the social sciences.* London: Routledge.

Roe, D., & Urquhart, P. (2001, May). Pro-poor tourism: Harnessing the world's largest industry for the world's poor. *International Institute for Environment and Development,* 1–8.

Romero-Daza, N., & Freidus, A. (2008). Female tourists, casual sex, and HIV risk in Costa Rica. *Qualitative Sociology, 31*(1), 169–187.

Sandbrook, C. G. (2008). Putting leakage in its place: The significance of retained tourism revenue in the local context in rural Uganda. *Journal of International Development, 22*(1), 124–136.

Scheyvens, R. (2002). *Tourism for development: Empowering communities.* London: Prentice Hall.

Scheyvens, R. (2009). Pro-poor tourism: Is the value beyond the rhetoric? *Tourism Recreation Research, 34,* 191–196.

Sheldon, P. J., & Park, S. Y. (2011). An exploratory study of corporate social responsibility in the US travel industry. *Journal of Travel Research, 50,* 392–407.

Smaoui, A. (1979). Tourism and employment in Tunisia. In E. Kadt (Ed.), *Tourism: Passport to development? Perspectives on the social and cultural effects of tourism in developing countries* (pp. 101–110). New York: Oxford University Press.

Trading Economics. (2011). International tourism; receipts (US dollar) in least developed countries UN classification. Retrieved February 2, 2011, from http://www.tradingeconomics.com/least-developed-countries-un-classification/international-tourism-receipts-us-dollar-wb-data.html

United Nations (UN). (2004). Managing corporate social responsibility for rural development in least developed countries. Retrieved from March 29, 2012, from http://www.un.org/esa/coordination/Alliance/documents/CSR%2014%20June%2004.pdf

United Nations World Tourism Organization (UNWTO). (1997). What tourism managers need to know: A practical guide for the development and application of indicators of sustainable tourism. Retrieved February 2, 2011, from http://www.world-tourism.org/cgi-bin/infoshop.storefront/EN/product/1020-1

United Nations World Tourism Organization (UNWTO). (2006). *Tourism and least developed countries: A sustainable opportunity to reduce poverty.* Madrid: Author.

United Nations World Tourism Organization (UNWTO). (2010a). Tourism and the Millennium Development Goals. Retrieved November 3, 2011, from http://www.unwto.org/tourism&mdgsezine

United Nations World Tourism Organization (UNWTO). (2010b). Tourism highlights. Retrieved February 3, 2011, from http://www.unwto.org/facts/eng/highlights.htm

Wheeler, B. (2005). Ecotourism/egotourism and development. In C. M. Hall & S. Boyd (Eds.), *Nature-based tourism in peripheral areas: Development or disaster?* (pp. 263–272). Clevedon, England: Channel View.

Wilson, T. D. (2008). Economic and social impacts of tourism in Mexico. *Latin American Perspectives, 35*(160), 37–52.

World Business Council for Sustainable Development (WBCSD). (1999). *Corporate social responsibility: Meeting changing expectations.* Geneva, Switzerland: Author.

Wunder, S. (2000). Ecotourism and economic incentives: An empirical approach. *Ecological Economics, 32*(3), 465–479.

Wunder, S. (2001). Poverty alleviation and tropical forests: What scope for synergies? *World Development, 29*(11), 1817–1833.

Xel-Há. (2011). Corporate social responsibility in Xel-Há. Retrieved February 3, 2011, from http://xelhacsr. com/perfil.php

Yunis, E. (2004, May 10). *Sustainable tourism and poverty alleviation.* Paper presented at the World Bank–ABCDE Conference–Europe, Brussels.

Zhao, W., & Ritchie, B. (2007). Tourism and poverty alleviation: An integrative research framework. *Current Issues in Tourism, 10*(2), 119–143.

Outer Island Tourism in the South Pacific and the Millennium Development Goals: Understanding Tourism's Impacts

Joseph M. Cheer

LEARNING OBJECTIVES

- To appreciate the need to substantiate tourism's nonfinancial and financial impacts in developing country contexts to establish whether tourism is assisting the mitigation of MDGs
- To outline some of the tensions that surround the exploitation of cultural heritage in developing country contexts
- To explain the critical importance of questioning the legitimacy of tourism as a development mechanism
- To understand that the interpretation and ownership of cultural heritage is largely problematic
- To appreciate that for many developing country communities their unique cultural heritage offers the best chance for joining the tourism economy
- To understand that the notion of cultural heritage as an "authentic, unchanging" phenomenon is undermined as a result of commercialization for tourism

This chapter examines tourism development in the Republic of Vanuatu, a small island state in the South Pacific, and reports on findings from exploratory fieldwork conducted on Pentecost Island examining the impacts of tourism in an outer island context. Pentecost is one of the country's largest, northernmost islands and is located outside the tourist enclave of the capital, Port Vila. The perspectives in this chapter have been extracted from a broader, ongoing study on tourism livelihoods in the region, conducted by the author, juxtaposing tourism livelihoods and peripherality (typically the consequence of geographic isolation from the center of economic activity).

In general, scholars and practitioners assume that where tourism is being conducted in a sustainable manner, it must in some way be making a contribution to meeting the Millennium Development Goals (MDGs) and, thus, be making positive development and livelihood impacts (Cheer, 2010; Hawkins & Mann, 2007; Mitchell & Ashley, 2010; Seetanah, 2011). However, to appraise the inroads tourism is making toward the successful mitigation of MDGs, research examining tourism's impact on livelihoods, poverty alleviation, rural development, gender equality, employment, and socioeconomic progress is needed to ensure that perspectives are informed.

As is the case in many small island states in the region and elsewhere, with the exception of one-off, piecemeal, and ad-hoc studies examining tourism's impacts, little is understood about the short-, medium-, and long-term impacts of tourism. Although tourism often is lauded for its ability to stimulate economic development, little is understood about its link to and subsequent impact on nonfinancial and traditional livelihoods (Cheer, 2010; Cheer & Peel, 2011). Therefore, the purpose of this chapter is to explain the extent of tourism's financial and nonfinancial impacts in an outer island setting where traditional lifestyles predominate and where development concerns are pressing. One of the key questions that must be asked of tourism development in the island nations of the South Pacific is at what point does the exploitation of unique cultural heritage become problematic and counterproductive to the advancement of islander communities? This tension is explored in this chapter, with particular focus placed on the unique heritage of land diving or the *naghol* of Pentecost Island. The *naghol* is widely accepted as the genesis behind the modern-day bungee jumping phenomenon (Kellett, 2010) and the foremost basis for tourism development in situ.

Background

Despite over two centuries of integration into global affairs, the mythologizing of the South Pacific as a paradise and the attendant depiction of islanders as some of the most contented people in the world has not abated. Such depictions have been reinforced by the *Happy Planet Index* (New Economics Foundation, 2006) judging Vanuatu to be the happiest country in the world. Typical of the romanticization of the region is Theroux's *The Happy Isles of Oceania* (1992), which presents reportage of a region that although weighed down by isolation, disadvantage, and underdevelopment, and despite the many limitations of the region and its peoples, retains an exotic allure. The unforgiving nature of the region is underlined by its location in an ocean bigger than all of the earth's land surfaces combined and with islands in inverse proportion— diminutive and mere specks (Scarr, 1990).

In many ways, the smallness of island states in the region is the area's heaviest burden, creating diseconomies of scale and inhibiting development and economic progress (Connell, 2010). For most, if not all, of the island states in the region, the foreboding prospect of climate change is of principal concern. The grim truth is that those who already have the least have the most to lose (Wong, 2009). The contemporary reality of the South Pacific is such that the comparative advantage of smallness and isolation are few, so much so that five of the region's island states are officially classified as least developed countries (Connell, 2010). Connell also points out that island states in the region are relatively poor and that development problems have intensified with the shift from commodities (especially subsistence living) towards a more diversified but less protected economy, involving liberalization of trade, globalization of production, and intensified pressure on resources, lands, and seas (p. 116).

It is clear that the complexion of the region has undergone and continues to experience massive change. Consequently, the urgency for effective governance and political reform is critical to the region's future (Crocombe, 2001). The prevailing development mantra espousing modernization over traditionalism is resulting in seismic shifts from customary lifestyles to an increasing monetization of societies. This is manifest in greater individualism and a narrowing of ties among community and kin, exacerbating rising levels of hardship and poverty and increasing degrees of inequality and marginalization previously unseen (Abbott, 2007). It is argued that the attendant transition and rate of change will persist for all of the island states in the region—chiefly the result of becoming firmly integrated into a broader global context that finds them exposed and vulnerable to external forces, rarely matched elsewhere (Slade, 2009).

Within this milieu, tourism has emerged as the principle comparative advantage open to countries in the region and central to countering the inherent social and economic frailties (Harrison, 2004; Narayan, Narayan, Prasad, & Prasad, 2010). Tourism also is seen as a more favorable alternative to conventional extractive industries such as logging, fisheries, and mining and is heavily predisposed to grassroots islander participation (Scheyvens & Momsen, 2008). However, tourism's touted economic benefits are contentious on two accounts: first, it is difficult to ascertain the full cost of tourism-related infrastructure, and second, the extent and nature of tourism's economic impacts, especially the tourism multiplier and economic leakages, is poorly understood (Allcock, 2006). It is tourism's linkage to natural and cultural heritage, often the key assets of islanders, that present the biggest case for its expansion. However, this is contingent on policy makers ensuring that the type of tourism developed harmonizes with existing livelihoods and optimizes local involvement (Basu, 2000).

Despite the bullishness towards it, promoting tourism in the region is not without its difficulties. Gaining regional cooperation, infrastructure limitations, natural disasters, political upheaval, and the restricted and costly nature of air travel to and around the region are overwhelming constraints to growth (Drysdale, 2009; Kissling, 1989). Furthermore, the competitiveness of the South Pacific for tourism investment and visitation is under attack from destinations such as countries in the Mekong (Vietnam, Laos, Cambodia, and Myanmar), Bali, Malaysia, and Thailand, all of which carry substantial competitive advantages with regard to geographic proximity to source markets for the South Pacific, like Australia, and with superior economies of scale. In essence, although tourism holds immense potential for countries in the region, it should be seen as one part of a broader economic development strategy and not the centerpiece of economies, given its innate vulnerability and fickle nature (Milne, 1992).

Vanuatu: An Overview

The Republic of Vanuatu is an anomaly in the South Pacific because it was the only island state subject to both French and British colonial administration, more commonly referred to as the "condominium." Consisting of around 83 islands widely scattered throughout the Y-shaped archipelago (see **Figure CS 1.1**) and with a population of around 241,866 (Vanuatu National Statistics Office [VNSO], 2011), the island state lies some 3,700 kilometers from Australia's east coast. With the exception of the many *ni-Vanuatu* (Vanuatu's indigenous people) communities with distinct languages and cultural identities, a distinct legacy of the condominium is the establishment of a linguistic and cultural duality—Anglophones and Francophones, schooled and funded, respectively, by either British or French development programs. Although the country gained political independence in 1980, the legacy of its colonial past is still outwardly evident in contemporary life, especially reflected in the education and bureaucratic superstructure in situ.

Although the majority of *ni-Vanuatus* still reside in rural or outer island locations, increasing urbanization in the capital Port Vila is a growing concern. In particular, the pursuit of cash income, flight from disputes and social restrictions in traditional villages, land shortages, intermarriage among communities, and the growing appeal of a modern lifestyle are key factors driving urbanization (Cox et al., 2007). A consequence of the country's growing population and strengthening education system is the continuing rise in demand for employment from young people leaving school, steadily increasing the drift from rural and outer island locales to the capital Port Vila (de Fontenay, 2010). Currently Vanuatu maintains a dual economy—that is, it is dominated by both the informal and formal sectors. The country's economy is underlined by subsistence agriculture and piecemeal cash-cropping, and a large government sector funded principally through international development assistance from Australia, France, New Zealand, the European Union, the United States, Japan, and China.

Akin to other small island developing states in the region and elsewhere, Vanuatu is burdened with an exceedingly narrow-based economy with few alternatives for diversification and economic development. Bereft of extractive and manufacturing industries—with a relatively poor capacity for consistent agricultural and industrial production and a poor skills base—and hampered by practical constraints in

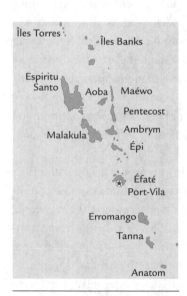

Figure CS 1.1   Map of Vanuatu.

terms of distance and cost to markets, the country has to rely heavily on international development assistance. Despite the country's inherited encumbrances, it is considered to have undergone faster growth in the 2000s, as compared to the period just after independence, mostly driven by foreign investment in tourism and land development, attracted by a liberal tax regime supported by a period of political stability, enhanced macroeconomic management, and successful institutional reforms (Cox et al., 2007). However, Cox et al. argue that little of the growth experienced in recent years has been of real benefit to *ni-Vanuatus*, calling for ongoing and urgent reforms to government and development policy. Not surprisingly, reform and good governance have become the catch cry of foreign aid donors and development partners, cognizant that the persistent specter of waning aid effectiveness must be overcome if the onerous demands of achieving the MDGs are to be realized.

Tourism in Vanuatu

The development of Vanuatu as a tourist destination had its beginnings in the 1960s and 1970s with the gradual development of a handful of small hotels and island-style resorts owned and operated by expatriates (Huffman, 1987). Shortly after independence in 1980 and during the period 1982–1983, annual international visitor arrivals peaked at 32,000, driven by foreign investment and private sector initiatives (United Nations Economic and Social Commission for Asia and the Pacific, 1995). It is argued that the country's growth over the first decade of the 2000s can be put down to tourism and real estate development, especially on the main island, Efate (Howes & Soni, 2009). Howes and Soni decry the popularly held notion that Pacific island economies cannot grow, citing tourism, active land markets, deregulation, and macroeconomic and social stability as key strategies. Whether tourism is the best choice for rapid growth in the country is arguable, and it is thought that as long as its competitiveness is not impaired by misguided labor market measures, it can be developed relatively rapidly (de Fontenay, 2010).

In the latter half of the 1980s, international visitor arrivals reached a low of around 15,000 annually (Milne, 1990). A steady increase to fewer than 60,000 in the mid-1990s followed, before this plummeted to around 20,000 in the early 2000s but then reclaiming the highs reached earlier in the 1990s (Niatu, 2007). From the mid-2000s visitation continued its upward trajectory, reaching a record high of around 90,000 in 2008, plus cruise ship arrivals of just over 100,000 (Cheer, 2010). Most recently, international visitor arrivals continue to grow, despite seasonal fluctuations, reaching record highs in 2009; remarkably this occurred amid the throes of the global economic crisis (see **Figure CS 1.2**). The motivation for the vast majority (77%) of visitors to Vanuatu during this period was primarily leisure (see **Figure CS 1.3**). Australians have traditionally dominated visitation to Vanuatu, and during the period 2009–2010, they comprised 54% of all visitors; Australia, New Zealand (11%), and neighboring New Caledonia (9%) made up 74% of all visitors during this period (see **Figure CS 1.4**).

The impact of increased competition in the airline sector, especially the introduction of low-cost carrier Pacific Blue, offshoot of the global Virgin organization, also is lauded as another principal reason for tourism's growth in the period from 2005 to 2010 (Vanuatu Tourism Office [VTO], 2006). According to the World Travel and Tourism Council (WTTC, 2010), the

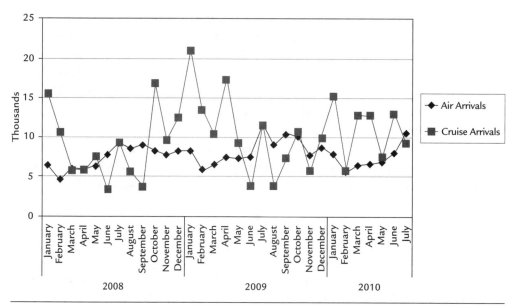

Figure CS 1.2   Vanuatu international visitor arrivals, 2008 to July 2010.
Source: From Vanuatu National Statistics Office. (2011). Live population of Vanuatu. Retrieved April 24, 2011, from http://www.vnso.gov.vu

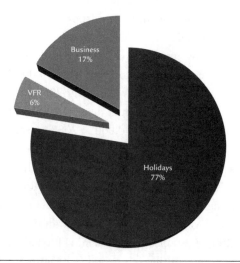

Figure CS 1.3   Purpose of visit, 2009 to July 2010.
Source: From Vanuatu National Statistics Office. (2011). Live population of Vanuatu. Retrieved April 24, 2011, from http://www.vnso.gov.vu

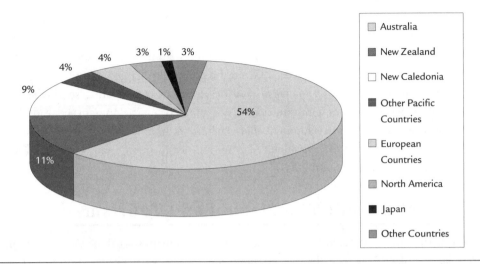

Figure CS 1.4   Visitor country of residence, 2009 to July 2010.
Source: From Vanuatu National Statistics Office. (2011). Live population of Vanuatu. Retrieved April 24, 2011, from http://www.vnso.gov.vu

magnitude of tourism's contribution to the Vanuatu economy can be seen across a number of key indicators (see **Table CS 1.1**). Importantly, WTTC's 10-year trend forecast projects continued strong growth through 2020.

Tourism in Vanuatu has not been free of detractors, who point especially to the impact that tourism has had on the alienation of traditional land (Slatter, 2006; Stefanova, 2008). Further questions about tourism's impacts also are being asked, particularly the veracity of claims that tourism is advancing the interests of the region's peoples (Cheer, 2010; Slatter, 2006). Of particular concern is the growth of tourism-induced real estate development that has resulted in more than 90% of coastal land on Vanuatu's main island Efate now being alienated

Table CS 1.1   Vanuatu Tourism Economic Indicators and 10-Year Forecast

Indicator	Status in 2011	10-Year Trend Forecast to 2022
Gross domestic product (GDP) total contribution	VUV38.583 billion, or 53% of total GDP	Rise to VUV60.104 billion
Tourism contribution to employment	31,000 jobs, or 47% of total employment	Rise to 43,000 jobs, or 48.2% of total employment
Visitor exports	VUV24.752 billion, or 74.1% of total exports	Rise to VUV36.986 billion, or 64.5% of total exports
Tourism investment	VUV4.847 billion, or 24.87% of total investment	Forecast to reach VUV9.397 billion, or 31.4% of total investment

Note: VUV, also known as the Vatu, is the national currency in Vanuatu (VUV100 is equivalent to approximately $1.06USD as at May 2012; see http://www.xe.com/ucc).
Source: Data from World Tourism and Travel Council (WTTC). (2012). Travel and tourism economic impact 2012–Vanuatu. London: WTTC.

from traditional land-owning communities (Stefanova, 2008). With limited and ineffectual land-use planning, residential subdivisions primarily targeted at expatriates are taking over prime beach frontage and preventing local communities from utilizing traditional fishing grounds and limiting right-of-way access. Given the politically charged nature of traditional land security in Vanuatu, poorly managed land development is generating serious tensions (Slatter, 2006). Yet *ni-Vanuatu* communities are not opposed to development, instead ideally welcoming sensitive tourism development that generates economic growth, particularly jobs and business opportunities for marginalized communities in outer islands and rural areas (Cox et al., 2007; Howes & Soni, 2009).

Pentecost Island: The *Naghol* and Tourism

The northern island of Pentecost is located around 200 kilometers north of Vanuatu's capital Port Vila. The island is practically and geographically distant, with a population of just over 15,000 living mainly in the southern and northern villages, and covering an area of around 438 square kilometers. Like most outer island locations in the South Pacific, access to Pentecost is constrained by costly and irregular air and shipping schedules. Moreover, the island's infrastructure is deficient, including generally impassable roads, especially in the wet season, and poor health, education, and government services characteristic. Copra (a dried meat or kernel of the coconut used in making coconut oil), once the economic mainstay of many outer island communities, has declined in value and importance, leaving islanders with even fewer options for livelihood diversification. Such constraints present a host of impediments that prevent islanders from actively engaging in the mainstream national economy, especially for the trade in primary commodities (kava, yams, and copra), the development of tourism, and access to education and employment.

Undoubtedly, outer island communities such as those on Pentecost are the most marginalized and disadvantaged in the region. This highlights why development concerns, especially making headway on the metrics related to poverty and the provision of basic needs, particularly health and education, in outer islands is pressing. Yet, although the urgency for MDGs abatement is especially pertinent for outer island communities like those on Pentecost, much development funding and attention has tended to focus on the main island of Efate, such as the US$62 million USAID funded "ring road" infrastructure project (U.S. Government Accountability Office, 2007). Consequently, alongside nongovernment, government, donor, and volunteer (e.g., U.S. Peace Corps, Australian Youth Ambassadors for Development) development impetus, tourism has become one of the key economic vehicles available to outer islander communities whose cultural heritage and natural assets are heavily predisposed to a range of tourism development.

It is no surprise, then, that the unique cultural heritage of the *naghol* or land diving has become the primary motivation for tourist visitation to Pentecost. The *naghol* is described as a ritual with profound sacred ancestral significance (Jolly, 1994) and is the traditional property of the Sa communities in the south. During the colonial era and with the arrival of Christian missionaries, traditional rites, symbols, and rituals such as the *naghol* were discouraged, and in many cases ceased to exist (Scarr, 1990). It was not until the 1970s with the onset of increased tourist numbers and a return to traditionalism that the *naghol* regained prominence (Huffman, 1987). Although the *naghol* narrative and its significance is far more complex and layered (Jolly, 1994) than can be described in this chapter, the bounds to its appropriation define how it can be used for tourism. The limits to the utilization of the *naghol* for tourism include questions over the nature of its performance, ownership, custodianship, traditional power structures, and debate over authenticity and commodification.

Traditionally, the performance of the *naghol* was restricted to the Sa and could only be appropriated by them and take place in the villages of the south. Furthermore, construction of the *naghol* tower is restricted to Sa men, using only locally sourced logs and yam vines (see **Figure CS 1.5**). The preeminent *naghol* narrative is of an annual celebration of the yam harvest (Huffman, 1987), during which men with yam vines attached to their ankles hurl themselves off a 60-meter tower (see **Figure CS 1.6**). It is thought that the success of the next season's yam harvest will be enhanced if the jumper's hair brushes the ground. Conversely, the alternative mythology of the *naghol* is of domestic upheaval, where in response to what was thought of as the suicide of his spouse, a man jumps to his death not realizing the deception at hand (his wife had tied vines to her feet and feigned jumping to her death from the treetops). Moreover, the performance of the *naghol* was traditionally restricted to the months of April and May in accordance with the yam cycle; in the 1980s it occurred five to eight times annually (Huffman, 1987). This stands in stark contrast to the situation today where performances are barred only on Sundays from March to June to allow the predominantly Christian community to attend church services.

The unique nature of the *naghol* has been appropriated for tourists eager to witness a ritual of immense uniqueness, power, and tradition. Symbolically for the Sa, the *naghol* is steeped in traditionalism and is sacred and critical to their identity on the island within

Figure CS 1.5 Construction of the *naghol* tower.

Figure CS 1.6 *Naghol* in flight.

Vanuatu and beyond. Thus, contention surrounding its utilization for tourism often is around the breaching of traditional values through excessive commercialization, enforcing what many consider to be crass and demeaning practice (Vanuatu National Cultural Council, 2006). For many scholars and practitioners, particularly culture guardians and anthropologists, tourism is viewed with some disdain, and its development is seen as antithetical to the spirit of anthropological research (Jolly, 1994). Jolly suggests the use of the *naghol* for tourism is somewhat profane in relation to the outward deference toward *kastom* (i.e., traditions) that is insisted on in all areas of *ni-Vanuatu* life (Tonkinson, 1982). It can be argued that famed documentary maker and naturalist Sir Richard Attenborough was the initial catalyst behind the foisting of the *naghol* into the global gaze in the 1960s, and he suggested that the *naghol*, in some respects, was already distorted then (Attenborough, 1966).

The discourse around the commodification of cultural heritage in indigenous settings, especially for tourism, suggests that tourism can serve to protect and conserve cultural heritage on one hand, while conversely serve to irrevocably despoil and transform it through excessive commodification (Busse, 2009; Butler & Hinch, 2007; Ryan & Aicken, 2005). Ensuring its longevity and authenticity, and accordingly enhancing sustainable tourism, should be a major preoccupation for the people of Pentecost and those responsible for the effective governance of tourism in the country. In particular, the question of whose voices should be loudest in the debate about the commodification of the *naghol* and the terms under which it is appropriated are key anxieties. Most importantly, the issue of ensuing financial recompense is central to the discourse around the use of the *naghol* for tourism, and to Sa concerns because of the way in which financial proceeds are distributed between culture brokers or agents on the main island, and the Sa themselves.

The Impact of Tourism on Pentecost Island: Preliminary Study Findings

Whether tourism is making an impact on MDGs mitigation on Pentecost is contentious and largely unsubstantiated. At a country level, recent strong growth in tourism arrivals and international tourist expenditure in Vanuatu over the period 2005–2010 suggests that coupled with continued expansion, a parallel growth in opportunities for *ni-Vanuatu* participation is taking place. Increased access to formal sector employment, microenterprise development, improved services, and the spill-over into the broader economy are considered some of the more desirable outcomes. However, evidence suggesting that tourism is aiding MDGs progression is limited owing to the chronic absence of reliable baseline data and on-going longitudinal investigations (Cheer, 2010). Consequently, the depth of understanding with respect to micro- and macro-level tourism impacts in the outer islands, and the country in general, is conspicuously lacking. Preliminary findings from this study suggest a number of principal inhibitors exist that curtail the impact that tourism is having on broad MDG indicators and the development and modernization on Pentecost Island. These are discussed in the following sections.

Culture Brokers and Booking Agents

The overriding influence of culture brokers or booking agents (typically outsiders including expatriates and *ni-Vanuatu* from elsewhere) on the main island Efate and the capital Port Vila is regarded as one of the key inhibitors preventing Pentecost islanders from accruing a fair and reasonable financial benefit from staging the *naghol*. Culture brokers in many tourism contexts are regarded as critical to meeting the supply and demand for cultural tourism products (Smith, 1977), and the same applies here. In this case, in the main, booking agents hold sway over the Sa because they have initial and primary contact with tourists, and overwhelmingly command the terms of *naghol*-induced tourism. This includes the determination of what tourists are charged, the particular *naghol* they attend, and, most importantly, the level and speed at which remittances are made to the particular Sa community. Furthermore, in the rare instance where tourists would opt to stay over on Pentecost, booking agents determine with whom they are accommodated and hold sway over the negotiated rates with bungalow operators. Given the Sa's reliance on and vulnerability to booking agents, in practical terms, they hold little control over the nature of tourism.

Distribution of Naghol-*Induced Income*

Another concern raised in this study is the extent to which *naghol*-induced income is distributed among islanders. Traditionalism very much governs societal processes within Sa communities and is typically led by elders or chiefs who hold authority through lineage. The implication here is that governance and control of tourism incomes is under the control of community elders, meaning that the broader community is vulnerable to their decisions and practices. Consequently, the collection, disbursement, consumption, and investment of *naghol*-related income is centralized and presided over by senior members of the community. In the event that tardiness, poor decisions, misappropriation, or corruption occurs, this potentially jeopardizes community prospects and subsequent development progress.

Naghol-*Induced Employment*

Evidence encountered in this study demonstrates that few long-term employment prospects are created on Pentecost Island. There a number of reasons for this, primary among them the overwhelming practice of tourists flying in from the capital Port Vila on day visits only. This is largely attributed to booking agents in Port Vila looking to maximize the sales of tours to other islands for the same groups of tourists. Thus, the need for accommodation, tours, and other services is minimal, consequently preventing the development of associated enterprises. The only way new employment opportunities can be created is through lengthening the period of stay in situ utilizing locally owned bungalow accommodation and participating in non–*naghol*-related activities.

Packaging the Naghol

The relative costs of visiting Pentecost Island for the *naghol* are prohibitive to its inclusion in the majority of vacation packages offered. Most tourists to the country are on a package vacation, so the small numbers who choose to visit Pentecost Island are independent tourists or expatriates based in Port Vila. Furthermore, average tourists stay in the country for just under a week as part of a vacation package in which multiple experiences are packaged into already time-constrained and price-sensitive itineraries. Thus, the practicality of including the *naghol* in packages is severely limited, meaning that any growth in international visitation for the country does not necessarily lead to greater benefits to Pentecost Island tourism.

Tourism and Traditionalism

Tourism's demonstration effects are widely discussed as key negative sociocultural impacts of tourism. In societies such as those on Pentecost Island, lifestyles, customs, and rules are governed by traditional mechanisms, often the very ones vulnerable to growing tourism and the attendant influence of tourists. However, the prevailing nature of tourism on Pentecost Island—where most tourists make day visits only and spend little, if any, time making direct contact with their hosts—mitigates any chance of social interaction. Although such a mode of tourism is decried as financially limiting for hosts, it is responsible for traditionalism remaining largely intact here. This is especially critical for traditionalists and suited to the growing agenda pushing for a return to traditional ways in the country.

Conclusion

Naghol-led tourism is a paradox. On the one hand it is a vehicle through which islanders are hoping to advance on the marginalization and poverty characteristic of their existence and in doing so incrementally moving away from traditional lifestyles. Conversely, it promotes traditionalism as an ideal worth saving given its inherent financial and cultural value and through which cultural practice symbolic to Sa identities is maintained, thereby strengthening traditionalism. It is unclear that widespread financial benefit is accruing from *naghol*-induced tourism, and this is a key concern. The concern for islanders is the increasing need for cash incomes. Tourism offers the best prospects in this regard but only if proceeds are distributed equitably. In particular, the influence of culture brokers must be curtailed and a *modus operandi* for community-based tourism that respects traditional structures and, at the same time, maximizes equitable distribution of revenues, is essential.

The tyranny of expensive airfares and irregular services are a key barrier to growing visitation to outer island locations. This is unlikely to improve in the short-term, meaning that the *naghol* will remain a niche experience with little prospect for new growth. Such circumstances are commonplace in outer island communities that, despite having outstanding tourism products and experiences, fail to capitalize because of the inherent frailties of peripherality, especially in relation to time, distance, and costs to markets. The "burden" of traditionalism must be reconciled if communities such as those on Pentecost Island are going to join the country's mainstream economy. This is not to say that traditionalism must be expunged; instead the call must be to find a compromise that helps advance islanders' modern existence and not leave them marginalized and poor, removed from the successes of MDGs advancement.

References

Abbott, D. (2007, December). Poverty and pro-poor policies for Pacific island countries. *Asia-Pacific Population Journal*, 59–74.

Allcock, A. (2006). *Pacific 2020: Background paper: Tourism*. Canberra, Australia: AusAID.

Attenborough, D. (1966). The land-diving ceremony in Pentecost, New Hebrides. *Philosophical Transactions of the Royal Society of London. Series B, Biological Sciences: A Discussion on Ritualization of Behaviour in Animals and Man, 251*(772), 503–505.

Basu, P. K. (2000). Conflicts and paradoxes in economic development tourism in Papua New Guinea. *International Journal of Social Economics, 27*(7/8/9/10), 907–914.

Busse, M. (2009). Epilogue: Anxieties about culture and tradition—property as reification. *International Journal of Cultural Property, 16*, 357–370.

Butler, R., & Hinch, T. (Eds.). (2007). *Tourism and indigenous peoples: Issues and implications*. London: Elsevier.

Cheer, J. (2010). Kicking goals or offside: Is tourism development in the Pacific helping progress towards the MDGs? *Pacific Economic Bulletin, 25*(1), 151–161.

Cheer, J., & Peel, V. (2011). The tourism-foreign aid nexus in Vanuatu: Future directions. *Tourism Planning and Development, 8*(3), 253–264.

Connell, J. (2010). Pacific islands in the global economy: Paradoxes of migration and culture. *Singapore Journal of Tropical Geography, 31*, 115–129.

Cox, M., Alatoa, H., Kenni, L., Naupa, A., Rawlings, G., Soni, N., . . . Bulekone, V. (2007). *The unfinished state: Drivers of change in Vanuatu*. Canberra, Australia: AusAID.

Crocombe, R. (2001). *The South Pacific*. Suva, Fiji: USP Institute of Pacific Studies.

de Fontenay, P. (2010). An educated, healthy and wealthy Vanuatu. *Pacific Economic Bulletin, 25*(2), 25–41.

Drysdale, A. (2009, December/2010, January). Pacific aviation needs new era of trust and cooperation. *Aviation Business Asia Pacific*, 14–17.

Harrison, D. (2004). Tourism in Pacific islands. *Journal of Pacific Studies, 26*(1&2), 1–28.

Hawkins, D. E., & Mann, S. (2007). The World Bank's role in tourism development. *Annals of Tourism Research, 34*(2), 348–363.

Howes, S., & Soni, N. (2009). Fast growth in the Pacific is possible—look at Vanuatu. *Briefing 10* (pp. 1–4). Port Vila, Vanuatu: Pacific Institute of Public Policy.

Huffman, K. (1987, October 26–November 7). *Socio-cultural considerations in tourism development: The case of Vanuatu*. Paper presented at the Tourism Foundation Course, Tourism Council of the South Pacific and World Tourism Organisation.

Jolly, M. (1994). The land dive as indigenous rite and tourist spectacle in Vanuatu. In L. Lindstrom & G. White (Eds.), *Culture, kastom, tradition: Developing cultural policy in Melanesia* (pp. 131–146). Suva, Fiji: USP Institute of Pacific Studies.

Kellett, P. (2010). AJ Hackett—a giant of tourism. In R. Butler & R. Russell (Eds.), *Giants of tourism* (Chapter 14). Oxfordshire, UK: CABI.

Kissling, C. (1989). International tourism and civil aviation in the South Pacific: Issues and innovations. *GeoJournal, 19*(3), 309–315.

Milne, S. (1990). Tourism and economic development in Vanuatu. *Singapore Journal of Tropical Geography, 11*(1), 13–26.

Milne, S. (1992). Tourism and development in South Pacific microstates. *Annals of Tourism Research, 19*, 191–212.

Mitchell, J., & Ashley, C. (2010). *Tourism and poverty reduction: Pathways to prosperity*. London: Earthscan.

Narayan, P., Narayan, S., Prasad, P., & Prasad, B. (2010). Tourism and economic growth: A panel data analysis for Pacific Island countries. *Tourism Economics, 16*(1), 169–183.

New Economics Foundation. (2006). *The happy planet index*. London: New Economics Foundation.

Niatu, A. (2007). *Dosalsal, the floating ones: Exploring the socio-cultural impacts of cruise ship tourism on Port Vila, Vanuatu residents, and their coping strategies*. Master's thesis, Master of Tourism Management, Lincoln University, Christchurch.

Ryan, C., & Aicken, M. (Eds.). (2005). *Indigenous tourism: The commodification and management of culture.* London: Elsevier.

Scarr, D. (1990). *The history of the Pacific islands: Kingdoms of the reefs.* Melbourne, Australia: Macmillan.

Scheyvens, R., & Momsen, J. H. (2008). Tourism and poverty reduction: Issues for small island states. *Tourism Geographies, 10*(1), 22–41.

Seetanah, B. (2011). Assessing the dynamic economic impact of tourism for island economies. *Annals of Tourism Research, 38*(1), 291–308.

Slade, T. N. (2009, August 3). *Keynote address: Responsibilities for tackling the economic crisis.* Paper presented at The Pacific Islands and the World: The Global Economic Crisis, Lowy Institute for International Policy, Brisbane, Australia.

Slatter, C. (2006). *The con/dominion of Vanuatu? Paying the price of investment and land liberalisation—a case study of Vanuatu's tourism industry.* Auckland, New Zealand: OXFAM New Zealand.

Smith, V. (1977). *Hosts and guests: The anthropology of tourism.* Philadelphia, PA: University of Pennsylvania Press.

Stefanova, M. (2008). The price of tourism: Land alienation in Vanuatu. *Justice for the Poor/World Bank, 2*(1), 1–4.

Theroux, P. (1992). *The happy isles of Oceania.* London: Hamish Hamilton.

Tonkinson, R. (1982). Kastom in Melanesia: Introduction. *Mankind, 13*(4), 302–305.

United Nations Economic and Social Commission for Asia and the Pacific. (1995). *Study on foreign investment in the tourism sector in Vanuatu: ST/ESCAP/1427.* New York: United Nations.

U.S. Government Accountability Office. (2007). *Millennium challenge corporation: Vanuatu compact overstates projected program impact.* Washington, DC: Author.

Vanuatu National Cultural Council. (2006). *Moratorium on commercial filming of Nagol.* Port Vila, Vanuatu: Author.

Vanuatu National Statistics Office. (2011). Live population of Vanuatu. Retrieved April 24, 2011, from http://www.vnso.gov.vu

Vanuatu Tourism Office. (2006). *Vanuatu tourism office, strategic plan 2007–2010.* Port Vila, Vanuatu: Author.

Wong, P. (2009). *Official closing address.* Paper presented at The Pacific Islands and The World: The Global Economic Crisis, Lowy Institute for International Policy, Brisbane, Australia.

World Travel and Tourism Council. (2010). *Travel and tourism economic impact—Vanuatu 2010.* London: Author.

Poverty Alleviation

Tourism and the Explicit Concern with Poverty Reduction: A Review

Ferry Van de Mosselaer and René Van der Duim

LEARNING OBJECTIVES

- To understand the development of the tourism–poverty nexus
- To comprehend the main concepts and principles of pro-poor tourism
- To be able to discuss the state-of-the-art in research in pro-poor tourism
- To provoke critical thinking on the future of tourism and poverty alleviation

September 22, 2010. Delegates have arrived from all over the world for this week's United Nations Millennium Development Goals Summit in New York to discuss how to tackle poverty, illness, and hunger in developing countries. Although New Yorkers may grumble about the extra traffic, this upswing is nothing compared to the some 46 million tourists that descend on the city annually. Debates this week at the UN revolve around ways to raise the necessary resources to meet the Millennium Development Goals (MDGs) by 2015, and one of the solutions for the next 5 years might lie in these astounding numbers behind tourism today.[1]

Over the last 10 years, the relationship between tourism and the MDGs has been subject to many debates (see, e.g., Saarinen, Rogerson, & Manwa, 2011). These debates have especially focused on the question of how and to what extent tourism can address MDG 1: the eradication of extreme poverty and hunger. However, policies and practices aiming at poverty alleviation through tourism are not new. Ever since the 1940s, aid programs have been developed to try to transfer wealth and expertise to what used to be known as the Third World. Already in the 1950s and 1960s tourism was identified as a potential modernization strategy that could help newly independent Third World countries to earn foreign income, and tourism was promoted as a development strategy to transfer technology, increase employment, amplify the GDP, attract foreign capital, and promote a modern way of life with Western values (see Scheyvens, 2007; Sharpley & Telfer, 2002). Supporters of the Washington consensus (Williamson, 2000), in particular, assumed that economic growth would eventually trickle down to the poorer categories of society (Dollar & Kraay, 2002), and hence create positive impacts for destinations at large. But these attempts have often been met with skepticism, especially among academics, and these doubts sometimes have been accompanied with virulent hostility to large-scale tourism (Harrison, 2008).

In the 1990s, poverty alleviation became the leading development agenda, and the World Bank, followed by many multilateral and bilateral donors, increasingly propagated the concept of pro-poor growth (Scheyvens, 2011). The central assumption of pro-poor growth was that economic growth is beneficial for development and should be encouraged as long as the "poor" benefit overproportionally (Meyer, 2011; Ravallion, 2004). Development organizations, technical assistance agencies, and donors started incorporating the concept into existing rural development and natural resource management programs and also hesitantly started to tailor it to the specific characteristics of the tourism industry. Research into the possibilities of tourism to contribute to poverty reduction (Bennett, Roe, & Ashley, 1999), commissioned by the United Kingdom's Department for International Development (DFID), and research undertaken by the Pro-poor Tourism Partnership (see Goodwin, 2011) were especially instrumental in this new way of thinking. Step by step, pro-poor tourism (PPT) became a focal concept for many involved in trying to link tourism to development and MDG 1.

From the start, the advocates of PPT have explicitly focused on the question of how tourism could help to reduce poverty by increasing net benefits to the poor (Ashley et al., 2001; Bennett et al., 1999). Pro-poor tourism supporters are not introducing yet another type of tourism but instead look at all types of tourism and how they can contribute to poverty reduction (Meyer, 2011).

---

[1] Millennium Foundation. Newsfeed 322. Retrieved September 23, 2011, from http://www.massivegood.org.

However, PPT, just like *sustainable* or *responsible* tourism, is a catchall term, a "fuzzy" but inherently valued thing, a "category of the good" (Neuman, 2005 in Gunder, 2006). It is fuzzy because it represents diverse views and competing values (Chok, MacBeth, & Warren, 2007), is based on the divergent agenda of various stakeholders, and is inspired and influenced by various approaches to relations between tourism and development (Scheyvens, 2007, 2009). It comprises a set of discourses and practices that came to occupy—although rather marginally and in many cases also contested—a place within development organizations as the organizing principle of the discursive field on tourism and development (Gunder, 2006). PPT slowly became a discursive construction that was used, built upon, and reinforced through a loose alliance of scholars and development practitioners. On the one hand, particular staff members of development organizations, technical assistance agencies, and donors used the PPT discussions to legitimize courses of action (see, e.g., Hummel & van der Duim, 2011). To these PPT practitioners, underlying concepts and premises such as linkages and leakages, pro-poor growth, and values chains became—although hesitantly— legitimate starting points for applied research and development practices. In their studies they attempted to find realistic solutions and workable market intervention strategies that enable the poor to participate in the industry (Meyer, 2009). On the other hand, PPT also became subject to academic debates, predominantly inspired by scholars influenced by poststructuralism and dependency paradigms. As part of this, the concept of PPT increasingly was accused of serving particular neo-liberal, bureaucratic, and corporate interests (Chok et al., 2007) and lacking academic rigor (Harrison, 2008; Scheyvens, 2007, 2009; Sharpley & Naidoo, 2010). Although PPT practitioners have never made claims to theoretical substantiation, the core of the PPT coalition now also supports the quest for a critical reflection into the concepts, premises, and methods of PPT (Mitchell & Ashley, 2010). This quest also is supported by another tendency. The development industry in general, accelerated by critical publications from economic scholars (see, e.g., Easterly, 2006; Moyo, 2009) and government reports (see, e.g., Scientific Council for Government Policy [WRR], 2010), has become subject to fierce debates on the effectiveness of current aid and development strategies, leading to development policy restructuring. This discussion also indirectly impacts the future of PPT. For example, SNV Netherlands Development Organization, with 65 tourism advisors in over 25 countries in 2010, when confronted with large budget cuts, recently had to decide to phase out pro-poor sustainable tourism as a practice area (see Hummel & van der Duim, 2011).

This chapter provides a review of some of the basic principles of PPT. We first look at the emergence of the idea of PPT. From this short historical account we then introduce and discuss the main concepts and premises associated with PPT. We look at how these premises serve as a framework for research and strategy development in PPT. Finally, we briefly discuss research into PPT and conclude with an outlook on future research and practice on tourism and poverty reduction.

The Rise of Pro-Poor Tourism

At the end of the 1990s, the U.K. Department for International Development (DFID) commissioned consultants Deloitte and Touche, in cooperation with the International Institute for Environment and Development (IIED) and the Overseas Development Institute (ODI), to develop an overview of the current and planned tourism-related activities of other development organizations (Bennett et al., 1999). They also considered the scope for working in partnership with the private sector. The work was undertaken in relation to three broad issues being considered by the DFID in relation to the seventh Commission on Sustainable Development (CSD-7):

1. What is the potential to develop initiatives in the tourism sector to promote pro-poor economic growth and contribute to poverty elimination?
2. How to ensure that the environmental and social costs of tourism initiatives are minimized and that environmental, social, economic, and overall net benefits are maximized?
3. What are the scope and mechanisms for working in partnership with the private sector in relation to first two?

Based on the outcome of the report of Bennett et al. (1999), supplemented by Goodwin's (1998) report a year before, the concept of pro-poor tourism was developed (see also Goodwin, 2008). Bennett et al. concluded that tourism in general has the potential to contribute to poverty alleviation in developing countries and that earlier concepts like sustainable tourism and community-based tourism had not addressed poverty reduction explicitly enough. During the CSD-7, information Bennett at al. provided was used to get tourism on the agenda as a means for poverty alleviation (Scheyvens, 2011). The potential for tourism to contribute to poverty alleviation is based on a number of related arguments, as summarized in **Box 3.1**.

Following the CSD-7, the UK Overseas Development Institute (ODI) initiated a research project conducted by the Pro-Poor Tourism Partnership, a collaboration of Harold Goodwin (International Centre for Responsible Tourism), Dilys Roe (International Institute for Environment and Development), and Caroline Ashley (ODI). This partnership has been very influential, with Ashley, Goodwin, and Roe collaborating on many of the early reports on PPT (Scheyvens, 2011).

During the Johannesburg World Summit on Sustainable Development in 2002, the UN World Tourism Organization (UNWTO) endorsed the PPT concept and launched the Sustainable Tourism—Eliminating Poverty (ST-EP) initiative. During that occasion, the UNWTO

Box 3.1   Arguments for Pro-Poor Tourism

- *Reverse supply chain:* Significant cross-selling opportunities at destinations because the consumer moves to the product.
- *Intersectoral linkages:* Potential of connecting other sectors, particularly agriculture and handicrafts, to the tourism industry.
- The labor-intensive character of tourism creates opportunities for employment.
- Tourism often takes place in marginal areas with a high poverty rate.
- Tourism generally employs a high level of females, youth, and unskilled workers.
- There are low entry barriers to the tourism sector.
- There is disproportionate growth of tourism in developing countries.

Source: Data from Meyer, D. (2010, April). *Value chain analysis and tourism.* Presentation at 3A-ST-EP meeting, Dar es Salaam; and Meyer, D. (2011). Pro-poor tourism: Can tourism contribute to poverty reduction in less economically developed countries? In S. Cole & N. Morgan (Eds.), *Tourism and inequality: Problems and prospects* (pp. 164–182). Wallingford, England: CAB International.

invited UN agencies, governments, donor agencies, nongovernmental organizations (NGOs), and other stakeholders to unite in a concerted effort to use the benefits that derive from tourism to actively combat poverty throughout the world (UNWTO, 2004). The ST-EP projects aim to enhance the local economic impact from tourism in various ways, such as by improving the performance of small and medium tourism enterprises, establishing PPT business linkages between the tourism business and neighboring communities, and using fees, taxes, and donations generated from tourism development (Leijzer, 2007). The ST-EP program includes four main components. The first component is a research base to identify linkages, principles, and model applications. There is also an operating framework for promoting and developing incentives for good practice among companies, consumers, and communities. Forums for sharing and exchanging information, ideas, and plans are another component designed to bring together private, public, and nongovernmental stakeholders. Finally, there is the ST-EP Foundation, which was originally concerned with attracting new, dedicated financing from business, philanthropic, and government sources (see http://www.unwtostep.org for more information). In the publication *Tourism and Poverty Alleviation: Recommendations for Action*, the ST-EP program presented seven different mechanisms through which the poor can benefit directly or indirectly from tourism (see **Box 3.2**). These mechanisms have become an important philosophy of the ST-EP initiative.

The emerging PPT approaches aimed to create a bridge between the development of mainstream and mass-market tourism (often referred to as the "boosterism" approach) and poor communities moving beyond small-scale and alternative tourism development approaches, such as community-based tourism (CBT) and ecotourism, which became popular at the end of the twentieth century. It was acknowledged that whereas CBT projects could empower communities to take part in the development and management of tourism, they often failed to deliver significant poverty reduction impacts (Bennett et al., 1999; see also Meyer, 2011). A review of 200 CBT projects across the Americas (Goodwin & Santilli, 2009; Jones & Wood, 2007; Mitchell & Muckosy, 2008) showed that many accommodation providers had only 5% occupancy. According to the review, the most likely outcome for a CBT initiative is a collapse after funding dries up. The main causes of collapse are poor market access and poor governance.

Box 3.2   Seven Mechanisms of UNWTO ST-EP

1. Employment of the poor in tourism enterprises
2. Supply of goods and services to tourism enterprises by the poor or by enterprises employing the poor
3. Direct sales of goods and services to visitors by the poor (informal economy)
4. Establishment and running of tourism enterprises by the poor (e.g., micro, small, and medium-sized enterprises [MSMEs], or community-based enterprises [formal economy])
5. Tax or levy on tourism income or profits with proceeds benefiting the poor
6. Voluntary giving/support by tourism enterprises and tourists
7. Investment in infrastructure stimulated by tourism also benefiting the poor in the locality, directly or through support to other sectors

Source: Data from United Nations World Tourism Organization and the Netherlands Development Organization. (2010). *SNV 2010 manual on tourism and poverty alleviation: Practical steps for destinations.* Madrid, Spain: Authors.

Similarly, Spenceley (2008) analyzed 217 community-based tourism enterprises in 12 southern African countries—Botswana, Lesotho, Madagascar, Malawi, Mauritius, Mozambique, Namibia, South Africa, Swaziland, Tanzania, Zambia, and Zimbabwe—and identified that next to accessibility, the important limitations in the development of community-based enterprises are market access and advertisement. As in other fields, such as agriculture, community-based tourism initiatives are unlikely to succeed if the community is unable to penetrate the market (see Nel & Binns, 2000).

The concept of pro-poor tourism is now seen as an overall approach specifically focusing on unlocking opportunities for the poor through tourism. Essential to this approach is that PPT is not necessarily just a small-scale or niche type of tourism, as previously proposed in alternative approaches but instead seeks to work with all types of tourism businesses (Meyer, 2007, 2010). A pro-poor approach pays specific attention to obstacles constraining greater participation in tourism by the poor and discerns three pathways by which tourism affects different poor people (Mitchell & Ashley, 2007, 2010):

1. *Direct effects from tourism to the poor:* Labor income from tourism jobs or small enterprise, other forms of tourism income, and nonfinancial livelihood changes (negative as well as positive).
2. *Secondary effects from tourism to the poor:* Indirect earnings from nontourism sectors that supply tourism (e.g., food). Added to these are induced effects from tourism workers respending their earnings in the local economy.
3. *Dynamic effects on the economy:* Impacts on entrepreneurialism, market factors, other export sectors, or the natural environment are all included here. They may be experienced in the macroeconomy or limited to the local destination economy. The poor may be affected more or less than the nonpoor by changes in, for example, wages and land prices.

According to pro-poor tourism advocates, all three pathways by which tourism impacts poverty need consideration (Mitchell & Ashley, 2010).

Concepts and Premises in PPT

Pro-poor tourism is a blended approach, deriving ideas, concepts, and thoughts from a variety of approaches: liberal and neo-liberal, critical, and alternative development approaches all have in some way contributed to the growth of interest in PPT (Scheyvens, 2007, 2011; Telfer & Sharpley, 2008).

Consequently, the PPT discourse, like the sustainable development debate, is shaped by diverse views and competing values: ". . . it is a morally-charged concept valued for its unifying qualities, yet remains vulnerable to political hijacking" (Chok et al., 2007, p. 146). The indefinite positioning of PPT is, according to Harrison (2008), due to the fact that (as summarized in **Box 3.3**) it is principally defined by what it is not, rather than what it is: "[I]t is neither capitalist nor hostile to mainstream tourism, on which it relies; it is neither a theory nor a model, and it is not a niche form of tourism; it has not a distinctive method and is not only (and sometimes not at all) about the poor" (Harrison, 2008, p. 864).

Box 3.3   Characteristics of Pro-Poor Tourism

PPT is not . . .	PPT does . . .
anti-capitalist	focus on incorporating the poor into markets
separate from the rest of tourism	depend on existing structures and markets
a niche type of tourism (e.g., community-based tourism)	orientate to net benefits of tourism to the poor
a specific method	use different methods to collect and analyze data, including value chain analysis
only about the poor	recognize that the poorest may not be touched by PPT and that the nonpoor may benefit disproportionately
just about hunger and incomes	use a broad definition of *poverty*; it is basically about *development*
only about individual benefits	focus on family and community benefits, including water, sanitation, health, education, training, and the like

Source: Data from Harrison, D. (2008). Pro-poor tourism: A critique. *Third World Quarterly, 29*(5), 851–868; and van der Duim, V. R. (2008). Exploring pro-poor tourism research: The state of the art. In H. De Haan and V. R. van der Duim (Eds.), *Landscape, leisure, and tourism* (pp. 179–196). Delft, The Netherlands: Eburon.

As a consequence, PPT proponents have taken on board a number of concepts that aim to substantiate the logic of pro-poor development interventions. In the following paragraphs we will discuss some of the main concepts and premises of PPT. First, there is the concept of poverty. Obviously, the main merit of PPT is that the poor are the central focus of concern (Zhao & Ritchie, 2007, p. 120). Yet, Scheyvens (2011, p. 19) recently argued that a fundamental weakness with PPT is that it is "dislocated from a theory of poverty." However, influenced by ideas of sustainable livelihoods, empowerment, and Sen's (2001) seminal philosophical elaboration on poverty as "capability deprivation," and the alleviation of poverty as "substantial freedom enhancement," increasingly the multidimensionality of poverty has been recognized. On poverty, the Pro-Poor Tourism Partnership (2004) commented that

> There is no agreed definition of poverty or how it should be measured. What may be considered poverty in one setting may be considered comparative wealth in another. At the international scale, the World Bank has defined poverty as an income of less than US$1 per day. However, it is important to note that poverty is multi-dimensional and includes not just lack of income but lack of power, inequality, insufficient food, poor health, etc.

Pro-poor tourism proponents acknowledge the multidimensionality of poverty, whereby not only economic growth and providing jobs and income is considered important but also reducing vulnerability, increasing self-reliance, building up capabilities and assets, and securing rights (see Scheyvens, 2011). But at the same time they have recognized the difficulties of working with a multidimensional conceptualization of poverty. For example, Mitchell and Ashley (2010, p. 12) recently argued that "to avoid falling at this definitional hurdle," one must retain "an agnostic view on what is the correct poverty level to apply to tourism studies." The sustainable livelihood approach, especially applied in early PPT research, often has been used to move beyond mere income and job-related benefits to identify other assets of the poor (human, social, natural, and physical capital) and to learn more about their strategies of coping and adapting (Meyer, 2011). Nevertheless, income and employment-related definitions are still central (see van der Duim, 2008) and have been particularly important in value chain analyses. The focus on quantifying employment and income impacts illustrates the pragmatism and accountability needs of development organizations that work with the poor. It also reflects the increased "institutionalization" of poverty by multilateral development organizations and development banks (Green, 2007). Poverty Reduction Strategy Papers (PRSPs), issued by the World Bank and International Monetary Fund (IMF), have become key in addressing poverty eradication by national governments as well as development organizations. As such, Green argued that PRSPs have become the exponents of institutionalized poverty and "the vehicles for the formalization of what are in effect national development strategies based on the development visions of multilateral organizations" (p. 38).

Second, and related, the pro-poor growth idea has been central to the concept of pro-poor tourism. It essentially builds on the premise that the benefits of economic growth do not naturally trickle down to the poorer sections of society (Meyer, 2010); hence, intervention is legitimized and needed. It argues that economic growth is essential to development, and tourism can contribute to poverty reduction as long as the poor benefit overproportionally (Meyer, 2010; Ravallion, 2004). Pro-poor growth requires strategies that are deliberately biased in favor of the poor (Kakwani & Pernia, 2000). However, consensus is lacking on when a strategy or intervention can be actually considered as pro-poor. A restrictive definition of pro-poor growth competes with an undemanding one (Meyer, 2010; Mitchell & Ashley, 2010). At one end of the spectrum is the undemanding definition, implying that any type of benefits that trickles down to the poor can be viewed as pro-poor, even if the main beneficiaries of growth are nonpoor and growth is associated with rising inequality. At the other end of the spectrum is a restrictive definition of pro-poor growth, meaning that growth is only pro-poor if the poor benefit overproportionally (Meyer, 2010; Mitchell & Ashley, 2010). Mediating between the two views makes development practice only more fragile and prone to critique, seemingly adapting the ends to a means, rather than vice versa. In this respect, Schilcher (2007, p. 166) argued that "in order to be pro-poor, growth must deliver disproportionate benefits to the poor to reduce inequalities which have been found to limit the potential for poverty alleviation. Hence, it is necessary to shift policy focus from growth to equity, which calls for strong institutions capable of regulating the tourism industry and distributing assets in order to facilitate 'pro-poor growth.'"

Third, the concept of *tourism* in pro-poor tourism also has been subject to discussions. The emergence of the PPT approach clearly reflected, especially in the first decade of the twenty-first century, an increasing awareness of development organizations and donors for tourism as an instrument for development. The ideas put forward by, for example, Bennett, Roe, and Ashley (1999) and by Ashley, Roe, and Goodwin (2001) caught on and resulted in significant programs of organizations such as ODI in the UK, GTZ in Germany (now part of the Deutsche Gesellschaft für Internationale Zusammenarbeit GIZ), and SNV Netherlands Development Organization. However, in line with the pragmatism of PPT they evidentially had to adopt not only a workable notion of poverty but also a particular notion of tourism, suggesting that tourism was generally conceptualized as an industry or sector (Goodwin, 2008). According to Mitchell and Ashley

(2010, p. 8), defining the *tourism sector* or *tourism industry* is surprisingly difficult: "this is partly because tourism is an economic activity, which is a composite of services and goods surrounded by rather unclear boundaries—so it is inherently a slippery animal." Related, Lickorish and Jenkins (1997 in Holden, 2005) argue that tourism does not employ an independent production function with a physical measurable output like agriculture (e.g., tons of wheat), nor can the impacts or contribution of tourism be easily isolated from the contribution of other sectors. To find practical answers and workable solutions, PPT practitioners have, often implicitly, narrowed their scope. Most research and projects are confined to the destination area, the place where tourists and tourism businesses can be encouraged to purchase in ways that benefit the poor. As such, the focus has been on the destination rather than on the global tourism industry (Goodwin, 2008). Within the destination, most studies and efforts have been directed at the accommodation sector and the role of the informal sector (e.g., guiding, crafts, taxi drivers, fruit and juice sellers). Further, also due to the fact that PPT was initially introduced as part of existing rural development and natural resource management programs, more emphasis was on the rural than on the urban. As Chok et al. (2007, p. 159) assert, "in urban slums, the poor do not have the same comparative advantage that PPT is currently promoting—namely pristine landscapes, abundant wildlife, indigenous cultural heritage and traditions. For the poor living in urban slums, their comparative advantage tends to be undervalued."

Fourth, the attention to PPT also has led to a revival of the discussion on linkages and leakages, which already has influenced tourism and development literature for decades. *Leakage* is a term used to describe the percentage of the price tourists paid for a vacation that leaves a destination in terms of imports or expatriated profits, or that never reaches the destination in the first place because of the involvement of especially northern-based tour operators and airlines (Meyer, 2007, 2010). It is argued that leakages tend to be high when the local destination economy is weak and lacks the quality and quantity of inputs required (Meyer, 2010). Tourism is increasingly entangled with the global economy and, in fact, it prospers because of it. Less economically developed countries often depend on stronger economies to build accommodations and infrastructure and to transport tourists. Arguably, the benefits that developing countries reap from tourism are higher than when they had not imported the required inputs. The strong emphasis on leakages in studies on tourism and development, as well as the way they have actually been calculated and measured, has been subject to criticism. For example, Harrison (2009, p. 10) recently questioned the focus on leakages by stating, "It is like suggesting that staff and accommodation costs for serving a cappuccino in a London café are 'leakage' from coffee plantations in Ethiopia!" In a similar line of thought, does anyone ever question how much money or how big a percentage of mobile phone sales or computer hardware sales *leaks out* of the Chinese economy? Revenues for design, wholesale, distribution, retailing, and taxes often are not reaped by the Chinese economy. Besides, the percentage that trickles down to the countries where the goods are actually sold also is fairly limited, namely distribution, retail margins, and value-added tax (VAT). Referring back to tourism, Sharpley (2009) recently proposed to focus on "destination capitals" as a basis for optimizing the benefits of tourism and internalizing its costs while reflecting both destination needs and tourism development opportunities. According to Sharpley, central to this process is the identification of human, sociocultural, technological, environmental, economic, and political capitals to establish "what resources or assets should be exploited for tourism, the extent to which they might generate a flow of benefits to the destination and, through the analysis of political capital in particular, who has access and control over the use of these capitals" (p. 181).

Fifth, PPT has reintroduced the concept of value chains as one of the main methodological tools to identify pro-poor tourism impacts of tourism and to go beyond tourism by focusing on intersectional linkages, especially between tourism and agriculture. Although the concept of value chains was used in the 1960s and 1970s, it made an important reentry into the development arena in the last decade, partly as a consequence of the writings of Michael Porter. Many sectors of industry have embraced the idea of value-chain enhancement as a path for sustainable development through active dialogue and collaboration with all stakeholders that are linked to the processing of goods and services. Development organizations also have started to adopt the concept as a means for integrative development, and particularly linked it to pro-poor development. Related to PPT, value chain analysis (VCA) "has been extended beyond individual firms and amplified to the whole supply chain and distribution network. Capturing the value generated for the poor along the chain and identifying supply/distribution nodes were interventions to increase poverty impacts are possible is at the heart of the VCA used in tourism" (Meyer, 2011, p. 176). Unlike concrete and tangible products, such as cocoa beans and cotton, value chains in tourism are difficult to delineate as a result of the indistinctness of what exactly delineates the tourism industry. Ashley and Mitchell (2008, p. 1) defined value chains as "a way of representing the series of transactions involved in providing a good or service, starting with the provision of inputs for production, and going through production, transformation, marketing to final consumption and subsequent recycling." Often the components of the value chain based in tourism-generating countries, like tour operators and airlines, have been put outside the equation of these VCAs. As Harrison (2008, p. 857) argues, "probably because of funding and time constraints, VCA has been applied somewhat simplistically. In particular, attention has focused primarily on linkages within tourism destinations, rather than on the wider global context." More generally, VCA has given few insights on the grounds for poverty and inequality and the barriers of entry to tourism value chains for poor people. VCA projects also faced important methodological problems (see Mitchell & Ashley, 2010, for an overview). For example, according to the often cited VCA study in Luang Prabang (Laos), "It seems likely that at least [US]$6 million per year of tourist expenditure is flowing directly to semi-skilled and unskilled producers, suppliers and workers, which is around 27% of the total receipts of around [US]$22.5 million into Luang Prabang" (Ashley, 2006). However, "[t]he estimates of expenditure and income are extremely rough . . . [and] . . . they could easily be wrong by a factor of two in either direction, and some gaps in the analysis have been filled with mere guesstimates" (p. vi). This type of research still has to face important conceptual and methodological challenges related to the definition and measurement of what counts as poor, and the inclusion of context analysis, including market relations and trends that influence impacts and possible interventions (Ashley & Mitchell, 2007, p. 29). Moreover, VCA focuses on the financial benefits and costs but has not yet found a way to reconcile objectives related to PPT interventions with environmental and social objectives, including other livelihood impacts, distributional priorities, and social and

---

Box 3.4   Some Strengths and Weaknesses of the Pro-Poor Tourism Approach

Strengths	Weaknesses
Putting poverty on the agenda	Indistinct definition of poverty
Link of poverty reduction to all types of tourism	Little insight into grounds for inequality and poverty, and power and governance issues
Linking tourism to other economic sectors	Strong local focus, little attention to international value chains and trade barriers
Practical orientation	Too many "hit and run" studies

Source: Data from Harrison, D. (2008). Pro-poor tourism: A critique. *Third World Quarterly, 29*(5), 851–868; Meyer, D. (2010, April). *Value chain analysis and tourism.* Presentation at 3A-ST-EP meeting, Dar es Salaam; and van de Mosselaer, F., & van der Duim, V. R. (2010). Pro-poor toerisme moet kleur bekennen. *Vrijetijdstudies, 28*(3), 25–34.

---

environmental change (Ashley & Mitchell, 2008). Nevertheless, VCA has been a welcomed first step to understand tourism's diverse poverty-reducing impacts (Meyer, 2011).

This short discussion of some of the main concepts and premises of PPT reveals some of the strengths and weaknesses of the PPT approach, which are summarized in PPT research (see **Box 3.4**).

The concepts of poverty, tourism industry (or sector), leakages, linkages, pro-poor growth, and value chain have predominantly shaped the conceptual framework from which problem-oriented research on PPT has been conducted. Recently, Mitchell and Ashley (2010) summarized the state of the art of this applied research, based on an extensive search for published and "grey" literature on the impacts of tourism on poverty (see also Goodwin, 2011). They point out the evidence is "scattered across a range of approaches using different methods and scale of analysis that are developing in splendid, and almost total isolation, from each other" (Mitchell & Ashley, 2010, p. 2). Their findings reflect the view of those who have argued that the number of publications on tourism in relevant and recognized academic journals with an explicit focus on poverty reduction or alleviation has been limited and, as a consequence, the PPT approach has remained at the margins of tourism research and has not been subject to stringent scrutiny (Harrison, 2009; Meyer, 2007; Scheyvens, 2007). Harrison (2009) has credited this lack of academic rigor primarily to the absence of permanent positions in academia among its proponents and to deficient funding. So far, PPT research has mainly been commissioned and/or executed by donor and development organizations (e.g., SNV Netherlands Development Organization, the IIED, ODI, the German Development Organization GTZ, the World Bank, the Asian and American Development Bank), making the scope and methods largely problem-oriented (Tassone, 2008). The sum of grants and funds dedicated to explicit academic research on tourism and poverty has been negligible. Most of the academic research on tourism and poverty has been incorporated in wider and divergent research agendas, resulting in the lack of critical academic mass and a platform for collaboration and knowledge exchange (see also van der Duim, 2008).

Nevertheless, in the last 5 years the number of studies on tourism and poverty in scientific journals has considerably increased. Compared to the results analyzed by Tassone (2008) and sequenced by Tassone and van der Duim (2008, 2010), who examined research papers across social sciences discussing tourism, poverty reduction, and nature conservation between 2003

Table 3.1 Tourism and Poverty Research

Concepts and critical assessment	Chok et al., 2007; Deller, 2010; Harrison, 2008, 2009; Meyer, 2007, 2009, 2011; Rolfes, 2010; Scheyvens, 2007, 2009; Scheyvens & Momsen, 2008; Schilcher, 2007; Sharpley & Naidoo, 2010; Zhao & Ritchie, 2007
Ex post impact evaluation	Akama & Keiti, 2007; Clifton & Benson, 2006; Dyer, Aberdeen, & Schuler, 2003; Harrison and Schipani, 2007; Mbaiwa, 2005; Mitchell & Faal, 2007; Muganda, Sahli, & Smith, 2010; Nyaupane, Morais, & Dowler, 2006; Saayman & Saayman, 2006; Sharpley & Naidoo, 2010; Spenceley & Goodwin, 2007; Spenceley, Habyalimana, Tusabe, & Mariza, 2010
Approaches to community and small and medium enterprise (SME) participation	Briedenhann & Wickens, 2004; Harris, 2009; Hawkins & Mann, 2007; Hill, Nel, & Trotter, 2006; Kennedy & Dornan, 2009; Lapeyre, 2010; Lepper & Goebel, 2010; Manyara & Jones, 2007; Manyara, Jones, & Botterill, 2006; Muhanna, 2007; Suntikul, Bauer, & Song, 2009; Threerapappisit, 2009; Tosun, 2006; Ying & Zhou, 2007; Zhao, 2009; Zorn & Farthing, 2007
The economics of tourism and poverty reduction	Blake, 2008; Blake, Arbache, Sinclair, & Teles, 2008; Christie & Sharma, 2008; Croes & Vanegas, 2008; Mshenga, Richardson, Njehia, & Birachi, 2010; Nadkarni, 2008; Riley & Szivas, 2009; Rogerson, 2006

and 2007, there has been a remarkable growth in the number of publications on pro-poor tourism in the last few years. **Table 3.1** gives a limited overview of publications in scientific journals addressing the tourism–poverty nexus.

The increasing popularity of pro-poor tourism around 2007 resulted in a number of critical studies on the concept of PPT (Chok et al., 2007; Scheyvens, 2008; Scheyvens & Momsen, 2008; Schilcher, 2008; Zhao & Ritchie, 2008) making use of insights from political sciences. More recently, a range of new studies on pro-poor impacts and community and small enterprise participation have been added to the research base, triggered by the publication of special journal issues from *Development Southern Africa* (2010) and *Asia Pacific Journal on Tourism Research* (2009). However, as Goodwin (2011) argues, to generate the body of empirical validated knowledge needed to inform policy choices, there is an urgent need for more detailed applied research on the outcomes of interventions. To do so, researchers not only "need to raise their game," as argued by Mitchell and Ashley (2010, p. 134), but also need access and funding (Goodwin, 2011).

Notwithstanding the importance of building a robust database of case studies on the impacts and effectiveness of pro-poor approaches, particularly for comparative analysis, more fundamental research into the enabling or obstructing conditions for PPT is needed as well as research that links theoretical ideas from well-established scientific disciplines. In this regard, recent contributions from, for example, scholars in tourism economics addressing underlying tenets in tourism and poverty focusing on the effect of information asymmetry (Nadkarni, 2008), causality relations between economic growth and poverty reduction (Croes & Vanegas, 2008), the role of labor markets behavior (Riley & Szivas, 2009), and the impacts of income distribution (Blake et al., 2008) must be welcomed for two reasons. First, reaching out to the discipline of economics is essential because poverty and human well-being are inherently socioeconomic dimensions. Second, they point to fundamental mechanisms that enable or hinder policy implementation or development intervention programs.

Despite these recent contributions, academic research on tourism and poverty is still frail and scattered. Little cross-reference has occurred, and many researchers are unaware of the existence of or are selective in the choice of relevant work on tourism and poverty "emanating from different stables" (Mitchell & Ashley, 2010, p. 2). This fragmentation persists for various reasons, including funding priorities, disciplinary self-isolation (Weaver & Lawton, 2007), and a still-existing gap among practitioners, consultants, and academic researchers (van der Duim, 2008).

When analyzing both the problem-oriented and academic studies on tourism and poverty, it appears that coalitions are formed around particular strands of research, predominantly working from and within their own knowledge circles. Apparently a large base of studies on tourism and poverty exists in China (see, e.g., Li, Zhong, & Cheng, 2009; Bowden, 2005; Donaldson, 2007), but there has been very little, if any, cross-reference between western-based and Chinese research institutes, partly due to language barriers.

To move forward, research is needed on the institutional environment in which tourism development is being advanced alongside the objective to eradicate poverty, such as governance arrangements, power imbalances, and the competitive value of tourism as a form of land and resource use. As Meyer (2011, p. 179) argues,

> . . . so far limited research has been undertaken that incorporates the many external factors that ultimately shape decision making, such as for example the policy environment, local cultures and traditions, gender inequalities, the global political economy, and global policy networks. An understanding of these factors, however, is fundamental when aiming to develop a type of tourism that aims to contribute to poverty reduction.

Conclusion

In this chapter we discussed the relationship between tourism and MDG 1 by focusing on the recent focus on pro-poor tourism (PPT) and related research. The idea of PPT rests on a variety of different and sometimes competing development approaches, and thus the relation between tourism and poverty alleviation has been, and will be, constantly debated, especially in international development cooperation. PPT has increasingly become a buzzword, and it is now almost common sense that tourism can have important pro-poor impacts and these benefits can be strengthened by deliberate public policy interventions, validated by research.

We have argued pro-poor tourism is a "fuzzy" concept; one that everyone purports to understand intuitively but somehow finds very difficult to operationalize into concrete terms (Gunder, 2006). On the one hand this ambiguity has given PPT its ideological power, has allowed tourism to be included in the development arena, and has given rise to new sources of funding for development organizations and new methods for identifying opportunities to unlock the poor from poverty. The work of PPT advocates, in terms of spreading the idea that tourism could be understood as a means for eradicating poverty, should be credited. Over the years, development organizations, multilateral institutions, governments, academia, and even the private sector increasingly have joined the bandwagon of PPT. On the other hand, the fuzziness of the concept has enabled it to be hijacked as a label for most of the socioeconomic interventions in tourism.

In the last decade, the work in PPT, as reviewed by Mitchell and Ashley (2010) and Scheyvens (2011), identifies valuable avenues for further research, particularly related to assessment of the multidimensional impacts of tourism on poor people's livelihoods. First, PPT research should provide evidence that pro-poor tourism can achieve impact on a large scale. According to Scheyvens (2011, p. 210), "evidence that tourism contributes directly to poverty alleviation is sporadic and often tokenistic." Similarly, Goodwin (2011) recently argued that we are still a long way from being able to provide policy makers with the evidence for informed decision making that the benefits of tourism reach the poor, not least because "policy makers and donors have denied themselves access to the knowledge they need to inform better policy making" (p. 340). Until we have sound data, based on comparative and longitudinal research projects, the question of whether PPT is rhetoric or reality will remain largely unanswered. Second, to improve the conceptual and methodological underpinnings of this research, the gap between different disciplines and between disciplinary research and the work of practitioners should be bridged. Third, research needs a stronger focus on the processes of governance. The degree to which tourism contributes to poor people's livelihoods is largely shaped by the modes of (destination) governance. It is these modes of governance that should be examined. How is tourism related to the destination's macroeconomic and trade policies? Which institutions shape these policies? How do these institutions come into existence and how are they monitored? Whose interests do these institutions represent?

Finally, we advocate making PPT practice and research itself an object of research; therefore, we question how and by whom "pro-poor" strategies are developed and translated into existing tourism practices, and what role research practices play in these processes of translation and stabilization (van der Duim, 2008). To fully grasp the mechanisms that can be used to reduce poverty through tourism, we also advocate action research in which the researcher follows development and donor organizations (see Mosse, 2005), incoming tour operators, hotel companies, or any other particular actor in the process of defining and executing PPT and creating associations that aim to produce an effect that is considered necessary—namely the increase of net benefits to the poor.

References

Akama, J., & Kieti, D. (2007). Tourism and socio-economic development in developing countries: A case study of Mombasa Resort in Kenya. *Journal of Sustainable Tourism, 15*(6), 735–748.

Ashley, C. (2006). *Participation by the poor in Luang Prabang tourism economy. Current earnings and opportunities for expansion.* ODI Working Paper 273. London: Overseas Development Institute.

Ashley, C., & Mitchell, J. (2007). *Assessing how tourism revenues reach the poor.* ODI Briefing Paper. London: Overseas Development Institute.

Ashley, C., & Mitchell, J. (2008). *Doing the right thing approximately, not the wrong thing exactly: Challenges for monitoring impacts of pro-poor interventions in tourism value-chains.* London: Overseas Development Institute.

Ashley, C., Roe, D., & Goodwin, H. (2001). *Pro-poor tourism strategies: Making tourism work for the poor: A review of experience.* London: International Centre for Responsible Tourism, International Institute for Environment and Development, and Overseas Development Institute.

Bennett O., Roe, D., & Ashley, D. (1999). *Sustainable tourism and poverty elimination study.* London: Deloitte and Touche, International Institute for Environment and Development, and Overseas Development Institute.

Blake, A. (2008). Tourism and income distribution in East Africa. *International Journal of Tourism Research, 10*(6), 511–524.

Blake, A., Arbache, J. S., Sinclair, M. T., & Teles, V. (2008). Tourism and poverty relief. *Annals of Tourism Research, 35*(1), 107–126.

Bowden, J. Y. (2005). Pro-poor tourism and the Chinese experience. *Asia Pacific Journal of Tourism Research, 10*(4), 379–398.

Briedenhann, J., & Wickens, E. (2004). Tourism routes as a tool for the economic development of rural areas—vibrant hope or impossible dream? *Tourism Management, 25*(1), 71–79.

Chok, S., Macbeth, J., & Warren, D. (2007). Tourism as a tool for poverty alleviation: A critical analysis of "pro-poor tourism" and implications for sustainability. *Current Issues in Tourism, 10*(2–3), 144–165.

Christie, I. T., & Sharma, A. (2008). Research note: Millennium development goals—what is tourism's place? *Tourism Economics, 14*(2), 427–430.

Clifton, J., & Benson, A. (2006). Planning for sustainable ecotourism: The case for research ecotourism in developing country destinations. *Journal of Sustainable Tourism, 14*(3), 238–254.

Croes, R., & Vanegas, M. (2008). Cointegration and causality between tourism and poverty reduction. *Journal of Travel Research, 47*(1), 94–103.

Deller, S. (2010). Rural poverty, tourism and spatial heterogeneity. *Annals of Tourism Research, 37*(1), 180–205.

Dollar, D., & Kraay, A. (2002). Growth is good for the poor. *Journal of Economic Growth, 7*(3), 195–225.

Donaldson, J. A. (2007). Tourism, development and poverty reduction in Guizhou and Yunnan. *China Quarterly, 190*, 333–351.

Dyer, D., Aberdeen, L., & Schuler, S. (2003). Tourism impacts on an Australian indigenous community: A Djabugay case study. *Tourism Management, 24*(1), 83–95.

Easterly, W. (2006). *The white man's burden*. New York: OUP/Penguin.

Goodwin, H. (1998). *Sustainable tourism and poverty alleviation*. Retrieved November 12, 2010, from http://www.haroldgoodwin.info/resources/dfidpaper.pdf

Goodwin, H. (2008). Pro-poor tourism: A response. *Third World Quarterly, 29*(5), 869–871.

Goodwin, H. (2011). Tourism and poverty reduction. *Annals of Tourism Research, 38*, 339–340.

Goodwin, H., & Santilli, R. (2009). Community-based tourism: A success? ICRT Occasional Paper 11. Leeds, United Kingdom: GTZ.

Green, M. (2007). Representing poverty and attacking representations: Perspectives on poverty from social anthropology. In D. Hulme & J. Toye (Eds.), *Understanding poverty and well-being: Bridging the disciplines* (pp. 24–45). Abingdon, United Kingdom: Routledge.

Gunder, M. (2006). Sustainability: Planning's saving grace or road to perdition? *Journal of Planning Education and Research, 26*, 208–221.

Harris, R. W. (2009). Tourism in Bario, Sarawak, Malaysia: A case study of pro-poor community-based tourism integrated into community development. *Asia Pacific Journal of Tourism Research, 14*(2), 125–135.

Harrison, D. (2008). Pro-poor tourism: A critique. *Third World Quarterly, 29*(5), 851–868.

Harrison, D. (2009). Pro-poor tourism: Is there value beyond "whose" rhetoric? *Tourism Recreation Research, 34*(2), 200–202.

Harrison, D., & Schipani, S. (2007). Lao tourism and poverty alleviation: Community-based tourism and the private sector. *Current Issues in Tourism, 10*(2–3), 194–230.

Hawkins, D. E., & Mann, S. (2007). The World Bank's role in tourism development. *Annals of Tourism Research, 34*(2), 348–363.

Hill, T., Nel, E., & Trotter, D. (2006). Small-scale, nature-based tourism as a pro-poor development intervention: Two examples in Kwazulu-Natal, South Africa. *Singapore Journal of Tropical Geography, 27*(2), 163–175.

Holden, A. (2005). *Environment and tourism*. London: Routledge.

Hummel, J., & van der Duim, V. D. (2011). *Tourism and development at work*. Working document. Wageningen, The Netherlands: Wageningen University.

Jones, H., & Wood, M. E. (2007). *Community-based tourism research initiative. Survey results demonstrating the connection that community-based tourism projects have to protected areas*. Washington, DC: EplerWood International.

Kakwani, N., & Pernia, E. M. (2000). What is pro-poor growth? *Asian Development Review, 18*(1), 1–16.

Kennedy, K., & Dornan, D. (2009). An overview: Tourism non-governmental organizations and poverty reduction in developing countries. *Asia Pacific Journal of Tourism Research, 14*(2), 183–200.

Lapeyre, R. (2010). Community-based tourism as a sustainable solution to maximize impacts locally? The Tsiseb Conservancy case, Namibia. *Development Southern Africa, 27*(5), 758–772.

Leijzer, M. (2007, December 12–13). *Using national tourism statistics for poverty reduction impact measurement*. Unpublished paper. Presentation during the IFC/SNV Conference Poverty Alleviation through Tourism—Impact Measurement in Tourism Chain Development. Phnom Penh, Cambodia.

Lepper, C. M., & Goebel, J. S. (2010). Community-based natural resource management, poverty alleviation and livelihood diversification: A case study from northern Botswana. *Development Southern Africa, 27*(5), 726–739.

Li, J., Zhong, L-S., & Cheng, S-K. (2009). Research progress on poverty elimination by tourism in China. *China Population Resources and Environment, 19*(3), 156–162.

Lickorish, L. J., & Jenkins, C. L. (1997). *An introduction to tourism*. New York: Butterworth-Heinemann.

Manyara, G., & Jones, E. (2007). Community-based tourism enterprises development in Kenya: An exploration of their potential as avenues of poverty reduction. *Journal of Sustainable Tourism, 15*(6), 628–644.

Manyara, G., Jones, E., & Botterill, D. (2006). Tourism and poverty alleviation: The case for indigenous enterprise development in Kenya. *Tourism, Culture and Communication, 7*(1), 19–37.

Mbaiwa, J. E. (2005). Enclave tourism and its socio-economic impacts in the Okavango Delta, Botswana. *Tourism Management, 26*(2), 157–172.

Meyer, D. (2007). Pro-poor tourism: From leakages to linkages. A conceptual framework for creating linkages between the accommodation sector and "poor" neighbouring communities. *Current Issues in Tourism, 10*(6), 558–583.

Meyer, D. (2009). Pro-poor tourism: Is there actually much rhetoric? And, if so, whose? *Tourism Recreation Research, 34*(2), 197–199.

Meyer, D. (2010, April). *Value chain analysis and tourism*. Presentation at 3A-ST-EP meeting, Dar es Salaam.

Meyer, D. (2011). Pro-poor tourism: Can tourism contribute to poverty reduction in less economically developed countries? In S. Cole & N. Morgan (Eds.), *Tourism and inequality: Problems and prospects* (pp. 164–182). Wallingford, England: CAB International.

Mitchell, J., & Ashley, C. (2007). *Can tourism offer pro-poor pathways to prosperity. Examining evidence on the impact of tourism on poverty*. ODI Briefing Paper 22. London: Overseas Development Institute.

Mitchell J., & Ashley, C. (2010). *Tourism and poverty reduction. Pathways to prosperity*. London: Earthscan.

Mitchell, J., & Faal, J. (2007). Holiday package tourism and the poor in the Gambia. *Development Southern Africa, 24*(3), 445–464.

Mitchell, J., & Muckosy, P. (2008). *A misguided quest: Community based tourism in Latin America*. ODI Opinions 102. London: Overseas Development Institute.

Mosse, D. (2005). *Cultivating development*. London: Pluto Press.

Moyo, D. (2009). *Dead aid: Why aid is not working and how there is another way for Africa*. London: Allen Lane.

Mshenga, P. M., Richardson, R. B., Njehia, B. K., & Birachi, E. A. (2010). The contribution of tourism to micro and small enterprise growth. *Tourism Economics, 16*(4), 953–964.

Muganda, M., Sahli, M., & Smith, K. A. (2010). Tourism's contribution to poverty alleviation: A community perspective from Tanzania. *Development Southern Africa, 27*(5), 630–646.

Muhanna, E. (2007). The contribution of sustainable tourism development in poverty alleviation of local communities in South Africa. *Journal of Human Resources in Hospitality and Tourism, 6*(1), 37–67.

Nadkarni, S. (2008). Knowledge creation, retention, exchange, devolution, interpretation and treatment (K-CREDIT) as an economic growth driver in pro-poor tourism. *Current Issues in Tourism, 11*(5), 456–472.

Nel, E., & Binns, T. (2000). Rural self-reliance strategies in South Africa: Community initiatives and external support in the former black homelands. *Journal of Rural Studies, 16*, 367–377.

Nyaupane, G. P., Morais, D. B., & Dowler, L. (2006). The role of community involvement and number/type of visitors on tourism impacts: A controlled comparison of Annapurna, Nepal and Northwest Yunnan, China. *Tourism Management, 27*(6), 1373–1385.

Pro-Poor Tourism Partnership. (2004). Pro-poor tourism information sheets. Retrieved January 15, 2011, from http://www.propoortourism.org.uk/ppt_pubs_infosheets.htm

Ravallion, M. (2004). *Defining pro-poor growth: A response to Kakwani.* Brasilia, Brazil: International Poverty Centre, United Nations Development Program.

Riley, M., & Szivas, E. (2009). Tourism employment and poverty: Revisiting the supply curve. *Tourism Economics, 15*(2), 297–305.

Rogerson, C. M. (2006). Pro-poor local economic development in South Africa: The role of pro-poor tourism. *Local Environment, 11*(1), 37–60.

Rolfes, M. (2010). Poverty tourism: Theoretical reflections and empirical findings regarding an extraordinary form of tourism. *GeoJournal, 75*(5), 421–442.

Saarinen, J., Rogerson, C., & Manwa, H. (2011). Tourism and Millennium Development Goals: Tourism for global development? *Current Issues of Tourism, 14*(3), 201–203.

Saayman, M., & Saayman, A. (2006). Estimating the economic contribution of visitor spending in the Kruger National Park to the regional economy. *Journal of Sustainable Tourism, 14*(1), 67–81.

Scheyvens, R. (2007). Exploring the tourism–poverty nexus. *Current Issues in Tourism, 10*(2–3), 231–254.

Scheyvens, R. (2009). Pro-poor tourism: Is there value beyond the rhetoric? *Tourism Recreation Research, 34*, 191–196.

Scheyvens, R. (2011). *Tourism and poverty.* London: Routledge.

Scheyvens, R., & Momsen, J. H. (2008). Tourism and poverty reduction: Issues for small island states. *Tourism Geographies, 10*(1), 22–41.

Schilcher, D. (2007). Growth versus equity: The continuum of pro-poor tourism and neoliberal governance. *Current Issues in Tourism, 10*(2–3), 166–193.

Sen, A. (2001). *Development as freedom.* Oxford: Oxford University Press.

Sharpley, R. (2009). *Tourism development and the environment: Beyond sustainability?* London: Earthscan.

Sharpley, R., & Naidoo, P. (2010). Tourism and poverty reduction: The case of Mauritius. *Tourism and Hospitality, Planning and Development, 7*(2), 145–162.

Sharpley, R., & Telfer, D. J. (2002). *Tourism and development: Concept and issues.* Clevedon. England: Channel View Publications.

Spenceley, A. (2008). *Responsible tourism.* London: Earthscan.

Spenceley, A., & Goodwin, H. (2007). Nature-based tourism and poverty alleviation: Impacts of private sector and parastatal enterprises in and around Kruger National Park, South Africa. *Current Issues in Tourism, 10*(2–3), 255–277.

Spenceley, A., Habyalimana, S., Tusabe, R., & Mariza, D. (2010). Benefits to the poor from gorilla tourism in Rwanda. *Development Southern Africa, 27*(5), 648–662.

Suntikul, W., Bauer, T., & Song, H. (2009). Pro-poor tourism development in Viengxay, Laos: Current state and future prospects. *Asia Pacific Journal of Tourism Research, 14*(2), 153–168.

Tassone, V. C. (2008). Systematizing scientific knowledge in sustainable tourism, poverty reduction and nature conservation. In H. J. de Haan & V. R. van der Duim (Eds.), *Landscape, leisure and tourism, socio-spatial studies in experiences, practices and policies* (pp. 159–187). Delft: Eburon.

Tassone, V. C., & van der Duim, V. R. (2008). An analysis of research developments and opportunities in tourism, poverty alleviation and nature conservation. In F. D. Pineda & C. A. Brebbia (Eds.), *Sustainable tourism III* (pp. 253–266). Southampton, England: WIT Press.

Tassone, V. C., & van der Duim, V. R. (2010). Tourism, poverty alleviation and nature conservation. The state of contemporary research. *Matkailututkimus Finnish Journal of Tourism Research, 6*(1–2), 7–29.

Telfer, D., & Sharpley, R. (2008). *Tourism and development in the developing world.* London: Routledge.

Theerapappisit, P. (2009). Pro-poor ethnic tourism in the Mekong: A study of three approaches in Northern Thailand. *Asia Pacific Journal of Tourism Research, 14*(2), 201–221.

Tosun, C. (2006). Expected nature of community participation in tourism development. *Tourism Management, 27*(3), 493–504.

United Nations World Tourism Organization (UNWTO). (2004). *Tourism and poverty alleviation, recommendations for action.* Madrid: Author.

United Nations World Tourism Organization and the Netherlands Development Organization. (2010). *SNV 2010 manual on tourism and poverty alleviation: Practical steps for destinations.* Madrid, Spain: Authors.

van de Mosselaer, F., & van der Duim, V. R. (2010). Pro-poor toerisme moet kleur bekennen. *Vrijetijdstudies, 28*(3), 25–34.

van der Duim, V. R. (2008). Exploring pro-poor tourism research: The state of the art. In H. de Haan & V. R. van der Duim (Eds.), *Landscape, leisure and tourism* (pp. 179–196). Delft: Eburon.

Weaver, B., & Lawton, L. J. (2007). Twenty years on: The state of contemporary ecotourism research. *Tourism Management, 28*(5), 1168–1179.

Williamson, J. (2000). What should the World Bank think about the Washington Consensus? *World Bank Research Observer, 15*(2), 251–264.

WRR (Scientific Council for Government Policy). (2010). *Minder pretentie, meer ambitie. Ontwikkelingshulp die verschil maakt.* Amsterdam/Den Haag: Amsterdam University Press.

Ying, T., & Zhou, Y. (2007). Community, governments and external capitals in China's rural cultural tourism: A comparative study of two adjacent villages. *Tourism Management, 28*(1), 96–107.

Zhao, W. (2009). The nature and roles of small tourism businesses in poverty alleviation: Evidence from Guangxi, China. *Asia Pacific Journal of Tourism Research, 14*(2), 169–182.

Zhao, W., & Ritchie, J. R. N. (2007). Tourism and poverty alleviation: An integrative research framework. *Current Issues in Tourism, 10*(2–3), 119–143.

Zorn, E., & Farthing, L. C. (2007). Communitarian tourism hosts and mediators in Peru. *Annals of Tourism Research, 34*(3), 673–689.

The Role of Indigenous Tourism in Supporting and Meeting the United Nations Millennium Development Goals

Holly Donohoe and Sylvie Blangy

LEARNING OBJECTIVES

- To understand that there is much to learn about indigenous tourism and a great deal to learn from indigenous peoples
- To understand that indigenous tourism is a tool to promote positive transformation within the communities and should be promoted as such in tourism research
- To identify the challenges associated with indigenous tourism, as tourism continues to develop into more environmentally and culturally sensitive areas, and the importance of critical analysis of the benefits and challenges associated therein

Indigenous cultures and destinations have become popular tourism attractions, and they are increasingly drawing the attention of tourists, tourism entrepreneurs, governmental and non-governmental agencies, and academics. Experiencing distinctive cultures, such as another people operating in their traditional manner or on their traditional lands, using traditional knowledge and local resources, is an important demand driver in the contemporary tourism market, and it promises benefits for host communities.

Since the publication of *Tourism and Indigenous Peoples* (Butler & Hinch, 1996) over 15 years ago, the myths and realities of indigenous tourism continue to be the subject of debate, and the fundamental and theoretical concern persists: Does indigenous tourism represent ". . . an opportunity for indigenous people to gain economic independence and cultural rejuvenation or . . . a major threat of hegemonic subjugation and cultural degradation"? (Hinch & Butler, 2007, p. 2). The literature addresses operational concerns related to the size of indigenous tourism markets (and measurement challenges), the appropriateness of Western or hegemonic business models in non-Western communities, and the challenge associated with sustaining community-based tourism in a highly complex economic and political environment (Tremblay, 2006).

Given the complexities associated with the global tourism exchange, the reality is that indigenous communities may encounter a range of opportunities and threats when engaging in indigenous tourism activities. External opportunities and threats such as economic recession, terrorism, or environmental crisis are factors over which indigenous people have little control, but governance and influence are possible when addressing internal factors such as community development, cultural empowerment, and self-determination.

The purpose of this chapter is to explore the role that indigenous tourism plays in supporting and meeting the United Nations Millennium Development Goals (MDGs). In order to fulfill this objective, indigenous tourism is defined, opportunities and benefits are presented, and the real and potential contribution of indigenous tourism within two select MDGs is examined through case studies of indigenous communities in Arctic and subarctic regions.

Indigenous Tourism

Indigenous tourism forms part of a cluster that Smith and Eadington (1992) call "tourism alternatives" that are characterized by visitor experiences different from traditional mass tourism. Destinations that possess rare and abundant biodiversity; remote, pristine, and unique landscapes; indigenous communities practicing cultural norms that are different than dominant Westernized traditions; and/or where the tourism experience is managed to reduce negative impacts on the environment and cultures (e.g., eco- and sustainable tourism) are popular alternatives that hold a competitive advantage in the tourism market (Blangy, 2006, 2010; Sinclair, 2003). Since the 1990s, indigenous tourism has flourished in the alternative market, and with growing stakeholder interest, definitional discourse has emerged (Blangy & Laurent, 2007).

For Smith (1996), indigenous tourism is the segment of the visitor industry that involves native peoples whose ethnicity is the main attraction. Sinclair (2003) argues that Smith's definition introduces a complexity of control that must be addressed in both the normative and operational stages of indigenous tourism. For Notzke (2006), the control factor is central to any definitional discussion, and she explains that indigenous tourism can be defined in two ways: first, tourism products and activities owned and/or controlled by indigenous peoples who are directly responsible for their management, and second, tourism products and activities based on indigenous culture and where control (ownership and management) is held by nonindigenous stakeholders. The relationship between indigenous culture as the attraction for tourism activities and indigenous control and ownership of tourism activities is identified as an important differential for distinguishing authentic indigenous tourism (Iankova, 2006; Zeppel, 2006). Although the literature contains definitions that include tourism activities in which indigenous groups have no control at all (and culture is the main attraction), the consensus on authentic or genuine indigenous tourism is that it includes tourism enterprises that both are controlled by indigenous people and feature an indigenous-themed attraction (Blangy, 2010; Butler & Hinch, 2007; Parker, 1993). This definitional framework is supported by indigenous communities and is reflected in operational definitions such as that of the Aboriginal Tourism Association of British Columbia, where indigenous tourism contributes over $35 million to the Canadian economy annually (2011b):

> An authentic Aboriginal cultural tourism experience is majority Aboriginal owned or controlled, satisfies industry standards for market readiness and sector requirements, has high operating standards, and sufficient cultural content that is culturally appropriate and recognized by the originators of that culture while providing an opportunity for visitors to interact with Aboriginal people during the cultural tourism experience. (Aboriginal Tourism Association of British Columbia, 2011a)

The indigenous tourism system can be defined by the variety of components, stakeholders, and the relationships between them (see **Figure CS 2.1**). Although the experience certainly varies in terms of time, space, and participants, Hinch and Butler (2007) argue that there is a set of universal components and patterns that define indigenous tourism and the variety of issues that arise in this unique context. Their model of the indigenous tourism system places the central emphasis on the role that culture plays not only in the visitor experience but also in the ways in which the experience is conceived, developed, and managed by the host. Culture is the distinguishing feature of the indigenous tourism system, and there often is a conscious effort to feature and/or commodify the "otherness" of the hosts as the central attraction. At the heart of their model is the dynamic that exists between the generating region where the tourist resides and the destination where the indigenous hosts are located. The flow is accompanied by additional flows from internal and external economic, political, social, and physical environments (e.g., financial resources, values, information). In the ideal case, the flows between hosts and guests are equal, as are the benefits to each respective stakeholder group. Hinch and Butler argue that this exchange is where many of the controversies and issues associated with indigenous tourism reside—inequality has traditionally defined the indigenous tourism system.

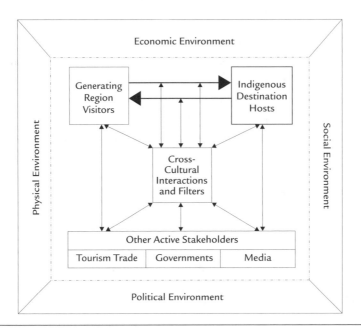

Figure CS 2.1   The indigenous tourism system.
Source: From Hinch, T., & Butler, R. (2007). Introduction: Revisiting common ground. Tourism and indigenous peoples: Issues and implications. In R. Butler and T. Hinch (Eds.), *Tourism and indigenous peoples: Issues and implications* (p. 7). Oxford: Butterworth-Heinemann.

Indigenous Tourism Opportunities and Benefits

The economic environment is considered the driving force for tourism, and the demand for tourism is primarily a product of the country of origin's level of economic development. Strong economic performance will result in higher levels of discretionary spending for travel (Mill & Morrison, 2006; Oh, 2005). Weak economic performance in destination areas, particularly where primary and secondary industries are struggling, results in tourism being pursued as a development alternative (Hinch & Butler, 2007). For example, the Caribbean islands that have lost their markets for sugar and tobacco now rely primarily on tourism (Goodwin, 2008). In indigenous communities where dependency on government social assistance is high and traditional subsistence activities have been submerged (for a variety of social, political, environmental, and economic reasons), governments and aid agencies are actively encouraging tourism development to support economic and sociocultural benefits such as employment opportunities as well as material and community well-being (Dyer, Aberdeen, & Schuler, 2003; Zeppel, 1998). In South Africa, the restitution of land to local indigenous communities is subject to a clause that mandates the establishment of tourism infrastructure and operations. The Makuleke community in Kruger National Park has rented its land to private tourism firms and is investing the revenues in community development and ecological restoration (Spenceley, 2008).

As a result of the potential economic benefits, indigenous tourism has become an important growth sector and an important alternative or complement to subsistence activities. But for indigenous communities, the motivations for tourism engagement transcend economic benefits, and these motivations have evolved over time (Blangy, 2010). In the 1990s, the first indigenous tourism initiatives emerged in the Amazon region of Latin America. One of the motivations for indigenous engagement was the potential to raise public awareness of the pressures on indigenous communities resulting from resource extraction on indigenous and near-indigenous lands (Jones, 2008). Visitors were solicited to become ambassadors and to disseminate key messages and issues to the international community. Concomitantly, indigenous communities perceived tourism to be a means of financing community development projects such as the construction of schools and other basic but much-needed infrastructure. For example, indigenous communities in Venezuela used tourism revenues to finance infrastructure projects that did not fall within government support parameters (Blangy, 2010). By extension, tourism is perceived as a means for reducing and alleviating poverty—a commonly shared demographic characteristic and condition that affects indigenous people throughout the world more often than it does nonindigenous people (Goodwin, 2007a, 2007b).

Today, the motivations are more complex and nuanced. Certainly, indigenous communities are using tourism as a platform for economic independence, but tourism also is perceived as a vector for cultural revitalization and social capital development (Stronza, 2008). Well-managed tourism is perceived as a means for increasing community interest and engagement with indigenous traditional values, languages, customs, and lands. For three indigenous communities in the Amazon, tourism engagement resulted in an enhanced sense of place, cultural identity, community organization, and empowerment while a reduction in social conflict was also observed (Stronza & Gordillo, 2008). For planning purposes, Williams and O'Neil (2007) led a series of community forums and focus groups in British Columbia, Canada, to determine indigenous community perspectives on the opportunities and benefits of indigenous tourism (see **Table CS 2.1**). The results provide a convenient reference and framework for discussion

Table CS 2.1   The Opportunities and Benefits of Indigenous Tourism

Economic development	Offering communities and individuals opportunities for economic diversification, employment, entrepreneurship, training and education, and business linkages with external partners
Cultural development	Providing important means and motivations to care for and maintain local heritage, traditional knowledge, and cultural practices, especially for youth
Social development	Offering indigenous communities and society opportunities for cultural exchange, understanding, and learning
Self-determination/ control	Providing indigenous people opportunities to pursue self-determination and control their own economic and cultural destinies
Political development	Raising public awareness of issues and opportunities associated with the politics surrounding local governance, land ownership, wildlife and environmental management, and resource sharing in indigenous communities

Source: From Williams, P., & O'Neil, B. (2007). Building a triangulated research foundation for indigenous tourism in B.C., Canada. In R. Butler and T. Hinch (Eds.), *Tourism and indigenous peoples: Issues and implications* (pp. 41–57). Oxford: Butterworth-Heinemann.

because they are relevant to indigenous communities around the world. Of particular interest to our focus on the MDGs is the potential for indigenous tourism to contribute to Goal 1, "to eradicate extreme poverty and hunger," and Goal 7, "to ensure environmental sustainability" (United Nations [UN], 2010). To explore the role of indigenous tourism in meeting these two goals, the following sections report the results of four case studies where participatory action research was conducted in indigenous communities.

Method

The case studies presented here are from several projects conducted in the Arctic and subarctic regions with the Saami reindeer herders of Övre Soppero in Northern Sweden; the nine First Nations of the Cree territory of Eeyou Istchee in Quebec, Canada; the Cree of Moose Factory in Ontario, Canada; and the Caribou Inuit of Baker Lake in Nunavut, Canada. Building on a decades-long research relationship with the communities that focused on land and wildlife management, sustainable tourism became an opportunity around which to build a new research agenda—one with support from the aforementioned indigenous communities. The project goal was to analyze indigenous tourism resources in each community and collaboratively identify opportunities and challenges as the basis for future tourism development.

In order to initiate the research, Chevalier and Buckles's (2010) social analysis system (SAS) was judged to be a best-fit methodological framework because it is well-suited to collaborative inquiry and social engagement. SAS offers a set of 50 or so tools and techniques for exploring and tapping into local knowledge and value systems in different and/or complex cultural settings. A dozen of these techniques were incorporated into the structure of 20 workshops that were con-

Figure CS 2.2 Floor mapping is a social analysis system technique that was used to share and capture traditional knowledge regarding indigenous issues and tourism resources.

ducted in the case study communities (Blangy, McGinley, & Lemelin, 2010). For example, the development of floor maps, narratives, small group issue identification, prioritization, and scoring were popular techniques that successfully resulted in active engagement (and were well-liked by community collaborators), a productive collaborative process, and the capture of high-quality data (see **Figure CS 2.2**). The SAS approach proved to be well-suited to the research context because it satisfied the fundamental basis of the research approach and method; that is, the collaborative engagement of the indigenous communities throughout the research process. Drawing from case studies in the Saami, Cree, and Inuit communities, the potential for indigenous tourism to contribute to MDGs 1 and 7 are explored.

MDG 1: Eradicate Poverty

Defined by the International Monetary Fund and the International Development Association (1995, p. 5):

> Poverty means a lack of basic capacity to participate effectively in society. It means not having enough to feed and clothe a family, not having a clinic or school to go to, not having the land on which to grow one's food or a job to earn one's living, not having access to credit. It means insecurity, powerlessness and exclusion of individuals, households and communities.

Poverty is not only about a lack of financial resources, it is multidimensional. As a result of this multidimensionality, the sociocultural components of the definition and the fact that poverty is a relative concept, there are little data available to demonstrate the impacts of tourism on poverty (Goodwin, 2007a). Academic views on the relationship between tourism and poverty are diverse, but criticism is consistent regarding the industry's ability to deliver financial benefits to local people (Scheyvens, 2011). The sociocultural and economic well-being opportunities linked with tourism are hard to ignore, particularly in small rural and/or indigenous communities where families struggle to meet their basic needs (Schellhorn, 2007). The proximity of a tourism attraction promises quality of life improvements through employment, aid, and poverty reduction, but the paradox is that poor countries, communities, and people are often excluded from or disadvantaged by tourism (Scheyvens, 2011). In the 1970s, Turner and Ash (1975, p. 53) warned that "tourism has proved remarkably ineffective as a promoter of equality and as an ally of the oppressed." The response was the development of the pro-poor tourism (PPT) concept to address tourism's shortcomings in delivering meaningful benefits to marginalized groups: " . . . tourism that generates net benefits for the poor (benefits greater than costs). Strategies for pro-poor tourism focus specifically on unlocking opportunities for the poor within tourism, rather than expanding the overall size of the sector" (Bennett et al., 1999, p. ii).

PPT garnered support from academia and industry and, in the last decade, the concept's alignment with the MDGs was noted (Goodwin, 2007b). For indigenous communities, PPT is perceived as a framework that has the potential to mitigate the negative impacts of tourism and to maximize the benefits when it is operationalized. However, Goodwin (2008) reports that very few of the PPT initiatives have provided published results, and there is still much to learn about the potential for tourism to reduce poverty in indigenous communities. In Scheyvens's (2011) *Tourism and Poverty*, she expresses a need for continued caution: "Is there any reason for us to believe that things have changed radically due to the emergence of the PPT concept?" (p. 5).

MDG 1: Indigenous Tourism Case Studies

The four case study communities are located in industrialized countries and therefore may not be characterized by poverty in absolute terms. The communities are facing challenges similar to those of indigenous communities in developing countries or poverty-stricken regions where safe drinking water, health, education, and access to information often are compromised. They also have to deal with industrialization and associated environmental issues such as climate change, habitat loss, and species extinction. Social issues also are present, as are overcrowding and housing problems leading to language, local knowledge, and cultural tradition loss, and an increasing generation gap between the young and elders are common. These conditions have contributed to cultural and social impoverishment.

In Eeyou Istchee, the traditional territory and homeland of the Cree of northern Quebec, tourism is helping to address poverty in a number of different ways. The Cree Outfitting and Tourism Association (COTA) was established by the James Bay and Northern Quebec Agreement (JBNQA) in 1975. COTA's mission was to implement a vision for a world-class sustainable tourism industry by positioning Eeyou Istchee as an indigenous tourism destination. More than 25 years after the association's establishment and despite considerable investment by government, few market-ready tours had been developed; social, cultural, and economic benefits were not being realized; and indigenous community engagement was limited (Blangy & McGinley, 2009). In hopes of renewing interest in the potential for tourism to contribute to community and individual quality of life, a research partnership was established. Several 3-day workshops were organized over the course of a 1-year period with a group of 20 community tourism leaders in order to collaboratively assess the market readiness of existing and potential tourism packages. The process was designed to act as a way to create synergies between the nine Cree First Nations in the region so as to share knowledge and resources and to collaboratively benefit from the outcomes. Twelve theme routes were created using SAS techniques such as floor maps and narratives. The routes are Cree trails used in the past and present for trading (fur), travel (family visits), and healing purposes (with a focus on youth). The trails link the five coastal and four inland communities of the Cree homeland. In the tourism context, the trails are intended to disperse tourism activity and any resultant benefits (i.e., tourist expenditures) across the nine communities. The process of creating the routes led to a new destination management organization. Eeyou Istchee Tourism (http://www.creetourism.org) works to market indigenous-controlled tourism in the region, support the development of the indigenous tourism product portfolio, and ensure that the Cree community has a voice and role in shaping regional tourism policies. The Cree of Eeyou Istchee are rediscovering their assets, strengthening their territorial identity, and by extension, reducing poverty in their communities by developing strong value-added cultural tourism packages.

The Moose Factory First Nation of Ontario, Canada, engaged in a similar exercise. Trapline tourism packages (of traditional hunting trails) were developed and participants learned that tourism on the land was empowering people and reducing the gaps between the "haves" and the "have nots" in the community. The immediate benefit of this initiative for the community, beyond the economic benefits resulting from tourist dollars, was that the community was able to regain access to their traditional territory. Moreover, the infrastructure developed to support the tourist experience (e.g., cabin refurbishment and development) is being used to encourage single parents to spend time on their traditional lands with their children in order to reconnect with Cree traditions such as storytelling and trapping (see **Figure CS 2.3**). In a community where many individuals have lost access to their traditional territory and/or do not have a trapline or a cabin anymore, this initiative is helping to address the social and cultural impoverishment that is now endemic in this community.

Figure CS 2.3   Tourist cabins are being used by the Cree of Moose Factory in Ontario, Canada. Spending time on their traditional lands helps them to reconnect with Cree traditions such as storytelling and trapping.

Although these case studies fail to provide evidence that indigenous tourism is contributing to the eradication of absolute poverty on a global scale, they do suggest that it can have a significant and lasting impact on relative poverty at the local scale. Visitation is generating financial gains for individuals and communities, and these benefits are translating into community development projects such as the revitalization of traditional hunting and trapping routes. Moreover, the tourism development process has resulted in renewed interest in cultural traditions, community cohesion, and a revaluing of indigenous assets—both tangible and intangible. For the Inuit and Cree communities profiled here, tourism is valued as an alternative to government aid dependence, a focal point for self-determination, and an important tool for addressing the multidimensionality of poverty in their communities.

MDG 7: Environmental Sustainability

The destruction of natural areas resulting from urbanization, unsustainable agriculture and resource extraction practices, pollution, and climate change are having a serious cumulative effect (Donohoe & Karlis, 2010). The situation is of particular concern in natural areas near core development areas where traditional indigenous land is found and in peripheral areas where indigenous people have been relocated through expropriation or environmental crisis (Westing, 1992). By virtue of their undeveloped state, these lands are increasingly being prized as scarce resources that are attractive for tourism development, and this trend is likely to continue if environmental degradation continues worldwide (Hinch & Butler, 2007; Kirkpatrick, 2001).

Nonindigenous people tend to see the land and its services as resources for human use; this view is distinct from the traditional relationship between indigenous people and the land (Mitchell, 1997; Notzke, 2006). Indigenous peoples do not view the land and its cohabitants (animals, plants) as commodities or natural resources to be bought and sold in global markets. Instead, the land is endowed with sacred meanings that are embedded in social relations that are fundamental to a definition of their existence and identity (Carr, 2007). In this way, indigenous people "believe they are conjugated inseparably with nature" (Hinch & Butler, 2007, p. 11). This attachment to the land is considered the defining characteristic of indigenous peoples; in a philosophical or cosmological sense, it is what links geographically and culturally disparate peoples throughout the world (Davis, 1993). In the last few decades, there has been a growing interest in the role that indigenous peoples and their traditional knowledge can play in sustainable development and environmental management (Berkes, Colding, & Folke, 2000; LaDuke, 1994). The World Commission on Environment and Development (1987) included the following statement in *Our Common Future*:

> These communities are the repositories of vast accumulations of traditional knowledge and experience that links humanity with its ancient origins. Their disappearance is a loss for the larger society, which could learn a great deal from their traditional skills in sustainably managing very complex ecological systems. It is a terrible irony that as formal development reaches more deeply into rain forests, deserts, and other isolated environments, it tends to destroy the only cultures that have proved able to thrive in these environments. (pp. 114–115)

The view that traditional ecological knowledge has value, coupled with the ongoing settlement of indigenous land claims in many countries, has resulted in increasing indigenous control of traditional lands (Blangy, 2006). "Greater control of the land base has allowed indigenous people to pursue land-based tourism as an attractive compromise between involvement in a wage economy and traditional subsistence practices tied to the land" (Hinch & Butler, 2007, p. 11). By extension, it has facilitated the active involvement (direct and indirect) of indigenous communities in environmental sustainability initiatives and movement towards the MDG environmental sustainability goal.

MDG 7: Indigenous Tourism Case Studies

Baker Lake (or *Qamani'tuaq*, meaning "where the river widens") is the only inland community in the Canadian Arctic, and it is home to 11 Inuit groups. The area is known to tourists and art aficionados for its Inuit art (e.g., wall hangings, basalt stone sculptures, stone cut prints) and its magnificent landscapes and wildlife. Tourism was a modest but significant activity at Baker Lake until gold and uranium sites were found in the vicinity. The community is now surrounded by more than 20 active mining or mineral exploration sites. The most recent mining proposal is the Areva's Kiggavik Uranium Mine—the first mine of its kind in Nunavut (Blangy, 2009). Concerns have been raised by indigenous and nonindigenous communities alike about the impacts of mining on human health and development and the long-term impacts on environmental sustainability. Given that the project will set a precedent for future uranium projects in the province, the community is calling for extensive social and environmental impact assessments to be completed before the project goes any further.

Baker Lake was once the host of a small but steady flow of visitors interested in the Inuit culture, but the hotels are now fully booked with miners and explorers. Few of the original tourism

Figure CS 2.4   Traditional Inuit camp: Avaala family's tourism enterprise, Baker Lake, Nunavut, Canada.

operators remain active with the exception of a few family-run local charter boats and businesses that specialize in paddling expeditions on the Thelon River. For these families, tourism serves as a means to financially subsidize the long and expensive trips to the traditional birthplace of the Elders (abandoned in 1957 when communities were relocated to Baker Lake by the Canadian government) where traditional caribou hunting and berry collecting are common activities. Tourism also serves as a way to communicate concerns with visitors who are asked to share their experiences and observations of the impacts of mining on the cultural traditions of the Inuit people and the environmental resources upon which they depend. This is made possible by close and personal contact with the Inuit community. By way of their tourism enterprise (see **Figure CS 2.4**), the Avaala family has developed a network of visitor ambassadors who are actively sharing information about mining activities and advocating for environmental sustainability in the Baker Lake area. The family also is now actively engaged in community-based research to assess the environmental impacts of mining. It is through tourism that the community is able to share their traditional ecological knowledge and express their concerns about the environmental sustainability of Baker Lake and surrounding areas.

The Saami of Övre Soppero in northern Sweden face similar environmental threats as the Inuit people in Baker Lake. The Saami rely on reindeer herding for their livelihood and the sustainability of their traditional way of life. Since the 1990s the reindeer herd size has been diminished by repetitive early autumn freezing rainfalls (herd reduced from 25,000 to 5,000) and it is further threatened by policy changes that would see the Norwegian border closed and access to reindeer calving grounds on the Norwegian side blocked.

In recognition that the environment was changing and that outside political and social factors were likely to further impact their traditional subsistence activities, the Saami invested in an alternative to reindeer herding as their primary economic activity. Unlike the government-driven tourism development agenda in Baker Lake (that has not been successful), the tourism agenda in Övre Soppero has been driven by the Saami people, and tourism is thriving (Blangy & Laurent, 2007). For example, Per Nils Päiviö and Britt-Marie Labba built a tourist center that includes a restored traditional Kota hut made of birch wood, peat moss, and grass and a Saami

Figure CS 2.5   Tourists can stay in the traditional Saami Kota hut when visiting Övre Soppero, Sweden.

museum in a restored heritage farm (see **Figure CS 2.5**). They consulted the elders to learn the old ways of packing reindeers so that they could take visitors on reindeer-supported treks through their traditional lands. The family also offers visitors the opportunity to go salmon fishing, follow the traditional reindeer migration path, learn traditional methods for smoking and drying reindeer meat, bake Saami bread, make traditional handicrafts from reindeer antlers and hide, visit the old Saami hunting camps, and learn to read the landscape. Visitors also are invited to join the Sameby (Saami village unit) when they journey to the summer reindeer camps on the Norwegian plateau. This tourism enterprise was originally developed to promote the Saami culture, but it has evolved to include environmental education about the landscapes and species upon which this indigenous community depends.

The investment in tourism development has brought the Saami people together, renewed their sense of community, and contributed to the development of an environmental agenda. Tourism is perceived as a vector for positive outcomes and a means through which the voice of the Saami can be heard beyond the boundaries of their territories. The immediate result has been increased awareness of the Saami culture and the environmental issues that affect the Saami people both within and beyond the boundaries of Övre Soppero. Looking to the future, the Saami are now working with the Swedish government to develop and co-manage a protected area that includes the reindeer calving grounds and traditional Saami camps. Tourists have been invited to participate in the planning process, and the Saami people are optimistic about the initiative because it promises to attract more tourists while conserving the cultural and natural resources upon which their people depend.

It may be of interest to the reader to learn that the indigenous communities profiled in this chapter were given the opportunity to meet and exchange knowledge at an SAS workshop in Ottawa, Canada (see Figure CS 2.2). Although the purpose of the workshop was to develop a collaborative research agenda that included research projects in their communities, the development of knowledge sharing tools, and the dissemination of indigenous tourism best practices, the most significant outcome of the workshop was the connections established between the Cree and Inuit of Canada and the Saami of Sweden. They are working in their own communities and collaboratively with each other to develop adaptation strategies to environmental change, to revitalize and reclaim their cultural heritage, and to promote environmental and cultural sustainability through indigenous tourism. Their shared optimism that tourism can improve the quality of life for their people is the driving force behind their collaboration. This outcome truly reflects the rather serendipitous nature of community-based participatory research and the sharing of knowledge enabled by the SAS approach (Blangy et al., 2010; Caine, Daison, & Stewart, 2009). Although formal research consultations, meetings, and procedures can be planned and implemented with varying degrees of success, direct and powerful lessons are also derived from spontaneous opportunities to interact with research participants in their own communities and on the land.

Conclusion

The adoption of the Millennium Development Goals by the United Nations has encouraged the World Tourism Organization and national and regional tourism and economic development agencies to adopt new approaches to tourism that focus on local economic development, poverty alleviation, and environmental sustainability. Although research suggests that these efforts have made *some* contribution to achieving the MDGs and other sustainable development imperatives, the reality is that methodological tools remain in the development stage and reporting is inconsistent. For indigenous communities, concern persists about the potential for tourism to perpetuate economic dependency, cultural insensitivity, social and environmental injustice, and disconnects between indigenous and nonindigenous values, experiences, and expectations (Scheyvens, 2011). The evolving sociopolitical environment and the current economic crisis further complicate the aforementioned concerns because they directly affect the governance systems in indigenous communities (Blangy et al., 2010; Notzke, 2004). However, the work of Goodwin (2007b) on measuring and reporting the impacts of tourism on the MDGs, the case studies discussed in this chapter, and the increase in publications on place-based indigenous tourism issues and applications are cause for renewed optimism. Goodwin (2007b) and Ryan (2005) establish assessment and reporting as a key research need so that an understanding of the beneficiaries can be improved and comparisons across time and space can be completed. Blangy and colleagues (2010) developed a geo-collaboratory—an Internet-based global knowledge-sharing portal—and it is contributing to an enhanced understanding of the benefits of tourism for thousands of indigenous operators around the world. Although this body of work identifies significant challenges for the realization of tangible and intangible benefits for indigenous people, the case studies discussed here suggest that they are benefiting from the sociocultural and economic outcomes of indigenous tourism. The research of Nepal (2002) and Schellhorn (2010) in Asia; Kirkpatrick (2001) and Dyer et al. (2003) in Oceania; Sinclair (2003) and Stronza (2008) in South America and the Caribbean; Spenceley (2008) in Africa; Notzke (2004), Iankova (2006), and Loverseed (1998) in North America; and Petterson and Viken (2007) in Europe suggest that a "space of hope" is emerging for indigenous tourism in communities around the world (see Harvey, 2000).

As tourism continues to develop into more environmentally and culturally sensitive areas, the call for a critical analysis of the benefits, challenges, and impacts resonates. In the context of the MDGs where significant concern exists about meeting the targets by 2015, it is possible that indigenous tourism is improving the lives of indigenous people, reducing poverty in indigenous communities, and contributing to environmental sustainability on local-to-global scales. The push for economic, social, and environmental justice supported by international agencies such as the United Nations, the World Tourism Organization, and others has inspired a new generation of tourism entrepreneurs, developers, planners, and managers. A new generation of tourists is demanding responsible tourism experiences that are congruent with the principles and practices of the global sustainable development paradigm. As a community of tourism stakeholders, we can actively assume a role by:

- Viewing indigenous tourism as a tool to promote positive transformation
- Encouraging indigenous tourism as being integral to economic, sociocultural, and environmentally sustainable development
- Promoting social and environmental justice as a core responsibility for individuals, communities, and nations
- Advocating for human, social, and environmental rights (including justice for indigenous communities)
- Developing strategies for indigenous tourism engagement (between hosts, hosts and tourists, hosts and governments, and hosts and development agencies)
- Promoting ethical governance, entrepreneurship, leadership, and innovation for and through indigenous tourism
- Engaging in collaborative research with indigenous communities so as to collectively improve understanding of the unique and complex context in which indigenous tourism exists

As this field of research and practice continues to evolve, it is the experience and the opinion of the authors that there is much to learn about indigenous tourism and a great deal to learn from indigenous peoples.

Acknowledgments

This project was made possible through the financial support of the European Commission Marie Curie Fellowship, the French Polar Research Institute, Carleton University, and the University of Florida.

References

Aboriginal Tourism Association of British Columbia. (2011a). Cultural authenticity program. Retrieved from March 7, 2011, http://www.aboriginalbc.com/corporate/info/cultural-authenticity-program

Aboriginal Tourism Association of British Columbia. (2011b). Industry facts. Retrieved March 7, 2011, from http://www.aboriginalbc.com/corporate/info/industry-facts

Bennett, O., Roe, D. & Ashley, C. (1999). *Sustainable tourism and poverty elimination study: A report to the Department for International Development.* London: DFID.

Berkes, F., Colding, J., & Folke, C. (2000). Rediscovery of traditional ecological knowledge as adaptive management. *Ecological Applications, 10*(5), 1251–1262.

Blangy, S. (2006). *Le guide des destinations indige`nes.* Montpellier, France: INDIGENE.

Blangy, S. (2009). *ECOTRAD: Étude comparative entre les Inuit chasseurs de caribous de Baker Lake au Nunavut et les Sami éleveurs de rennes de Övre Soppero en Suède.* Rapport d'Activité de L'IPEV 2008-2009. Plouzané, France: IPEV.

Blangy, S. (2010). *Co-construire le tourisme autochtone par la recherché-action participative et les Technologies de l'Information et de la Communication.* Unpublished doctoral thesis. Université Paul Valéry, Montpellier III, France.

Blangy, S., & Laurent, A. (2007). Le tourisme autochtone: Un lieu d'expression provilégié pour des formes innovantes de solidarité. *Téoros, 26*(3), 38–45.

Blangy, S., & McGinley, R. (2009). Géoportail, routes thématiques et recherche collaborative; des outils en appui au territoire traditionnel cri d'reyou istchee au Québec. In A. Laurent (Ed.), *Chronique sociale, tourism responsable: clés d'entrée du développement territorial durable* (p. 508). Lyon, France: Chronique Sociale.

Blangy, S., McGinley, R., & Lemelin, R. H. (2010). La recherche action participative et collaborative autochtone peut-elle améliorer l'engagement communautaire dans les projets touristiques? *Téoros, 29*(**1**), 69–80.

Butler, R., & Hinch, T. (1996). *Tourism and indigenous peoples.* London: International Thompson Business Press.

Butler, R., & Hinch, T. (2007). *Tourism and indigenous peoples: Issues and implications.* Oxford: Butterworth-Heinemann.

Caine, K., Daison, C., & Stewart, E. (2009). Preliminary field-work: Methodological reflections from North Canadian research. *Qualitative Research, 9*(4), 489–513.

Carr, A. (2007). Māori nature tourism businesses: Connecting with the land. In R. Butler & T. Hinch (Eds.), *Tourism and indigenous peoples: Issues and implications* (pp. 113–127). Oxford: Butterworth-Heinemann.

Chevalier, J., & Buckles, D. (2010). Social analysis systems. Retrieved May 1, 2011, from http://www.sas2.net/sites/default/files/sites/all/files/manager/pdf/sas2_module3_sept11_red_en.pdf

Davis, S. (1993). *Indigenous views of the land and the environment.* World Bank Discussion Papers, 188. Washington, DC: International Bank for Reconstruction and Development/World Bank.

Donohoe, H., & Karlis, G. (2010). Tourism, transformation and environmental sustainability: A Canadian geographic perspective. *Loisir et societé/Society and Leisure, 32*(2), 261–298.

Dyer, P., Aberdeen, L., & Schuler, S. (2003). Tourism impacts on an Australian indigenous community: A Djabugay case study. *Tourism Management, 24*, 83–95.

Goodwin, H. (2007a). Indigenous tourism and poverty reduction. In R. Butler & T. Hinch (Eds.), *Tourism and indigenous peoples: Issues and implications* (pp. 84–94). Oxford: Butterworth-Heinemann.

Goodwin, H. (2007b). Measuring and reporting the impact of tourism on poverty. In D. Airey & J. Tribe (Eds.), *Tourism research: New directions, challenges and applications* (pp. 63–75). Oxford: Elsevier.

Goodwin, H. (2008). Tourism, local economic development, and poverty reduction. *Applied Research in Economic Development, 5*(3), 55–64.

Harvey, D. (2000). *Spaces of hope.* Berkeley, CA: University of California Press.

Hinch, T., & Butler, R. (2007). Introduction: Revisiting common ground. In R. Butler & T. Hinch (Eds.), *Tourism and indigenous peoples: Issues and implications* (pp. 1–12). Oxford: Butterworth-Heinemann.

Iankova, K. (2006). Tourism and the economic development of native communities in Quebec. *Recherches amérindiennes au Québec, 36*(1), 69–78.

International Monetary Fund and the International Development Association. (1995). *Poverty reduction strategy: Operational issues.* Washington, DC: Authors.

Jones, H. M. (2008, May). Community-based tourism enterprise in Latin America. EplerWood International, May 2008. Retrieved March 7, 2011, from http://www.eplerwood.com/pdf/Community_Based_Tourism_Enterprise.pdf

Kirkpatrick, J. (2001). Ecotourism, local and indigenous people, and the conservation of the Tasmanian World Heritage area. *Journal of the Royal Society of New Zealand, 31*(4), 819–829.

LaDuke, W. (1994). Traditional ecological knowledge and enviromental futures. *Colorado Journal of International Environmental Law and Policy, 5*(1), 127.

Loverseed, H. (1998). Aboriginal tourism in North America. *Travel and Tourism Analyst, 6*, 42–61.

Mill, R., & Morrison, A. (2006). *The tourism system.* Dubuque, Iowa: Kendall/Hunt.

Mitchell, B. (1997). *Resource and environmental management.* Essex, England: Addison Wesley Longman.

Nepal, S. (2002). Involving indigenous peoples in protected area management: Comparative perspectives from Nepal, Thailand, and China. *Environmental Management, 30*(6), 748–763.

Notzke, C. (2004). Indigenous tourism development in Southern Alberta, Canada: Tentative engagement. *Journal of Sustainable Tourism, 12*(1), 29–54.

Notzke, C. (2006). *The stranger, the native and the land: Perspectives on indigenous tourism.* Concord, Onatario, Canada: Captus Press.

Oh, C. (2005). The contribution of tourism development to economic growth in the Korean economy. *Tourism Management, 26,* 39–44.

Parker, B. (1993). Developing aboriginal tourism: Opportunities and threats. *Tourism Management, 14*(5), 400–404.

Petterson, R., & Viken, A. (2007). Saami perspectives on indigenous tourism in northern Europe: Commerce or cultural development. In R. Butler & T. Hinch (Eds.), *Tourism and indigenous peoples: Issues and implications* (pp. 176–187). Oxford: Butterworth-Heinemann.

Ryan, C. (2005). Introduction: Tourist-host nexus—research consideration. In C. Ryan & M. Aicken (Eds.), *Indigenous tourism: The commodifcation and management of culture* (pp. 1–14). Oxford: Elsevier.

Schellhorn, M. (2007). *Rural tourism in the "third world": The dialectic of development. The case of Desa Senaru at Gunung Rinjani National Park in Lombok Island.* Unpublished doctoral thesis. Lincoln University, New Zealand.

Schellhorn, M. (2010). Development for whom? Social justice and the business of ecotourism. *Journal of Sustainable Tourism, 18*(1), 115–135.

Scheyvens, R. (2011). *Tourism and poverty.* New York: Routledge.

Sinclair, D. (2003). Developing indigenous tourism: Challenges for the Guainas. *International Journal of Contemporary Hospitality Management, 15*(3), 140–146.

Smith, V. (1996). *Hosts and guests: The anthropology of tourism* (2nd ed.). Philadelphia: University of Pennsylvania.

Smith, V., & Eadington, W.R. (1992). *Tourism alternatives.* Chichester: Wiley.

Spenceley, A. (2008). Local impacts of community-based tourism in Southern Africa. In A. Spenceley (Ed.), *Responsible tourism: Critical issues for conservation and development* (pp. 285–303). London: Earthscan, IUCN.

Stronza, A. (2008). Through a new mirror: Reflections on tourism and identity in the Amazon. *Human Organization, 67*(3), 244–257.

Stronza, A., & Gordillo, J. (2008). Community views of ecotourism: Redefining benefits. *Annals of Tourism Research, 35*(2), 444–468.

Tremblay, P. (2006). The demand for indigenous tourism: Are there really "disagreements" on how little we know? In P. Whitelaw & B. O'Mahoney (Eds.), *CAUTHE 2006: To the city and beyond* (pp. 1642–1652). Footscray, Victoria, Australia: Victoria University, School of Hospitality, Tourism and Marketing.

Turner, L., & Ash, J. (1975). *The golden hordes: International tourism and the pleasure periphery.* London: Constable.

United Nations. (2010). Millennium development goals. Retrieved March 7, 2011, from http://www.un.org/millenniumgoals

Westing, A. (1992). Environmental refugees: A growing category of displaced persons. *Environmental Conservation, 19,* 201–207.

Williams, P., & O'Neil, B. (2007). Building a triangulated research foundation for indigenous tourism in B.C., Canada. In R. Butler & T. Hinch (Eds.), *Tourism and indigenous peoples: Issues and implications* (pp. 41–57). Oxford: Butterworth-Heinemann.

World Commission on Environment and Development (WCED). (1987). *Our common future.* New York: Oxford University Press.

Zeppel, H. (1998). Come share our culture. *Pacific Tourism Review, 2*(1), 67–81.

Zeppel, H. (2006). Indigenous ecotourism: Sustainable development and management. *Ecotourism Series No. 3.* Wallingford, UK: CABI.

Ecotourism as a Potential Tool for Poverty Eradication and Wild Tiger Conservation

Steve Noakes and Jack Carlsen

LEARNING OBJECTIVES

- To understand the potential for ecotourism to contribute to the UN Millennium Development Goals
- To explore the role of wildlife tourism in contributing to tiger conservation in the tiger range countries (TRCs) of Asia
- To introduce to the sustainable tourism literature new international networks focusing on wild tiger conservation
- To examine the potential for wildlife tourism in TRCs to contribute to poverty eradication as well as conservation of tiger species and habitat

Even though tigers are a critically endangered umbrella species they continue to have charismatic appeal in selling a wide range of products such as gasoline, breakfast cereals, sporting goods, toys, candy, tobacco, and pool and billiard products as well as tourism destinations and travel services. In the competitive tourism marketing of tropical Asian countries, tiger landscapes and the relevance of tigers as religious, cultural, or national icons are key attributes of destination attractiveness. As a flagship species for public relations and biodiversity fundraising, Walpole and Leader-Williams (2002) suggest that tigers play a strategic socioeconomic role for commercial sectors such as tourism rather than an ecological role that can support broader conservation priorities. All of the 13 tiger range countries (TRCs) of Bangladesh, Bhutan, Cambodia, China, India, Indonesia, Lao People's Democratic Republic (PDR), Malaysia, Myanmar, Nepal, Russian Federation, Thailand, and Vietnam include tiger images and information within some aspect of the marketing of their destinations and individual tourism products. (For more information on where tigers are located see http://www.globaltigerinitiative.org.)

Simultaneously, levels of extreme poverty in most of these TRCs remain unacceptably high, with 81.3% of Bangladeshis, 49.5% of Bhutanese, 57.8% of Cambodians, 36.3% of Chinese, 75.6% of Indians, 60% of Indonesians, 76.8% of Laotians, 77.6% of Nepalese, and 48.5% of Vietnamese living on less than US$2 per day (World Bank, 2011). There is an inextricable link between these pervasive problems in TRCs because poverty gives rise to illegal practices of logging, poaching, and land clearing that threaten the very existence of tigers in the wild. However, with a concerted effort by all organizations involved in conservation and poverty eradication, the potential for ecotourism development can be realized as an alternative that can achieve the dual MDGs of eradicating poverty and ensuring environmental sustainability in the future for TRCs.

At the opening of the Convention on Biodiversity in Nagoya, Japan, in 2010, Robert B. Zoellick, president of the World Bank Group, noted the link between biodiversity loss and poverty when he stated, ". . . successful conservation of our natural resources, our ecosystems, and our biodiversity is central to addressing all development challenges and to improving the lives of the poor" (Zoellick, 2010). In a postmodern approach to international development and a shift in its environment strategy from the "do no harm" principle to the "do measurable good" approach (Adams, 2010), biodiversity conservation as a partner in poverty alleviation has become the focus of a number of World Bank development programs. This includes the World Bank's high-profile commitment to the alliance of governments, international agencies, civil society, and the private sector known as the Global Tiger Initiative (GTI).

Basu and Kiess (2010) identify four funding sources that could generate revenues for tiger conservation:

1. Ecotourism
2. Parks management
3. Payments for ecosystem services
4. Wildlife-friendly certification

This chapter considers ecotourism as a tool for both wild tiger conservation and poverty eradication in the TRCs. We report on the current status of the world's wild tiger population with particular focus on the plight of the Sumatran tiger in Indonesia and provide comments on current ecotourism policy issues and challenges for the GTI partners (e.g., illegal trade in endangered wildlife networks in Southeast Asia and South Asia). In addition, we discuss the advantages for a common TRC tiger-ecotourism definition for effective, achievable, and measurable public policy consistency among the nations where wild tigers can still be found. The chapter also refers to the philanthropic tourism approach of a private sector company applying small-scale ecotourism as a wildlife conservation tool and contributing to improving local livelihoods in Indonesia.

The objectives of this case study are (1) to report on the current status of tiger conservation and poverty eradication in TRCs through the activities of the World Bank, Smithsonian Institute, World Wildlife Fund, and numerous other agencies involved in conservation and poverty eradication; (2) to explore the potential of ecotourism as part of the toolbox for the conservation of wild tigers in Asia; and (3) to examine the objectives and operations of international organizations involved in tiger conservation, poverty eradication, and tourism in the context of TRCs. A further outcome of this chapter is to provide new insights on and knowledge of the issues associated with the GTI with reference to Indonesia as well as to progress the dialogue of poverty eradication through ecotourism development by private philanthropic tourism organizations such as Ecolodges Indonesia.

The Current Status of Tiger Conservation

Wild tigers are on a trajectory to extinction. First evolving some 2 million years ago in East Asia, wild tigers have disappeared from southwest and central Asia (Afghanistan, Iran, Kazakhstan, Pakistan, Tajikistan, Turkey, Turkmenistan, Uzbekistan) as well as from the Indonesian islands of Java and Bali and from other large range areas of Southeast and Eastern Asia, such as the Korean Peninsula. From an estimated 100,000 tigers a century ago (Smithsonian National Museum of Natural History, 2011), the species is now under the threat of extinction, with best estimates putting the global tiger population living in their natural habitats at between 3,000 and 5,000 adults (International Union for Conservation of Nature and Natural Resources [IUCN], 2011). The expanding economies and populations of most of the TRCs in South and Southeast Asia over recent decades has resulted in large areas of tiger habitats being converted for agricultural use, urbanization, plantations, mining, tourism, and other uses leading to tiger–human conflicts. Poaching to supply tiger products and retributive killing of tigers also remains a real threat to the survival of the species.

Improving the livelihoods of poor people in landscapes that historically contained rich biodiversity depends upon healthy ecosystems, symbolized through healthy wildlife populations including top predator species and biodiversity beacons such as the tiger. To support viable populations, tigers in the wild require large areas of land. They are an umbrella species for other animal and plant species that share their habitat. Their top predator status can assist in regulating the number and distribution of prey, impacting forest structure, composition, and regeneration (Ale & Whelan, 2008; Wegge, Morten, Pokharel, & Storaas, 2009).

Officially designated and effectively managed tiger conservation landscapes can help protect tigers from being hunted and give them access to sufficient prey and adequate hunting territory.

As an apex predator it is difficult for tigers to coexist with humans, but examples from the Terai Arc Landscape project in Nepal and South West India illustrate that effective wildlife conservation can occur with appropriate spatial planning and ecological zoning, which include development, human settlements, wildlife core areas, buffer zones, and corridors as an integrated landscape to support coexistence between humans and wildlife (Dinerstein et al., 2006).

A significant problem for tiger conservation is inadequate law enforcement and intergovernmental coordination to combat illegal wildlife trade. This requires the engagement of environmental management agencies, police, and customs officials to markedly increase the risk of arrest and prosecution of tiger poachers and traffickers. One important regional initiative that recognizes wildlife crime as a major threat to the natural systems that sustain human life is the Bangkok-based Association of Southeast Asian Nations Wildlife Enforcement Network (ASEAN-WEN), launched December 1, 2005, at the Special Meeting of ASEAN Ministers responsible for the implementation of the Convention on International Trade in Endangered Species of Wild Fauna and Flora (CITES). ASEAN-WEN includes 7 of the 13 TRCs (Cambodia, Indonesia, Lao PDR, Malaysia, Myanmar, Thailand, and Vietnam). The other three ASEAN-WEN states are Brunei Darussalam, Philippines, and Singapore, with the latter two having small captive zoo-based tiger populations rather than free-ranging wild tigers. Echoing a call from Dr. Surin Pitsuwan, Secretary General of ASEAN (CITES, 2009) for all TRCs to "build upon the success of ASEAN-WEN and reach out to all of Asia in this effort to develop a region wide effort to protect our endangered species for our future generations to enjoy and benefit from," international partners such as Interpol, the United Nations Office on Drugs and Crime, the World Customs Organization, the World Bank, IUCN, World Wildlife Fund (WWF), and others provide support to ASEAN-WEN. To date, there is no evidence that regional Southeast Asian government tourism networks such as the ASEAN Tourism Forum have addressed tourism and wildlife conservation interfaces.

Further to the west, the South Asia Cooperative Environment Program (SACEP), which includes the TRCs of India, Bangladesh, Bhutan, and Nepal, was established under the South Asian Association for Regional Cooperation (SAARC) to work on environmental issues in South Asia. In relation to tourism issues, SAARC leaders identified the benefits from more regional cooperation on tourism in 1986 and then formed a Technical Committee on Tourism in 1991, held the first meeting of SAARC Tourism Ministers in 1997, and in 1999 assigned tourism issues to the SAARC Chamber of Commerce and Industry (SCCI) Tourism Council (SAARC, 2011). As in Southeast Asia, there is no evidence the South Asian tourism cooperation networks have addressed tourism and wildlife conservation interfaces.

Independent of SACEP activities, and signaling a new era in regional cooperation on wildlife law enforcement, in January 2011, the South Asia Wildlife Enforcement Network (SAWEN) was announced at an intergovernmental meeting in Bhutan attended by government delegates from Afghanistan, Bangladesh, Bhutan, India, Nepal, Pakistan, and Sri Lanka (Traffic, 2011).

> SAWEN is a powerful signal that South Asia is ramping up efforts to combat poaching and illegal wildlife trade in the region. Illegal wildlife trade does not exist in a vacuum and if it continues unabated we risk losing species like rhinos and tigers, jeopardizing local livelihoods, and in the bigger picture, affecting the delicate natural ecosystems that make this corner of our living planet so unique and irreplaceable. (WWF, 2011)

Following the November 2010 International Tiger Forum in Saint Petersburg, Russia, the secretary-general of CITES, the secretary-general of Interpol, the executive director of the United Nations Office on Drugs and Crime (UNODC), the president of the World Bank, and the secretary-general of the World Customs Organization (WCO) signed a letter of understanding to establish an International Consortium on Combating Wildlife Crime (ICCWC) (Interpol, 2010). Among its activities in 2011 were providing training support to officials in SAWEN, conducting senior-level seminars for customs and police from all of the TRCs, and completing a toolkit on wildlife and forest crime for use by the TRCs to review their current response to such crimes.

The Global Tiger Initiative

The Global Tiger Initiative (GTI) is about mainstreaming wildlife conservation into international development expressed through the contemporary MDG agenda. It is a network that harnesses the convening power of the World Bank and a coalition of international organizations including the WWF, Wildlife Conservation Fund (WCF), and Smithsonian Institution. Each of the governments of the 13 TRCs are participants in the GTI, as are conservation agencies, zoos, and benevolent foundations such as Conservation International, International Fund for Animal Welfare, Save the Tiger Fund, Wildlife Conservation Society, World Association of Zoos and Aquariums, Zoological Society of London, Smithsonian's National Zoological Park, Animals Asia Foundation, Born Free, Corbett Foundation, Freeland Foundation, and others. Launched by the president of the World Bank, the Smithsonian Institution, the Global Environment Fund (GEF), and an alliance of governments and international organizations in June 2008, the GTI aims to:

- Make the world aware of the tiger and wildlife crisis
- Harvest knowledge from the world's top scientists and practitioners
- Secure high-level political support and influence public policy

Proposing that saving the tiger from extinction would help to energize world efforts to protect the planet's threatened life-blood of biodiversity, the GTI identifies the tiger's presence in natural ecosystems as a barometer of the critical question: Are we making the right choices to sustain the planet? (GTI, 2011).

Ecotourism as a Tool for Conservation and Poverty Eradication

Complementing improved enforcement and protection measures, ecotourism is often cited as one of the new mechanisms that can be tailored to local conditions to address the root causes in the decline of tiger populations and their habitats such as weak incentives, market failures, and institutional impediments. Similar causes contribute to ongoing poverty, particularly institutional corruption and a lack of integration between public and private sector initiatives. Seeing the need for a tiger conservation model that also can contribute to the dual MDGs of conservation and poverty eradication and "blend incentives for conservation (carrots) with deterrence and enforcement (sticks)," Damania et al. (2008, p. 20) cite the experiences from successful and sustainable wildlife tourism case studies in Africa.

Research by Lepp (2002) on gorilla-induced tourism in the Bwindi Impenetrable National Park (BINP) in Uganda illustrates how income sources for local people from timber and gold mining and subsistence from hunting and gathering within the park could be replaced with host participation as guides, trackers, porters, and other employment opportunities. The gorilla conservation outcome through ecotourism has reduced threats to the forest biodiversity from logging and mining and reportedly resulted in host community satisfaction with wildlife ecotourism.

Two further examples of ecotourism as a tool for conservation and poverty eradication emerge from the Asian destinations of the Philippines and Cambodia. The first is in the former 19th-century Spanish naval center of Puerto Princesa, self-proclaimed as the "Ecotourism Capital of the Philippines" (Puerto Princesa City, 2011). It is located in Palawan province, the largest of the Philippine provinces, stretching from Mindoro in the northeast to Indonesian Borneo in the southwest and lying between the South China Sea and the Sulu Sea. The Puerto Princesa Subterranean River National Park is a key visitor natural attraction, contributing to the growth in tourist numbers to Puerto Princesa from 12,000 in 1992 to 425,000 in 2010 (Palawan Tourist Council, 2011). Many local people rely on food from the sea for their livelihoods, and killing dolphins and turtles was a common occurrence. Destructive trawl net fishing and other methods including the use of dynamite and cyanide not only depleted the mammal and reptile life, but also ruined or damaged the local coral reef systems. With the realization that marine life such as dolphins and turtles are more valuable as ongoing tourist attractions than as a food source, local fishermen have been trained as ecotourism guides and adapted their fishing boats to become island-hopping passenger-carrying vessels (France 24, 2011).

Increasingly throughout Asia, the value of live tigers is being acknowledged as considerably greater than that of dead or captive tigers. This provides the context for the second example, in the Southern Cardamom Mountains in the southwest of Cambodia near the border with Thailand, home to numerous threatened species, including tigers, Asian elephants, Siamese crocodiles, and pileated gibbons. Located at the foothills of the mountains, the village of Chi Pat in the remote province of Koh Kong was until recent times ". . . infamous for its abundant poachers, loggers and slash-and-burn farmers, who were forced to turn to illegal practices to make a living" (Lindt, 2011, p. 1). Community participation in ecotourism ventures provides income to improve their livelihoods and provides incentives to protect the forest and its wildlife, rather than to exploit it in an unsustainable manner. Former wild animal hunters who know the forest well have become tour guides. Local families have become guesthouse owners or have started businesses making biodegradable soap and locally harvested honey to be purchased by visitors. Local people are working in appropriately designed and operated ecolodges where expatriate residents of Cambodia have been able to assist with equity and working capital to support the financial sustainability of the enterprise.

Ecotourism is not a panacea for wildlife conservation, poverty reduction, and related MDG targets; however, ecotourism can play an important part in wild tiger conservation efforts (Noakes, 2010; Sproule, 2010). Two key first steps to undertake are (1) to enable the TRCs to generate a consensus on a shared cross-cultural TRC-relevant meaning of the concept of "tiger ecotourism" and (2) to establish workable partnerships among government, private sector, community, conservation, and development sectors to achieve effective conservation outcomes from tiger ecotourism.

Ecotourism depends on the natural environment; hence the loss of habitat damages the destination's ecotourism profile and potential (Weaver, 2008). Studies into this potential for wildlife as an attraction for tourists can be traced back to Grinnell and Storer (1916), who advocated the use of "wildlife imagery" to promote parklands to tourists and saw wildlife experiences "[a]s a stimulant to the senses of far sight and far hearing, faculties largely neglected in the present scheme of civilization, they are no less consequence than the scenery, the solitude and the trails. To the natural charm of the landscape they add the witchery of movement" (p. 377). Research reported by Damania et al. (2008) and Hill (2001) find there is a growing demand to observe wildlife as part of the tourist experience. In his report *Ecotourism and Tiger Conservation—Summary of the Main Messages* from the Hua Hin Asian Ministerial Conference (AMC), World Bank economist Richard Damania stated: "[ecotourism] . . . is worth doing and it will work for conservation if and only if it substantially alters the balance between the payoffs from destruction relative to the payoffs from conservation" (AMC, 2010). He argues a key challenge will be to clearly illustrate how habitats thriving with living wild animals are worth more than empty landscape converted to the monoculture of oil palm plantations or other agriculture, roads, mines, factories, and other forms of economic enterprise, destructive to the natural environment required for tiger existence. The model of economic extraction can also apply to tourism, particularly where it is developed as an "enclave industry" that profits from the existence and attributes of a rich natural environment but makes little, if any, contribution towards its conservation and protection. Importing goods and services to deliver within the resorts results in high levels of economic leakage, exporting profits out of the region and providing few local benefits apart from low-paid and low-skilled employment opportunities that do not contribute to a sustainable development approach as per the goals of the MDGs.

Ecotourism in the TRCs is largely underdeveloped and undermanaged due to factors such as remote tiger landscapes and difficulties in accessing and seeing tigers in the jungle environments of Asia. India is host to the largest tiger tourism industry in the world with more than 1.29 million tourists visiting tiger reserves each year and a further 2 million visiting the reserves for pilgrimage purposes. India currently has 27 tiger reserves; low entry fees to these result in approximately 60,000 tourists, on average, annually at each reserve. However, overall, tourists generate insufficient funds for wild tiger conservation measures (Damania et al., 2008).

Indonesia: Progress Toward the MDGs and Tourism Performance

The Republic of Indonesia rates 124th on the global Human Development Index (United Nations Development Programme [UNDP], 2011). The World Bank (2011) reports that out of a national population of over 232 million, more than 32 million people live below the poverty line and approximately half of all households remain clustered around the national poverty line, set at 200,262 rupiah per month (US$22 as of March 2010). After more than three centuries of Dutch colonial rule, Japanese occupation during World War II, and decades of repressive rule, in 1999 the first free and fair legislative elections took place (Central Intelligence Agency [CIA] Indonesia, 2012). The 33 provinces within Indonesia combine to make the country the world's third most populous democracy and home to the world's largest Muslim population. The high human population density has resulted in an expansion of human activity, including agriculture, into areas that once were dominated by wildlife. Large-scale monoculture of palm, wood extraction, and other plantation development have created a dramatically changing landscape and also have impacted Indonesia's capacity to achieve MDGs relating to environmental sustainability. The continuous forcing of wild tigers to move increases the scale and extent of encounters between humans and wildlife, as has been similarly reported by Lee and Priston (2005) in their research on human attitudes and perceptions of primates as pests and sources of conflict, and the consequences for primate conservation.

The MDGs are relevant to the National Development Planning documents of the government of the Republic of Indonesia. The *Report on the Achievement of the Millennium Development Goals in Indonesia* (Ministry of National Development Planning, 2010) records the three MDG targets that have already been achieved:

- *MDG 1:* The proportion of people having per capita income of less than US$1 per day declined from 20.6% in 1990 to 5.9% in 2008.
- *MDG 3:* Gender equality in all types and levels of education has almost been achieved.
- *MDG 6:* The prevalence of tuberculosis decreased from 443 cases per 100,000 population in 1990 to 244 cases per 100,000 in 2009.

However, problems persist, and data on the status of the MDGs in Indonesia as of March 2011 (UNDP, 2011) indicates that the proportion of the population with sustainable access to clean water and sanitation has not increased significantly and the maternal mortality rate of 228 per 100,000 remains one of the highest in Southeast Asia. The rate of HIV/AIDS infection has accelerated, particularly in high-risk urban areas and the province of Papua. Enrollment of children in primary school is positive at 95%, the same level as the literacy rate for the population between ages 15 and 24.

In 2009, Indonesia received a record 6,452,259 international visitor arrivals, an increase of 0.36% over the previous year. On average, visitors stayed for 7.8 nights, spent US$1,000 per visit, and underpinned the contribution of tourism to 4.8% of Indonesia's gross domestic product (Ministry of National Development Planning, 2010). After gas/petroleum (US$19 billion) and palm oil (US$10.3 billion), tourism (US$6.29 billion) was the third major foreign exchange earner for the country from 2006 to 2009, coinciding with a drop-off in earnings from rubber products and garments (Ministry of National Development Planning, 2010). The World Economic Forum's *Travel and Tourism Competitiveness Report* (WEF, 2011) rates the factors and policies that make development of the travel and tourism sectors attractive in 139 countries. In the 2011 report, Indonesia ranked as #74, improving its position from #83 in 2009.

Tiger Conservation in Indonesia

The Republic of Indonesia's biodiversity wealth across its vast archipelagic network of over 17,000 islands is well recorded (Center for International Forestry Research [CIFOR], 2011).

Driven by the expansion of plantation crops and pulp wood production, deforestation in Indonesia is currently 2.97 acres (1.2 million hectares) per annum (Verchot et al., 2010). Indonesia also carries the burden of containing the highest number of IUCN Red Listed species of any country in the world (IUCN, 2011). Exploitation of vast areas of natural forest for agricultural use such as the monoculture of oil palm plantations results in a poor habitat for most terrestrial mammal species, including wild tigers. Although Maddox et al. (2007) found that the compatibility of such plantations and most mammal species is very low, they highlighted the importance of marginal or degraded habitats found within palm oil concessions to retain high conservation values that could guide new planting to reduce impacts on local wildlife populations.

Critically endangered due to poaching and habitat destruction, the Sumatran tiger is the last of three tiger subspecies remaining in Indonesia, following the extinction of the Bali tiger between the 1930s and 1950s and the Java tiger in the 1970s (Seidensticker & Suyono, 1980). It is the smallest among all existing tiger subspecies and has a remaining population of some 400 living in fragmented and isolated habitats (World Wildlife Fund [WWF], 2012). The Indonesian government issued its first action plan for the conservation of the Sumatran tiger in 1994, and 10 tiger conservation areas currently have been designated on Sumatra: TN Bukit Barisan Selatan, TN Way Kambas, Bukit Balai Rejang Selatan, TN Kerinci Seblat, Riau/Lansekap Tesso Nilo-Bukit Tigapuluh, Senepis/Buluhala, Jambi/PT Asiatic Persada, Sumatera Barat, TN Batang Gadis, and Ekosistem Leuser.

Ecolodges Indonesia

Ecolodges Indonesia, which currently offers five ecolodge experiences on the islands of Bali, Flores, Borneo, and Sumatra, is a private company with strong links to wildlife veterinarians and conservationists. Supported by a small number of international investors and mentors, the enterprise only employs local Indonesians and places an emphasis on applying small-scale ecotourism as a wildlife conservation tool and contributing to improving local livelihoods and poverty eradication (Ecolodges Indonesia, 2011).

In close proximity to Way Kambas National Park in Lampung Province, Sumatra, Ecolodges Indonesia owns and operates the eight-room Satwa Elephant Ecolodge and plays an active role in developing and delivering a range of biodiversity, wildlife, wildcat, and community training and support mechanisms in the local community and for National Park staff. First established by the Dutch colonial rulers as a game park in 1937, Way Kambas National Park was inaugurated in 1989 and includes the Elephant Training Center (ETC), which houses about 150 captive elephants, and the Sumatran Rhino Sanctuary, which can house up to 10 of this most threatened of the five living rhino species (International Rhino Foundation, 2011). This lowland tropical forest is also host to the rare white-winged wood duck, along with over 400 other bird species as well as various deer species, the Asian tapir, sun bears, and wild cats including the tiger, leopard cat, clouded leopard, flat-headed cat, golden cat, fishing cat, and marbled cat (Tiger Trust, 2011).

A rapid business and economic assessment undertaken on the contribution by Satwa Ecolodge to local employment and economic impacts (Thomas, 2009) provided a baseline understanding of the factors that impede an improvement of business success and support to local communities. Utilizing several methods (i.e., attractions inventory and access analysis, market demand analysis), results indicated that the key attractors to the National Park and the ecolodge were trekking, bike tours, boat trips, and bird watching, along with cultural experiences and the opportunity to visit the Rhinoceros Sanctuary and the Elephant Training Center. The four significant markets identified were research tourists, specialized niche tourists, local and Asian tourists, and those from NGO-type organizations. Thomas's research illustrated that the salary of Satwa Ecolodge's 10-member staff represented 75% of the resources of the staff's families, supporting an additional 28 persons including four families considered "poor." Two-thirds of the staff was living in the immediate vicinity of the ecolodge, and most of them secured their employment via word of mouth. Satwa Ecolodge contributed benefits not only through employment at the ecolodge but also to the local community through local suppliers and/or producers, taxes to the local authorities, and the provision of tourist activities inside the national park and the Rhinoceros Sanctuary.

Ecolodges Indonesia has undertaken preliminary site inspections for a possible tented tiger-safari-type eco camp near the 3.46 million-acre (1.4 million-hectare) Kerinci Seblat National Park in Sumatra (established in 1992 and World Heritage–listed in 2005). Home to an estimated population of 150 wild tigers as well as endangered elephants, clouded leopards, sun bears, and more than 370 bird species, this national park is divided by the Barisan mountain range and fringed by extensive palm oil plantations. Along with the encroaching palm oil plantation development, the park is under threat from a number of sources, including wildlife poaching (eight dedicated tiger-cable snares were uncovered by a Fauna and Flora International field team in March 2011; FFI, 2011), illegal road construction, and government proposals to build several highways through the national park to serve as evacuation routes in the event of volcanoes, earthquakes, flooding, or other natural disasters (Kutarumalos, 2011).

At this stage, the only evidence that the operations of Ecolodges Indonesia and its affiliated not-for-profit conservation organization, Save Indonesian Endangered Species (SIES), are having any positive impact on tiger conservation is largely through their collective efforts to bring local, national, and international attention and support to the plight of this endangered species. The company continues to consider new commercially viable ecolodge facilities in wild tiger precincts such as Sumatra's Kerinci Seblat National Park and to enhance the flow of quality information on wild tigers to its guests and local community around Satwa Ecolodge.

Conclusion

The world's wild tiger population is under severe threat. Substantial challenges remain for wildlife law enforcement networks in Southeast Asia and South Asia to halt the trade in endangered species such as the wild tiger. Concurrently, poverty remains not only an acute problem for the population in the majority of TRCs but also a problem that perpetuates the threat to habitat and protection of tigers globally. Ecotourism has the potential to contribute to the two MDGs of poverty eradication and environmental sustainability, but a number of barriers remain in place. The efforts and initiatives described in this chapter exemplify how some TRCs are progressing towards achieving conservation and poverty eradication through ecotourism.

Indonesia has one of the highest deforestation rates in the world. Apart from losses to the archipelago's biodiversity, deforestation is a significant contributor to climate change, which threatens millions of people living on over 17,000 islands across Indonesia. The recent history and future outlook for the remaining Sumatran tigers are relevant to Indonesia's MDG ambitions, particularly in relation to environmental sustainability, poverty eradication, and global partnerships for development, which is evidenced through the work of international networks such as the GTI. In the case of sustainable tourism, these global partnerships could include the International Ecotourism Society, Global Sustainable Tourism Council (GSTC), and UNWTO's World Committee on Tourism Ethics (which hosted the 2011 seminar on Responsible Tourism and its Socio-Economic Impact on Local Communities in Asia Pacific in Bali, Indonesia) to bring attention to the role and practices ecotourism can contribute to improving local livelihoods and biodiversity conservation.

Human beings depend on a healthy ecosystem. Ecotourism as an economic generator also depends on a healthy ecosystem. Hence, the loss of tigers and tiger landscapes in any one of the TRCs degrades not only the quality of life for individuals living in these areas but also a destination's tourism profile and potential. There is no evidence that the 13 TRCs have the will or mechanisms in place to develop tiger sensitive ecotourism policies that have some degree of consistency of definition and intent across international borders. There is a need to undertake a process to enable the TRCs to generate a consensus on a shared cross-cultural meaning of the concept of "tiger ecotourism" before any effective, achievable, and measurable public policy can be applied to the positive benefits that ecotourism can contribute to wild tiger conservation efforts. There also is the need to establish workable partnerships among the government, private, community, conservation, and development sectors to achieve effective conservation outcomes from tiger ecotourism.

A range of international conservation, wildlife protection, customs agreements, and sustainable tourism and guidelines can provide the foundation for national-level legislation, policy statements, and codes of conduct for tiger ecotourism. Each TRC is a party to multilateral agreements such as CITES, the National Tiger Action Plans (NTAPs), and international treaties such as the Convention on Biological Diversity (CBD), resulting in legally binding responsibilities under international law.

Where the private sector can be mobilized to finance and develop ecotourism business structures in an efficient, effective, and results-oriented and sustainable manner, it should be encouraged by public policy makers. Tiger ecotourism has unique challenges to alternative forms of wildlife viewing, given the solitary nature of the species and the forest environment it inhabits. Ecotourism companies need to partner with local protected area management agencies to develop innovative interpretive and wildlife viewing opportunities for ecotourists.

There is evidence that the philanthropic tourism approach of private sector companies such as Ecolodges Indonesia can successfully apply small-scale ecotourism as a wildlife conservation tool and contribute to improving local livelihoods in Indonesia.

References

Adams, J. (2010, January 27). *Keynote opening remarks by the vice president, East Asia and the Pacific, World Bank group.* Presented at the 1st Asia Ministerial Conference on Tiger Conservation, Hua Hin, Thailand.

Ale, S. B., & Whelan, C. J. (2008). Reappraisal of the role of big, fierce predators. *Biodiversity Conservation, 17,* 685–690.

Asian Ministerial Conference (AMC). (2010). Government of Thailand hosts world's first inter-ministerial meeting on wild tiger conservation. Retrieved April 5, 2011, from http://www.globaltigerinitiative. org/2010/01/13/government-of-thailand-hosts-world's-first-inter-ministerial-meeting-on-wild-tiger-conservation

Basu, P., & Kiess, J. (2010). *Innovative finance for tiger conservation.* Washington, DC: World Bank.

Central Intelligence Agency (CIA) Indonesia. (2012). Retrieved March 28, 2012, from https://www.cia. gov/library/publications/the-world-factbook/geos/id.html

Center for International Forestry Research (CIFOR). (2011). Living and working in Indonesia. Retrieved May 1, 2011, from http://www.cifor.org/about-us/careers-with-cifor/living-and-working-in-indonesia. html

Convention on International Trade in Endangered Species of Wild Flora and Fauna (CITES). (2009). *Manifesto on combating wildlife crime in Asia.* Geneva, Switzerland: Author.

Damania, R., Seidensticker, J., Whitten, T., Sethi, G., Mackinnon, K., Kiss, A., & Kushlin, A. (2008). *A future for wild tigers.* Washington, DC: World Bank.

Dinerstein, E., Loucks, C., Heydlauff, A., Wilramanayake, E., Brya, G., Forrest, J., . . . Songer, M. (2006). *Setting priorities for the conservation and recovery of wild tigers: 2005–2015. A user's guide.* New York: World Wildlife Fund, Wildlife Conservation Society, Smithsonian, and Save the Tiger Fund.

Ecolodges Indonesia. (2011). About us. Retrieved April 2, 2012, from http://www.ecolodgesindonesia. com/ecolodge/?page_id=239

Fauna and Flora International (FFI). (2011). Tiger snares active in Kerinci Seblat National Park Sumatra. Retrieved May 10, 2011, from http://www.fauna-flora.org/news/tiger-snares-active-in-kerinci-seblat-national-park-sumatra

France 24. (2011). Ecotourism offering a feast of opportunities in Asia. Retrieved March 22, 2011, from http://www.france24.com/en/20110322-ecotourism-offering-feast-opportunities-asia

Grinnell, J. & Storer, T. I. (1916, September 15). Animal life as an asset on national parks. *Science,* 375–380.

Global Tiger Initiative (GTI). (2011). Themes. Retrieved December 2, 2011, from http://www. globaltigerinitiative.org/html/themes-all.php

Global Tiger Initiative (GTI). (2012). Indonesia. Retrieved March 28, 2012, from http://www. globaltigerinitiative.org/english-map-indonesia

Hill, B. (2001). *Kangaroos in the marketing of Australia: Potentials and practice.* Gold Coast, Queensland, Australia: Sustainable Tourism Cooperative Research Centre.

International Union for Conservation of Nature and Natural Resources. (2011). Redlist, Panthera tigris. Retrieved February 28, 2011, from http://www.iucnredlist.org/apps/redlist/details/15955/0

International Rhino Foundation. (2012). Sumatran Rhino Sanctuary, Indonesia. Retrieved March 28, 2012, http://www.rhinos-irf.org/srs

Interpol. (2010). Powerful alliance to fight wildlife crime comes into effect. Retrieved May 24, 2012, from http://www.interpol.int/News-and-media/News-media-releases/2010/PR098

Kutarumalos, A. (2011, April 28). Road-building plans threaten Indonesian tigers. *Jakarta Post.* Retrieved May 5, 2011, from http://www.thejakartapost.com/news/2011/04/28/road-building-plans-threaten-indonesian-tigers.html

Lee, P., & Priston, N. (2005). *Human attitudes to primates: Perceptions of pests, conflict and consequences for primate conservation.* Cambridge, England: Department of Biological Anthropology, University of Cambridge.

Lepp, A. (2002). Uganda's Bwindi Impenetrable National Park: Meeting the challenges of conservation and community development through sustainable tourism. In B. Johnston (Ed.), *Life and death matters: Human rights and the environment at the end of the millennium* (pp. 211–220). London: Sage.

Lindt, N. (2011, March 4). In Cambodia, Koh Kong emerges as an eco-tourism destination. *New York Times.* Retrieved March 6, 2011, from http://travel.nytimes.com/2011/03/06/travel/06nextstop-kohkong.html?pagewanted=1

Maddox, T., Priatna, D., Gemita, E., & Salampessy, A. (2007). *The conservation of tigers and other wildlife in oil palm plantations: Jambi Province, Sumatra, Indonesia.* ZSL Living Conservation Report No. 7. London: Zoological Society of London.

Ministry of National Development Planning, Republic of Indonesia. (2010). Report on the achievement of the Millennium Development Goals Indonesia 2010. Retrieved April 3, 2011, from http://www.undp.or.id/pubs/docs/MDG%202010%20Report%20Final%20Full%20LR.pdf

Noakes, S. (2010, January 27–30). *Ecotourism and wild animals in wild habitats.* Address at First Asian Ministerial Conference (ACM) on Tiger Conservation, Hua Nin, Thailand.

Palawan Tourist Council. (2011). Tourism. Retrieved April 3, 2011, from http://www.palawan.gov.ph/tourism.html

Puerto Princesa City. (2011). Puerto Princesa Philippines: Exploring the ecotourism capital of the Philippines. Retrieved April 3, 2011, from http://www.puertoprincesaphilippines.com

Seidensticker, J., & Suyono, I. (1980). *The Javan tiger and Meru Betiri Reserve, a plan for Management.* Gland, Switzerland: International Union for Conservation of Nature.

Smithsonian National Museum of Natural History. (2011). Mammals: It isn't easy being the world's top cat. Retrieved February 28, 2011, from http://www.mnh.si.edu/exhibits/mammals/tiger.htm

South Asian Association for Regional Cooperation (SAARC). (2011). Area of cooperation: Tourism. Retrieved February 28, 2011, from http://www.saarc-sec.org/areaofcooperation/cat-detail.php?cat_id=49

Sproule, K. (2010, January 27–30). *The untold success story . . . and a real comparative advantage for destination Namibia. The Communal Conservancy Sector.* Address at First Asian Ministerial Conference (ACM) on Tiger Conservation, Hua Nin, Thailand.

Thomas, F. (2009). *Rapid business assessment: Satwa Ecolodge, Way Kambas National Park, Sumatra, Indonesia. Internal report to Ecolodges Indonesia.* Jakarta, Indonesia: Ecolodges Indonesia.

Tiger Trust. (2011). Way Kambas National Park. Retrieved May 5, 2011, from http://www.tigertrust.info/sumatran_tiger_where.asp?ID=NP1&catID=8

Traffic, The Wildlife Trade Monitoring Network. (2011). South Asia Wildlife Enforcement Network (SAWEN) formally launched at Paro. Retrieved April 3, 2011, from http://www.traffic.org/home/2011/1/30/south-asia-wildlife-enforcement-network-sawen-formally-launc.html

United Nations Development Programme (UNDP). (2011). International human development indicators: Indonesia. Retrieved April 3, 2012, from http://hdrstats.undp.org/en/countries/profiles/IDN.html

United Nations Development Programme (2011). Indonesia Millennium Development Goals. Retrieved April 3, 2011, from http://www.undp.or.id/mdg/index.asp

Verchot, L. V., Petkova, E., Obidzinski, K., Atmadja, S., Yuliani, E. L., Dermawan, A., . . . Amira, S. (2010). Reducing forestry emissions in Indonesia. CIFOR, Bogor, Indonesia. Retrieved April 29, 2011, from http://www.cifor.org/publications/pdf_files/Books/BVerchot0101.pdf

Walpole, M. J., & Leader-Williams, N. (2002). Tourism and flagship species in conservation. *Biodiversity and Conservation, 11*, 543–547.

Weaver, D. (2008). *Ecotourism.* Milton, Australia: John Wiley & Sons.

Wegge, P., Morten, O., Pokharel, C. P., & Storaas, T. (2009). Predator-prey relationships and the responses of ungulates and their predators to the establishment of protected areas: A case study of tigers, leopards and their prey in Bardia National Park, Nepal. *Biological Conservation, 142*, 189–202.

World Bank. (2011). Poverty head count ratio at $2 a day (PPP) (% of population). Retrieved January 3, 2011, from http://data.worldbank.org/indicator/SI.POV.2DAY

World Economic Forum (WEF). (2011). *The travel and tourism competitiveness report 2011.* Geneva, Switzerland: Author.

World Wildlife Fund (WWF). (2011). Wildlife enforcement in South Asia gets a boost. Retrieved April 3, 2011, from http://www.worldwildlife.org/who/media/press/2011/WWFPresitem19802.html

World Wildlife Fund (WWF). (2012). WWF camera traps capture first images of tiger with cubs in Central Sumatra. Retrieved March 28, 2012, from http://www.savesumatra.org/index.php/newspublications/pressdetail/17

Zoellick, R. B. (2010, October 27). Remarks for the opening plenary of the high level segment—COP10. Retrieved January 3, 2011, from http://www.globaltigerinitiative.org/wp-content/uploads/2010/11/Plenary-Remarks-Nagoya-Japan.pdf

Education, Empowerment, and Building Community Capacity

High-End Ecotourism's Role in Assisting Rural Communities in Reaching the Millennium Development Goals

Anna Spenceley and Sue Snyman

LEARNING OBJECTIVES

- To demonstrate the main mechanisms for sustainable tourism to reduce poverty and for sustainable tourism's progress towards fulfilling the Millennium Development Goals
- To identify the three main mechanisms for reducing poverty through tourism—employment, value chain linkages, and equity
- To learn from across Africa through examples that demonstrate how each mechanism can be used to reduce poverty (and where it does not work)

Rural African communities are largely characterized by a lack of economic development, remoteness, high levels of poverty and unemployment, low levels of skills and education, and a heavy reliance on subsistence agriculture and natural resources for survival. Natural resources provide essential services to communities, including watershed protection, fuel, food, pollination, building materials, and climate regulation. Living alongside conservation areas also entails human–animal conflict costs: loss of crops and livestock. In the past, communities were able to survive through subsistence farming and, in some cases, government rations and grants. As population growth has escalated people are finding it harder to survive in this manner, and there is a greater need for permanent employment and a steady, reliable income. The increasing role of climate change and its effect on subsistence lifestyles is also resulting in a growing dependence on the market economy and a declining ability of traditional subsistence lifestyles to sustain rural populations. There is therefore an urgent need for alternative income-earning opportunities that are sustainable: the panacea often thought to reside in high-end ecotourism. For ecotourism to be viable and sustainable as a land use it is essential that there are tangible benefits for communities living in and around the conservation areas that exceed the costs they bear in the form of human–wildlife conflict and lack of access to resources.

This chapter looks specifically at communities living alongside conservation areas in Zimbabwe and Malawi and examines the impact of high-end ecotourism on reducing poverty, improving primary education, and ensuring environmental sustainability. Structured one-on-one questionnaire interviews were used to ascertain the socioeconomic situation of local communities around Hwange National Park in Zimbabwe and Liwonde National Park in Malawi and the impacts of conservation and tourism on the communities. Two types of community members are identified in this case study: those employed in a high-end ecotourism operation and those living adjacent to the conservation area where the ecotourism operation is located. The role of ecotourism employment in reducing poverty and improving rural social welfare was analyzed from the data collected in these surveys. A total of 150 staff surveys were conducted in 6 high-end ecotourism lodges and a total of 472 community surveys were conducted in 10 rural villages, covering 10 different ethnic groups.

Analysis of income sources, dependency ratios, and average household income indicates there is a heavy reliance in many rural areas on the market economy, in the form of ecotourism, for support. This highlights the important role that ecotourism plays in rural economic and social development. Tourism employment and tourist philanthropy can go a long way in assisting rural communities in reaching some of their Millennium Development Goals (MDGs) through education support, infrastructure development, feeding schemes, and water provision programs.

Overview

This chapter is based on 622 lodge staff and community socioeconomic surveys conducted in villages alongside Hwange National Park in Zimbabwe and Liwonde National Park in Malawi. Analysis of the impact of ecotourism employment on household incomes and social welfare will highlight the important role of ecotourism in terms of poverty reduction. Various philanthropic projects will be discussed that have assisted these communities in moving towards the achievement of some of their MDGs. This chapter is based on quantitative data as well as having a qualitative dimension, which ensures a rigorous analysis of the impact of ecotourism on local communities in rural Africa. To ensure sustainability, tourism needs to provide tangible benefits to local communities that are impacted by the protected/conservation area. This chapter will look at whether this is in fact occurring.

Key Mechanisms for Sustainable Tourism to Reduce Poverty in Africa

Tourism has been promoted as an economic option for community development and poverty alleviation in Africa through employment (Binns & Nel, 2002; Mahony & van Zyl, 2002; Poultney & Spenceley, 2001), equity in enterprise ownership (Mahony & van Zyl, 2002; Ntshona & Lahiff, 2003), and procurement through value chain linkages (Ashley, 2007; Steck, Wood, & Bishop, 2010). Tangible socioeconomic benefits have been documented in South Africa in relation to community-based tourism enterprises (Biggs, Turpie, Fabricius, & Spenceley, 2011; Ntshona & Lahiff, 2003), joint ventures with the private sector (Ashley & Jones, 2001; Poultney & Spenceley, 2001), and where tourism enterprises have channeled donations into community initiatives (e.g., Spenceley, 2001, 2010). In addition, protected area managers have used tourism concessions across South Africa to commercialize parks and leverage quantifiable local economic benefits through concession contracts (Fearnhead, 2004; Relly, 2004; Spenceley, 2004).

A comparison of some of the economic impacts of seven African tourism case studies conducted for the World Bank finds some interesting patterns (Spenceley, 2010):

- *Number of jobs:* Mount Kilimanjaro has an estimated 35,000 climbers each year, and an average of US$1,376 is spent on each trip (US$275 per day). The climbing generates around 10,900 jobs, but these are seasonal, informal jobs, and salary levels are low.
- *Number of tourists and their expenditure:* The number of tourists visiting the Seychelles and business travelers visiting Nairobi, Kenya, is similar, but the average expenditure is much higher in the Seychelles (US$230 vs. US$128 per day).
- *Length of stay and amount spent per day:* Encouraging tourists to stay longer and spend more money locally each day generates more income in destinations. For example, an average expenditure of US$2,303 per trip (or US$230 per day) in the Seychelles for a 10-day trip generates three times the revenue of a 7-day business trip to Nairobi at $762 per trip (or $108 per day).

Table 4.1 illustrates a framework of different ways in which local people can be involved in tourism economically, and therefore options that can be used to reduce poverty.

The next few sections provide an overview of three of the main ways that sustainable tourism can contribute to mitigating social challenges in Africa. We will specifically explore employment, value chain linkages, and equity.

Table 4.1   Types of Participation by Local People in Tourism

Type of Participation	Level of Skill Required	Level of Empowerment	Security of Return (risk)	Direction of Benefits	Contribution to Local Development
Independent community enterprise	High	High	Insecure	Active individuals and community as a whole	High
Individual local enterprise	High	High	Insecure	Active individuals	High
Community–private sector joint venture enterprise	Moderate	Moderate to high	Fairly secure	Active individuals and community as a whole	High
Supply of goods and services	Low to moderate	Low to moderate	Fairly secure	Individuals (favoring more active members)	Moderate
Employment by outside investor	Low to moderate	Low	Fairly secure	Individuals (potentially including poorest members)	Moderate
Rental of land or delegation of use rights	None	Low	Secure	Individuals or community as a whole	Low
Sale of land to investor	None	Low	Very secure	Individuals or community as a whole	Low
Reception of protected area use fees	None	None	Secure	Community as a whole	Low

Source: Reproduced from Strasdas, W., with Corcoran, B., & Petermann, T. (2002). *The ecotourism training manual for protected area managers.* Zschortau, Germany: German Foundation for International Development (DSE)/Centre for Food, Rural Development, and the Environment (ZEL).

Employment

A number of tourism operations are located in remote, rural areas of Africa, with little development and very few employment opportunities for the communities living in these areas. Consequently, unemployment rates and poverty levels are generally high. Employment, both direct and indirect, that results from tourism operations in these areas can thus make a large contribution to poverty reduction and an overall improvement in social welfare in these areas (Ashley, 2006; Mitchell & Ashley, 2010; Spenceley, 2003). Direct employment opportunities (direct participation in tourism; e.g., lodge workers, guides) are limited in terms of the size of the ecotourism operation, but indirect employment opportunities can be substantial (Ashley, 2006; Mitchell & Ashley, 2010; Spenceley, 2008c). These can include craft-makers, local suppliers to the tourism industry (supply chains), and the transport industry. Employment includes those working directly in the tourism industry and relying specifically on the tourism industry for support as well as self-employment, individual entrepreneurship, or micro-enterprise (Mitchell & Ashley, 2010) that exists as a result of the tourism industry but is not always entirely dependent on it.

Tourism's ability to generate employment in the informal sector of the economy has been cited as one of the key opportunities presented by tourism growth in developing countries (de Kadt, 1979 in Mitchell & Ashley, 2010). Despite the fact that this informal labor may often be seasonal, variable, and unreliable, it can constitute a very important and useful supplement to other poor household livelihood strategies (Mitchell & Ashley, 2010). The scale of spending in the local economy will determine the magnitude of the impact on informal employment and from there the magnitude of the impact on poverty reduction. The contribution of formal-sector tourism employment to the total income of the poor ranges from 12% to 76% (Mitchell & Ashley, 2010). This is a very wide range but indicates the overall importance of formal sector employment in terms of poverty reduction.

Empowerment and Skill Development

The creation of employment opportunities is one of the key indicators of how successful tourism can be in promoting rural livelihoods (Mbaiwa, 2008) and reducing poverty (Mitchell & Ashley, 2010). It has been found (Mbaiwa, 2008; Salafsky & Wollenberg, 2000; Stem, Lassorie, Lee, Deshler, & Schelhas, 2003) that skills training, development, and the empowerment of local communities through employment, along with other indirect benefits of tourism, have the potential to improve rural livelihoods and social welfare and encourage the sustainable use of natural resources.

Direct and indirect employment impacts not only those who are employed but also all those whom they support, and in this way extends the poverty reduction impacts of tourism employment, in many cases quite substantially (Mitchell & Ashley, 2010; Snyman, 2010; Spenceley, 2008c). Poultney and Spenceley (2001) found that waged employment makes a dramatic difference to the well-being of the poor and often may lift a family out of poverty on a sustainable basis. Tourism wages are generally attractive in comparison with the alternatives available in many developing countries (Mitchell & Ashley, 2010), and the security of a reliable monthly income can improve overall security and social welfare. Research in the Eastern Cape of South Africa, whereby seven private game reserves were surveyed, demonstrated that the number of employees increased by a factor of 3.5 when properties converted their use to wildlife-based tourism (from 175 people to 623), and employees also received additional benefits that were not normally received by farm employees, including accommodations, training, food, pension contributions, and medical insurance (Sims-Castley, Kerley, Geach, & Langholtz, 2005). The next section explores the impact of employment within one safari company, Wilderness Safaris.

Wilderness Safaris in Malawi and Zimbabwe

An extensive socioeconomic study by Snyman (forthcoming) on the impact of high-end ecotourism on rural communities in six southern African countries highlights the important role of tourism employment in poverty reduction. Data were collected from two Wilderness

Safaris (http://www.wilderness-safaris.com) camps in Liwonde National Park, Malawi (327 surveys), and four camps in Hwange National Park, Zimbabwe (295 surveys), using structured questionnaire interviews with 150 staff employed in ecotourism operations and 472 community members living in and around the conservation areas where the ecotourism operations are situated.

The results of the socioeconomic surveys in this case study indicate that education plays an important role in terms of securing permanent employment. Staff had, on average, a statistically significant higher mean number of years of education (M = 8.9) compared to community respondents (M = 4.94). An analysis of average total monthly household income revealed that respondents employed in ecotourism had, on average, a statistically significant higher total mean monthly household income (M = US$117.12) than the average community household in the area (M = US$44.29).

The difference in the average number of people that each staff and community member supported was also statistically significant. On average, staff had 7.7 dependents, whereas community respondents had just 4.74, which illustrates a heavy reliance of these communities on employment in ecotourism for support. For a broader view, **Table 4.2** illustrates the number of dependents per staff member in five of the six countries analyzed by Snyman (forthcoming) as well as the average monthly amount given directly to dependents. Over US$10,000 is paid per month out of 12 camps to support dependents in rural communities. This amount excludes payments for food, education, clothes, and the like that is also paid to support dependents. The multiplier effects of this spending in rural areas further assists in reducing poverty in remote, rural communities in Africa. Nearly 5,000 people have been lifted above the poverty line (US$1.25) through tourism employment in the 12 camps (an average of approximately 408 people per tourism camp or 15 people per bed).

Value Chain Linkages

A value chain is defined as "a sequence of related business activities (functions) from the provision of specific inputs for a particular product to primary production, transformation, marketing, and up to the final sale of the particular product to consumers" (Springer-Heinze, 2007). A diverse set of organizations (including multilateral, bilateral, NGO, and research) is re-evaluating its approach to tourism along the lines of improving value chain linkages. Theses organizations are developing interventions that consider the entire tourism value chain and boost market access of the poor, often through mainstream tourism. At the same time there is change within the private sector, where good practices are no longer just the domain of small owner-operated or niche companies. Hotel chains, international tour operators, and a range of NGOs and commercial networks are now developing more socially oriented practices, or what are often called *inclusive businesses*. Inclusive business explicitly incorporates engagement with the local economy, but organizations may engage in the arena under the terms of sustainable tourism, responsible tourism, or corporate social responsibility/investment (Mitchell & Ashley, 2008, cited in Ashley, Mitchell, & Spenceley, 2009). A model developed from Spenceley, Ashley and de Koch (2009) describes the linkages among the tourism industry, supply chains and related sectors, and the poor (see **Figure 4.1**).

Table 4.2   Beneficiaries and Financial Benefits

Country	Total No. of Staff in Surveyed Camps	Average Monthly Wage per Staff Member (US$)[1]	Average No. of Dependents per Staff Respondent	Total No. of People Indirectly Impacted by Camp Employment[2]	Average Monthly Amount Given to Dependents per Staff Respondent (in US$)[3]	Total Payments to Dependents per Month (in US$)[4]	Total Number of People Lifted Above Poverty Line (US$1.25 per day): Staff and dependents	Average Number of People Lifted Above Poverty Line (US$1.25 per day) per bed: Staff and dependents
Namibia (1 camp surveyed, 40 beds)	78	180.44	6.63	517.14	$20	$1,560.00	595.14	14.87
Botswana (3 camps surveyed, 58 beds)	173	219.18	7.84	1,356.32	$36.54	$6,321.42	1,529.32	26.37
Malawi (2 camps surveyed, 42 beds)	108	85.59	7.95	858.6	$5.64	$609.12	966.6	23.01
Zimbabwe (4 camps surveyed, 96 beds)	119	298.11	7.75	922.25	$9.98	$1,187.62	1,041.25	10.85
South Africa (2 camps surveyed, 74 beds)	95	334.36	6.16	579.04	$19.75	$1,876.25	674.04	9.11
Average/total (12 camps, 310 beds)	573	223.60	7.27	4,233.35	$18.38	$10,531.74	4,806.35	15.5

[1] Over and above wages, employees receive gratuities (not included in this analysis) as well as other non-monetary benefits of employment such as accommodations, food, a uniform, and a company HIV awareness/testing and education program. These figures are based on preliminary results from socioeconomic surveys conducted by Snyman (2010) and are not official wage figures.

[2] This result is calculated by multiplying the number of people employed in the surveyed camps by the calculated average number of staff dependents.

[3] These figures were obtained from the expenses section of the surveys conducted in the countries. All figures were converted to US$ for comparison purposes using http://www.xe.com exchange rates on December 2, 2010.

[4] These figures were calculated by multiplying the total number of staff by the average monthly payment to dependents.

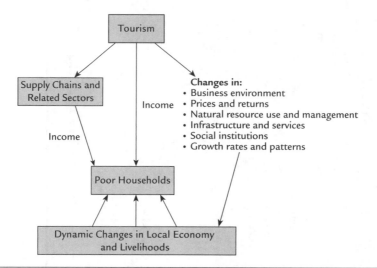

Figure 4.1 Dynamic effects of tourism on local development and poverty reduction.
Source: Reproduced from Spenceley, A., Ashley, C., & de Koch, M. (2009). *Tourism and local development: An introductory guide* (p. 42, Figure 13). Geneva, Switzerland: International Trade Centre.

Development agencies and NGOs working on tourism value chains (such as SNV Netherlands Development Organization) tend to concentrate their efforts on four main sectors that appear to have the greatest potential for poverty reduction: accommodations, food and drink, handicrafts and shopping, and excursions. A series of Value Chain Analyses (VCAs) undertaken in Africa have illustrated the following impacts on poverty from these sectors in Tanzania, Rwanda, Mozambique, and the Gambia.

Looking at a nature-based tourism destination, Mitchell and Keane (2008) evaluated the value of tourism value chains on Mount Kilimanjaro in Tanzania. They estimated that the revenue from 35,000 mountain climbers on a typical climbing package provides in-country tourist expenditure of just under US$50 million per year. Of this, US$13 million is considered to be pro-poor expenditure. Mitchell and Keane estimated that all expenditure on climbing staff (wages and tips) was pro-poor (US$8.5 million). About 90% of food and beverage expenditure on Kilimanjaro is sourced from local markets in Moshi, and the suppliers of this market are overwhelmingly local small-holder farmers. The average climber spends US$58 each on cultural goods and services, half of which is considered to have a pro-poor impact (US$1 million). Total park revenue is estimated at US$22 million, of which 5% is having some pro-poor impact (over US$1 million). Finally, expenditure on accommodations is around US$2.5 million, of which around 16% is considered to have a pro-poor impact (almost US$500,000).

In Rwanda, Spenceley et al. (2010) considered the impacts on the poor of gorilla tourism in the Parc National des Volcans, which is famed for being inhabited by endangered mountain gorillas. The overall value of the accommodation, food and beverage, tour operator, and shopping value chains around the park was estimated at US$42.7 million per year, with an associated US$2.8 million in expenditure on wages, fruits and vegetables, and nonfood purchases. The pro-poor income was an estimated US$1.8 million (4.3% of destination turnover).

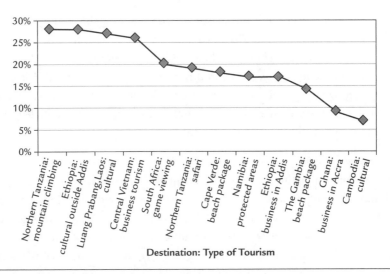

Figure 4.2   Pro-poor income as a percentage of destination spending.
Source: Data from Mitchell, J., & Ashley, C. (2010). *Tourism and poverty reduction: Pathways to prosperity.* London: Earthscan.

Zanzibar is a tourism destination that is promoted as a beach destination with a rich cultural background. Here Steck et al. (2010) found that the pro-poor benefit from accommodation was 7–47% from restaurants, 27% from the retail sector, and 19% from tours and excursions. Therefore, of the total revenue of US$172 million per year, US$10.2 million (6%) reached the poor. In the Gambia, another beach tourism destination, Mitchell and Faal (2007) found that the value of the Gambian tourism value chain was around £96 million (US$153 million) per year, and about half of this money is spent within the Gambia. They found that 7% of expenditure on accommodations (£1.2 million [US$1.9 million]), 11% of money spent on food and beverage (£1.7 million [US$2.7 million]), 50% of money spent on shopping (£2.4 million [US$3.8 million]), and 25% of excursions revenue (£1.1 million [US$1.8 million]) reached the poor. This equated to 7% of the total benefits of the tourism value chain being retained by the poor.

To provide an idea of how destinations' pro-poor income compare to one another, Mitchell and Ashley (2010) compiled a comparative analysis (see **Figure 4.2**). Considering the previously summarized studies, this demonstrates that mountain climbing on Kilimanjaro provides a far higher pro-poor income than beach tourism in the Gambia. In general, there are greater local benefits to the poor from tourism value chains when local people can participate in the tourism sector by providing labor, products, and services. Interventions by development agencies focus on reducing barriers to entry into the tourism sector and enabling the poor to participate.

Equity

There are a number of different equity/ownership arrangements for tourism operations in Africa. Benefits from such arrangements vary depending on the agreements between the parties; the extent of impacts on poverty reduction also varies with the chosen equity agreement. The level of community involvement depends on the specific conditions of the equity arrangement, with a large amount of involvement occurring in community-based tourism (CBT) and a more limited amount in public–private partnerships. However, in the majority of cases, the tourism sector operates without community equity, and a pure private sector model is observed. There also are cases of partnerships between the private sector, communities, and government (see, e.g., Mahony & van Zyl, 2001; Reid, 2001; Steenkamp & Uhr, 2000 for the case of the Makuleke community/ Wilderness Safaris and South African National Parks).

Community-Based Tourism

Since the 1980s, community involvement in tourism has been widely supported in the literature as essential from a moral point of view, an equity perspective, and a developmental perspective (Brohman, 1996; Cater, 1987; de Kadt, 1990; Wilkinson, 1989). Proponents suggest that community ownership provides livelihood security, minimal leakage, efficient conflict resolution, increases in the local population's social carrying capacity, and improved conservation (Steele, 1995). As a result of interventions by NGOs and development agencies, community-based tourism initiatives have proliferated across Africa, Asia, and the neotropics (Walpole, 1997). There also have been a series of theoretical and practical studies (mostly through case studies) examining them (see, e.g., Steenkamp & Uhr, 2000; Wells & Brandon, 1992).

In relation to poverty reduction, the level and distribution of economic benefits from CBTs depends on many factors including the attractiveness of the tourism asset, the type of tourism operation, the nature and degree of community involvement, and whether earnings become private income or are channeled into community projects or other benefit-spreading mechanisms (Kiss, 2004; Wunder, 2000).

Problems associated with developing community tourism projects include that they are expensive to establish and they generate high expectations that may not be feasible. Also, new conflicts may arise as marginal groups become more empowered and elites gain greater benefits through networks (Zazueta, 1995). They also may fail because authority has not been devolved to the appropriate lowest level, so benefits from activities are not returned to the community (Attwell & Cotterill, 1999) (see **Box 4.1**). Furthermore, donor support may be fickle and may be removed at any time because there are seldom contracts to state that a donor must remain until

---

Box 4.1   Example of a Commercially Unsustainable Approach: Wild Coast Community-Based Tourism

This project (2002–2005) developed community-based accommodations (lodges and campsites) at three sites along a very rural stretch of the South African coast. It supported hospitality training, craft development, community empowerment, hiking trail development, environmental management, and tourist promotion. It established community trusts to manage receipts from tourists. It was funded by the European Union at a cost of €12.9 million (US$16.4 million). In the end, it created 87 jobs for the 3 years the project was running—none of them sustainable. Thus, the average cost per job per year was US$50,000. It generated about US$20,000 in a community trust, much of which did not benefit anticipated beneficiaries. The private sector concessions collapsed due to community conflict and local government resistance. A major beneficiary was a European consultancy company.

Source: Reproduced from Spenceley, A., Ashley, C., & de Koch, M. (2009). *Tourism and local development: An introductory guide* (p. 71, Box 22). Geneva, Switzerland: International Trade Centre.

a project is sustainable. In addition, communities are frequently unable to provide the standard of service foreign tourists require, leaving large tourism operations without competition or any incentives to distribute wealth (Yu, Hendrickson, & Castillo, 1997).

A systematic review of the impacts of 215 community accommodation enterprises in Botswana, Lesotho, Madagascar, Malawi, Mauritius, Mozambique, Namibia, South Africa, Swaziland, Tanzania, Zambia, and Zimbabwe revealed that although there are some success stories, the majority struggle to survive with problems of accessibility in remote locations, limited market access, poor promotion, low motivation, and constrained communication (Spenceley, 2008c). The study implied that interventions by third parties (e.g., NGOs, donor agencies) have not promoted business plans or market-led approaches of the community-based tourism enterprises (CBTEs) because the intermediaries were primarily focused on capacity building and empowerment of the poor rather than commercial viability. Despite operating from a difficult basis, the CBTEs demonstrated tangible benefits to local people, including employment of 2,504 people and providing access to finance, community infrastructure, education, and product development. Local procurement totaled nearly US$1 million per annum on products such as crafts, food, décor, building materials, and services including entertainment, guiding, catering, and construction from all of the enterprises. Most of the enterprises considered themselves to be practicing sustainable tourism, with many having policies and commitments on conservation and local benefits. However, until CBTEs adopt a business perspective, many will continue to struggle and frustrate the intended beneficiaries, who have not been empowered to recognize their failings and adapt to improve, or to move on and pursue alternative livelihood options (Spenceley, 2008c). Similar findings on CBT have come from Tanzania (Nelson, 2008) and Zambia (Dixey, 2008). Key determinants of success in Zambia were linkages to tourism companies, proximity to main tourism routes, competitive advantage, financial management, visitor handling, and community motivation (Dixey, 2008). Dixey ascertained that community-based tourism has to be market related with regard to consumer demand, if it is to be viable and benefit the poor in the long term. However, when Barnes (2008) undertook an analysis of community-based natural resource management (CBNRM) and conservancies in Namibia, he demonstrated positive impacts of community-based tourism at both a local and a national level. By using cost benefit analyses of five conservancies (Torra, ≠Khoadi || Hôas, NyaeNyae, Mayuni, and Salambala), Barnes found that communities derive positive net returns from their investments in tourism-related CBRNM, particularly in arid and semi-arid areas. In addition, he reported that donor and government grants significantly enhanced the returns that communities obtained (although some would be viable without grants).

In recent years, practitioners have effectively shaken the premise that community-based tourism enterprises are always a useful development tool in poor, rural areas. Although CBT can provide greater economic benefits than agriculture in some areas, it is imperative that these projects are planned and operated as commercial entities. There is little value in establishing a CBT enterprise that tourists do not know about (because of poor promotion), cannot reach (because of poor infrastructure), where the establishment is product-led rather than demand-led (because no market research was done), where a low level of service is given (because of poor training), and that does not make a profit (because expectations remain unrealized and third parties have to subsidize the operations in the long term). It is clear that the concept of community-based tourism should be reconfigured to take a market-led approach that concentrates on small business development and maximizing linkages between tourism and communities through the supply chain, rather than stressing collective owner-ship and management. Where donors and NGOs work with the poor to establish small tour-ism businesses, they have a responsibility to provide an enabling framework for partnerships with tourism professionals to ensure a realistic and commercial approach is adopted. Policy makers also have a key role to play, by providing a consistent enabling policy framework that empowers communities to capitalize on their natural environment and heritage in a sustain-able way (Spenceley, 2008b).

Public–Private Partnerships and Joint Ventures

The case of public–private partnerships (PPPs) in African ecotourism is well illustrated by the commercialization of South African National Parks (SANParks). SANParks is a government-run organization that embarked on a commercialization strategy in 2000 (Varghese, 2008). The main objective of this strategy was to reduce dependence on government funding (which amounted to 20% of its operational requirements [approximately US$80 million]) and to improve existing operational efficiencies (Varghese, 2008). To date the strategy has resulted in increased market segmentation and product and price differentiation (Varghese, 2008). An additional 380 guest beds resulted in an increased contribution to the local economy through increased employment and other associated multiplier effects. The commercialization through PPPs has proved to be a successful funding mechanism for SANParks and therefore conservation (Varghese, 2008). According to Varghese, the strategy's most significant benefit has been its ability to reduce poverty in remote areas through the creation of sustainable employment. The combination of the conservation expertise from national parks (public sec-tor) and the business expertise of private enterprises allows for the maximization of ben-efits through increased employment, improved service delivery, increased infrastructure, and improvements in skills training and development of local people. PPPs can, undercertain circumstances, therefore be an effective mechanism for reducing poverty and promoting con-servation in the long term by bringing together the strengths of various public and private enterprises.

With the vision of creating successful tourism businesses that local people can benefit from, there has been a trend away from community-based tourism towards joint-venture partnerships in sub-Saharan Africa. This trend has recognized that partnerships in which communities bring resources (e.g., land, natural attractions) and the private sector brings business acumen and net-works (e.g., existing client bases, linkages with tour operators, business planning and promotion experience) create "win–wins" for both parties. Wilderness Safaris has taken the joint-venture model in Africa a step further, evolving the joint-venture model (Spenceley, 2010). In its new venture at Rocktail Beach Lodge, Wilderness Safaris is not only a partner in the commercial enterprise but also in the company that represents the community. With this linkage, Wilderness Safaris can assist on the financial governance of the enterprise to avoid problems of misappro-priation of community funds (Spenceley, 2008a, 2010).

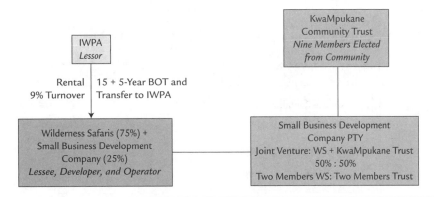

Figure 4.3   Institutional arrangements at Rocktail Beach Camp, South Africa, by Wilderness Safaris.

Joint ventures between community groups and private tourism operators might have the greatest potential for generating significant revenues for communities. They also might be more likely to succeed than wholly community-run enterprises. However, communities will often need outside assistance to organize, obtain, and assert their legal rights and understand their obligations in such partnerships.

Figure 4.3 illustrates an example of the institutional structure of a second-generation joint-venture model, in this case Wilderness Safaris' Rocktail Beach Camp. In this instance, the iSimangaliso Wetland Park Authority (IWPA) leases the land to a joint venture between Wilderness Safaris (WS) and a small business development company (SBDC). The SBDC is another joint venture, this time between WS and the KwaMpukane Community Trust. The reason for having the SBDC as another joint venture was due to lessons learned from an earlier initiative, Rocktail Bay Lodge. Here a joint-venture arrangement did not work well. Few jobs were realized, and there was consistent mismanagement of dividends that were distributed to a community trust formed within the Mqobela community (despite three separate community elections of trustees).[1] Some observers say that the expectations of the Mqobela community were not realistic, and that the benefits of social capital and natural resource assets were offset by the negative elements of conflicts, mistrust, and restrictions in access and use of natural resources (Simpson, 2008). The evolution of the community company (the Small Business Development Company PTY) allowed Wilderness Safaris to participate as a joint partner, and to provide technical expertise in business and financial management (Spenceley, 2010).

With respect to &Beyond, the example of Phinda is a notable innovation that has created a win–win situation from the land-claims process in South Africa (see **Figure 4.4**). Previously a privately owned, developed, and operated venture, Phinda became a joint venture with local communities in 2007, following a land claim that had been declared in 2002. &Beyond did not oppose the claim, and was paid 268 million rand (approximately US$34.5 million) by the South African government for the return of 12,000 hectares to the communities. Now &Beyond pays rental agreements for areas of land it leases from the communities, and also has traversing

---

[1] Personal communication, Poultney, cited in Spenceley, 2008c; Poultney and Spenceley, 2001.

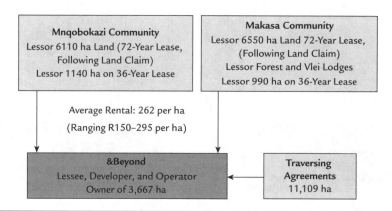

Figure 4.4   Joint venture operation institutional arrangement: Phinda and &Beyond.

agreements to operate game drives.[2] The rental income is being used for projects including electrification and education[3] (Spenceley, 2010).

Pure Private Sector

Largely due to the lack of the necessary commercial focus to generate sufficient revenues from natural resources, African governments and state conservation departments have been turning to the private sector to assist with the management and maintenance of conservation areas (Spenceley, 2003). The private sector appears to be best placed to identify opportunities, realize the potential of a destination, and drive forward the development of a product, and it also has the potential to adopt a range of highly effective strategies for the benefit of communities and their livelihoods (Simpson, 2008). The degree to which pure private sector ownership can contribute to poverty reduction depends on the particular private sector operator and its desire to contribute to local community development through employment opportunities, philanthropic donations, and the construction and development of infrastructure and community projects. This varies depending on the particular business and ethical objectives of the private sector operator (Spenceley, 2003). For example, safari operators such as &Beyond have responded constructively to the HIV/AIDS issue by developing health education programs among communities neighboring its lodges (Spenceley, 2008c). Also, companies practicing significant levels of corporate social responsibility (CSR), such as Wilderness Safaris, have produced ethical policies that are advertised in their brochures and in their annual report (see **Box 4.2**).

Motivations for the private sector to engage in tourism operations include obligations to provide benefits to rural communities through concession arrangements, being driven by corporate social responsibility, seeking market advantage, or ethical tendencies to do so (e.g., Ngala Private Game Reserve in Kruger National Park; Jackalberry Lodge; Vilanculos Lodge in Mozambique; Wilderness Safaris in various southern African countries) (Spenceley, 2003, p. 111). These motivations also are driven by a number of forces, including market forces, the diversification of commercial activities,

---

[2] Personal communication, Pretorius & Campbell, cited in Spenceley, 2008c.
[3] &Beyond, undated.

Box 4.2   Wilderness Safaris' Policy Regarding Work with Neighboring Communities

The honest, mutually beneficial and dignified engagement of our rural community partners (staff, equity partners, landlords, neighbours) in ways that ensure sustainability beyond the lifespan and aegis of our organisation and which deliver a meaningful and life-changing share of the proceeds of responsible ecotourism to all stakeholders.

These mechanisms include community-centric employment, joint ventures (e.g., equity, revenue share, traversing fees), education (e.g., children's camps, bursaries) and training, social benefits, capacity building and infrastructure development (e.g., schools, crèches, clinics).

Source: Reprinted with permission of Wilderness Safaris, 2010.

---

and the availability of new, competitive opportunities (Spenceley, 2003). The private sector has the capital available for the development of new tourism ventures, as well as marketing capabilities, greater advertising opportunities, economies of scale, and financial management skills.

In general, the private sector is oriented more toward generating revenue and making a profit from selling tourism products and services (Buckley, 2002; Spenceley, 2003). The private sector can also play a very important role in catalyzing the development of new community institutions, facilitating and financing projects, and assisting with the management of community projects (Spenceley, 2003). These empowerment and skills enhancement benefits are important in terms of long-term poverty reduction and local economic development.

Critical to the long-term success of private sector tourism operations and the development of tourism in Africa is that local governments create an enabling environment in which the private sector can operate effectively and efficiently and that can also stimulate economic growth (Spenceley, 2003). The degree to which private sector ownership impacts poverty reduction varies greatly depending on the particular private sector operator and its objectives, but it can be enhanced by a commitment to the development of local communities in the area through employment, equity shares, empowerment, and skills training and development.

Conclusion

Some of the successes in improving the economic impacts of tourism in Africa have included capital investment, increased yield per tourist, job creation, market linkages, commercial opportunities for small businesses, and diversification of markets (Spenceley, 2010). Some of the constraints include high costs of taxes, levies, and government fees; insufficient economies of scale to develop viable market linkages; and the fact that "many" jobs may not necessarily mean "many good quality and well-paid jobs," with decent working conditions.

A number of mechanisms have been identified and applied to enhance the economic impacts of tourism (Spenceley, 2010). These include:

- Creating incentive and taxation instruments that support, rather than punish, commercial success
- Providing mechanisms to ensure living, or minimum, wages across the sector, in participation with the private sector

- Promoting value for money in tourism products and destinations, coupled with quality service and experiences
- Investing in marketing and promotion
- Establishing strong market linkages between the destination and source markets
- Promoting strong local value chains so local businesses can overcome barriers to engaging in tourism markets and sell their goods and services to the tourism sector
- Monitoring and evaluating the economic and financial returns to society and local people

Current thinking in tourism focuses on interventions that are more strategic and based on an open-minded assessment of where impact can be created at scale. In summary, these attempt to engage the private sector in expanding opportunities for poor people, and take advantage of the growing business case for the tourism sector to demonstrate its commitment to destination development; link poor people to opportunities in mainstream tourism, not just niche tourism; assess and then tackle the main market blockages that limit participation of the poor; work at any point in the tourism value chain, wherever there is greatest potential for pro-poor change; and evaluate the potential environmental, cultural, and social impacts of the intervention and the type of enterprise being developed. This should be done during the planning stage and in participation with local stakeholders to ensure the overall impacts will be beneficial (Spenceley, Ashley, & de Koch, 2009).

In conclusion, there is a range of ways that pro-poor interventions can be scaled up (Spenceley, 2010). These include joint venture partnerships, value chain linkages, and community capacity building and skills training. The uniqueness of Africa's natural resources, its abundant and diverse wildlife, and its cultural diversity make it very attractive for tourism. The concurrent high levels of poverty and unemployment on the continent make it even more important that tourism is truly pro-poor focused and that local rural communities benefit from conservation and tourism in a sustainable manner that will assist them in achieving the Millennium Development Goals.

References

Ashley, C. (2006). *How can governments boost the local economic impacts of tourism? Options and tools.* London: Overseas Development Institute.

Ashley, C. (2007). *Pro-poor analysis of the Rwandan tourism value chain: An emerging picture and some strategic approaches for enhancing poverty impacts.* Unpublished research report for SNV-Rwanda. London: Overseas Development Institute.

Ashley, C., & Jones, B. (2001). Joint ventures between communities and tourism investors: Experience in southern Africa. *International Journal of Tourism Research, 3*(5), 407–423.

Ashley, C., Mitchell, J., & Spenceley, A. (2009). *Tourism-led poverty reduction program: Opportunity study guidelines.* Report to the International Trade Centre's tourism-led poverty reduction program. Geneva, Switzerland: International Trade Centre.

Attwell, C. A. M., & Cotterill, F. P. D. (1999). Postmodernism and African conservation science. *Biodiversity and Conservation, 9,* 559–577.

Barnes, J. I. (2008). Community-based tourism and natural resource management in Namibia: Local and national economic impacts. In: A. Spenceley (Ed.), *Responsible tourism: Critical issues for conservation and development* (pp. 343–357). London: Earthscan.

Biggs, D., Turpie, J., Fabricius, C., & Spenceley, A. (2011). The value of avitourism for conservation and job creation: An analysis from South Africa. *Conservation and Society, 9*(1), 80–90.

Binns, T., & Nel, E. (2002). Tourism as a local development strategy in South Africa. *Geographical Journal, 168*(3), 235–247.

Brohman, J. (1996). New directions for tourism in Third World development. *Annals of Tourism Research, 23*(1), 48–70.

Buckley, R. (2002). Public and private partnerships between tourism and protected areas: The Australian situation. *Journal of Tourism Studies, 13*(1), 26–38.

Cater, E. A. (1987). Tourism in the least developed countries, *Annals of Tourism Research, 13*, 202–226.

de Kadt, E. (1990). *Making the alternative sustainable: Lessons from development for tourism* (discussion paper no. 272). Brighton, United Kingdom: Institute of Development Studies.

Dixey, L. M. (2008). The unsustainability of community tourism donor projects: Lessons from Zambia. In: A. Spenceley (Ed.), *Responsible tourism: Critical issues for conservation and development* (pp. 323–342). London: Earthscan.

Fearnhead, P. (2004, May 5–7). Commercialisation in national parks. In: A. Spenceley (Ed.), *Proceedings of the SASUSG Annual Members Meeting, Addo Elephant National Park* (pp. 54–61). Pretoria, South Africa: Southern African Sustainable Use Specialist Group.

Kiss, A. (2004). Is community-based ecotourism a good use of biodiversity conservation funds? *TRENDS in Ecology and Evolution, 19*, 232–237.

Mahony, K., & van Zyl, J. (2001). *Practical strategies for pro-poor tourism. Case studies of Makuleke and Manyeleti tourism initiatives.* Working paper no. 2. London: CRT/IIED/ODI.

Mahony, K., & van Zyl, J. (2002). The impacts of tourism investment on rural communities: Three case studies in South Africa. *Development Southern Africa, 19*(1), 83–103.

Mbaiwa, J. (2008). The realities of ecotourism development in Botswana. In: A. Spenceley (Ed.), *Responsible tourism: Critical issues for conservation and development* (pp. 205–224). London: Earthscan.

Mitchell, J., & Ashley, C. (2010). *Tourism and poverty reduction: Pathways to prosperity.* London: Earthscan.

Mitchell, J., & Faal, J. (2007). Package holiday tourism in the Gambia. *Development Southern Africa, 24*(3), 445–464.

Mitchell, J., & Keane, J. (2008). *Tracing the tourism dollar in Northern Tanzania, final report.* London: Overseas Development Institute.

Nelson, F. (2008). Livelihoods, conservation, and community-based tourism in Tanzania: Potential and performance. In: A. Spenceley (Ed.), *Responsible tourism: Critical issues for conservation and development* (pp. 305–321). London: Earthscan.

Ntshona, Z., & Lahiff, E. (2003). Community-based eco-tourism on the Wild Coast, South Africa: The case of the Amadiba Trail. Cape Town, South Africa: Program for Land and Agrarian Studies.

Poultney, C., & Spenceley, A. (2001). *Practical strategies for pro-poor tourism, Wilderness Safaris South Africa: Rocktail Bay and Ndumu Lodge.* Pro-poor tourism working paper no. 1. Cape Town, South Africa: ODI/CRT/IIED.

Reid, H. (2001). Contractual national parks and the Makuleke community. *Human Ecology, 29*(2), 135–155.

Relly, P. (2004). *Employment and investment in Madikwe Game Reserve, South Africa.* Masters dissertation in Tourism Studies. Witswatersrand, the Netherlands: University of Witswatersrand.

Salafsky, N., & Wollenberg, E. (2000). Linking livelihood and conservation: A conceptual framework and scale for assessing the integration of human needs and biodiversity. *World Development, 28*(8), 1421–1438.

Simpson, M. C. (2008). The impacts of tourism initiatives on rural livelihoods and poverty reduction in South Africa: Mathenjwa and Mqobela. In: A. Spenceley (Ed.), *Responsible tourism: Critical issues for conservation and development* (pp. 239–266). London: Earthscan.

Sims-Castley, R., Kerley, G. I. H., Geach, B., & Langholtz, J. (2005). Socio-economic significance of ecotourism-based private game reserves in South Africa's Eastern Cape Province. *Parks, 15*(2), 6–18.

Snyman, S. (2010). *Various unpublished socio-economic reports based on extensive surveys conducted for Wilderness Safaris in six southern African countries.* Cape Town, South Africa: Wilderness Safaris.

Spenceley, A. (2001). *Integrating biodiversity into the tourism sector: Case study of South Africa.* Paris, France: United Nations Environment Programme, Biodiversity Planning Support Programme (UNEP-BPSP).

Spenceley, A. (2003). *Tourism, local livelihoods, and the private sector in South Africa: Case studies on the growing role of the private sector in natural resource management, sustainable livelihoods in southern Africa.* Research paper no. 8. Brighton, England: Institute of Development Studies.

Spenceley, A. (2004). Responsible nature-based tourism planning in South Africa and the commercialisation of Kruger National park. In: D. Diamantis (Ed.), *Ecotourism: Management and assessment* (pp. 267–280). London: Thomson Learning.

Spenceley, A. (2008a). "Rocktail Beach Camp, KwaZulu-Natal, South Africa." African Safari Lodge Foundation: Practitioners Workshop [conference presentation]. Grace Hotel, South Africa. 19–21 May 2008.

Spenceley, A. (2008b). "Phinda Private Game Reserve, KwaZulu-Natal, South Africa." African Safari Lodge Foundation: Practitioners Workshop [conference presentation]. Grace Hotel, South Africa. 19–21 May 2008.

Spenceley, A. (2008c). Impacts of wildlife tourism on rural livelihoods in Southern Africa. In: A. Spenceley (Ed.), *Responsible Tourism: Critical issues for conservation and development*. London: Earthscan.

Spenceley, A. (2010, December 27). *Tourism product development interventions and best practices in sub-Saharan Africa. Part 1: Synthesis report.* Washington, DC: Report to the World Bank.

Spenceley, A., Ashley, C., & de Koch, M. (2009). *Tourism and local development: An introductory guide.* Geneva, Switzerland: International Trade Centre.

Spenceley, A., Habyalimana, S., Tusabe, R., & Mariza, D. (2010). Benefits to the poor from gorilla tourism in Rwanda. *Development Southern Africa, 27*(5), 647–662.

Springer-Heinze, A. (Ed.). (2007). *Value links manual: The methodology of value chain promotion.* Eshborn, Germany: GtZ.

Strasdas, W. (2001). Ecotourism in practice: The implementation of the socioeconomic and conservation-related goals of an ambitious tourism concept in developing countries. (Available in German: Ökotourismus in der praxis: Zurumsetzung der sozio-ökonomischen und naturschutzpolitischen Ziele eines anspruchsvollen Tourismuskonzeptes in entwicklungsländern.) Ammerland, Germany: Studienkreisfür Tourismus und Entwicklung. Cited in Strasdas, W., Corcoran, B., & Petermann, T. *The Ecotourism Training Manual for Protected Area Managers.* Zschortau, Germany: German Foundation for International Development (DSE), Centre for Food, and Rural Development and the Environment (ZEL).

Steck, B., Wood, K., & Bishop, J. (2010, February 3). *Tourism: More value for Zanzibar, value chain analysis.* Final report. Zanzibar, Tanzania: VSO/SNV/ZATI.

Steenkamp, C., & Uhr, J. (2000). *The Makuleke land claim: Power relations and community-based natural resources management.* Evaluating Eden Series discussion paper no. 18. London: International Institute for the Environment and Development.

Steele, P. (1995). Ecotourism: An economic analysis. *Journal of Sustainable Tourism, 3*, 29–44.

Stem, C. J., Lassorie, J. P., Lee, D. R., Deshler, D. D., & Schelhas, J. W. (2003). Community participation in ecotourism benefits: The link to conservation practices and perspectives. *Society and Natural Resources, 16*, 387–413.

Varghese, G. (2008). Public-private partnerships in South African national parks: The rationale, benefits and lessons learned. In: A. Spenceley (Ed.), *Responsible tourism: Critical issues for conservation and development* (pp. 69–84). London: Earthscan.

Walpole, M. (1997). Dragon tourism in Komodo National Park, Indonesia: Its contribution to conservation and local development (PhD thesis). Kent, United Kingdom: Durrell Institute of Conservation and Ecology.

Wells, M. P., & Brandon, K. E. (1992). *People and parks: Linking protected area management with local communities.* Washington, DC: World Bank/WWF/USAID.

Wilkinson, P. F. (1989). Tourism in small island nations: A fragile dependency. *Leisure Studies, 6*(2), 127–146.

Wilderness Safaris. (2010). *Wilderness annual report, 2010.* Gaborone, Botswana: Wilderness Holdings.

Wunder, S. (2000). Ecotourism and economic incentives: An empirical approach. *Ecological Economics, 32*(3), 465–479.

Yu, E. W., Hendrickson, T., & Castillo, A. (1997). Ecotourism and conservation in Amazonian Peru: Short-term and long-term challenges. *Environmental Conservation*, 24(2), 130–138.

Zazueta, A. E. (1995). *Policy hits the ground: Participation and equity in environmental policy making.* Washington, DC: World Resources Institute.

A Partnership for Education and Environmental Awareness: Outreach in Fiji's Upper Navua Conservation Area

Jeremy Schultz and Nathan Bricker

LEARNING OBJECTIVES

- To understand how tourism, communities, and conservation stakeholders have implemented educational programs to assist with conservation efforts
- To understand the importance of education in ecotourism
- To demonstrate competing forces in the conservation of natural landscapes

---

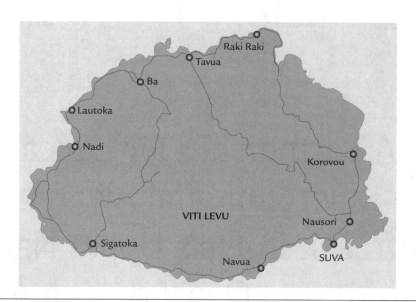

Figure CS 4.1   Map of Upper Navua Conservation Area.

The case of Rivers Fiji highlights how an ecotourism operation expanded its conservation efforts to include an educational community outreach program for schoolchildren. The program also shows how a unique lease for conservation contributes to the protection of one of Fiji's rare and fragile ecosystems in the interior highlands of Viti Levu, the largest of 332 islands within the country. Revenue generated from Rivers Fiji whitewater rafting programs provides economic benefits directly to local communities in the form of wages and conservation-based lease payments, which support the protection of the Upper Navua Conservation Area (UNCA). Since the establishment of the UNCA in 2000 it has become a destination for tourists to experience the geologic and natural attributes of the Upper Navua River and surrounding environment (see **Figure CS 4.1**).

To date, the primary threats to maintaining the UNCA area are illegal logging, mining upstream, and hydroelectric power. Such practices have the capability of causing irreparable damage to the dense tropical rainforest where the UNCA is located. To optimize and promote less extractive use of the river canyon, environmental outreach programs were developed by tourism operator Rivers Fiji, a whitewater rafting company, and NatureFiji-MareqetiViti, a locally based NGO focused on the protection and conservation of the country's natural environment (NatureFiji-MareqetiViti, 2011). These two organizations worked collaboratively to offer local young people and their parents living in the river communities rafting trips that emphasized the economic, environmental, and cultural importance of the region. In an effort to reach the future UNCA decision makers, the programs were designed to inspire children and their families to think about sustainable development and conservation aspects of the ecologically unique river corridor.

History of the Upper Navua Conservation Area

In 1998, Rivers Fiji began running whitewater rafting and kayaking trips on the Upper Navua and Wainikoroiluva Rivers (Rivers Fiji, 2010b). These rivers are located in the remote regions of Fiji's tropical interior on the largest island, Viti Levu (see Figure CS 4.1).

In 1999, the Fijian government adopted a national ecotourism policy (NEP) that aimed to provide economic alternatives for people in rural areas, typically away from mainstream tourism opportunities of the coastal areas (Bricker, 2003). Historically, tourism in the rural highlands was nonexistent. Because Rivers Fiji was offering a new type of tourism activity (whitewater rafting) with significant economic and employment opportunities, the communities embraced the concept and agreed to collaborate and open the highlands to ecotourism.

In the late 1990s, the primary threats to the Upper Navua River were commercial gravel extraction and extensive logging. Given that logging is only restricted to within 30 feet of the river's edge, this unique corridor was facing ecological threats to the riparian zone of the canyon. The Navua River is Fiji's third largest freshwater drainage, and these types of activities also created downstream threats to Beqa Lagoon, an important soft coral area.

Rivers Fiji engaged stakeholders from local communities to discuss a long-term collaborative effort to conserve the unique biological and geological ecosystem of the Upper Navua River corridor, as well as provide benefits to local communities (Bricker, 2001). By protecting these key elements, the success of the whitewater rafting experience, and subsequent economic contribution from river trips to the community, could be ensured. As a result, efforts by Rivers Fiji were centered on obtaining protection of the river canyon through a lease for conservation, the first time this had been done in Fiji.

During 2000, Rivers Fiji, in cooperation with the nine *mataqali* (landowning families) of the region, two local villages, Fiji's Native Land and Trust Board (NLTB), a logging company, and the government of Fiji, obtained official permission to establish the 26-kilometer corridor of the Upper Navua River Canyon as the Upper Navua Conservation Area (UNCA) (Bricker, 2001). The UNCA was created to help protect the area as a living museum for biodiversity, culturally significant heritage sites, and spectacular scenery within the corridor (Rivers Fiji, 2010a) (see **Figure CS 4.2**).

As part of the lease for conservation, no commercial logging or harvesting of natural resources is allowed within the conservation area. However, the nine *mataqali* are allowed to have traditional access to the resources, should they desire to harvest noncommercial subsistence products from farming and fishing for their individual needs using traditional methods. This agreement does not

Figure CS 4.2   Upper Navua River.

separate the people from their land but rather encourages conservation of other areas within their realm for such needs. Just like a healthy ecosystem, the economics of the area are at their healthiest when a diversity of opportunities for economic enhancement and ecosystem protection are present.

The UNCA's lease for conservation not only protects the biodiversity but, through an attractive tourism product, also provides economic diversity for the needs of the local communities that depend upon resources in the highlands. This type of agreement is an excellent example of how ecotourism can directly support conservation and provide tangible benefits to local communities. For the local people living in the UNCA, the conservation area provides all the necessary food and supplies for their daily living routines. The lease for conservation also offers financial compensation via direct payments to the *mataqali* as well as numerous employment opportunities for many community members. All of these opportunities were made possible through collaboration with local communities to create a sustainable tourism product that favors a diversity of opportunities, rather than a unidimensional approach to conservation.

To further the integrity and recognition of the UNCA, Rivers Fiji pursued a Ramsar International Wetlands of Importance classification for the area. Ramsar (2011) promotes "the conservation and wise use of all wetlands through local, regional and national actions and international cooperation, as a contribution towards achieving sustainable development throughout the world" (p. 1). Currently, there are more than 1,200 Ramsar wetlands globally (Ramsar, 2011). Obtaining a Ramsar designation offers international support to the protection and preservation of fragile wetlands that face surmounting challenges. In 2006, the UNCA was awarded Fiji's first Ramsar designation (Rivers Fiji, 2010a).

The UNCA Environmental Education Outreach Program

Despite the overall success of the UNCA in protecting its fragile ecosystem, the area continues to face influences that threaten the ecological balance of the river corridor and forests of the area. Issues such as illegal logging within the boundaries of the UNCA have generated a need for further action to ensure the conservation goals. Such prohibited activities threaten the biodiversity of the river corridor and have downstream impacts on coral reefs. These destructive activities pose a long-term threat to the vitality of the UNCA and its people, which are the attributes that attract tourists to the area.

Rivers Fiji and the establishment of the UNCA provide continual economic stability to the *mataqali* through the ongoing long-term lease for conservation funds and employment. However, the immediate financial benefits offered by the logging industry, which supplement income to the same *mataqali*, can be difficult for some community members to resist. Such immediate payoff to *mataqali* has been a significant challenge for Rivers Fiji in maintaining the environmental integrity of the conservation area. The ecotourism operations provided by Rivers Fiji have offered proven economic viability over many years for the *mataqali*. The economic benefits of the ecotourism venture, when compared to the short-term payoffs commonly associated with logging, demonstrate the capacity of ecotourism to provide stable long-term economic support to the communities. In an effort to promote the conservation benefits of ecotourism to the local communities, Rivers Fiji worked with the communities and a conservation NGO (Nature Fiji) to develop community outreach programs.

Through a Ramsar Small Grants Fund, Rivers Fiji was able to expand protection and conservation of the UNCA through environmental outreach programs. The programs were developed with the goals of educating and informing the children of the *mataqali* and their communities about areas of ecological and cultural significance, and economic viability (Rivers Fiji, 2010a, p. 2). The overall objective of the program was to foster the development of intrinsic values among the young people who will be the future decision makers of the UNCA. Such values possess the capability of influencing current debates about the area as well as future decisions regarding conservation of the UNCA.

Stakeholder Support

As Wight (1994) and others have suggested, ecotourism "should promote understanding and involve partnerships between many players, which could involve government, non-governmental organizations, industry, scientists, and locals" (p. 11). The UNCA environmental outreach programs were built with the cooperation of NatureFiji-MareqetiViti, entities within the Fijian government, and the nine UNCA *mataqali* as well as two additional villages that mark the beginning and end boundaries of the conservation area. Working upon the foundation of collaboration, Rivers Fiji also concentrated on the delivery of the program content. Together they decided a place-based, experiential approach, such as whitewater rafting trips, would be the most effective method of delivering the program while also highlighting the unique attributes and importance of the river ecosystem.

Planning for the UNCA outreach programs began in 2010. The planners believed that by creating a program through which the children could experience the UNCA firsthand, there was a greater chance of recall and their taking pride in the ecological and cultural lessons they learned during the programs. Place-based experiential forms of environmental outreach programs have been applied in other tourism destinations around the world that promote sustainability and conservation (Ruhanen, 2005).

Permission was required from each of the *mataqali* involved with the UNCA to allow their children to participate in the river trips. Meetings were held with the *mataqali* leaders to explain the purpose and delivery of the outreach programs. During the meetings, chaperones (members of each child's family) from each *mataqali* were also selected to accompany the children during the river trips. All the *mataqali* offered full support for the involvement of their children in the UNCA environmental outreach programs.

Having established a cooperative team and an educational philosophy to work from, the UNCA environmental outreach programs were developed into guided river trips overseen and led by Rivers Fiji and its guides. All of the guides employed by Rivers Fiji represent each of the nine *mataqali* involved in the project.

Conservation and Tourism

A key player in the implementation of the UNCA outreach programs was NatureFiji-MareqetiViti. The aim of NatureFiji-MareqetiViti is to "generate enthusiasm and local expertise in all matters associated with wildlife conservation and management through raising the

level of conservation and environmental awareness and education" (NatureFiji-MareqetiViti, 2011). NatureFiji-MareqetiViti played a key role in the delivery of the educational component of the outreach programs. Representatives from NatureFiji-MareqetiViti accompanied the children on each river trip, providing ecological lessons about the UNCA. Various stopping points along the river corridor were turned into living classrooms where the children learned about the flora and fauna of the area. These riverside classrooms also allowed for the guides (see **Figure CS 4.3**) and chaperones to share stories about the UNCA they had been taught by their families and friends.

Student Involvement

Figure CS 4.3   Rivers Fiji guide with a participant of the outreach program.

The children, ranging in age from 6–17 years, were given waterproof cameras to use during the river trips and were instructed to take pictures along the river that they thought were beautiful or important (see **Figure CS 4.4**). The pictures were then incorporated into slideshow presentations that were delivered to the children's communities and villages, providing them with an opportunity to share what they had learned during the river trips and to express their emotions. Eighty-nine children and their chaperones from nine *mataqali* and three Fijian villages (often composed of several *mataqali* or family groups) participated in the UNCA environmental outreach programs (Rivers Fiji, 2010a).

Student Reflections

The children were asked to express their thoughts about the river trip experience. Results of their reflections and evaluation forms indicated they appeared to have a deeper appreciation for

Figure CS 4.4   Children photographing a waterfall.

the area in the highlands communities compared to an appreciation for the ecology of the river. Some of the students commented:

> I was brought up on this river to fetch for food with my dad when I was a young girl. We used to walk through small creeks and follow tracks then, but coming on this trip makes me realize that there is more to what it has to offer. Its beauty and what I have seen living within the Upper Navua Conservation area today is a gift from God. I personally need to be grateful and appreciative of what lies within our land.

> This is my first time on the trip and I have learned so much about the wildlife, the endangered birds, fish and trees, and especially the Sago Palm.

The children living in the UNCA were not the only ones inspired by the outreach programs; many of the chaperones were also affected by their experience on the river. Some of them commented:

> I will help to conserve and protect the Upper Navua because it is so beautiful.

> Even though I knew the river existed, I took it for granted. I did not realize how important it was to me.

> I am grateful that this opportunity was given to our children to have a firsthand experience about this adventure trip and also learn the importance of wildlife and how we the land-owners should make the right decision in conserving this place in the future.

These comments suggest the children and adults value the UNCA area and river. Without long-term follow-up of the children and chaperones we cannot know if the program has had an effect on them in terms of their views and perceptions of the area. However, delivering programs like this may instill an appreciation of local surroundings. It will be vital for future ecotourism initiatives within the UNCA to support the hope seen within the quotes taken from participants in the outreach programs.

Conclusion

The results of the UNCA educational outreach programs support the importance of education as one of the fundamental functions of ecotourism for all stakeholders involved (Ross & Wall, 1999). For conservation outcomes, it is clear education plays a role in establishing meaning and understanding of the complex systems that, in the end, support quality of life for communities, including not only economic support but also resources depended upon for daily subsistence.

The UNCA outreach programs exhibited a direct positive awareness of environmental education as expressed by participants; however, these were not the only benefits resulting from the programs. From a values perspective, ecotourism has the potential to transform the political, social, religious, and moral values of a local community (Wearing, 2001). For those who reside within the rural highlands, these values are often the basis for decisions that affect the entire community. This value system begins to develop in children through formative experiences and education as well as family influence and upbringing. According to Sinha and Bushell (2002), "tourism [can] contribute to biodiversity conservation and maintenance of cultural identity by reinforcing stories about local histories and promoting respect for traditional culture and use of natural resources" (p. 35).

Another benefit resulting from the UNCA environmental outreach program was marketing and national publicity for the conservation area. Representatives from Fiji's national newspaper, *The Fiji Times*, and reporters from national television stations attended some of the river trips to document the outreach programs. The resulting articles and television segments were seen throughout Fiji and via the Internet. This type of publicity is vital in gaining the support of government officials for further conservation efforts in Fiji.

Considering the future of the UNCA and the downstream watershed, the activities that occur upstream affect the health of ecosystems downstream. At the delta where the Navua River reaches the Pacific Ocean lies what was formerly a healthy, flourishing coral reef. Runoff from the Navua River and its tributaries is a contributing factor to the degradation of the coral reef. Activities such as illegal logging that increase the amount of sediment and pollution in the run-off have effects that reach the distance of the entire watershed and its destination. Hence, the importance of ecologically healthy river systems extends well beyond the communities of the highlands to the coastal regions.

Overall, the UNCA environmental awareness outreach programs were successful in providing an enjoyable opportunity for local children to learn about the importance of conservation in supporting their communities and their way of life. The UNCA's *mataqali* have all expressed a desire to continue the program. Education is a critical piece in developing ecotourism, which supports conservation. Without it, short-term economic gain will continue to override conservation efforts, increasing the likelihood that degradation of the natural environment will continue despite formal lease agreements. Education is one strategy that helps promote the value of conservation and potentially ensures a level of awareness for future generations.

References

Bricker, K. (2001). Ecotourism development in the rural highlands of Fiji. In: D. Harrison (Ed.), *Tourism and the less developed world: Issues and case studies* (pp. 235–250). Wallingford, United Kingdom: CABI.

Bricker, K. (2003). Ecotourism development in Fiji: Policy, practice, and political instability. In: D. Fennel & R. Dowling (Eds.), *Ecotourism policy and planning* (pp. 187–204). Wallingford, United Kingdom: CABI.

NatureFiji-MareqetiViti. (2011). Welcome. Retrieved April 9, 2012, from http://www.naturefiji.org

Ramsar Convention on Wetlands. (2011). About the Ramsar convention. Retrieved April 5, 2012, from http://www.ramsar.org/cda/en/ramsar-about/main/ramsar/1-36_4000_0

Rivers Fiji. (2010a). *Ramsar environmental awareness workshops in the Upper Navua Conservation Area.* Pacific Harbour, Fiji: Rivers Fiji (unpublished report).

Rivers Fiji. (2010b). Upper Navua Conservation Area. Retrieved April 9, 2012, from http://www.riversfiji.com/ecotourism/upper-navua-conservation-area

Ross, S., & Wall, G. (1999). Ecotourism: Towards congruence between theory and practice. *Tourism Management, 20*, 123–132.

Ruhanen, L. (2005). Bridging the divide between theory and practice: Experiential learning approaches for tourism and hospitality management education. *Journal of Teaching in Travel and Tourism, 5*(4), 33–51.

Sinha, C., & Bushell, R. (2002). Understanding the linkage between biodiversity and tourism: A study of ecotourism in a coastal village in Fiji. *Pacific Tourism Review, 6*(1), 35–50.

Wearing, S. (2001). Exploring the socio-cultural impacts on local communities. In: D. Weaver (Ed.), *The encyclopedia of ecotourism* (pp. 395–410). Wallingford, United Kingdom: CABI.

Wight, P. (1994). Environmentally responsible marketing of tourism. In: E. Cater & G. Lowman (Eds.), *Ecotourism: A sustainable option?* (pp. 39–56). Brisbane, Australia: John Wiley & Sons.

Breaking Gender Barriers: A Market-Based Approach to Women's Empowerment Through Tourism

Lucky Chhetri and Wendy Brewer Lama

LEARNING OBJECTIVES

- To promote understanding of the socioeconomic conditions and obstacles rural women in developing countries face in becoming tourism professionals as a basis for designing intervention strategies
- To discuss how tourism can be harnessed as a mechanism for achieving the Millennium Development Goals (MDGs) of empowering women and promoting gender equality using a market-driven approach as an alternative to a supply-driven strategy
- To share and apply lessons learned from private sector tourism development with donor-funded development programs, addressing complementary objectives of sustainable tourism, market security, and women's empowerment
- To profile the synergetic relationship of an adventure travel company and a women's empowerment and livelihood development NGO in Nepal

Figure CS 5.1   The three sisters.

A women-owned-and-operated trekking company in Nepal, 3 Sisters Adventure Trekking, is breaking down gender barriers and opening up employment opportunities for rural Nepalese women as tour guides. Responding to the calls of solo-women trekkers for hassle-free guiding services in the early 1990s, three sisters—Lucky, Dicky, and Nicky Chhetri (see **Figure CS 5.1**)—tapped their entrepreneurial skills as lodge operators and money their parents had saved for their weddings to start a trekking company that caters to independent travelers, particularly women.

Having seen first-hand the desperate social conditions facing women in the remote mountain regions of Nepal, they have embraced a business model that helps disadvantaged Nepalese women transform their lives through tourism (see **Box CS 5.1**).

3 Sisters Adventure Trekking now supports a nongovernmental organization (NGO), Empowering Women of Nepal (EWN), that trains and mentors village women to become trekking professionals. Training-certified Nepalese women, with greater confidence and on-the-job experience, find gainful employment guiding female adventure travelers—now one of the fastest growing tourism markets—and earn respect as community leaders and bread-winners in a traditionally gender-imbalanced society.

This is a story of a trekking company that helps to boost rural women's economic and social status in Nepal. It considers the role of the women's adventure travel market in moving women out of the shadows and into the limelight as valued tourism professionals. It examines a private sector approach to market-based gender-equitable tourism and considers what strategies can be shared with donor-funded tourism development programs, and suggests measures for motivating, supporting, and sharing lessons learned and promoting market linkages among women tourism entrepreneurs.

Box CS 5.1   The Motivation to Transform Women's Lives

Lucky Chhetri, founder of 3 Sisters Adventure Trekking, works as a consultant and trainer for development programs in rural Nepal. In 2003, Lucky and her sister Nicky were trekking from Humla to Jumla, one of the poorest, most isolated, and marginalized regions of Nepal. The Maoist conflict had had a significant impact on people's lives: tourism was down, and most men had been swept up in the Maoist movement and lived away from their families or were in India seeking employment. The women had been left behind with the full responsibility of caring for their families and animals. They were out of cash resources and did not have sufficient food; healthcare facilities had been destroyed, and education and communications were nonexistent. Due to the insurgency, government and development assistance was on hold. This situation was widespread throughout western Nepal. As in many war-time situations, women bore the brunt of the hardship. The Chhetri sisters decided to do something about the women's desperation that they observed, and the idea for training women as trekking guides was born.

Response to a Need: 3 Sisters Adventure Trekking

The story of 3 Sisters Adventure Trekking, a small home-grown tourism enterprise with a social and ethical mission, tells how one company responded to a niche market demand (solo women travelers) and is now riding a wave of market growth in women's adventure travel. This uncommon model of investing profits in training and empowering women has earned 3 Sisters Adventure Trekking and EWN international recognition, including winning the Geotourism Challenge, sponsored by Ashoka's Changemakers and National Geographic. The 3 Sisters' mission has evolved into a unique marketing profile among Nepal's more than 700 registered trekking agencies.

The Chhetri sisters were running a guest house in the lakeside tourist destination of Pokhara in the early 1990s when they decided to open a trekking company that would employ Nepalese women as guides. Lucky, the oldest sister, recalls:

> In the beginning, female guides were not well received by Nepalese society. People discouraged and excluded us and tried to spoil our reputation. We went through rough times but somehow we were sure that women's involvement in the trekking and tourism industry would build women's self-esteem and generate income to help lift women out of poverty and above the exploitation and discrimination they face.

Tourism began to boom in Nepal in the mid-1990s, and the demand for female guides began to grow exponentially. The stories of 3 Sisters' young women guides' life-changing experiences inspired the sisters to reach out to others; they targeted women from low-caste and impoverished families, the uneducated, and those who had been abandoned by their husbands. The company realized immediately that for women to become professional guides, they needed more knowledge and skills. This led to the inception of EWN, which provides training to women in basic first aid, culture and religion, the environment, flora and fauna, map reading, cross-cultural communication, women's human rights, women's health issues, and conversational English (see **Box CS 5.2**).

Although 3 Sisters Adventure Trekking and EWN are governed by the same directors and work collaboratively to promote and involve women in adventure tourism, the two organizations have different functions. EWN extends educational and practical skills, and 3 Sisters Adventure Trekking provides employment and entrepreneurial opportunities to EWN trainees

---

Box CS 5.2 From Outcast to Professional

Kamala Devi Sunar was already divorced from her husband when she joined the program in 1999. She is Dalit (a disadvantaged caste in Nepal) and has minimal education. She regularly attended the EWN training programs and began working as a trekking guide. She married again and has a 4-year-old daughter. She now has a permanent job with 3 Sisters and is using her income to send her daughter to school. She is well accepted by her and her husband's Muslim family and by society because she is considered a professional woman. She is now able to make her own decisions about her life.

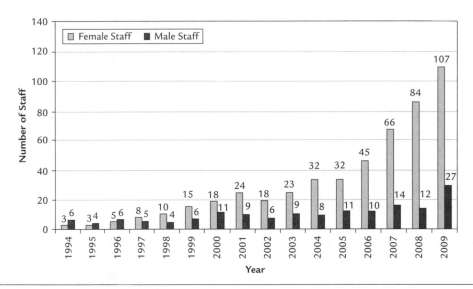

Figure CS 5.2   Staffing for 3 Sisters Adventure Trekking: female and male staff (1994–2009).

(see **Figure CS 5.2** and **Box CS 5.3**). Fifteen to 20 percent of 3 Sisters' profit goes to EWN for female trekking guide training held twice a year and supports a children's home that provides food, accommodations, medical care, and educational scholarships to 20 girls in need. Some of the older children are rescued from bondage labor from the nearby Annapurna trekking area, and others come from impoverished families from west Nepal and other remote districts.

Recognized for its training expertise, EWN offers it services to sustainable tourism development programs including SNV Netherlands Development Organization, Norwegian Development Fund, the Global Fund for Women, and others. Through the Women's Initiation in

---

Box CS 5.3   Changing Nepalese Women's Lives Through Tourism

Ways in which tourism has impacted women's lives directly in Nepal:[1]

- Over 800 disadvantaged or rural women have been trained as guides through EWN.
- 3 Sisters Adventure Trekking seasonally employs up to 100 female and 20 male staff.
- Five trainees run their own trekking business; two run a tea house in the Annapurnas.
- Over 50 trainees work part-time to support their higher education.
- Eighty-seven trainees are working with NGOs and international NGOs (INGOs) in west Nepal; some run businesses.
- Over 100 trainees have taken advanced rock climbing training; 12 have taken technical ice climbing training, of whom four have received extensive climbing training in Nepal and abroad.
- Other trekking companies are hiring EWN trainees.
- Young, educated, middle class women are now taking up trek guiding, whereas in the past mostly disadvantaged rural women were interested in the field.
- Eight trainee graduates work full-time at the EWN office.
- About 20 senior female guides hold leadership positions or are trainers within EWN.

[1] EWN, 2011. Personal communication.

Figure CS 5.3   Training future female trekking guides.

Ecotourism project, it has trained 435 rural women and 66 men in west Nepal since 2000 (see **Figure CS 5.3**). According to Lucky Chhetri

> Our work is very interactive with the locals; we listen to the people and encourage them to be "agents of change" in their communities. We support and encourage locals to take leadership positions and make decisions for their community. For this, we provide an enabling environment where we give ideas, help them identify their needs and opportunities and support their aspirations to achieve their goals.[2]

This case study describes a private sector market-based approach to empowering women through tourism and illustrates how market demand can drive investment by a private company, an NGO, and the women guides who pay for their training and the immeasurable benefits it brings.

Hurdles to Women's Equality

The women of Nepal face many obstacles in gaining an economic footing, particularly in remote rural areas and among certain ethnic groups. Gender equality in Nepal is hampered by a number of social and political conditions, including:

- A highly patriarchal society
- Women's ignorance of the law
- Unequal opportunities and discrimination in access to basic education, health care, nutrition, and employment
- Unequal rights to inheritance and the ability to own property (see also **Box CS 5.4**)

According to a National Planning Commission survey (Upadhyay & Grandon, 2008), only 17% of Nepalese women work in the nonagricultural sector compared to 82.5% of men, and census data show that only half of these women earn a wage (National Sample Census of

---

[2] Lucky Chhetri, personal communication, 2011.

Box CS 5.4   A Portrait of Rural Women of Nepal

- Women have far less access to education. One reason is the opportunity costs of educating girls: When girls are in school they are unavailable for work at home and on the farm. Secondly, the investment in educating girls (though schooling and books are now free for girls up to mid-level) is considered a waste in preparing for a life as a wife and mother.[3]
- Women's literacy rates in the mid- and far-western regions are 8–24%, compared to those of men at 41–60% (United Nations Development Programme [UNDP], 2004, in Leduc, 2011).
- Women have more health problems than men, are more exposed to the effects of poverty, face more discrimination, and are more vulnerable to violence (Leduc, 2011).
- Only 17.5% of Nepalese women work in wage employment in the nonagricultural sector, compared to 82.5% men (National Sample Census of Agriculture Nepal, 2001/2002). Note: 2011 census data were not available at the time this book went to print.
- Extreme poverty, a high unemployment rate, and political strife drive the rural poor to out-migration; women often are subjected to and forced into prostitution (U.S. Department of State, 2010).
- Women have very limited access to financial resources and the right to own land. In 2001, only 0.8% of women in Nepal owned a house, 5.3% owned land, and 5.4% owned livestock (Dabadi, 2009, in Leduc, 2011).
- Women are rarely represented on decision-making bodies, and their needs are seldom addressed by development plans (International Centre for Integrated Mountain Development, 2012). Between 1997 and 2002, women's representation in local government institutions in Nepal was 6.7% in the district development committees, 7.7% in the village development committees, and 2.1% in village councils (UNDP, 2004, in Leduc, 2011).

---

[3] Lucky Chhetri, personal communication, 2011.

Agriculture Nepal, 2001/2002). Women's contributions to the well-being of their households and communities is not calculated and seldom acknowledged when measuring economic productivity (Lama, 2000).

Tourism is a significant contributor to the economic and social development of Nepal. The direct contribution of travel and tourism to Nepal's gross domestic product is Rs37.3 billion (US$517 million), which accounted for 2.8% of total gross domestic product in 2011. Tourism and travel directly support 293,000 jobs (2.4% of total employment) and indirectly affect 726,000 jobs (5.9% of total employment) (World Travel and Tourism Council, 2011). Trekking and mountaineering are a major component of the tourism industry and "have helped uplift thousands of mountain people out of poverty" (Sherpa, 2007, p. 1). Trekking tourism was launched 50 years ago on the backs of poor farmers who worked as porters and mountaineering guides. Young men have worked their way up to become trekking cooks, guides, and business owners; some now own successful hotels and airline companies and have children studying abroad.

Women, however, seldom move beyond the home. Whereas rural Nepalese women are physically strong and able, household chores, child-rearing responsibilities, and social stigmas largely preclude their taking jobs in tourism that require traveling away from home. As "tea house trekking" evolved along Nepal's popular trekking routes, women's home duties and hospitality skills have channeled them into the role of managing trekking lodges, particularly when male family members working as trekking staff are away for long periods.

Besides the societal hurdles to Nepalese women's participation in trekking tourism, other political and gender-bias factors (which may be good for the tourism industry but not necessarily for women) are creating barriers:

- Participation in government-certified trekking guide training requires documentation of Nepalese citizenship, 2 years of work experience in trekking, literacy, and a fee of Rs 5,000, all of which are very difficult to satisfy by many women.[4]
- A competitive trekking guide market demands that would-be guides have good communications skills in English, guide training certification, good work performance, and confidence with strangers—all of which many women lack due to inferior education and pressure to abide by social norms.
- Trekking management jobs hire from within their ranks of long-experienced staff, into which females are just now entering.

"Women's Work": Overcoming Exploitation

Studies of women involved in the tourism industry worldwide agree that the type of tourism work available to rural women is usually low-skill, low-paying jobs such as cleaning and cooking, seen as an extension of their normal (unpaid) domestic roles (United Nations World Tourism Organization [UNWTO], 2011). In addition to their tourism sector work, women are expected to continue fulfilling their domestic responsibilities, with tourism adding to their already heavy workload. Furthermore, women working in home-based tourism businesses are often doing so without pay, lending little to their potential empowerment as contributors to household income and questioning the viability of such enterprises (Sherpa, 2007).

The degree to which tourism elevates a woman in society varies considerably across cultures, ethnic groups, and even households. According to the *Global Report on Women in Tourism 2010 Preliminary Findings*:

> [Tourism] has the potential to be a vehicle for empowerment of women in developing regions. Tourism provides better opportunities for women's participation in the workforce, women's entrepreneurship, and women's leadership than other sectors of the economy. Women in tourism are still underpaid, under-utilized, under-represented; but tourism offers pathway to success. (UNWTO, 2010, p. ii)

Such is the case in the village of Dhampus, within the popular Annapurna Conservation Area Project (ACAP) trekking area of Nepal. Women who operate tea shops and lodges or provide services to tourists earn greater respect for having contributed financially to their households versus women who earn no income. Male family members will even take up "women's work" and allow female lodge managers to attend community meetings to further tourism development (Apostolopoulos, 2001).

---

[4] Lucky Chhetri, personal communication, 2011.

Women are valued as "tourism assets" in the Helambu-Langtang region of Nepal. Community members brainstormed the unique attributes and skills that women offer tourism and realized how much they bring to the tourists' well-being and the villages' reputation as a tourist destination (Lama, 2000). This open appreciation of women may only be possible, however, within societies where females already share a relatively egalitarian relationship with males. Sherpa points out that among women of certain ethnic groups of highland Nepal (e.g., Sherpas, Gurungs, Yolmos, and Humlis) "even when roles are defined as per gender, they are not necessarily of an unequal nature" (Sherpa, 2007, p. 3).

Beyond Nepal, in Gunung Rinjani National Park on the Indonesian island of Lombok, women who have turned traditional weaving skills into profitable enterprises have gained a higher level of status within their families, opening the door to their participation in community forums. It also has emboldened them to interact with outsiders. Once they began bringing home money for their efforts, household divisions of labor changed. The notion that a woman's social status reflects her economic worth is reflected in the same Lombok case study that measured whether enhanced skills alone (without income) or a lesser contribution to household revenue also elevates a female. It found that women who were trained as tour guides but were not hired due to a lack of language skills and confidence did not attain a significantly higher level of social standing, and women whose home enterprises (snack-making) did not generate significant income gained no social advantages. On the contrary, their efforts generated resentment from husbands for spending time away from home (Scheyvens, 2007).

Whereas women's social value may be linked to the money they contribute to household income and the benefits they bring to tourism-based economies, it does not necessarily earn them equal footing in the legal system. In India, "the interesting aspect of tourism development is that it has exploited the productivity of women without conferring (property) ownership rights on them" (Rao, 1998, p. 170).

Empowerment, Tourism, and the MDGs

Recognizing the tourism-related variables that affect a women's place in society (i.e., the cultural context, government policies, access to education and training opportunities, level of contributions to household or village income, and no doubt the personalities and abilities of individual women), can tourism be harnessed as a mechanism for achieving the Millennium Development Goals (MDGs) of empowering women and promoting gender equality, and if so, how?

An aspect of this case study is to see what lessons can be learned from a private sector–led market-based approach to delivering gender equality to women through tourism against a background of the more widely employed donor-funded sustainable tourism development program.

Although a strong sense of ethics plays a significant role in 3 Sisters Adventure Trekking's business plan, the market is the engine that drives and enables women's professionalism in tourism. Responding initially to a perceived unfulfilled market niche of solo women trekkers, 3 Sisters has demonstrated that tourism can turn a profit while empowering women and contributing to gender equality. Riding the growth of the women's adventure travel market, 3 Sisters' need for women guides has increased, promoting more opportunities for women's advancement in tourism.

Women now make up more than half of the soft adventure travel market and nearly two-thirds of other travel markets, giving female travelers considerable leverage in changing how tourism affects the disadvantaged women of the world (George Washington University School of Business et al., 2010). As a group, adventure travelers place a higher level of importance on exploring new places and engaging with local cultures, and have a desire to give back to their host communities on their vacations (Centre for Responsible Tourism [CREST], n.d.). With women at the forefront, adventure travel holds promise for delivering benefits to people living in remote areas commonly visited by adventurers. Women-to-women travel does this by design.

Reaching for new markets and marketing messages, women's travel companies and a handful of international tour operators offer women's tours and social service trips that benefit women in host countries. Many contract with in-country women tourism professionals to foster women-to-women exchanges. Such interactions can snowball into educational and travel sponsorships for local women who befriend women visitors. Women visitors to local NGOs or artisan cooperatives bring about new marketing linkages, technical "voluntourism," and greater pride and confidence among women entrepreneurs whose products attract international attention. Tour companies and travelers contribute financially and in-kind to support the revival of traditional arts and culture and to support programs for destitute women. In the words of a frequent organizer of women-to-women travel:

> I travel with women because of the bonds that develop among the group members as well as the women we meet. Our trips feature a community-service donation to needy women; for example, we deliver eye glasses to women embroiderers in rural Vietnam and India whose livelihoods and the survival of traditional skills depend upon good eyesight. It is a win-win situation, and is a big selling point to our trips.[5]

By necessity, the success of the tourism industry relies on its ability to anticipate and respond to market demand. The development sector has taken decades to learn that lesson. After years of supply-side tourism planning, international donor-funded programs are finally using a market-based approach to promoting tourism products that meet travelers' demands; however, they seek market support for moving women into tourism to a lesser degree.

One such program is the Great Himalayan Trail Development Programme (GHTDP) in Nepal. This program focuses equally on identifying and nurturing tourism markets and developing sustainable tourism products and services that match market trends. Moving beyond the traditional "build it and they will come" attitude, the program helps link national and local tour operators with small and micro local tourism entrepreneurs; business partnerships and exchanges of product–market information are ensuing. Gender-sensitive policies and training quotas require female participation. Tourism plans help facilitate small-scale tourism enterprises such as tea houses and home stays in which women are traditionally involved.

However, engaging women in sustainable tourism has proved challenging. The duration of development programs is often too short to see the needed changes to education, health, legal, and social policies and perspectives. Program efforts are frustrated by the limited number of

---

[5] Christina Wilson, in collaboration with KarmaQuest Ecotourism and Adventure Travel.

women who are willing or able to step outside of their social bounds. With no or limited business experience or capital resources, women are wedded to a low risk and low return (i.e., do more of the same business strategy). EWN is a consultant agency in the GHTDP and serves as a role model for women participants; however, it is too early to measure the true impacts on women.

Conclusion

The adventure travel market for women and a small but growing number of highly motivated entrepreneurs and NGOs hold promise for contributing to women's empowerment and equality and achieving the MDGs. More important than the size of this impact is what drives it: the desire to improve disadvantaged women's lives through tourism, and to foster the delivery of gender-sensitive tourism in a highly competitive market. As donor-funded tourism development programs and the market move closer together, where are the synergies for a win–win outcome? The following sections describe some strategies and mechanisms that could be used to ensure the meaningful involvement of women in the tourism industry.

Facilitating Dialogue

Facilitate two-way dialogue, wherein development planners and tourism market representatives clearly understand the objectives, aims, and constraints of each other, and seek to support and encourage mutually beneficial approaches. As Yankila Sherpa, past president of the Trekking Agents Association of Nepal (TAAN) and State Minister of Tourism for Nepal, and current president of the Federation of Women Entrepreneurs Association of Nepal (FWEAN) and owner of Snow Leopard Trekking Pvt. Ltd., a woman-owned trekking company in Nepal, recommends:

> . . . public and private sectors could join hands in providing training and promoting women related indigenous skills. . . . women should be prioritized for receipt of loans to support tourism related micro enterprises such as home stays, tea shops, local lodges, handicraft sales, etc. (Sherpa, 2007, p. 8)

Reward System

Reward and assist tour operators in promoting women's involvement in tourism through measures targeted at reducing the investment risks and valuing women's roles as market strengths. For example:

- Sponsor mentorships and on-the-job training programs for beginning female tourism professionals, including trekking staff.
- Support market research to target tour operators that promote women-to-women travel.
- Share market research results with women tourism entrepreneurs and service providers to enhance linkage opportunities.
- Provide technical support for women-in-tourism blogs and inexpensive and accessible information sharing venues.

- Subsidize "fam" (familiarization) trips to tourism destinations that feature women artisans, women entrepreneurs, and women leaders as the basis for a women's tourism product.
- Aid entrepreneurs in qualifying for loan assistance to foster female-friendly business practices.

Increase Awareness

Increase awareness among women tourism professionals and would-be entrepreneurs:

- Publicize women's conditions in remote regions to inspire more tour operators to contribute to their betterment.
- Help to bring tourists and tour operators into first-hand contact with women beneficiaries to motivate "north-south" women-to-women relationships, exchanges, and sponsorships.
- Foster well-planned and managed "south-to-south" study tours and workshops in peer-to-peer learning exchanges.

References

Apostolopoulos, Y. (2001). *Women as producers and consumers of tourism in developing regions.* Westport, CT: Greenwood.

Centre for Responsible Tourism. (2009). *The market for responsible tourism products in Latin America and Nepal: Summary of report prepared for SNV Netherlands Development Organisation.* Quito, Ecuador: SNV Netherlands Development Organisation.

George Washington University School of Business, Adventure Travel Trade Association (ATTA), & Xola Consulting. (2010). Adventure tourism market report. Retrieved April 10, 2012, from http://www.xolaconsulting.com/Adventure-Market-2010.pdf

International Centre for Integrated Mountain Development, (2012). *Mainstreaming gender in mountain development: From policy to practice.* Retrieved January 1, 2012, from http://books.icimod.org/index.php/downloads/publication/740

Lama, W. B. (2000). Community-based tourism for conservation and women's development. In: P. M. Godde, M. F. Price, & F. M. Zimmermann (Eds.), *Tourism and development in mountain regions* (pp. 225–363). Wallingford, England: CABI.

Leduc, B. (2011). *Mainstreaming gender in mountain development: From policy to practice.* Kathmandu, Nepal: International Centre for Integrated Mountain Development.

National Sample Census of Agriculture Nepal. (2001/2002). Kathmandu, Nepal: Central Bureau of Statistics. Government of Nepal National Planning Commission Secretariat.

Rao, N. (1998). India's mountain women kept in the background. In: P. East, L. Kurt, & K. Inmann (Eds.), *Sustainability in mountain tourism* (pp. 170–206). New Delhi: Book Faith India.

Scheyvens, R. (2007). Ecotourism and gender issues. In: J. Higham (Ed.), *Critical issues in ecotourism: Understanding a complex tourism phenomenon* (pp. 185–213). Oxford, England: Elsevier.

Sherpa, Y. (2007). *Mountain tourism: A boon or a bane? Impacts of tourism on Himalayan women.* Paper submitted to Women of the Mountains Conference, Orem, Utah. Retrieved April 9, 2012, from http://www.womenofthemountains.org/files/Microsoft%20Word%20-%2007-03-01-From-Yankila-Sherpa-FINAL-PAPER-Final_paper_sent_to_Baktybek.pdf

United Nations World Tourism Organization (UNWTO) & United Nations Entity for Gender Equality and the Employment of Women (UN Women). (2011). *The global report on women in tourism 2010 preliminary findings.* Madrid, Spain & New York: Authors.

Upadhyay, R., & Grandon, R. (2008). *Labor force survey 2008, Central Bureau of Statistics.* Women in Nepalese Tourism. Hotel Association of Nepal 39th Annual General Meeting report, Kathmandu, Nepal.

U.S. Department of State. (2010). Country narratives: Nepal. Retrieved April 10, 2012, from http://www.state.gov/g/tip/rls/tiprpt/2010/142761.htm

World Travel and Tourism Council. (2011). Nepal Economic Impact Report. Retrieved April 5, 2012, from http://www.wttc.org/research/economic-impact-research/country-reports/n/nepal

Local Empowerment in a Rural Community Through Ecotourism: A Case Study of a Women's Organization in Chira Island, Costa Rica

Marieloz Bonilla Moya

LEARNING OBJECTIVES

- To explore women's roles as agents of change for community benefit through networking and governance of public resources resulting in local empowerment
- To illustrate how responsible tourism development enhances community well-being via environmental stewardship while maintaining local values among a small group of women
- To illustrate how ecotourism can reduce poverty and support micro-business via networking with other groups in the community
- To explore specific impacts and inputs on environmental practice and social conditions

This case study illustrates how a women's group in a rural island community can reduce poverty and improve local empowerment through the creation of ecotourism in a community that has traditionally survived on fishing and farming. A change via pro-poor projects is directly illustrated through participation of a small group of rural women in a project supplying lodging, meals, and nature-based tours. The women involve other groups in the community such as producers of food, goods, and handicrafts as part of their project. This case is relevant because this group of women took leadership for change in Chira, Costa Rica, an island unknown as a tourist destination. They started a process of empowerment that is not always possible in rural areas. The women have overcome numerous obstacles (e.g., few financial resources, lack of participation, lack of technical skills), resulting in an increased sense of empowerment and political influence in the community. The impact on environmental practice and social conditions is explored as well. Qualitative data supplemented with anecdotal evidence illustrate how responsible tourism development improves local community well-being, while protecting the environment and positively impacting the value system of some local people, especially among a small group of women and their families.

Origins

This case study merges concepts this author deems relevant after 20 years of working with community organizations in Costa Rica as a facilitator of tourism product development in rural areas. The approach explores how a women's group can be empowered as individuals via an ecotourism project, and how they can have a positive impact on the community as a result of the project. These women have gone through a process that has changed their roles within the community. This case study proposes that if women are empowered individually and their social and environmental needs satisfied, they could become agents of change for the common good of their community through networking for governance of public resources.

Figure CS 6.1 depicts the reflective features of the local empowerment process discussed in this case study. This figure suggests three components (lessons learned, social impacts, and environmental practices) necessary to empower a community. The first component, *lessons learned*, addresses the project from its inception. The project was a concrete activity that encouraged a process of change. However, obstacles in the form of barriers appear; some people drop out and others continue. The obstacles vary according to the groups and communities involved in the project, such as a lack of financial support for the project or lack of local participation. Such obstacles present in such a way as to either stop a project or move it forward. If financial benefits are not achieved, there is an inverse connection to social and environmental benefits. However, financial contributions from government and NGO donations can bias the process if women have not been empowered to overcome obstacles to their success. Awareness and capacity building are major factors in ensuring empowerment that are attributed to lessons learned in the development and implementation of a project.

The second component, *social impacts*, refers to the satisfaction of basic needs (food, clothing, home, leisure), followed by health care, education (for themselves and their children), and decision-making autonomy. By being part of a sustainable tourism project, awareness about the environment was increased through the capacity-building process, which most of the rural ecotourism community projects in Costa Rica have been part of.

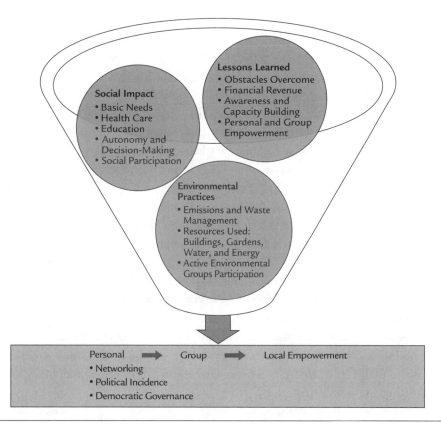

Figure CS 6.1   Personal, group, and local empowerment: reflective features of the process.

The third component, *environmental practices*, are placed later in the process because the author's experience in Costa Rica reveals that conservation within communities is not possible if financial and social needs are not satisfied first or at least are in progress at the same time. Environmental practices include approaches to reduce CO_2 emissions, waste management, conservation of water and energy, and incorporating environmentally friendly designs of buildings and gardens.

It was conceptualized that these three components empower individuals, groups, and local communities. If individual and group empowerment succeeds, a broad influence in the community can be expected, resulting in local community empowerment. Results of local community empowerment can lead to enhanced networking, political activism, and governance. Women's involvement in networking and politics is necessary to influence local governance and is relevant to women´s empowerment within a community (Bonilla Moya, 2008).

A qualitative approach was used within this case study, involving 2-hour in-depth interviews with 3 of the original 12 women who started the Chira Island ecotourism project in 2002. These are the women who overcame numerous obstacles throughout the process. Additional data were obtained from four brief interviews among members of the local women's craft association, informal conversations with some locals and visitors, informal observations, and the author's witnessing of changes throughout this project's development since its inception.

Chira Island

Chira Island (Isla de Chira) is a Costa Rican island of approximately 7,400 acres in the Gulf of Nicoya. It is the biggest island in the Nicoya gulf and the second largest of the country (see **Figure CS 6.2**). There are approximately 3,000 people living in four communities on the island—Bocana, San Antonio, Montero, and Palito—which are located along a road crossing the island from east to west. The main economic activities on the island are fishing and farming (crops and cattle). Chira's biological importance is relevant due to the tropical dry forest, one of the most endangered biodiversity areas in Central America. There is a large estuary leading to a canal with vast mangrove forests. These biological resources host many species of birds and marine wildlife. The rural landscape of traditional fishing and farming communities of the dry forest lends itself well to a tourism project. Local groups have formed in the last 10 years in order to improve their financial outlook. These groups include a women's group of *piangua* producers (a sort of oyster), a fishing association, a women's craft association, and the organization described in this study: the rural ecotourism project. The origin of these four groups is a result of the National University of Costa Rica's extension program (UNA).

The Women's Association of Isla de Chira (*Asociación de Damas de la Isla de Chira*) was one of the first women's groups supported by the National University of Costa Rica (UNA) in 1997. The UNA's intent is to support potentially productive groups to develop alternatives to the uncertainty of fishing. It is important to meet the basic needs of rural communities, which is a critical situation in the region.

At first, the idea of how to encourage tourism was not clear. While considering a variety of options, in 2000 the UNA officially formed an association to address tourism issues,

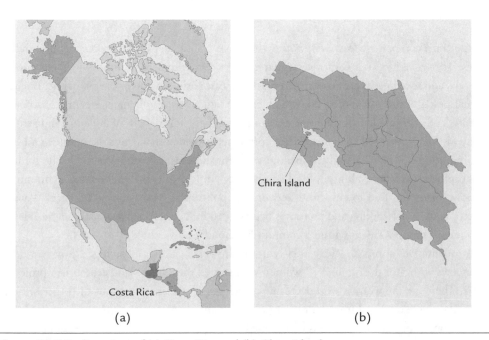

(a)   (b)

Figure CS 6.2   Locations of (a) Costa Rica and (b) Chira Island.

the *Asociación de Damas de la Isla de Chira*. The group envisioned the eventual development of a lodge but decided to start slowly. They began by building a boat to operate 1-day tours to visit mangroves and lead bird-watching trips. As the first form of economic income generation, they were delighted by the opportunity: "the biggest happiness was to buy food for the kids." The next step was to buy a small property in order to start the lodge. They received aid from donors to build the first cabin, which they built with their own hands. There were many challenges because their property did not have electricity or drinking water on the island, nor was there road access to the project site to facilitate transport of materials.

The group received further donations to build a dining area and kitchen. A group of volunteers from England volunteered to assist. Once completed, they added breakfast and lunch services to their 1-day tours. This increased opportunity for additional income and also increased their motivation to continue. Two more cabins were built to accommodate growing visitation (see **Figure CS 6.3**).

They now own three cabins and can accommodate up to 24 guests. There are private bathrooms, a campsite with two showers and two toilets, a dining room, and a kitchen. They operate nature and cultural tours on the island and the gulf of Nicoya and rent bikes. In addition, they offer visits to other groups within the community in order to support their initiatives. One project that is directly supported is the craft project. When the association has groups, it takes them to the artisans' workshop or invites the artisans to display their art at the lodge. They are expanding their hosting services within the communities by recommending cabins of their neighbors as well. They have a home-stay network as well for groups or individuals that wish to volunteer on social projects in the community. Their target market includes visitors motivated by education, university research, voluntourism, and communing with local culture and nature (see **Figure CS 6.4**).

Figure CS 6.3   Blending with the landscape: the first cabin design.

Goals for the future include:

- To learn English.
- To implement a greenhouse of native trees of the dry forest to introduce a reforestation program in the area.

Figure CS 6.4   Visitor experiencing local flora.

- To improve the infrastructure by providing some single or double rooms. Current accommodations are not practical for smaller groups needing private rooms.
- To diversify the promotion and marketing channels to allow them to target people that respect their environment and community.
- To have consistent visitation throughout the year. The low season is a challenge.

This small group of women agrees that becoming a designated tourist destination, as some of Costa Rica's communities are, is not a concern. They would like to keep the rural authenticity that Chira offers. They are afraid of losing it as some other touristic destinations have experienced. In addition, they believe that by staying small scale, they will minimize their impact on the natural dry forest landscape. They also wish to keep their project affordable for Costa Ricans. The three women reject the notion of becoming an expensive traditional tourist destination in Costa Rica. They would rather represent the rural community from the perspective of a traditional natural and cultural landscape of a dry forest.

Women and Local Empowerment

The following summarizes some of the problems women faced when initiating this project:

- *Internal fears:* "The main obstacle was to face ourselves. It was like a soap opera." They mentioned feeling fear, insecurity, and uncertainty in learning new tasks and roles such as driving a boat (see **Figure CS 6.5**), traditionally a "man's job." This situation made them face their fears to experience change and handle difficulties.
- *Lack of building conditions:* At that time, there was no drinking water, electricity, and road access to the island. Infrastructure development was a big challenge. They had donations for the materials but not for the labor. They started building by themselves under very harsh conditions. For example, to work with concrete, water was brought from a well 600 meters away. They transported materials bought by boat, hired a truck, and carried the materials by foot the last 500 meters to the construction site. In addition to the physical construction work, they had duties during the evenings and took turns each week.

Figure CS 6.5 Women's empowerment through a tourism project.

- *Hard work and lack of income:* It was difficult to work the extra hours and maintain their households, construction, and guard duty. In addition, the minor income received came from 1-day tours only, which were barely enough to sustain their families.
- *Community rejection and gossip:* Initially, the local people stopped greeting the women in public and gossiped about them behind their backs. They were called "the crazy ladies" because they were doing jobs different from the cultural norm. These women were disappointed by the lack of community support; one woman received threats about reporting her to the national child's institute because she insisted on working outside her home.
- *Community rejection of tourism:* The community was against their tourism project because they believed that tourists would spoil the island with drugs, prostitution, and child kidnapping.
- *Resignations:* The three women felt bad when their partners began to leave the group, not only because there were fewer hands on the project but also because those former partners reverted back to the traditional "macho roles of staying at home taking care of hungry kids." They wanted a better quality of life for themselves and their partners.

The principal obstacles were primarily the scarcity of financial resources, community rejection, and resignation of the other women. However, the three women overcame the initial difficult beginning stage and gained strength from the experience in the end.

Women's Empowerment: Lessons Learned from the Obstacles

Overcoming the obstacles, the women learned to face adversity while taking advantage of the opportunities to grow personally. They recognized the strength they gained from the challenges they faced, which represents self-empowerment. This in turn led to self-confidence. The tourism project taught the women that they could achieve things if they tried hard enough.

> It has been marvelous to feel one-self empowered; to dream about things because we now have this infrastructure after having nothing more than mud under our nails, we see that it is possible to dream of more.

One person also stated that "in this life there are no barriers, when one really wants to fight for what one believes."

- *Addressing interpersonal relationships:* The women all agreed that fishing was very different from tourism. They mentioned that it is totally different working on the sea than working in tourism where they had to interact with diverse people. Therefore, one of the greatest challenges for them was learning how to deal with interpersonal relationships and talk to people from outside the island. They learned to speak with visitors and other stakeholders from the tourism projects from Costa Rica and Central America, the government, NGOs, university people, and suppliers of services and goods for their business services, such as banks, tour operators, and supply stores.
- *Community acknowledgment:* Nowadays many locals know the "women of the lodge." They are no longer referred to as the crazy ladies. The community now shows them respect.

Figure CS 6.6 Women's empowerment through local crafts.

- *Community benefits:* The women believe it is important that they benefit the community by "calling on the artisan women, buying eggs from a lady's farm, buying food at the corner store, buying gasoline for the boat and buying the fish directly from our husbands" (see **Figure CS 6.6**).
- *Team building:* The women realized that they could work together on projects regardless of the challenges they had, and that if they do not know how to do something, there will always be people and organizations to approach for help. The women learned how to take care of each other, to face problems together, and to rejoice together. The strength they give to each other and how it helps to empower themselves is important to them.
- *Income:* The women learned that it was worthwhile to follow their dream and work hard on the project. They realized that they were satisfying their children's needs by having money when necessary. Since their first payment, they felt the rewards of hard work because they could feed their kids. "There were 3000 colones left and we divided them by the six at that time. Therefore, we could buy a bag of rice. That was the first payment."
- *Conflict management:* The women learned that there would always be different opinions and conflicts. They learned not to remain silent but to discuss and resolve the conflicts. They learned to get along no matter their differences. Today they speak more openly about their conflicts.
- *Family leadership:* The women gained a leadership role in their families related to the income they make.
- *Capacity building:* They mentioned the importance of training (e.g., leadership, self-esteem, teamwork) to overcome obstacles related to participating in a capacity-building program. Based on their experiences, the project is successful because of their hard work as a team and their strong partnerships but also because they have invested donations wisely. They have seen many projects fail when the donor funding ran out.

These strengths are evidence of the personal growth that these women experienced as individuals. A summary of obstacles and strengths is illustrated in **Figure CS 6.7**. Before discussing how this growth affected the community, it is important to review the specific social and environmental impact caused by the women's experience participating in the ecotourism project.

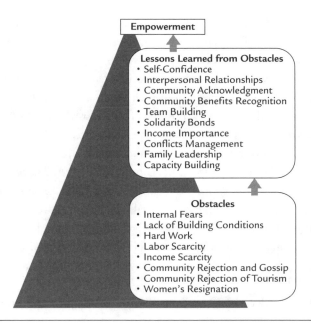

Figure CS 6.7   Women's empowerment framework: Chira Island, Costa Rica.

Social Impact

The social impact of the association includes benefits such as satisfaction of basic needs like food, clothing, housing, and leisure, followed by health care, education, and autonomy in decision making. This section does not include the larger influence on social issues of the community as a whole. The following are the initial individual and family results:

- *Basic needs:* The women now have monthly revenue that provides their families with food, clothing, house maintenance, and some recreational activities. In some cases, they can help their relatives or sustain their households alone when the fishing activity of their husbands takes a downturn.
- *Health care:* They have access to the national health system and are able to pay for insurance for the whole family. If they need to visit the clinic or the hospital in the city, they have the means to get there. When necessary, they also can afford private health care.
- *Education for themselves:* The women have had the opportunity to create a "career for life," as they call it, because they now feel confident that they have a job they were trained for. Concerning their own knowledge, they mentioned learning the following skills:

  - Hosting travelers
  - Guiding tours in the mangroves, for bird watching, in the dry forest, and in the community
  - Driving a motorboat
  - Providing interpretive talks about their own project history
  - Cleaning and decorating a room well and folding towels in different shapes
  - Participating in fairs and other public events
  - Traveling outside the island
  - Communicating via phone or directly with tourists

- *Education for their children:* Their children are now completing middle school, high school, and university courses. They have the financial resources to help and encourage their children to pursue a professional career.
- *Autonomy and decision-making:* This is self-evident among these women. Their opinions are well defined and independent from each other, and even when they disagree, they readily reconcile the differences. This is one of the most relevant signs of empowerment.
- *Social participation:* The women support the committee against drugs in the community. They received a certificate of recognition from the national institution in charge of working against destructive drugs in the country (the IAFA; *Instituto sobre Alcoholismo y Farmacodependencia de Costa Rica*—Drugs Dependence and Alcoholism Institute of Costa Rica). They participate in committees at local schools and churches. The community recognizes their participation not only with groups on the island but also that they exhibit the rural community project at national and international events.

Environmental Impact

Environmental impacts refer to CO_2 emissions, resource use, and educational impact. These results included:

- *Emissions and waste management:* Project guests are asked to remove their own waste and recycle, treat, or dispose of it off the island. Sometimes they are hesitant to ask their guests to take their garbage with them, but they recognized that this is something they must do. They have a worm compost project to process organic waste and to produce materials to use for growing vegetables. Most of their guests ask them not to change their beds and towels during their stay, a policy they plan to put into practice for all the guests.
- *Resource use at buildings and gardens:* The buildings were designed to fit the natural landscape. They continue to work on removing many exotic species in the gardens to stay true to their "keep it local" policy.
- *Use of water and energy:* They use solar stoves to cook most of their meals. Despite guests' requests, they believe they should not use water to fill a swimming pool because it is precious for the dry forest and it belongs to the community.
- *Active environmental group participation:* The women implement policies of the environmental initiative known as COVIRENAS. This is an official program through which the government trains citizens about the environment, and educates them on how to report illegal practices that damage the environment or violate environmental laws. From this training, the project women are more conscious of the resources they protect and the ways to protect them.

In addition, this group formed the first group of trained volunteer firefighters on the island. Fires are a constant threat to the forest, particularly in the dry season (February to April) when a small spark with little wind can destroy an entire forest. Because there were previously no firefighters, the women took initiative and got themselves trained as firefighters. They involved the local farmers in the training because they were quick to recognize the benefits.

These women took initiative to protect the natural resources of the island due to their participation in the ecotourism project. "The project has taught us to love nature. Therefore we care for our island and its mangroves." Their initiative and participation in active environmental actions on the island has had a positive impact on the community. Now, community members refer to them as the role models for local development.

Community Empowerment

Figure CS 6.8 illustrates the most relevant issues in the community empowerment process. These issues are described as follows:

- *Support to community organizations:* The direct support the women provide to the women's crafts group is an excellent example of community support. They call the group when they receive visitors or recommend individual visitors to visit the artisans association. This is a women's association that started in 2002 with the intention of generating income from local crafts. The group initially started with 35 women; 9 were successful in overcoming the initial obstacles of starting a business. They now have a building that accommodates their workshop and a store to sell arts and crafts. Although minimal, the revenue satisfies basic needs such as food and provides support for their children's schooling. The profitability of this project further illustrates empowerment, along with the social aspect of working together as a group of artisans. Other beneficiaries of tourism include fishermen, egg farm producers, vegetable and fruit stores, the public boat transporter, and the bus and staff they hire when they receive large groups or when they need to go off the island.
- *Influence on community behavior:* Although the women recognize their own self-empowerment, they see even greater change in the community over the past 10 years. They feel they have influenced positive changes in their community, including:

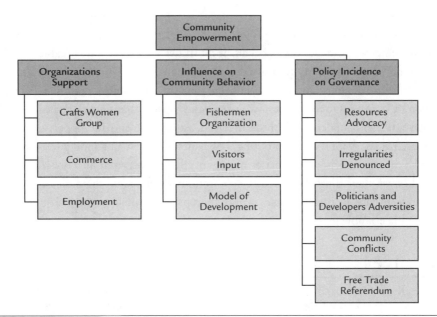

Figure CS 6.8   Community empowerment through the ecotourism project: Chira Island, Costa Rica.

- A fishermen's organization that manages coastal resources (coral reefs, fisheries, and mangroves). This collaborative effort is a result of the women's cooperative.
- Educated visitors to the project provide local incentive for advanced study to pursue professional careers and the desire for travel.
- Enhanced community pride. Project participants are proud of their efforts in lieu of public appreciation and acknowledgement of their efforts. The community recognizes the need for additional lodging projects similar to theirs, and consults with this group about future developments. Locals are following their environmental practice more readily than previously. It's important the projects belong to the *chireños* (people from Chira). They are proud to know their efforts have been worthwhile to their community, which gives them the most satisfaction. "More than my personal growth; the most important thing is to see this change in my community."

Policy on Governance

As COVIRENAS (citizen environmental rangers), these women are the caretakers of the island resources. They defeated an airport construction initiative because of potential damage to the mangroves. It was a difficult situation to handle that involved politicians and foreign investors. They faced external political advisors as well as those from the community. Later, a government institution in charge of the initiative stopped the airport construction. Those who initially wanted the project eventually changed their minds in support of the women caretakers. This is a political manifestation because this group stood up to defend their principles for community development and defend the island's natural resources.

Conclusion

This case study illustrates how a small project can transform a community, even if there are just three people empowered to act on its behalf. It illustrates how three individuals as a collective unit can empower a community to provoke positive change for a community, despite political adversity. This case demonstrates how sustainable tourism can improve poor living conditions. In addition, it is relevant to recognize how income and capacity-building programs can enhance self-esteem and self-confidence for those involved. Autonomy and the opportunity to make decisions are necessary for social networking, policy development, and local governance.

These women initially sought a better quality of life in their attempt to extend benefits to their families, yet their efforts benefited the community overall amid the difficulties they faced and continue to face in their struggle against the obstacles. Their positive attitudes in these efforts set a life example for everyone.

References

Bonilla Moya, M. (2008). Respuestas del mercado al turismo rural comunitario en Costa Rica: Diversificando la oferta nacional. Revista TECNITUR de ACOPROT. San José, Costa Rica. Retrieved April 5, 2012, from http://www.greenactioncr.com/downloads/Respuestas_Mercado.pdf

Health, Welfare, and Well-Being

The Role of Sustainable Tourism in Mitigating HIV/AIDS, Malaria, and Other Major Diseases

Keri A. Schwab, Daniel L. Dustin, and Kelly S. Bricker

LEARNING OBJECTIVES

- To explore the interrelationships between sustainable tourism and disease mitigation
- To learn about ways in which tourism can help mitigate the spread of disease
- To understand the power of tourism to affect positive change with respect to disease mitigation

For better or worse, tourism is going to play an increasingly important role in global affairs. Although the world itself is finite, increasing numbers of people are going to populate the world, and travel to and fro is going to make it possible for the world's peoples to get to know one another and impact one another in ways we have yet to imagine. The prospect of an international community increasingly transmigrating and transmingling brings with it reasons for optimism and pessimism. The optimism resides in the possibility that tourism, when practiced sustainably, can lead to greater cross-cultural understanding, peace, and prosperity. The pessimism resides in the possibility that tourism, when practiced unsustainably, can lead to cross-cultural misunderstanding, disease, and poverty.

Nowhere is this dual-edged prospect more pronounced than in the context of human and environmental health. Sustainable tourism can promote health in its broadest ecological sense, whereas unsustainable tourism can promote disease in its broadest ecological sense. This is because tourists, wittingly or unwittingly, are "carriers" of things good and bad for themselves, their host culture, and the environment that nourishes them all. Much like migratory birds that carry new beginnings in the form of seeds they transport from one continent to another, tourists also carry new beginnings and new seeds of one sort or another as they crisscross the globe.

The purpose of this chapter is to discuss how sustainable tourism should be managed to ensure that tourists are carriers of good things rather than bad things. Specifically, we examine the role of sustainable tourism in mitigating HIV/AIDS, malaria, and other major diseases. We then move from the specific question of disease mitigation to the more general question of sustainable tourism's role in health promotion. This requires us to define what we mean by "health" at the chapter's outset, and then to illustrate how sustainable tourism can contribute to the kind of health we have in mind. We conclude the chapter by offering some guidelines for the delivery of sustainable tourist practices to assist tourism professionals in the work they do in the name of health promotion.

An Ecological Model of Health Promotion

In a recent issue of *Leisure Sciences* (Dustin, Bricker, & Schwab, 2010), the authors of this chapter conceptualized a new way of thinking about health that combines its human and environmental dimensions. We characterized our thinking as an "ecological model of health promotion" and we described what we perceive to be health's symbiotic nature. We reasoned that people cannot be healthy in an unhealthy environment, and an environment cannot be healthy if it is populated by unhealthy people.

Our ecological model of health promotion (see **Figure 5.1**) is useful as an organizing principle for discussing the interrelationships and interdependencies that characterize human/environment interactions as they play out in the context of sustainable tourism. The model makes it easier to visualize the complex array of linkages that tie humans to each other as well as to the environment. It indicates how individual health affects family health, how family health affects community health, how community health affects national health, how national health affects international health, and back again. The model also suggests that ecosystem health underpins human health and that human health impacts ecosystem health. In sum, an ecological model of health promotion

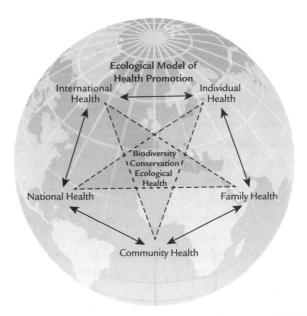

Figure 5.1   An ecological model of health promotion.
Source: Reproduced from Dustin, D., Bricker, K., & Schwab, K. (2010). People and nature: Toward an ecological model of health promotion. *Leisure Sciences, 32*(1), 3–14.

conveys a sense of the highly complex web of interrelationships and interdependencies that characterize health's symbiotic nature. As we concluded in our *Leisure Sciences* article, "Health, from an ecological perspective, is a measure of the wellness of the individual and the community considered together" (Dustin et al., 2010, p. 7).

The relevance of our ecological model of health promotion to a discussion of touristic practices rests on the inference that, when practiced sustainably, tourism can deliver health-related benefits from people to the environment, and the environment, in turn, can deliver health-related benefits to people. The potential for this reciprocal relationship to make a lasting positive impact on the world's overall health is heartening, and nowhere is the potential good that can come from this complex mix of mutually beneficial relationships more evident than in a discussion of sustainable tourism's role in mitigating HIV/AIDS, malaria, and other major diseases.

Disease in the Context of Tourism

We begin this discussion with the unsettling reminder that tourism can be a negative as well as a positive force in health promotion. Indeed, most of the tourism literature related to HIV/AIDS, malaria, and other major diseases focuses on tourism's role in spreading disease, not in stopping it. Consequently, before we consider sustainable tourism's potential for disease mitigation, it is necessary to consider ways in which tourism, as it is commonly conceived, perpetuates disease. In so doing, we will better understand what needs to be changed in the tourism industry to make it more sustainable and health promoting.

HIV/AIDS

Human immunodeficiency virus (HIV) causes acquired immune deficiency syndrome (AIDS). It is one of the most serious diseases facing the world today, and sub-Saharan Africa and the Caribbean are regions of the world most affected by HIV/AIDS. They also are regions of the world heavily visited by tourists. HIV/AIDS is spread through sexual contact, and drug and alcohol use exacerbate the risks of contracting HIV/AIDS. Research suggests that tourists on holiday adopt a more carefree and devil-may-care attitude when it comes to sexual conduct, which heightens their vulnerability to contracting or spreading HIV/AIDS. Whether they are infecting themselves or others, individuals engaging in "sexual tourism" are prime candidates to carry HIV/AIDS home with them, leave the disease in the host country, or pass it on to other countries as well. The spread of HIV/AIDS in this manner is a prime example of tourists as "carriers" of bad things. Knowingly or not, they return home from their touristic experience worse, rather than better, for the wear.

Just as sad, the spread of HIV/AIDS in the host country contributes to a relentless downward cultural, economic, and environmental spiral. It has been estimated, for example, that 67% of all people in the world living with HIV/AIDS reside in sub-Saharan Africa (U.S. Department of Health and Human Services [USDHHS], 2011). This means shortened life spans, confinement to poverty, and the likelihood that the virus will live on in generations of children yet unborn. What starts out as a solitary act of irresponsibility is soon written large as a social problem of the highest magnitude. The negative effect on the health of the ecosystem at large is devastating.

Ironically, tourism professionals are reluctant to own up to this connection between HIV/AIDS and tourism because of what bad publicity might mean for business. The tourism industry thus becomes complicit in the spread of HIV/AIDS and thereby opens itself up for criticism regarding its failure to live up to its ethical and professional obligations (Padilla, Guilamo-Ramos, Bouris, & Reyes, 2010). Clearly, there is much work to do in clarifying the tourism profession's "standard of care" when it comes to protecting the health of tourists, tourism providers, the host community, and the surrounding environs. By not assuming a leadership role, the tourism industry risks having its tourist destinations turn into breeding grounds for HIV/AIDS (Padilla et al., 2010).

Malaria

Malaria presents a different kind of problem. Unlike HIV/AIDS, which is human induced, malaria is a disease the environment inflicts on people by way of mosquitoes. Once again, sub-Saharan Africa and other tropical climes are prime breeding grounds for mosquitoes that carry the parasite causing malaria. Tourists visiting these regions of the world who do not take the necessary medical precautions are particularly susceptible to contracting the disease. And although most Western travelers survive malaria, it ravages impoverished Third World peoples, especially children. It is estimated that more than 300 million people are afflicted with malaria every year worldwide, resulting in 1 million deaths (Roll Back Malaria, 2006). Ninety percent of the cases are in sub-Saharan Africa.

Like HIV/AIDS, the threat of contracting malaria is a deterrent to tourism and consequently has serious negative effects on local economies. It has been estimated, for example, that the gross domestic product (GDP) of some African countries would be 30% greater than it is today without the specter of malaria, and that malaria reduces the GDP of Africa by US$12 billion a year (Gallup & Sachs, 2001). The detrimental rippling effects on the physical and economic health of Third World peoples are staggering, and those effects are intensifying.

The combination of global warming and vector-borne (insect-carried) diseases that require warm climates for carriers (mosquitoes and other insects) to thrive is also expanding the range of countries now at risk for contracting malaria. Europe, for example, once considered to be malaria-free, has seen a 10-fold increase in outbreaks over the past 30 years (World Health Organization Regional Office for Europe, 2007). Malaria also is spreading across Asia, and Southeast Asia now has the highest incidence of drug-resistant malaria (Roll Back Malaria, 2006). Although malaria is not endemic in the United States, the threat of contracting the disease is expected to grow due to increasing international tourism and changes in migration patterns (Centers for Disease Control and Prevention [CDC], 2006a). Of the 1,300 cases of malaria reported in the United States every year, most are attributed to travelers to other malaria-endemic regions of the world (CDC, 2006b). Nevertheless, the prospect of malaria becoming endemic in the United States, especially in the warmer southern states, is likely to increase with climate change (Rogers & Randolph, 2000).

Deforestation also exacerbates the malaria problem in the world's tropical areas. Deforestation creates new edges and interfaces between undisturbed forest ecosystems and human developments, which in turn create new breeding grounds for a variety of vector groups, including *Anopheles*, the mosquito species that transmits the malaria parasite (Molyneux, Ostfeld, Bernstein, & Chivian, 2008). Essentially, deforestation brings the mosquito carrier and humankind into closer proximity, which heightens the opportunity for infection. These edges and interfaces are frequently prime locations for eco-lodges and other tourism enterprises that are designed to put people in close contact with nature. Even more disturbingly, research has shown that the destruction of forest habitat can favor the replacement of more benign vector species with more effective disease vectors like *Anopheles* (Walsh, Molyneux, & Birley, 1993). Once again, this complex web of relationships illustrates how human health and environmental health are intertwined.

Other Major Diseases

HIV/AIDS and malaria, although monumental in their impact on the ecology of human and environmental health, are by no means the only diseases that plague the tourism industry. One need only think of the recent outbreaks of West Nile virus in the United States brought on by mosquitoes and infected migratory birds. The West Nile virus now is present in mosquitoes and birds in every state in the continental United States (National Institute of Allergies and Infectious Diseases, 2007). Other highly debilitating diseases that threaten tourists throughout the world are cholera (transmitted through contaminated food and water), Lyme disease (transmitted through bites from infected ticks), salmonellosis (transmitted through contaminated food and water), severe acute respiratory syndrome (SARS; transmission method not entirely clear), and yellow fever (transmitted through bites by infected mosquitoes). These, and a multitude of other serious diseases, are potential "carry-on baggage" for anyone who is part of the rapidly expanding population of global travelers (Molyneux et al., 2008, pp. 289–293).

As the world gets "smaller," and as people from all walks of life travel more and more internationally, opportunities to unintentionally spread disease are bound to multiply. As we have seen, the deleterious effects of disease on tourists, the host culture, and the larger ecosystem are far ranging and long lasting. And although tourism is by no means the only accomplice to this cavalcade of unhealthy events, the tourism industry does have a professional obligation—indeed an ethical obligation—to assume a leadership role in mitigating the spread of disease through the work it does. It is to this daunting challenge that we now turn.

Sustainable Tourism's Role in Disease Mitigation

We should reiterate at this juncture that tourism's role in mitigating disease is a shared international responsibility. Having said that, we believe the tourism profession is well-suited to assist in achieving the United Nations' Millennium Development Goals (MDGs) (United Nations Department of Economic and Social Affairs, 2010), which include combating HIV/AIDS, malaria, and other diseases (MDG 6), the topic of this chapter. But as we have shown via our ecological model of health promotion, the factors that contribute to increasing incidence of disease across the globe are also interrelated, including poverty and hunger (the elimination of which is MDG 1), lack of universal education (the eradication of which is MDG 2), gender equality, and child and maternal health care (the attainment of which is incorporated in MDGs 3, 4, and 5), environmental sustainability (the assurance of which is embodied in MDG 7), and the need to work together to solve the world's multifaceted problems (MDG 8). All of these issues are interconnected and they must be addressed simultaneously. That, in turn, requires an unprecedented degree of international cooperation and collaboration.

Assuming a Leadership Role

Tourism professionals are ideal candidates for taking the lead in working toward the United Nations' MDGs for a variety of reasons. First and foremost, they are "on the ground" working closely with indigenous peoples to provide tourism services to visitors from afar. Second, they understand host cultures as well as the visitors' cultures. They are in a good position to mediate cultural differences, to educate about cultural differences, and to facilitate enhanced cross-cultural understanding. Third, their strategic position as go-betweens provides a readymade educational forum for discussing all eight of the United Nations' MDGs, including the goal of combating HIV/AIDS, malaria, and other diseases. They are, then, in the midst of the unfolding of everything the United Nations wants to change. They are on the cutting edge.

Are tourism professionals up to the challenge? To take on such a leadership role and to do justice to it requires a highly educated cadre of professionals who understand the workings of the vast web of ecological interrelationships and interdependencies, and who can effectively communicate the implications of that ecological reality to the constituencies they serve—customers, service providers, host communities, and host nations. Their motivation, of course, can be driven merely by wanting to stay in business, and by understanding that deteriorating health is bad for business and that it threatens their livelihood. Or their motivation can be driven by higher sensibilities—for example, wanting to make the world a better place. Either way, the work to be done is critical and urgent.

Developing an Ecologically Based Business Model

Recognizing that tourism is a business, it also is appropriate at this point in our discussion to encourage tourism professionals to revisit the notion of the "bottom line." It is common to think of the bottom line in terms of the residual dollars and cents left over (i.e., profit) after the costs of production are deducted from revenues generated. It is also customary to think of the bottom line in quarterly increments, as if taking the "temperature" of the business every 3 months gives a good indication of how the business is faring. But if there is one lesson to be learned from our ecological model of health promotion, it is that the bottom line is really about ensuring the long-term viability of a region to deliver health benefits on a sustainable basis. Consequently, when taking the long view, it profits the tourism industry to do everything in its power to conduct its business in a way that guarantees good health in its broadest ecological context over the long haul. It is a form of selfishness wrapped in selflessness. It is a business model that sustainable tourism would do well to embrace.

Sustainable Tourism's Role in Health Promotion

The tourism industry has an important role to play in fostering sustainable tourism in a way that also promotes health. Sitting at the crossroads of tourism employees, travelers, and government agencies, the tourism industry is ideally situated to mitigate the spread of HIV/AIDS, malaria, and other major diseases. Fulfilling this responsibility can take place in three ways: educating and protecting tourism workers, educating travelers, and collaborating with government agencies, ministries, and healthcare providers to create policies and practices that promote health.

Working from Within: Caring for Tourism Employees

A first step in promoting health and mitigating the spread of major diseases through tourism is to address practices regarding education and mitigation efforts among tourism employees. Travel industry workers are at high risk for exposure to HIV/AIDS for a variety of reasons, including misperceptions about disease transmission, lack of access to education or health care, and promiscuous behaviors while working with foreign clients. Tourism professionals can begin mitigating the spread of disease by educating their own employees about the health risks attendant to each of these areas.

Many tourism employees working in developing nations do not have access to formal education and may have misperceptions about the spread or prevention of HIV/AIDS and other diseases. Further, such misperceptions can lead to stigmatization and mistreatment of workers who do have diseases, causing many workers either to not reveal their diagnosis and risk further spread of the disease or to leave the workforce altogether. A study of Egyptian workers found that employees often held misperceptions about the spread of disease, such as thinking HIV could be transmitted through insects, shaking hands, or sharing utensils. The study also found that some workers afflicted with HIV/AIDS ultimately quit their job because they experienced stigmatization from other staff members (El-Sayyed, Kabbash, & El-Gueniedy, 2008).

The tourism industry should be more proactive in mitigating the spread of HIV/AIDS and other diseases by providing accurate information about disease transmission, prevention, and treatment to its workers. Tourism operators should provide education pamphlets in a variety of languages informing staff members about disease transmission and prevention, and place posters in employee break rooms, living quarters, and offices. Tourism operators should also invite doctors or other medical professionals to provide in-house informational sessions or health clinics to answer questions and provide medical advice for tourism workers. Such informational sessions and increased knowledge may help correct misperceptions about the transmission of diseases and reduce fear and stigmatization among tourism workers. Finally, discouraging staff members from engaging in sex with one another while on duty or having sex with tourists can help mitigate the spread of disease.

Another reason HIV/AIDS may spread more easily among tourism workers is due to promiscuous behaviors. Many employees, especially in developing countries, leave their remote villages and families to find work in urban tourist destinations. Research has found that tourism workers far away from their loved ones are more likely to engage in extramarital affairs or have sex with tourists or with members of the local population and then possibly carry a disease back to their spouse. One possible remedy is for tourism operators to provide family housing, or to employ married couples together in order to prevent unsafe sexual behaviors (Forsythe, 1999).

Tourism operators can take several measures to help protect their staff. One step in helping to mitigate the spread of sexually transmitted diseases is for tourism operators to provide basic sex education and condoms to all workers along with information on how to correctly use condoms (Orisatoki, Oguntibeju, & Truter, 2009). Although cultural norms and traditions must be considered when discussing sex, condom use is one of the best ways to prevent the spread of HIV/AIDS and other sexually transmitted diseases. To prevent the spread of nonsexually transmitted diseases, such as malaria, tourism operators can provide mosquito nets, clean water, sanitary living quarters, and access to preventative health care, including time off to visit local health clinics, to all staff. Although these preventative healthcare measures might cost more up front, in the long run they will prevent the spread of disease and help lower staff turnover.

Health Promotion and Education Among Tourists

Tourists themselves constitute the second major group to be educated. They are the primary carriers of disease from one country to another. Historically, tourism operators, ministries, and government agencies have been reluctant to engage in this kind of education because they have felt that providing educational information about disease prevention might scare off tourists and jeopardize the much-needed economic boost tourism provides to developing nations (Forsythe, 1999).

Mixing tourism and public education about the HIV/AIDS epidemic has been called a "controversial business" (Lewis & Bailey, 1992/1993) in the tourism literature. Some researchers have noted that increased public education efforts about the existence of diseases in foreign countries have led to increased xenophobia or fear of foreigners from that country or toward locals when outsiders visit. Because so many developing nations rely on the tourism industry to create jobs and support the economy, many governments are hesitant to reveal the extent of communicable diseases in the country, or to provide public education or awareness campaigns about diseases. Some governments are also afraid xenophobia will extend further than tourism into business and foreign investments (Lewis & Bailey, 1992/1993). However, this lack of public education and accurate information only serves to allow diseases and misinformation about transmission and prevention to continue to spread.

Educating the public does not have to be at the expense of tourism; rather, it can help promote tourism by providing strategies that empower visitors to take their own precautions. Rather than fear public education and assume negative effects on the perception of a country, the tourism industry is well positioned to help change beliefs and attitudes about disease and potentially help end the risky behaviors that lead to disease transmission. Tourist education can start with travel agent Web-based services and guide books used to make travel plans. A critical first step in empowering tourists involves taking advantage of these outlets to let travelers know about the increased risk of disease transmission when engaging in certain behaviors while traveling.

A good strategy would be to educate travelers about the distinction between risky behaviors and risky places. For example, unprotected sex or sharing intravenous needles are risky behaviors that can be engaged in anywhere. They represent poor behavioral choices, not poor destination choices. Emphasizing behaviors rather than places moves the focus off the country as the place of danger and puts the onus on the traveler to take his or her own precautions when traveling abroad. A study of travelers to Thailand, for example, found that tourists supported the idea of receiving more information about disease epidemics so they could protect themselves while visiting the country. This desire for additional information indicates that knowledge about disease prevalence may not drive tourists away but rather lead to a desire for increased knowledge about disease prevention (Forsythe, 1999). Host countries willing and ready to share this information may actually boost tourism while at the same time slowing the spread of disease. Indeed, the state of Hawaii provided information to tourists demonstrating that HIV/AIDS cannot be spread through insects, a toilet seat, or a lei greeting and then provided positive and accurate information about transmission through unprotected sex (Lewis & Bailey, 1992/1993).

An additional consideration when educating the public is that all information must be culturally sensitive and reflect the values and norms of both the host country and the tourist groups targeted by the message. This can be a complicated process when trying to address a population that is a mix of religions, gender roles, and social values. For example, because of the strong influence of Christian churches, open discussion of sex and sexuality in most Pacific countries is uncomfortable, yet the topic must be discussed if the spread of diseases is to be stopped.

Finally, the notion of tourism needs to be expanded to include all travelers who move between cities and countries. Military personnel, fishermen, truck drivers, residents or students returning from an extended stay abroad, diplomats, mission workers, international volunteers, or those working for foreign aid agencies also need to receive disease mitigation information (Lewis & Bailey, 1992/1993). All traveler groups need appropriate education about personal safety while traveling as well as an understanding of the prevalence and transmission of disease among travelers.

An Ecological Approach to Health Promotion

When problems exist that involve many intertwined aspects of a country—such as health, economics, employment, and education—multiple stakeholders will need to be involved to create and implement effective disease prevention measures. An ecological perspective provides a good vantage point from which government agencies can think about the relationships among health, education, economies, communities, and individuals. Such complex systemic interrelationships require collaborative systemic responses.

Governmental agencies should welcome partnerships among ministries of health, tourism, and education, as well as collaborations with businesses in the private sector, such as tourism operators. Such collaborations can help everyone involved better understand the relationships among tourism, public health, and the economy; how these relationships are playing out in their locality; and how to best work together to mitigate the spread of disease. For example, the Ministry of Tourism in Barbados recently worked closely with the Barbados Hotel and Tourism Association and the National HIV/AIDS Commission to draft a policy that reduces discrimination and stigma, and promotes supportive services and education among tourism workers about the transmission and prevention of HIV/AIDS. In thinking about the final draft, the Deputy Chairman of the National HIV/AIDS Commission noted that views and opinions from all industries, including government, transportation, tourism, trade unions, and all subsectors, were critical in helping craft an effective policy (Hutchinson, 2011).

Understanding that a nation can only be healthy if its communities are healthy, and communities can only be healthy if individuals are healthy, governmental agencies and those in the tourism sector would be well-advised to begin collaborating in several ways to create policies that help mitigate the spread of disease in individuals, communities, and nations. First, government agencies should work with the private sector to create policies that protect all workers in the tourism industry. The current draft policy in Barbados is a good example of government efforts to acknowledge the importance of all workers, including those living with HIV/AIDS. It emphasizes the need to reduce stigma and discrimination in the workplace, and anchor all prevention efforts in evidence-based research with a results-focused orientation. Second, collaborating agencies must commit to public awareness campaigns that provide adequate and accurate information about diseases that do not under-report disease rates or dangers. One study of health policies in the Caribbean suggested that HIV/AIDS awareness campaigns that emphasized the benefits of prevention and safe sex would be well-received among tourists and local tourism workers (Cessens & Gin, 1994; Padilla, Reyes, Connolly, Natsui, Puello, & Chapman, 2011). Third, government agencies should consider not supporting the sex industry, or offering protection for sex workers if the industry is supported. Many studies have found that political leaders often directly or indirectly support the sex-tourism industry (Orisatoki et al., 2009). At a minimum, government agencies should regulate the sex industry. In Antigua, for example, "houses of entertainment" are reviewed regularly by government health officers who make sure workers and clients are regularly tested, treated, and given condoms. Finally, policies should be enacted that ensure equal employment opportunities for men and women in a variety of fields. Policies relating to disease prevention among tourism workers must address equality between the sexes and the often limited opportunities for women in many counties to have a voice in their government or even their personal relationships, and to choose from a variety of occupations (Lewis & Bailey, 1992/1993).

Any governmental interventions must be chosen, planned, and implemented carefully so as not to ignore certain groups or further perpetuate stereotypes or stigmatizations. When implementing any intervention, governmental agencies need to be aware of the local context in which the problem or situation occurs, and the local groups with whom they are working. There are often specific and unique underlying beliefs and attitudes that perpetuate a problem. Talking to local leaders or locals affected by the spread of diseases should provide better insights into how to effectively implement interventions and create conditions necessary for change. A good strategy is not to just listen to "crisis narratives" about health and poverty but to listen to all stories that help ferret out underlying problems and create appropriate and useful interventions (Steele, Oviedo, & McCauley, 2007).

Parting Thought

It is easy to be overwhelmed by the sheer magnitude of the problems associated with the spread of HIV/AIDS, malaria, and other major diseases. It is equally easy to assume tourism can offer little in the way of disease mitigation. Yet as ecologist Garrett Hardin admonishes us, we should never globalize a problem if it can be dealt with locally (Hardin, 1985). If individual tourism professionals each makes a difference in his or her own immediate sphere of influence, the cumulative effect on the prevention and mitigation of HIV/AIDS, malaria, and other major diseases will be felt globally. It is a daunting challenge, but it is a challenge that can be met through cooperation and collaboration between the private and public sectors within countries, and through cooperation and collaboration among countries. If carried out with conviction, the end result will be not only a healthier and more sustainable tourism industry but also a healthier and more sustainable planet.

References

Centers for Disease Control and Prevention (CDC). (2006a). *Areas where malaria is no longer endemic.* Atlanta: National Center for Infectious Diseases.

Centers for Disease Control and Prevention (CDC). (2006b). *Malaria surveillance: United States, 2004.* Atlanta: National Center for Infectious Diseases.

Cessens, J., & Gin, S. (1994). Tourism and AIDS: The perceived risk of HIV infection on destination choice. *Journal of Travel and Tourism Marketing, 3*(4), 1–20.

Dustin, D., Bricker, K., & Schwab, K. (2010). People and nature: Toward an ecological model of health promotion. *Leisure Sciences, 32*(1), 3–14.

El-Sayyed, N., Kabbash, I. A., & El-Gueniedy, M. (2008). Knowledge, attitude and practices of Egyptian industrial and tourism workers towards HIV/AIDS. *Eastern Mediterranean Health Journal, 14*(5), 1126–1135.

Forsythe, S. (1999). HIV/AIDS and tourism. *AIDS Analysis Africa, 9*(6), 4–6.

Gallup, J., & Sachs, J. (2001). *The economic burden of malaria.* Cambridge, MA: Harvard University.

Hardin, G. (1985). *Filters against folly: How to survive despite economists, ecologists, and the merely eloquent.* New York: Viking.

Hutchinson, N. (2011). *One step forward for tourism workplace HIV/AIDS policy.* Bridgetown, Barbados: Barbados Government Information Service.

Lewis, N. D., & Bailey, J. (1992/1993). HIV, international travel and tourism: Global issues and Pacific perspectives. *Asia-Pacific Journal of Public Health, 6*(3), 159–167.

Molyneux, D., Ostfeld, R., Bernstein, A., & Chivian, E. (2008). Ecosytem disturbance, biodiversity loss, and human infectious disease. In: E. Chivian & A. Bernstein (Eds.), *Sustaining life: How human health depends on biodiversity* (pp. 287–323). New York: Oxford University Press.

National Institute of Allergies and Infectious Diseases. (2007). *NIAD research on West Nile virus*. Bethesda, MD: National Institutes of Health.

Orisatoki, R. O., Oguntibeju, O. O., & Truter, E. J. (2009). The contributing role of tourism in the HIV/AIDS epidemic in the Caribbean. *Nigerian Journal of Medicine, 18*(2), 143–148.

Padilla, M., Guilamo-Ramos, V., Bouris, A., & Reyes, A. (2010). HIV/AIDS and tourism in the Caribbean: An ecological systems perspective. *American Journal of Public Health, 100*(1), 70–77.

Padilla, M. B., Reyes, A. M., Connolly, M., Natsui, S., Puello, A., & Chapman, H. (2011). Examining the policy climate for HIV prevention in the Caribbean tourism sector: A qualitative study of policy makers in the Dominican Republic. *Health and Policy Planning*, 1–11.

Rogers, D., & Randolph, S. (2000). The global spread of malaria in a future, warmer world. *Science, 289*(5485), 1763–1766.

Roll Back Malaria. (2006). *World malaria report 2005*. Geneva, Switzerland: World Health Organization.

Steele, P., Oviedo, G., & McCauley, D. (Eds). (2007). *Poverty, health, and ecosystems: Experience from Asia*. Gland, Switzerland, & Manila, Philippines: IUCN & Asian Development Bank.

U.S. Department of Health and Human Services (USDHHS). (2011). Global AIDS overview. Retrieved December 1, 2012, from http://www.aids.gov/federal-resources/around-the-world/global-aids-overview

United Nations Department of Economic and Social Affairs. (2010). *The Millennium Development Goals report 2010*. New York: Author.

Walsh, J., Molyneux, D., & Birley, M. (1993). Deforestation—effects on vector-borne disease. *Parasitology, 106*, S55–S75.

World Health Organization Regional Office for Europe. (2007). *Malaria in the WHO European region*. Copenhagen, Denmark: Author.

Yasawan Islanders' Perspective on Tourism's Impact on Health and Well-Being

Kelly S. Bricker and Deborah L. Kerstetter

LEARNING OBJECTIVES

- To understand the links between biodiversity conservation and community health and well-being
- To understand the impact of tourism on community health and well-being
- To learn how rural Fijians perceive the impact of tourism in small island communities

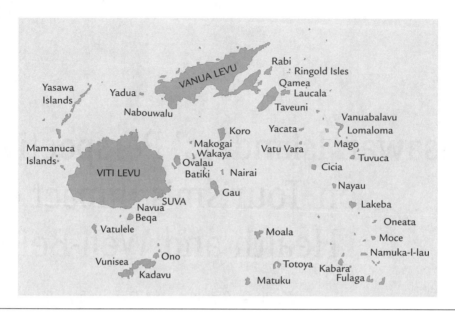

Figure 6.1   Republic of Fiji.

Tourism is the number one foreign exchange earner in the Republic of Fiji (Fiji Department of Tourism, 2007). After the 2000 coup, visitor arrivals increased 12%, on average, from 2002 to 2005 (Fiji Islands Business, 2006). In 2010, 631,868 tourists visited Fiji, generating earnings of nearly 980 million Fijian dollars (FD). The Fiji Visitors Bureau predicts that this growth will continue, allowing for a reduction in poverty and support for rural economies throughout the 332+ islands within the nation (see **Figure 6.1**) (World Bank, 2011).

Although the economic well-being of tourism appears to be steadily increasing, what are the implications for local residents' quality of life? More specifically, what are residents' perceptions of tourism and its impact on their quality of life? To answer these questions, we begin this chapter by discussing tourism in the Yasawa Islands (the western region of Fiji). Then, we follow with a review of the Millennium Development Goals (MDGs) in Fiji and literature regarding the connections between tourism and quality of life. We end the chapter by reviewing the results of a case study that provides insight into residents' quality of life and well-being in one area of the Yasawas—the Nacula Tikina.

Yasawa Islands

The Yasawa Islands (or Yasawas) chain lies northwest of the main island of Fiji, Viti Levu, and encompasses 6 primary islands and approximately 60 smaller islands, islets, and sandy cays (see **Figure 6.2**). The population of the Yasawas was estimated at 5,465 during the last census (Fiji Bureau of Statistics, 2007).

The people of the Yasawas live in traditional villages where they share customary land and are surrounded by their kin. Villagers pay homage to hereditary chiefs and observe many cultural traditions, including a cooperative approach to major tasks such as building homes, construction of churches, and certain types of planting and fishing.[1]

Over the past 20 years, the Yasawas has seen significant growth in the provision of backpacker-type accommodations. This is due in part to a concerted effort on the part of the Fiji Visitors Bureau (FVB) to increase visitor arrivals (Fiji Visitors Bureau, 2006). Today there are nearly 40 resorts in the Yasawas. Of the 40 resorts, 32 are community-based (i.e., the community is responsible for the management and maintenance of the resort), and most are directly linked to villages (Kerstetter & Bricker, 2009). Further, the Yasawas now host over 545,000 visitors per year (Fiji Department of Tourism, 2007), in part due to the advent of reliable transportation (i.e., Awesome Adventures Catamaran, the Yasawa Flyer).

Although the Yasawas have experienced economic growth, the infrastructure has not kept pace. There is an inadequate amount of fresh water; a lack of sewage treatment facilities (as of 2007, only two resorts had proper primary treatment and sustainable disposal); no coordinated solid waste disposal program; a number of unlicensed resorts, which impacts the quality and consistency of services; social tension among community members and resort development investors; a lack of funding for capital improvements; and additional problems (Fiji Department of Tourism, 2007). These issues—relevant to the pillars of sustainable development—may influence residents' relationship with their island environment.

Fortunately, the development issues faced by residents of the Yasawas have been noticed by the Department of Tourism. Through a consultation process, the department has developed a vision for the future. In response, a portion of the overall vision for the tourism industry within the Yasawas addresses a sustainable approach to tourism. It includes, but is not limited to, being an industry that embraces the social and cultural traditions and practices of all peoples of Fiji; supporting conservation and reducing its ecological footprint; and supporting poverty alleviation, reducing urban migration, and assisting in regional prosperity (Fiji Department of Tourism, 2007).

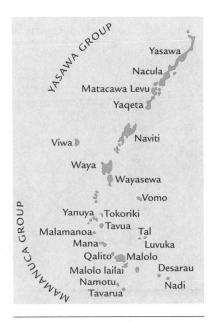

Figure 6.2   Yasawa Island group, including the Nacula Tikina.

The Nacula Tikina

The Nacula Tikina is a local governmental region of the Yasawa Island chain. A *tikina* is composed of several *koro* or villages, each with its own headman or *Turaga ni Koro* (United Nations Economic and Social Commission for Asia and the Pacific [UN ESCAP], 2011). When two or more *tikina* combine, they form a province. The Nacula Tikina, which has experienced an

---

[1] Nacula Tikina Tourism Association. (2005, May 1). Personal communication with Andrew Fairley, Secretary.

Table 6.1   Lodges and Resorts Within the Nacula Tikina

Island	Village	Lodge/Resort
Nacula Island	Nacula*	Oarsman's Bay Lodge
	Navotua	Blue Lagoon Beach Resort
	Malakati*	Nabua Lodge
Tavewa Island	—	Coral View Resort
		Otto and Fanny's
Nanuya Lailai	—	Nanuya Island Resort
		Sunrise Lagoon Resort
		Seaspray Resort
		Gold Coast Resort
Matacakawa Levu	Matacakawalevu*	Long Beach Resort
	Vuaki*	Bay of Plenty Resort
Yaqeta	Yaqeta*	Navutu Stars

* Villages included in the Tourism Quality of Life study.

increased number of backpacker-type accommodations (see **Table 6.1**) and attendant social and environmental impacts, formed the Nacula Tikina Tourism Association (NTTA). The vision for the Association is:

> To be a Tikina in which every village operates profitable and responsible tourism related businesses, enabling development in the Tikina of enduring education and health infrastructure, delivery of financial benefits to families, and the establishment of ongoing economic independence for each village.[1]

As stated in its mission statement, the NTTA is committed to many aspects of quality of life for its residents. From economic to health and education benefits, the NTTA sees tourism as a vehicle for positive change in its communities.

Millennium Development Goals in Fiji

In 2010, the Ministry of National Planning (MNP) reported on the status of the MDGs for the country. The report provided an overview of Fiji's national status on eight priority areas within the MDGs. The report concluded that despite scarce resources, Fiji had progressed well in achieving five of its eight goals (Fiji Ministry of National Planning [MNP], 2010, p. i). The three MDGs that remain in question are MDG 1 (eradicating poverty), MDG 3 (promoting gender equality and empowering women), and MDG 6 (combating HIV/AIDS and other diseases) (see **Table 6.2**).

Concerning MDG 1 and MDG 6, the ministry has concluded that Fiji is unlikely to achieve both goals. With respect to poverty, it has increased from around 25% in 1990 to around 40% in 2008 (MNP, 2010). HIV/AIDS, on the other hand, which is at a low level overall, has

Table 6.2   Status of Fiji's MDGs and Targets

Number of Targets	Targets for 2015	Status: Will Target Be Met?	State of Supportive Environment
MDG 1: Eradicate Extreme Poverty and Hunger			
1	Halve the proportion of people living below the national poverty line	Unlikely	Fair
2	Achieve full and productive employment for all including women and young people	Unlikely	Fair
3	Halve the proportion of people suffering from hunger	Potentially	Strong
MDG 2: Achieve Universal Primary Education			
4	All children will complete a full course of primary education	Potentially	Strong
MDG 3: Promote Gender Equality and Empower Women			
5	Eliminate gender disparity in education	Potentially	Strong
6	Promote gender equality and empower women	Unlikely	Fair
MDG 4: Reduce Childhood Mortality			
7	Reduce child mortality by two-thirds	Potentially	Strong
MDG 5: Improve Maternal Health			
8	Reduce maternal mortality by 75%	Potentially	Strong
9	Achieve universal access to reproductive health services	Inadequate data	Weak but improving
MDG 6: Combat HIV/AIDS, Malaria, and Other Diseases			
10	Halt and begin to reverse the spread of HIV/AIDS	Unlikely	Strong
11	Achieve universal access to treatment for HIV/AIDS for all who need it	Potentially	Weak but improving
12	Have halted by 2015 and begun to reverse the incidence of malaria and other major diseases	Potentially	Fair
MDG 7: Ensure Environmental Sustainability			
13	Integrate the principles of sustainable development into country policies and programs and reverse the loss of environmental resources	Potentially	Strong
14	Reduce biodiversity loss	Potentially	Fair
15	Halve the proportion of population without sustainable access to improved drinking water and sanitation	Potentially	Strong
16	Achieve significant improvement in the lives of urban slum dwellers	Unlikely	Fair

(continues)

Table 6.2   Status of Fiji's MDGs and Targets (*continued*)

Number of Targets	Targets for 2015	Status: Will Target Be Met?	State of Supportive Environment
MDG 8: Develop a Global Partnership for Development			
17	Develop further open, rule-based, predictable, non-discriminatory trading and financial system	Potentially	Fair
18	Address the special needs of small island developing states	Potentially	Fair
19	Deal comprehensively with the debt problems of developing countries	Potentially	Fair
20	Provide access to affordable essential drugs	Potentially	Strong
21	In cooperation with the private sector, make available the benefits of new technology	Potentially	Fair

Source: Data from Fiji Ministry of National Planning. (2010). *Millennium Development Goals: Second report, 1990–2009. Report to the Fiji Islands.* Suva, Fiji: Fiji Ministry of National Planning.

increased from 4 reported cases in 1989 to 333 cumulative cases at the close of 2009 (MNP, 2010). The incidence of noncommunicable diseases, such as diabetes and hypertension, which have been attributed to lifestyle changes and changes in physical activity, also has increased. In response, the government has focused on establishing specific efforts to contain the spread of HIV/AIDS through educational programs and health clinics.

Promoting gender equality and the empowerment of women (i.e., MDG 3) includes two specific targets: eliminating gender disparity in education, and promoting gender equality and empowering women. The target of eliminating gender disparity in education has already been achieved, according to the ministry. In 2008 there were slightly more females than males enrolled in primary education (MNP, 2010). However, there is uncertainty when it comes to the second target, which is to promote gender equality and empower women. The supporting data demonstrate that males' participation in the labor force is at least 2.5 times that of females'. Further evidence of the discrepancies in gender equality is that only 12% of the members of parliament are female (MNP, 2010).

Because tourism plays such a significant and positive role in Fiji's economy, understanding its impact on the MDGs should be of import to policy makers. This is especially true with respect to poverty reduction and employment.

Tourism and Quality of Life

Defined as "ecologically responsible, socially compatible, culturally appropriate, politically equitable, technologically supportive, and finally, economically viable for the host community" (Choi & Sirakaya, 2005, p. 382), sustainable tourism has significant potential to impact the lives of community residents both positively and negatively (Andereck & Nyaupane, 2011). Sustainable tourism embodies principles that support a healthy ecosystem and quality of life for local people, including conservation of land and marine resources, benefits to local communities, and environmental and cultural interpretations for both local populations and guests (Mehta, 1999). Best practices of sustainable tourism can be used to assist in sustainable development and increasing the health and well-being of community members (Mehta, Baez, & O'Loughlin, 2002). Hence, organizations are increasingly rallying around sustainable tourism development and identifying ways to enhance its potential benefits. For example, the World Health Organization's (WHO's) Healthy Tourism Initiative was established to "reduce the various negative impacts of tourism development, while also increasing the positive outcomes for quality of life of the local community as well as the visitor" (Bushell, 2002, p. 1). Healthy tourism considers the interconnectedness of humans, commerce, and the environment, but there is limited empirical evidence of its value as a component of sustainable tourism. This lack of empirical evidence should not be read as "not important," however, because concepts associated with healthy tourism are synonymous with "quality of life"—supporting community through conservation of environmental resources and enhancement of economic and social aspects of society (Bushell, 2002).

Healthy tourism is especially important within small island nations, where specific vulnerabilities to all types of development exist, such as vulnerability to external economic changes due to small domestic market base and insularity; impacts to coastal and marine ecosystems due to development, extraction, poor boating practices, and pollution; and limited freshwater resources (Bushell, 2002). Alternatively, research on quality of life relative to tourism development explores ways in which tourism affects the life satisfaction of community members.

In the next section of this chapter we will demonstrate tourism's effect on quality of life (i.e., an indicator of healthy/sustainable tourism), which encompasses emotions and values such as life satisfaction, happiness, feelings of well-being, and beliefs about standard of living (Davidson & Cotter, 1991; Diener & Suh, 1997; Dissart & Deller, 2000; Grayson & Young, 1994).

Resident Quality of Life and Well-Being in the Nacula Tikina

According to Cutter (1985), quality of life (QOL) in a community is based on an aggregate of community members' perceptions of and feelings about conditions that are most likely impacted by tourism development, such as the level of economic activity, social/cultural aspects of community life, and environmental conditions. Researchers have assessed the QOL of community residents using objective or subjective indicators. Perdue, Long, and Gustke (1991), Crotts and Holland (1993), and Diener and Suh (1997) suggest that objective indicators may be most useful because they can be quantified using objective items (e.g., health, population, crime, education, level of poverty) that go beyond economic benefit. Alternatively, subjective indicators include measures of what people view their life to be at a given moment in time and place. Because one's "QOL refers to one's satisfaction with life and feelings of contentment or fulfilment with one's experience in the world. It is how people view or what they feel about, their lives" (Andereck & Nyaupane, 2011, p. 248), many scholars believe QOL should be studied from the subjective or individual perspective (Andereck & Nyaupane, 2011; Taylor & Bogdan, 1990).

We chose to address tourism's impact on quality of life for residents of the Nacula Tikina using a modified version of the Tourism Quality of Life (TQOL) scale (Andereck & Nyaupane, 2011). The TQOL scale is a subjective measure of life circumstances for residents within each community; it is "relative because it compares the existing circumstance to their ideal standard; and specific because respondents evaluate specific characteristics of their communities" (Andereck & Nyapuane, 2011, pp. 250–251). The items in the TQOL scale represent several aspects of an individual's life, including emotional and psychological well-being; interpersonal and social relationships; material well-being; personal development; physical well-being; self-determination, individual control, and decision making; social inclusion, dignity, and worth; and rights, including privacy (Schalock, 1996, pp. 126–127, in Andereck & Nyapuane, 2011).

To understand tourism's influence on the Nacula Tikina, we surveyed several communities using a modified version of the TQOL. We wanted to learn what was important to residents and their level of satisfaction with their quality of life. Finally, we wanted to explore whether tourism decreased, had no effect, or increased the various quality of life factors.

The Questionnaire

The questionnaire was administered in the Fijian dialect and was divided into three sections. The first section included importance and satisfaction scales with respect to QOL items (see **Table 6.3**).

Table 6.3 Tourism Quality of Life Survey Questions

Importance Scale *Not at all important to extremely important (1–5)*	Satisfaction Scale *Not at all satisfied to extremely satisfied (1–5)*	Effect of Tourism Scale *How much tourism greatly decreases to greatly increases (1–5) each condition in your community*
Dimension: Cultural Preservation		
Opportunities to participate in local culture		Participation in local culture
Awareness of natural and cultural heritage		Same
The preservation of my way of life		Same
Having tourists who respect my way of life		Same
Dimension: Security		
Feeling safe		Same
Strong and diverse economy		The strength and diversity of the local economy
Enough good jobs for residents		Same
Fair prices for goods and services		Same

(continues)

Table 6.3   Tourism Quality of Life Survey Questions *(continued)*

Importance Scale *Not at all important to* *extremely important (1–5)*	Satisfaction Scale *Not at all satisfied to* *extremely satisfied (1–5)*	Effect of Tourism Scale *How much tourism greatly decreases to greatly* *increases (1–5) each condition in your community*
Dimension: Political Stability		
A stable political environment		Same
Resident participation in local government		Same
Proper land use		Conflicts over land use
Dimension: Community Well-Being		
Health care in my community		Same
Clean air		Same
Quality utility services		Same
The preservation of natural areas		Same
The preservation of wildlife habitat		Same
The beauty of my community		Same
Dimension: Cultural Pride and Leisure		
A feeling of belonging in my community		Same
The preservation of cultural/historical sites		Same
Community pride		Same
Quality leisure, sport, and recreation opportunities		Same
Dimension: Island Image		
Preserving peace and quiet		Peace and quiet
The prevention of crowding and congestion		Same
The image of my community to others		Same
Dimension: Crime, Substance, Litter		
The prevention of crime and vandalism		Crime and vandalism
The prevention of drug and alcohol abuse		Drug and alcohol abuse
Litter control		Litter
Dimension: Community Necessity		
Good transportation to other islands		Good inter-island transportation
The availability of clean water		Same
Dimension: Culture and Quality		
An understanding of different cultures		Same
My personal quality of life		Same

Results

Overall, respondents of the Nacula Tikina ranged in age from 17 to 85 years old. Approximately 53% of the respondents were male, 67% were married, and nearly half (47%) were unemployed (see **Table 6.4**).

When asked about their quality of life, 93% of the respondents rated it as "good" to "very good," and were "satisfied" to "very satisfied" with their health. In terms of tourism in the Nacula Tikina, residents felt that they were "moderately" or "slightly" knowledgeable, and most (9 out of 10) felt that they personally benefit from tourism in their village (see **Table 6.5**).

Table 6.4 Sociodemographic Characteristics of Respondents

Item	Number	Percentage
Sex		
Male	104	52.9
Female	117	46.0
What Is Your Marital Status?		
Living with partner	8	3.6
Divorced	2	0.9
Widowed	20	9.0
Single	44	19.7
Married	149	66.8
What Is Your Employment Status?		
Working full time	56	25.1
Working part time	44	19.7
Retired	19	8.5
Unemployed	104	46.6

Table 6.5 QOL of Respondents of the Nacula Tikina

Item	Number	Percentage
How Would You Rate Your Quality of Life? *(n = 226)*		
Poor	1	0.5
Neither poor nor good	12	5.4
Good	141	63.8
Very good	67	29.6
How Satisfied Are You with Your Health?		
Very dissatisfied	2	0.9
Dissatisfied	4	1.8
Neither satisfied nor dissatisfied	7	3.1
Satisfied	107	47.3
Very satisfied	103	45.6
How Would You Describe Your Level of Knowledge About the Tourism Industry in the Yasawas?		
Not at all knowledgeable	26	11.7
Moderately knowledgeable	55	24.8
Slightly knowledgeable	103	46.4
Very knowledgeable	38	17.1
How Much Do You Feel You Personally Benefit from Tourism in Your Village?		
Not at all	1	0.4
Very little	13	5.8
Some	50	22.4
Quite a bit	65	29.1
A lot	94	42.2

Residents and Quality of Life

To understand whether tourism had a positive, negative, or neutral role in residents' perceived quality of life, we followed the procedures suggested by Andereck and Nyaupane (2010). First, using factor analysis, we identified six dimensions of TQOL (see **Table 6.6**). The six dimensions had alpha reliability scores ranging from 0.71 to 0.90, so they had relatively high reliability.

Table 6.6 Factor Analysis of Tourism and Quality of Life Dimensions

Dimensions	Factor Loadings	Eigenvalue	Variance Explained
Village Pride and Well-Being			
Preservation of cultural and historical sites	0.874		
Having tourists who respect my way of life	0.835		
Community pride	0.792		
Participation in local culture	0.787		
The preservation of my way of life	0.751		
Clean air	0.627		
The beauty of my community	0.577		
Feeling safe	0.572		
Awareness of natural and cultural heritage	0.532		
$\alpha = 0.90$		5.80	18.69
Community Peace and Quality of Life			
The image of my community to others	0.774		
Preserving peace and quiet	0.770		
Health care in my community	0.696		
The prevention of crowding and congestion	0.622		
An understanding of different cultures	0.489		
My personal quality of life	0.467		
$\alpha = 0.79$		4.02	12.96
Daily Life and the Economy			
Enough good jobs for residents	0.828		
Strong and diverse economy	0.746		
Quality leisure and recreation opportunities	0.627		
A feeling of belonging in my community	0.569		
Quality utility services	0.556		
Fair prices for goods and services	0.500		
$\alpha = 0.80$		3.52	11.35

(continues)

Table 6.6   Factor Analysis of Tourism and Quality of Life Dimensions (*continued*)

Dimensions	Factor Loadings	Eigenvalue	Variance Explained
Land Use and Local Government			
Resident participation in local government	0.749		
Conflicts over land use	−0.707		
The preservation of wildlife habitats	0.700		
α = 0.84		3.35	10.79
Negative Societal Impacts			
Drug and alcohol abuse	0.879		
Crime and vandalism	0.756		
Litter	0.486		
α = 0.71		2.20	7.08
Critical Island Attributes			
Good inter-island transportation	0.691		
The preservation of the natural environment	0.556		
The availability of clean water	0.551		
α = 0.54		2.12	6.84

Excluded variable: A stable political environment.

"Pride and well-being," the first quality of life dimension identified, was rated the highest (M = 28.74) by residents (see **Table 6.7**). It was followed in level of importance by the "daily life and the economy" dimension (M = 28.23). The remaining dimensions in order of importance to residents were: "critical island attributes" (M = 25.93), "community peace and quality of life" (M = 24.58), "negative societal impacts" (M = 12.74), and "land use and local government" (M = 8.45). Unlike previous studies using the TQOL (see Andereck & Nyaupane, 2010), there were no negative scores related to these dimensions, suggesting that tourism plays a positive role in residents' perceived quality of life.

Table 6.7   Tourism and Quality of Life Dimension Scores

TQOL Dimensions	Mean	Standard Deviation
Village pride and well-being	28.74	10.85
Community peace and quality of life	24.58	18.00
Daily life and the economy	28.23	7.64
Land use and local government	8.45	26.98
Negative societal impacts	12.74	10.79
Critical island attributes	25.93	17.47

Conclusion

The purpose of this chapter was to explore tourism's impact on quality of life. The case study served to reinforce how important it is within the context of sustainable tourism to understand how residents of areas like the Nacula Tikina perceive the impact of tourism on their quality of life. As proposed by Andereck and Nyaupane (2010), this measurement may provide a more "accurate assessment of ways in which residents view tourism in their communities and the way it affects their lives" (p. 257).

Further, the information presented in this chapter illustrates the connection among the MDGs, sustainable tourism, and quality of life. We have demonstrated through this chapter, and other related studies, that quality of life can be a useful tool in understanding the impacts of developments and economic drivers such as tourism. This case study of one community has shown that tourism can be attributable to increased quality of life factors, which address many aspects of the MDGs. From economic to health and well-being aspects of daily life, the community members in the Nacula Tikina have identified positive impacts of the tourism initiated in the region.

References

Andereck, K. L., & Nyaupane, G. P. (2011). Exploring the nature of tourism and quality of life perceptions among residents. *Journal of Travel Research, 50*(3), 248–260.

Bushell, R. (2002, February). *Healthy tourism: A new approach to achieve sustainable outcomes.* Proceedings of Tourism Development, Community and Conservation: Shaping Ecotourism for the Third Millennium International Conference, Jhansi, India.

Choi, H. C., & Sirakaya, E. (2005). Measuring residents' attitude toward sustainable tourism: Development of sustainable tourism attitude scale. *Journal of Travel Research, 43*, 380–394.

Crotts, J. C., & Holland, S. M. (1993). Objective indicators of the impact of rural tourism development in the state of Florida. *Journal of Sustainable Tourism, 1*(2), 112–120.

Cutter, S. L. (1985). *Rating places: A geographer's view on quality of life.* Washington, DC: Association of American Geographers.

Davidson, W. B., & Cotter, P. R. (1991). The relationship between sense of community and subjective well-being: A first look. *Journal of Community Psychology, 19, 246–253.*

Diener, E., & Suh, E. (1997). Measuring quality of life: Economic, social, and subjective indicators. *Social Indicators Research, 40*(1–2), 189–216.

Dissart, J. C., & S. C. Deller. (2000). Quality of life in the planning literature. *Journal of Planning Literature, 15*(1), 135–161.

Fiji Bureau of Statistics. (2007). Census of population 1881–2007. Retrieved April 12, 2012, from http://www.statsfiji.gov.fj/cens&surveys/Popu_census.htm

Fiji Department of Tourism. (2007). *Regional tourism development strategy: Yasawa Islands—2007–2016.* Suva, Fiji: Department of Tourism.

Fiji Islands Business. (2006, April). New marketing image! *Islands Business* (Fiji), 30–31.

Fiji Ministry of National Planning. (2010). *Millennium Development Goals: Second report, 1990–2010. Report to the Fiji Islands.* Suva, Fiji: Fiji Ministry of National Planning.

Fiji Visitors Bureau. (2006). *Realizing the industry's potential through responsible tourism: 2006 Fiji Visitors Bureau marketing plan.* Nadi, Fiji: Fiji Visitors Bureau.

Grayson, L., & Young, K. (1994). *Quality of life in cities: An overview and guide to the literature.* London: British Library.

Kerstetter, D., & Bricker, K. S. (2009). Exploring Fijian's sense of place after exposure to tourism development. *Journal of Sustainable Tourism, 17*(6), 691–708.

Mehta, H. (1999). *International trends in ecolodge research.* Research paper presented at the 1999 World Ecotourism Conference and Field Seminar, Kota Kinabalu, Malaysia. Burlington, VT: International Ecotourism Society.

Mehta, H, Baez, A., & O'Loughlin, P. (Eds.). (2002). *International ecolodge guidelines.* Burlington, VT: International Ecotourism Society.

Perdue, R. R., Long, P. T., & Gustke, L. D. (1991). *The effect of tourism development on objective indicators of local quality of life. Tourism: Building credibility for a credible industry.* Paper presented at the 22nd Annual TTRA Conference, Travel and Tourism Research Association, Salt Lake City, UT.

Taylor, S., & Bogdan, R. (1990). Quality of life and the individual's perspective. In: R. Schalock and M. Begab (Eds.), *Quality of life: Perspectives and issues* (pp. 27–40). Washington, DC: American Association on Mental Retardation.

United Nations Economic and Social Commission for Asia and the Pacific (UN ESCAP). (2011). Country paper: Fiji. Retrieved April 9, 2012, from http://www.unescap.org/huset/lgstudy/country/fiji/fiji.html

World Bank. (2011). Fiji: East Asia and Pacific (developing only). Retrieved April 9, 2012, from http://data.worldbank.org/country/fiji

Environmental
Sustainability

Role of Ecotourism in Preserving Natural Areas and Biodiversity

Paul F. J. Eagles

LEARNING OBJECTIVES

- To understand the links between biodiversity conservation and parks
- To understand that park visitation helps visitors better understand biodiversity conservation in parks
- To know that the payments visitors make to visit parks pay for park management and biodiversity conservation
- To realize that environmental education, recreation, and tourism in parks help create a conservation constituency that argues for conservation
- To learn that private reserves and ecotourism contribute to biodiversity conservation

Goal 7 of the Millennium Development Goals concentrates on ensuring environmental sustainability. The overall target is to integrate the principles of sustainable development into country policies and programs and reverse the loss of environmental resources. Major identified problems include ongoing global deforestation, increasing levels of greenhouse gases in the atmosphere, increased levels of species endangerment, and increasing levels of species extinction.

Target 7B aims to reduce biodiversity loss by slowing the loss of forests, reducing carbon dioxide emissions, reducing the release of ozone-depleting substances, making fishing sustainable, increasing water use sustainability, and reducing species loss. The most effective approach to implement most of these goals is through the creation and conservation of parks and protected areas. The world's protected areas now cover about 12% of the global land surface and 1% of the ocean. In October 2010 the nations who adopted the Convention on Biological Diversity agreed to increase land coverage of parks to 17% and ocean coverage to 10% by 2020. Implementation of these laudable goals is dependent on two important issues: (1) political support and (2) sufficient funding. The best way to ensure political support for biodiversity conservation is through widespread and effective environmental education of citizens. This can be done successfully as citizens visit, learn about, and develop an appreciation of biodiversity in parks. There are many ways to fund the management of parks and protected areas, yet there are just two approaches with widespread utility: government grants, and tourism fees and charges. Globally, government grants are not keeping up with the current level of increase in parkland area, and the increase of parkland in the next decade must see this trend reversed. Globally, fees and charges paid by ecotourists who visit parks are increasingly funding park management. Therefore, ecotourism is critically important in creating a political imperative among citizens to conserve biodiversity through the creation of parks and paying taxes to fund those parks, and in helping pay for the conservation of nature in parks and protected areas through paying for using the parks. The purpose of this chapter is to establish the link between biodiversity conservation and parks and to highlight the contributions of visitor management (i.e., environmental education, recreation, and tourism) and ecotourism to biodiversity conservation.

Linking Biodiversity Conservation and Park Management

The world's national parks and other forms of protected areas have been established over the last several centuries. By 2008 protected areas that were based on land or sea occupied about 21.8 million square kilometers, or 4.3% of the entire Earth's surface, including the oceans (World Conservation Management Center [WCMC], 2010a; Yatsevich, 2009). To illustrate how large this is, compare it to Russia, the largest country in the world, which is 17.1 million square kilometers. This large protected area constitutes 12.4% of all terrestrial land and the territorial waters up to 22.2 km (12 nautical miles) from shore (Yatsevich, 2009). There is a marked difference between the coverage of terrestrial and marine conservation areas. About 12.4% of land is covered by protected areas, whereas marine protected areas currently cover 5.9% of the territorial seas of countries but only 0.5% of the extraterritorial seas (WCMC, 2010a). One of the targets set by the World Parks Congress (WPC) in 2003 was to vastly increase the amount

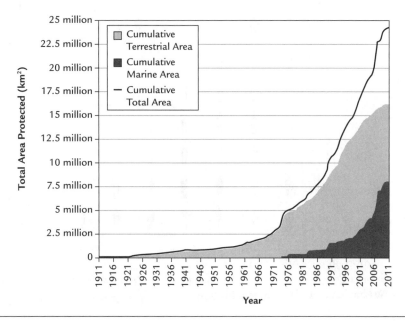

Figure 7.1   Global growth in the world's protected areas.
Source: Reproduced from International Union for Conservation of Nature & United Nations World Monitoring Programme. (2012). *The world database on protected areas (WDPA): February 2012.* Cambridge, United Kingdom: UNEP-WCMC.

of marine area in protected status (WPC, 2003). The creation rate of protected areas had been constant, but recently the creation of terrestrial areas has slowed down and the creation of marine areas has sped up (see **Figure 7.1**).

The protected areas contain the world's most important remnants of natural habitat. Virtually all of the most important ecosystems and habitats are represented in the system. However, there are large areas that have less than 5% coverage, such as much of the boreal forest in Canada, the central plains in the United States and Canada, and the grasslands of South America (WCMC, 2010b).

In 2004 the Convention of Biological Diversity set a target of 10% for each of the world's ecological regions to be effectively conserved. Coad et al. (2008) noted that by 2008 the terrestrial target had been achieved, but the marine target had not. Even though the overall terrestrial target had been achieved, many areas of the world were underrepresented, including Antarctica, the Pacific, South Asia, North Eurasia, North Africa, and the Middle East as well as Australia/New Zealand. The only areas of the world that had reached beyond 10%, which were for marine representation, were South America, North America, and Australia/New Zealand (Coad et al., 2008).

However, the amount of natural habitat remaining for inclusion in the system in the future is dwindling as agricultural, industrial, and urban development continues to damage such lands. In 2011 the world's human population reached 7 billion people (see **Figure 7.2**)

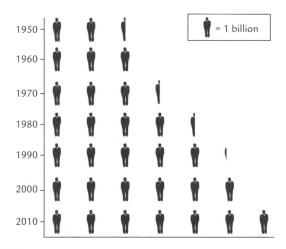

Figure 7.2   Growth in the world's population.
Source: Data from Engleman, R. (2010). *World population growth slows modestly, still on track for 7 billion in late 2011.* Washington, DC: Worldwatch Institute.

(Engelman, 2010). This massive and growing number of people is making unprecedented demands on the world's natural environments and their productive capacity. For example, throughout the 1990s 16 million hectares of forests were removed each year (United Nations, 2010). Consequently, the creation of new protected areas on natural land becomes less possible as undeveloped land continues to become scarcer.

The Living Planet Index produced by the World Wide Fund for Nature (WWF) found a 30% decline in the populations of 2,500 species between 1970 and 2007 (WWF, 2010). The 2008 List of Endangered Species, published by the International Union of the Conservation of Nature, listed 16,928 species as being threatened with extinction. The five principal pressures directly driving biodiversity loss (habitat change, overexploitation, pollution, invasive alien species, and climate change) are either constant or increasing in intensity (Secretariat of the Convention on Biological Diversity, 2010).

By 2010 it became obvious that the Millennium Development Goals for biodiversity conservation were not being achieved; therefore, the 10th meeting of the Committee of the Parties under the Convention on Biological Diversity (CBD) took definitive steps to set specific targets for global representation of terrestrial land in parks (17%) and marine parks (10%) by 2020 (CBD, 2010). This will mean about a 50% increase in land and marine area in parks and protected areas. This is an unprecedented global goal for biodiversity conservation through parkland creation across the entire planet. The world's parks and protected areas are critical for the conservation of the biodiversity of the planet. The burgeoning human population and rapid conversion of natural lands to human-dominated uses is causing massive loss of species.

Of the 193 members of the United Nations, 188 are party to the Convention on Biological Diversity. Two major holdouts are Somalia and the United States (Djoghlaf, 2008). It is important to note that the United States is a signatory to the Convention on Biological Diversity, but this convention has not been ratified by the U.S. Senate; therefore, it is not committed to increase its protected area according to COP 10 (the tenth meeting of the Conference of the Parties [COP 10] to the Convention on Biological Diversity [CBD]) goals. There are continued calls by environmental nongovernmental organizations and international bodies for the United States to officially join the Convention (United Nations Environment Programme, 2010). However, the United States has the largest amount of protected area in total of all countries at the present time, even though it is well down the list in terms of percentage of the country covered (Yatsevich, 2009).

This discussion has shown that the world's parks and protected areas are vitally important for the conservation of our planet's biodiversity. There is now an international movement to increase the effectiveness of biological conservation by a major expansion of parkland. This must be done globally but should be targeted in those ecosystems and habitats that are underrepresented now, such as the world's grasslands, boreal forests, and marine areas.

Linking Park Tourism and Political Support for Biodiversity Conservation

This section explores the connection between park visitation and support for biodiversity conservation. A review of concepts underlying both the negative and positive impacts of park tourism on conservation will be outlined.

Parks and protected areas have a dual mandate of conservation and human use. Conservation includes the long-term maintenance of both natural and cultural heritage. The use involves both direct use values and indirect use values. Direct use values include activities such as recreation, education, tourism, and sustainable resource extraction. All direct use values are also market value, meaning that they can be given a monetary exchange value. Indirect use values include ecological functions of an area, watershed protection, wildlife habitat conservation, and carbon sequestration. Many of the indirect values are nonmarket values, but attempts have been made to estimate their market values. The nonuse values include features such as existence value, option value, and bequest value. The existence value is the benefit to people who may not visit but are pleased that a park exists. Such people may be willing to donate money or encourage their governments to provide foreign aid for conservation. The option value is the concept that protected areas are a resource bank that can be drawn on in the future. The bequest value is a benefit that comes from providing special areas for future generations to use. The nonuse values are generally considered to be nonmarket values. All of these values are dependent upon human perceptions that parks and protected areas have utility to human society. How do people gain such ideas?

There are two important avenues whereby individuals can gain an understanding of the values of in situ conservation. One is through various educational programs. Informal education occurs through media, movies, television, and books. The wonders of nature are a major focus of many media operations. Formal education in schools often includes environmental education. However, the most powerful avenue is through direct contact with nature and biodiversity by visiting parks and protected areas.

Alegre and Cladera (2009) found that satisfaction with a visit to a park and the number of previous visits had a positive effect on park visitors' decision to return to this park. Powell (2008) found that interpretation programs offered during an ecotourism experience led to supportive attitudes toward conservation in the host area, more positive general environmental intentions, and philanthropic support for conservation. These studies reveal that visitors are influenced by visits to a park to have more positive attitudes towards environmental conservation in general, as well as at the specific park visited.

Walpole and Goodwin (2001) found that local people who lived around Komodo National Park in Indonesia showed positive attitudes towards tourism, high support for conservation, and recognition that tourism benefits obtained by local people are dependent upon the existence of the park. Sekhar (2003) had similar findings in a study with local people around Sariska Tiger Reserve in India. It makes intuitive sense that a local community will understand and appreciate institutions that provide positive economic impact, such as a park providing a base for ecotourism activity.

One of the most telling case studies of park visitation and conservation comes from Costa Rica. The creation of Santa Rosa National Park in 1969 was the start of the national park system in Costa Rica. In 1970 the national parks service was created, led by the first director Mario Boza (McNeil, 2001). By 2010 the country had 25 national parks covering 12% of the country (Franke, 2009). The other forms of protected areas, such as biological reserves, wildlife refuges, and the like, provide a total of 161 protected areas covering 25.6% of the country (SINAC, 2011). The primary purpose of this system is biodiversity conservation.

This developing large park and protected area system evolved along with an emerging ecotourism industry. The increasing positive economic impact from ecotourism encouraged the creation of more conservation reserves. These reserves, in turn, provided more opportunity for park-based ecotourism. By 2001, Weaver and Schluter declared that Costa Rica was the best-known ecotourism destination in the world at a national level. They stated that this status was "closely associated with Costa Rica's well developed national protected area system" and that this relationship between parks and ecotourism occurs with "most high profile destinations" (Weaver & Schluter, 2001, p. 177). From 1985 to 2005, visitation to national parks in Costa Rica increased from 250,000 to over 1 million (see **Figure 7.3**), revealing substantial growth of park tourism of 5.5% per year. Importantly this increase was in both domestic and foreign visitors. The domestic increases show increasing appreciation of park use as an important leisure activity within the country. The foreign tourism is an important export industry bringing in foreign exchange. In 2008 the international tourism expenditures within Costa Rica totaled US$718 million, up substantially from US$316 million in 1995 (Trading Economics, 2011). A major part of this large, nationwide tourism expenditure was due to international tourists coming to Costa Rica to visit the national parks and other forms of protected areas.

However, Costa Rican parks and protected areas are chronically underfunded (Weaver & Schluter, 2001). This leads to weak tourism infrastructure, such as eroded trails, nonexistent educational programs, and poor washrooms. It is alleged that some of the funds derived from tourism fees collected in the national parks is deflected out of park management and into other government agencies,[1] exacerbating the funding deficiency. Therefore, it is important to note

---

[1] Mario A. Boza, personal communication.

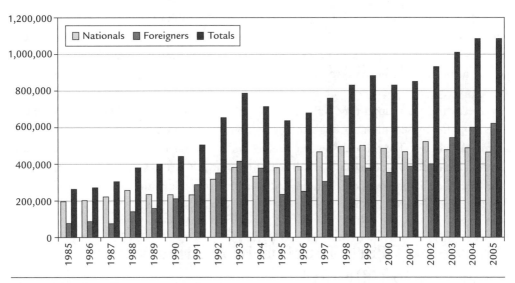

Figure 7.3   Costa Rica national park visitation.

that tourism income does not automatically lead to effective park management. The park agency must have efficient tourism and financial management for this to occur.

The private sector has responded to the demand for ecotourism services, programs, and facilities by creating a plethora of reserves and destinations. Additionally, international environmental conservation groups have been very active in purchasing private land for the creation of private reserves. Chacon (2006) reports there are 2,654 private protected areas in Costa Rica, covering 264,228 hectares. These areas are primarily dedicated to biodiversity conservation, but many supplement their income through ecotourism.

The total number of ecolodges in Costa Rica is not clearly documented, but the Responsible Travel (2011) website lists 11 ecolodges, Eco Tropical Resorts (2010) lists 14 rated lodges and 14 nonrated lodges, and InfoHub (2011) lists 26. Clearly, only a small number of private protected areas have developed ecolodges.

Fennell (1990) noted that the top-ranked ecotourism destination in Costa Rica is a private reserve, the Monteverde Cloud Forest Reserve in the mountains of central Costa Rica. Generally, the private ecotourism sector provides services and programs that do not exist in national parks, including accommodation, restaurants, trips and tours, and shops for souvenirs, clothing, and equipment. Unique ecotourism experiences can be illustrated by reference to those found around the Monteverde Cloud Forest Reserve. Here, the private sector provides unique experiences such as the Sky Walk trails and suspension bridges that enable ecotourists to safely experience the canopy of the rain and cloud forests in the Monteverde area. There also is a Frog Pond, a zoo of local frogs and amphibians; the Bat Jungle, an exhibit of local bats; the Orchid House, which displays 425 species of orchids; and the Butterfly Garden, which is a display and farm of local species of butterflies. Each of these five unique private destinations offers environmental education within specialized facilities and locales outside the Monteverde Cloud Forest Reserve. No environmental education programs of such sophistication occur in the national parks.

During a personal visit in 2006, the author observed a contrast between the weak tourism infrastructure in the national parks and the much better developed and safer infrastructure in ecolodges and other private ecotourism destinations. This observation revealed a lack of funding of the national parks, and a much better fiscal situation in the private tourism facilities.

Costa Rica is a good example of biodiversity conservation and ecotourism functioning as intertwined, self-supporting activities. The publically owned parks and reserves provide the spine for conservation, through the protection of large blocks of natural land scattered across the county. The privately owned reserves and ecolodges fill in the matrix between and around the national lands with the addition of innovative tourism services. The combination constitutes an impressive conservation and tourism consortium that serves as a model for conservation and ecotourism.

The Role of Park Tourism in Biodiversity Conservation Finance

This section explores options for the financing of parks and protected areas. Emphasis is placed on the issue of tourism funding for park management.

All management depends upon sufficient finance. Traditionally, the foundation of many protected areas has been public money from government. Increasingly, many park management agencies do not have sufficient funds to properly manage both tourism and conservation. Currently, most governments do not fund protected areas fully. Lindberg (2001) reported that protected area budgets in the early 1990s were only about 24% of the estimated US$17 billion required to maintain these areas properly. In addition, the global trend is for governments to increasingly create parkland for biodiversity conservation purposes but hold budgets static or decrease financial allocations. Geoghegan (1998) reported on the Caribbean region experience on protected areas: "While the political will to establish protected areas may be strong, the will to budget for their management has shown itself to be very weak, in the face of urgent national priorities and continuous fiscal crisis." In the absence of tax-based funds derived from governments, many protected areas are only paper parks; they exist in regulation and on maps but have no effective management. This type of situation is not conducive to long-term biodiversity conservation. Therefore, other sources of funds are necessary, and tourism is very promising.

Fundraising Opportunities for Protected Area Managers

Lindberg and Enriquez (1994) found that government grants are the most common source of park management funding, and the second most prevalent source is from tourism. Tourism affects park financing in two ways. The first and most obvious is through the direct contribution of funds through payments for recreation service such as entrance fees, camping fees, recreation program fees, concessionaire payments, and donations. The second, and often forgotten, is indirectly through the encouragement of governments to provide grants. Park visitors can be a powerful lobby group to domestic governments. However, foreign tourists also can contribute

Table 7.1 Protected Area Revenue Sources

Income Source	Comments
Government allocations	Common, but very often declining
Entrance fees	Commonly used, often strong resistance from local residents
Recreation Activity fees	Commonly used, but often through concessionaires or contracts who provide the service
Accommodation for visitors	Commonly used, but often through concessionaires or contracts who provide the service
Accommodation for staff	Common for remote parks
Concessions	Used for facilities and programs with high capital requirements
Equipment rental	Recreation equipment is often needed by visitors
Food sales	Food is required by all visitors
Merchandise sales	Souvenirs, recreation equipment and clothing are commonly sold in parks to earn income
Sales of intellectual property	Possible but difficult
Campfire wood sales	Important source of income for some parks
Cross-product marketing	Done on a small scale with those parks that are allowed to function like a business
Interest	Can be earned on all income
Land sales	Often not possible or desirable
Foreign aid	Frequent in developing countries
Debt for nature swap	Frequent in developing countries, but declining in use
Donations	Rare in public parks, very common in private reserves
Carbon offsets	A major potential source in the future
Lotteries	Possibly, but rarely used
Public good service payments	A potential source, especially payment for the use of water downstream from parks

Source: Data from Eagles, P.F., McCool, S., & Haynes, C. (2002). *Sustainable tourism in protected areas: Guidelines for planning and management.* Paris, France: United Nations Environment Programme, World Tourism Organization, and World Conservation Union.

by encouraging their home governments to contribute to park management through foreign aid. The author has observed this phenomenon in Tanzania where German tourists actively lobby their home government to provide foreign aid to Tanzania for national park management activities. Within a park, tourists provide funds through two main sources, fees for services and donations. Each will be discussed in turn.

Table 7.1 lists a number of tourism income sources potentially available to protected areas. Tourism has the potential to provide agencies with most of these income sources, as long as the management agency is capable of functioning like a business. A few examples are provided here and developed later in this chapter.

Visitor Fees

Many parks charge some form of entrance fees, either per person, per vehicle, or a combination of both. The purchase of these entrance tickets also provides managers with good information on the volume of use and when it occurs. Some parks provide specialized recreation services, such as guided tours or special events. These can be provided by licensed companies, park staff, allied non-governmental organizations (NGOs), and concessionaires. Parks that allow vehicle entrance must provide parking sites. Charging for parking can be a lucrative source of income. For example, some campgrounds allow one vehicle per campsite registration; other vehicles must pay a parking fee. Earmarking revenues for the protected area is important to improve stakeholder acceptance of fees.

Accommodations

One of the largest expenditure categories for travelers is accommodations. Some parks operate campsites, cabins, and lodges, and charge visitors accordingly. Accommodation charges can be one of the largest income sources available for protected areas. The management of accommodations (whether directly or through a concession) is a complicated activity that requires specially trained staff and proper business procedures.

Equipment and Food Services

Outdoor recreation often requires specialized equipment, much of which is difficult to transport over long distances. Therefore, the provision of such equipment in parks, either for sale or for rental, can be a source of revenue. All park visitors require food, either in the form of store-bought groceries or food prepared in restaurants. The purchase of food is a major expenditure item for travelers, and parks can earn a substantial income from this source. Managers must decide whether it is better to operate these services within the agency structure or utilize a concessionaire.

Consumer Products

Merchandise sales are potentially a very large source of income for parks, but one that is seldom utilized. However, in recent years the sale of tailor-made, specialized parks merchandise, such as clothing, equipment, and publications, has become quite successful. SANParks in South Africa uses specialized concessionaires who operate stores in the national parks. Some parks use community cooperatives to provide these products; others use specialized NGOs such as friends groups. Major crafting industries develop around parks through which the park agency facilitates contact between the craftspeople and the tourists, involving communities living within or around the areas, and bringing jobs and income to the people involved. For example, Algonquin Provincial Park in Ontario, Canada, has an art center in which local artists display and sell their work.

Public/Industry Donations

Satisfied park visitors are sometimes willing to make donations to protected areas. Such donations are most frequently provided toward specific initiatives, such as a new facility, research, or a special recreation program. Satisfied and concerned foreign visitors have been known to return to their home countries and lobby for foreign aid budgets to be applied to the parks they have visited.

Cross-Product Marketing and Image Sales

Cross-product marketing occurs when two allied products advertise and sell each other's products. An example in a protected area context might be a shared market program between a film company and a park. Each gains by cooperation in marketing their product. Protected areas represent a valuable intellectual property, as an image with which corporations wish to be associated. For example, park names often are very well-known and appreciated. Additionally, their sites are attractive and highly desired by some enterprises, such as advertisers and movie producers. A few protected areas earn substantial income from the sale of licenses to use their names and images. Cross-product marketing is a very popular business practice but is rare in protected areas.

Each year Ontario Parks publishes a guide that outlines all the provincial parks open for visitation, as well as the facilities and programs that are available. This is given for free to all visitors. Given that it is in full color and 92 pages long, it is expensive to produce. The costs are covered by advertisements from companies that offer services useful to park users, such as a food store chain, outdoor clothing brand, and equipment store. The agency has developed 32 corporate sponsors (Ontario Parks, 2011).

Private Biodiversity Conservation and Ecotourism

This section explores the role of private reserves and ecotourism. In the last 30 years there has been an explosion in the number of private reserves created by the private sector. The private nonprofit organization (NPO) conservation sector has a paramount purpose of buying ecologically valuable property for the purpose of conservation. Land acquisition often is funded by donations. Increasingly, the NPO sector is paying for site management through tourism fees. Later in this chapter the American Bird Conservancy, which uses this option, will be highlighted. The profit-making private sector has shared purposes of conservation and profit. There is documentation of several thousand ecolodges being created that cater to ecotourists through higher service levels than what is found in public parks.

The Size of the Nonprofit Conservation Sector

It is not possible to provide a definitive statement on the size of the nonprofit conservation sector globally. One must make do with a glimpse through published sources for specific areas of the world. Chacon (2006) documented the size of the private conservation lands in Central America. He found that the 7 countries had 2,941 reserves totaling 540,983 hectares (see **Figure 7.4**). There were substantial differences among the countries. Costa Rica, with its long tradition of very active NPO activity, had by far the most areas at 2,654, totaling 264,228 hectares. Nicaragua, with its history of social and military strife, had the smallest, with only 26 areas covering 5,534 hectares. Major differences in the size of the systems in different countries are found globally. The social stability of the country, the activity of the NPO sector, the environmental profile of the area, and the size of the ecotourism activity all contribute to the size of the private nature reserve system.

The private nature reserve system in Australia has been slow to develop compared to other countries, but major progress has been made recently. The Australian Wildlife Conservancy (AWC) owns 21 properties covering an immense 2.5 million hectares, possibly making it the largest NPO landowner in the world. This organization concentrates on establishing sanctuaries for the

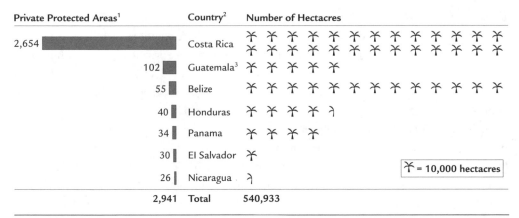

Figure 7.4 Private nature reserves in Central America.

[1] Private protected areas include nature reserves and privately protected properties. Examples of private protection include conservation easements, contracts of payments for environmental services, and forestry incentives for conservation.

[2] Data for South American countries remains incomplete because no exact data currently exists.

[3] The number of hectares shown for Guatemala includes private nature reserves and properties protected under PINFOR while the number of private protected areas includes only private nature reserves.

Source: Data from Chacon, C. M. (2006). Private lands conservation in Mesoamerica. Retrieved April 5, 2012, from http://www.privateconservation.net/mm/file/Taller%20Custodia%20 Barcelona-C%20Chacon-Mesoamerica.pdf

conservation of threatened endemic flora and fauna and ecosystems on the Australian continent. The AWC purchased Kalamurina, a huge area of central desert in South Australia, in 2007. This reserve covers 667,000 hectares, making it the largest private nature reserve in the world. Importantly, the Conservancy states that this land is a natural bridge between Lake Eyre National Park to the south and the Simpson Desert Regional Reserve to the north, thereby creating a vast system of linked public and private natural lands (AWC, n.d.). This concept of the private sector working with the public sector to create systems of linked lands can be found in many countries, with South Africa and Costa Rica being prime examples. Typically, the private sector buys lands near publicly owned lands, thus extending the conservation concept beyond and around the public parks.

The Royal Society for the Protection of Birds (RSPB), founded in 1889, is a very large NPO based in the United Kingdom. This organization owns, manages, and provides public recreation services for 190 nature reserves in the United Kingdom, covering approximately 130,000 hectares. It has over 1 million paid members and estimates over 1 million recreational visits to its reserves each year. The RSPB is the second largest landowner in Britain, second only to the National Trust, another major NPO. The RSPB concentrates on priority species, habitats, and sites. It operates through the funds coming from membership fees, donations, and the sale of merchandise. It has a very large volunteer operation (Birdlife International, 2011; RSPB, 2011).

Krug (2002) estimates that a minimum of 14 million hectares of land in southern Africa is devoted to some form of wildlife protection. Within that area, South Africa has an extensive private nature reserve system that contributes to both biodiversity conservation and ecotourism. Damm (2001) estimated that there were almost 10,000 game ranches in South Africa. These ranches function like wildlife farms, where native animals are raised for conservation, food, and tourism purposes. Krug estimates there are almost 1,000 private nature reserves in South Africa that undertake nature conservation largely for the income that can be earned from ecotourism. Southern Africa generally, and South Africa specifically, shows a wide diversity of private profit-making and nonprofit organizations involved in nature conservation. The combination of wildlife conservation and consumptive use of wildlife through hunting and game farming is relatively unique. Krug makes the important connections among viewing wildlife, hunting of wildlife, and producing funds for conservation directly through use fees but also indirectly through donations:

> Considering that much of the economic benefits resulting from wildlife viewing and hunting safaris are based on foreign demand, it can be concluded that the international community is paying for the private supply of biodiversity in southern Africa. The same applies to non-use values, as most donations to private reserves originate from northern countries. This important distinction helps to counter negative domestic incentives for under-investment in biodiversity by the state. (p. 34)

There are many NPOs in North America that are involved in ownership of land for both nature conservation purposes and ecotourism. Possibly the largest is the Nature Conservancy, based in the United States. This international organization works in all U.S. states and 30 other countries in nature conservation, largely through the purchase of biodiversity-rich natural lands. This organization uses a variety of mechanisms for nature conservation, including direct purchase and retention, conservation easements, and land purchase and resale to conservation groups. The overall funding largely comes from donations from corporations, foundations, and individuals. The Nature Conservancy states that it is involved with the conservation of 6 million hectares of land (Nature Conservancy, 2011).

One organization that combines land purchase and ecotourism for a targeted biodiversity conservation program is the American Bird Conservancy.

American Bird Conservancy

The American Bird Conservancy (ABC) is an NPO dedicated to the conservation of native birds and their habitats throughout the Americas. It operates through private donations allowed under U.S. law. The organization has four major fields of operations: to safeguard the rarest bird species; to conserve important bird habitat for breeding, wintering, and migration; to eliminate threats to birds such as long-line fishing and energy structures; and to build a conservation constituency for bird conservation through environmental education (ABC, 2011).

The ABC attempts to link the activity of birding with bird conservation. The ABC points out that research shows that almost 50 million Americans are bird watchers and that industry associated with bird watching generates over US$30 billion a year in the United States. The ABC works with other NPOs, such as the American Birding Association, to make sure that birders follow a code of ethics during their recreational activity. Most of the donors and supporters of the ABC are birders who enjoy watching birds and subsequently donate money for bird conservation programs (ABC, 2011).

The ABC purchases land throughout the Americas that is important for conservation of habitat for the 200 most endangered bird species, within a program called Alliance for Zero

Conservation. The Alliance is a joint initiative of 67 conservation organizations that aims to prevent species extinctions by identifying and safeguarding key habitats.

The ABC developed a conservation and ecotourism network, the Latin American Bird Reserve Network, that links birders and private nature conservation sites throughout the Americas. The goal is to attract birders who pay fees for ecotourism services necessary for bird watching. These fees are then used to manage the conservation of the sites. The network contains 35 private reserves in 12 countries, covering 101,000 hectares that contain 2,025 bird species. Importantly, 14 species that are critically endangered, 44 that are endangered, 80 that are vulnerable, and 107 that are near threatened are found in this reserve network (ABC, 2009). The conservation birding website provides information on regional areas for suggested birding travel routes, possible species to view, specialized tour operators, and places to stay. This targeted conservation program that is closely tied to bird watching tourism and environmental education is an excellent example of the connectedness of biodiversity conservation and ecotourism.

Conclusion

This chapter explored the role of ecotourism in preserving natural areas and biodiversity. It provided evidence that ecotourism plays a significant role in conservation of natural areas in many parts of the world, with examples from the United States, Australia, southern Africa, the United Kingdom, Costa Rica, and throughout Central America. The review has shown that the virtuous circle of ecotourism leads to a self-reinforcing activity of positive attitudes and site visitation (see **Figure 7.5**). The American Bird Conservancy recognizes the need to start positive attitude development early in life; therefore, it sponsors bird conservation programs in environmental education in schools in areas near the private conservation reserves. The ABC also capitalizes on international ecotourism by using bird watching tourism to fund the conservation of significant bird habitats throughout Latin America. When those bird watchers post positive reports on websites of seeing rare birds in the ABC reserves, this stimulates more bird watching tourism, thereby illustrating the concept of the virtuous circle of ecotourism.

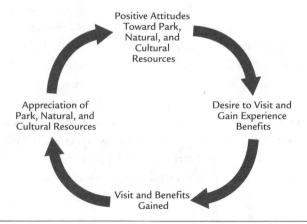

Figure 7.5   The virtuous circle of ecotourism.

All conservation ultimately depends on the support of society. This support is best developed through appreciative travel during which individuals experience conservation in the field. Travel visitation provides support for conservation in several ways. A primary impact is caused by tourism spending that supports local economies. Tourists are often stimulated to donate time or money to further conservation programs. In addition, tourists may lobby governments and other decision makers to create laws and policies that are supportive of biodiversity conservation.

The chapter illustrates how ecotourism assists with the implementation of the Millennium Development Goal Target 7B that aims to reduce biodiversity loss. Examples from many countries show this linkage. A major challenge for the future is to strengthen this linkage in a period of very high energy prices that will reduce travel, while expanding human populations place increasing pressure on the remaining natural lands.

References

Alegre, J., & Cladera, M. (2009). Analysing the effect of satisfaction and previous visits on tourist intentions to return. *European Journal of Marketing, 43*(5/6), 670–685.

American Bird Conservancy (ABC). (2009). *The Latin American bird reserve network.* Plains, VA: Author.

American Bird Conservancy (ABC). (2011). Conservation birding. Retrieved April 5, 2012, from http://www.conservationbirding.org/index.html

Australian Wildlife Conservancy (AWC). (n.d.). Kalamurina: Linking Lake Eyrie and the Simpson Desert. Retrieved April 5, 2012, from www.shapeourworld.com.au/download/Kalamurina_Property_Report.pdf

Birdlife International. (2011). United Kingdom: The Royal Society for the Protection of Birds (RSPB). Retrieved April 5, 2012, from http://www.birdlife.org/worldwide/national/united_kingdom/index.html

Chacon, C. M. (2006). Private lands conservation in Mesoamerica. Retrieved April 5, 2012, from http://www.privateconservation.net/en

Coad, L., Burgess, N., Fish, L., Ravillious, C., Corrigan, C., Pavese, H., . . . Besancon, C. (2008). Progress towards the Convention on Biological Diversity terrestrial 2010 and marine 2012 targets for protected area coverage. *PARKS, 17*(2), 35–42.

Convention on Biological Diversity (CBD). (2010). *A new era of living in harmony with nature is born at the Nagoya Biodiversity Summit.* Montreal, Quebec: United Nations Environment Programme.

Damm, G. (2001). *Saving Africa's wildlife: A guide to the African renaissance in nature conservation.* Johannesburg, South Africa: SCI African Chapter.

Djoghlaf, A. (2008). *The United States and the Convention on Biological Diversity.* Washington, DC: George Washington University Law School.

Eagles, P. F. J., McCool, S. F., & Haynes, C. (2002). *Sustainable tourism in protected areas: Guidelines for planning and management.* Paris, France: United Nations Environment Programme, World Tourism Organization, and World Conservation Union.

Eco Tropical Resorts. (2010). Costa Rica eco lodges. Retrieved April 5, 2012, from http://www.eco-tropicalresorts.com/centralamerica/costarica.htm

Engleman, R. (2010). *World population growth slows modestly, still on track for 7 billion in late 2011.* Washington, DC: Worldwatch Institute.

Fennell, D. (1990). *A profile of ecotourists and the benefits derived from their experience: A Costa Rican case study.* Master's thesis, Department of Recreation and Leisure Studies, University of Waterloo, Waterloo, Canada.

Franke, J. (2009). *Costa Rica national parks and reserves.* Seattle, WA: Mountaineers.

Geoghegan, T. (1998). Financing protected area management: Experiences from the Caribbean. CANARI Technical Report 272. Retrieved April 5, 2012, from http://www.canari.org/finance.pdf

InfoHub. (2011). Costa Rica eco hotel. Retrieved April 5, 2012, from http://www.infohub.com/Lodgings/eco_lodge/costa_rica_eco_lodges3.html

International Union for Conservation of Nature & United Nations World Monitoring Programme World Conservation Monitoring Centre. (2012). *The world database on protected areas: February 2012.* Cambridge, England: United Nations Environment Programme World Conservation Monitoring Centre.

Krug, W. (2002). *Private supply of protected land in southern Africa: A review of markets, approaches, barriers and issues.* Paris, France: Organisation for Economic Cooperation and Development.

Lindberg, K. (2001). *Protected area visitor fees: Overview.* Queensland, Australia: Griffith University, Cooperative Research Centre for Sustainable Tourism.

Lindberg, K., & Enriquez, J. (1994). *Summary report: An analysis of ecotourism's contribution to conservation and development in Belize.* Washington, DC: World Wide Fund for Nature.

McNeil, J. (2001). *The rough guide to Costa Rica.* London: Rough Guides.

Nature Conservancy. (2011). About us: Private land conservation. Retrieved April 5, 2012, from http://www.nature.org/aboutus/privatelandsconservation/index.htm

Ontario Parks. (2011). *Nearby and natural.* Peterborough, Canada: Ministry of Natural Resources.

Powell, R. B. (2008). Can ecotourism interpretation really lead to pro-conservation knowledge, attitudes and behaviour? Evidence from the Galapagos Islands. *Journal of Sustainable Tourism, 16*(4), 467–489.

Responsible Travel. (2011). Costa Rica ecolodges accommodation. Retrieved April 5, 2012, from http://www.responsibletravel.com/accommodation/costa-rica-ecolodges

Royal Society for the Protection of Birds (RSPB). (2011). *RSPB nature's voice.* Retrieved April 5, 2012, from http://www.rspb.org.uk

Secretariat of the Convention on Biological Diversity. (2010). *Global biodiversity outlook 3.* Montreal, Canada: United Nations Environment Programme.

Sekhar, N. U. (2003). Local people's attitudes towards conservation and wildlife tourism around Sariska Tiger Reserve, India. *Journal of Environmental Conservation, 69*(4), 339–347.

SINAC (National System of Conservation Areas). (2011). National system of conservation areas. Retrieved April 5, 2012, from http://www.costarica-nationalparks.com

Trading Economics. (2011). Costa Rica international tourism expenditures. Retrieved April 5, 2012, from http://www.tradingeconomics.com/costa-rica/international-tourism-receipts-us-dollar-wb-data.html

United Nations. (2010). *The Millennium Development Goals report 2010.* New York: Author.

United Nations Environment Programme. (2010). *Whatever happened to biodiversity? Conservation community urges United States ratification of the Convention on Biological Diversity.* Montreal, Canada: Secretariat of the Convention on Biological Diversity.

Walpole, M. J., & Goodwin, H. J. (2001). Local attitudes towards conservation and tourism around Komodo National Park, Indonesia. *Environmental Conservation, 28*(2), 160–166.

Weaver, D. B., & Schluter, R. (2001). Latin America and the Caribbean. In: D. Weaver, K. F. Backman, E. Cater, P. F. J. Eagles, & B. McKercher (Eds.), *The encyclopedia of ecotourism* (pp. 173–188). New York: CABI Publishing.

World Conservation Monitoring Center. (2010a). Coverage of protected areas. Retrieved April 5, 2012, from http://www.wdpa.org/Statistics.aspx

World Conservation Monitoring Center. (2010b). Protected area overlays with biodiversity. Retrieved April 5, 2012, from http://www.wdpa.org/Statistics.aspx

World Wide Fund for Nature (WWF). (2010). *Living planet report 2010.* Gland, Switzerland: Author.

World Parks Congress. (2003). *WPC recommendation 23: Protecting marine biodiversity and ecosystem processes through marine protected areas beyond national jurisdiction.* Gland, Switzerland: World Commission on Protected Areas.

Yatsevich, M. (2009). *Growth in protected areas slows.* Washington, DC: Worldwatch Institute.

The Role of Ecotourism and Sustainable Tourism in Ensuring Environmental Sustainability in the Marine Environment

Carl Cater

LEARNING OBJECTIVES

- To show the links between environmental sustainability and other MDGs in the marine environment
- To identify some of the specific challenges faced in protection of marine areas and their management through looking at the Great Barrier Reef World Heritage Area
- To consider the usefulness of the sustainable livelihoods approach in understanding community assets towards fulfillment of the MDGs

This chapter will discuss the role of ecotourism and sustainable tourism in supporting and meeting the Millennium Development Goal (MDG) of ensuring environmental sustainability, with a focus on the marine environment. Sustainable environmental development in the marine environment is highly dependent on the achievement of other MDGs due to high interdependencies. The interlinked nature of the marine environment means that all activities in this environment are likely to influence one another. Consequently there are a number of specific threats to environmental sustainability, of which tourism development is only one. Indeed, the two principal MDG targets of ensuring environmental sustainability most relevant to the marine realm are also closely linked. These are to "integrate the principles of sustainable development into country policies and programs and reverse the loss of environmental resources" (7a) and to "reduce biodiversity loss, achieving, by 2010, a significant reduction in the rate of loss" (7b) (United Nations [UN], 2008, p. 36). It would seem that the second aim is one of halting the tide of environmental destruction, whereas the former aim uses sustainability to reverse this decline. A useful framework for supporting the complexities of environmental sustainability is discussed in the Sustainable Livelihoods Approach and its evaluation of community assets, with natural capital at its core. The latter part of this chapter examines specific strategies to mitigate and even remove these threats, using the Great Barrier Reef as an example, in many cases using sustainable tourism as a galvanizing force for positive outcomes.

Environmental Sustainability and Biodiversity

It is widely acknowledged that the seas are a repository for global biodiversity, and yet paradoxically they are the least well documented habitat. Out of 33 animal phyla, 32 are found in the sea, 15 of which are exclusively marine, and oceans contain the world's largest (the blue whale) and smallest (meiofauna) animals. Compared with 1.5 million land species, only 275,000 marine species have been identified and described, and yet it is estimated that coral reefs alone may harbor in excess of 1 million species, with as many as 10 million in the deep ocean basins (International Union for Conservation of Nature/World Wide Fund for Nature [IUCN/WWF], 1998). It is no wonder that it has been claimed that, in light of the fact that "only around one-tenth of the 290 million km² of the seabed has actually been explored and charted . . . we know more about the moon than our own ocean world" (IUCN/WWF, 1998, p. 10). This lack of knowledge also reminds us of the vast potential of the marine environment for ecotourism activity.

Despite this lacuna of knowledge, it is clear that oceans are indispensable to our life support, livelihoods, and lifestyles. The oceans are "the engines that drive the world's climate, defining weather and storing huge quantities of solar energy in the process . . . the liquid heart of the Earth's hydrological cycle—nature's great solar-driven water pump" and ocean currents, "the blue planet's super highways, transfer great quantities of water and nutrients from one place to another. The Gulf Stream, for instance, pushes more water than is carried by all the rivers on Earth from the Gulf of Mexico and the Caribbean across the Atlantic into northern Europe" (IUCN/WWF, 1998, p. 7). Economically, oceans contribute 63% (US$20.9 trillion) of the goods and services provided by the world's ecosystems, over half of which (US$12.6 trillion) originate from coastal ecosystems (IUCN/WWF, 1998). Scottish waters generate £14 billion, or 21%, of Scottish GDP each year.[1] Oceans and coasts provide a myriad of products ranging from food to minerals, drugs, and medicines but also enhance our lifestyles in terms of opportunities for rest and recreation. As the former becomes increasingly corporatized and hidden, our divorce from this connection to nature spurs a need to reconnect through tourism and leisure activity. Millions of tourists are attracted to the sea every year by the proliferation of opportunities such as swimming, snorkeling, diving, water sports, boating, sailing, fishing, and wildlife viewing. Although efforts are underway to exploit space as the final frontier for tourism, it is clear that the penultimate frontier still offers much untapped potential.

Consequently tourism and recreation has an increasingly marine focus. Indeed, Hall (2001) describes how the ocean and marine environment is not only a "new frontier" but also one of the fastest growing tourism market segments, citing the U.S. National Oceanic and Atmospheric Administration's recognition of the fact that it is increasing, in terms of both volume and diversity, more than any other coastal activity. Partly this is a result of geographic trends because an increasing proportion of the world's population resides in coastal regions. For example, although coastal states make up only 11% of the contiguous United States in land area, they are home to over 50% of the population (Cordell, 2004). In Australia the situation is even more pronounced—over three-quarters of the population live within 40 km of the coast and one-quarter are within 3 km. It is no surprise, then, that recreational activities are likely to make heavy use of the marine environment.

At the same time, MDG reporting suggests that the marine environment is under significant threat. For example, the proportion of overexploited and depleted stocks in fisheries has increased over the past 20 years (UN, 2008). Total catches have been maintained at roughly the same level through the use of new resources, but this may become increasingly difficult because this is largely due to technological advances in what has been dubbed by some commentators "a war on fish" (End of the Line, 2009). Major efforts are now required to improve fisheries management and to improve the productive capacity of exploited stocks. Management action is also required to mitigate the impact of fisheries on aquatic ecosystems. These concerns can be addressed through the adoption of a holistic, participatory ecosystem approach to fisheries management. A number of initiatives have taken hold in this direction, such as reducing total allowable catches of commercial species, reducing bycatch of vulnerable species (e.g., seabirds, sea turtles), and establishing marine protected areas. However, reducing fishing capacity remains a key objective of global fisheries management (UN, 2008).

Climate change also has a major impact on the marine environment. Sea level change will clearly have the greatest impact in littoral zones where relationships with the marine environment are so important. Indeed, although no area can escape the adverse impact of climate change, "the Arctic, small islands, mega deltas in Asia and Africa, and the African region overall seem to be especially vulnerable because of their high exposure to the effects of climate change, their populations' limited capacity to adapt to the consequences, or both" (UN, 2008, p. 37). Warming of the oceans themselves is causing changes to ecosystems on a vast scale, such as the increased incidence of coral bleaching described later in this chapter. Furthermore, climate change models point to the disruption of the all-important ocean currents. However, solutions to this threat may be far from easy.

---

[1] Email from Cheales, N. (2005, February 25). Enquiry from website.

For example, despite the MDGs' call for "transition to cleaner and renewable energy sources" and the requirement for "large investments in energy projects over the coming years" (UN, 2008, p. 37), there is considerable concern about the local impacts of some of these schemes in marine settings. Many of the huge tidal, wave, and offshore wind energy schemes currently being planned and constructed around the world may have unintended environmental impacts in this realm.

Protecting Biodiversity

It is clear that biodiversity is central to environmental sustainability, and indeed many of the other MDGs. Furthermore, because biodiversity is the flagship for marine ecotourism (e.g., the scuba diving destinations of the "coral triangle"), it is fundamental to livelihood opportunities. Indeed, "loss of biodiversity will also hamper efforts to meet other MDGs, especially those related to poverty, hunger and health, by increasing the vulnerability of the poor and reducing their options for development" (UN, 2008, p. 55). One of the most widespread methods for protecting marine biodiversity has been through the creation of marine protected areas (MPAs). Much like their terrestrial counterparts, these have become important venues for ecotourism, although this is often spatially concentrated. Although the number of marine protected areas has grown rapidly in recent years, their performance remains highly variable. Kelleher et al. (1995) assessed the management level of 383 of the 1,306 MPAs they inventoried around the globe. They concluded that 31% could be classified as having a high management level (generally achieving their management objectives), 40% as moderate, and 29% as having a low level. The reasons for MPAs failing to achieve their management effectiveness are many and various, but recurrent factors were (Kelleher et al., 1995, p. 17):

- Insufficient financial and technical resources
- Lack of data
- Lack of public support and unwillingness of users to follow management rules
- Inadequate commitment to enforce management
- Unsustainable use of resources occurring within MPAs
- Impacts of activities in land and sea areas outside the boundaries of MPAs
- Lack of clear organizational responsibilities for management and lack of coordination between agencies with responsibilities relevant to MPAs

Burke and Maidens (2004) analyzed the effectiveness of Caribbean MPAs using expert assessment. They generated a simple measure of management effectiveness using only four broad criteria: (1) existence of management activity, (2) existence of a management plan, (3) availability of resources, and (4) extent of enforcement. Of the 285 parks examined in this way, only 6% were rated as effectively managed, 13% were partially effectively managed, and nearly 50% were judged to have an inadequate level of management.

These authors suggested two major reasons for such a high level of failure. The first is the lack of long-term financial support. Kelleher et al. (1995) suggested that a critical issue in financing marine protected areas was the assessment and publication of the economic benefits of MPAs, which often exceed those of any alternative use. They suggested that wider regional benefits, particularly in tourism, are ignored despite the fact that these extend beyond direct financial flows from entry fees to include improved overall fish catches; there is also revenue from the external tourism industry and employment in these industries. The identification and establishment of facilities to promote ecotourism in MPAs by management agencies in cooperation with local communities and other groups is advocated. The second major reason for failure of MPAs, as suggested by Burke and Maidens (2004), is the critical issue of a lack of support from the local community. This is usually attributable to a lack of local involvement in planning and a failure to share financial or other benefits. It is this human dimension that has been increasingly recognized as being paramount in determining the success or failure of MPAs. Mascia (2003) suggests that, rather than biological or physical variables, social factors are the primary determinants. The local acceptance of regulatory measures is a crucial factor in the establishment of an effective MPA. In general, the ownership of responsibility and compliance to rules increase as more and more users of resources are directly included in the management decisions and the responsibility becomes local. The most important predictors of success, determined by a study of 45 community-based marine protected areas in the Philippines by Pollnac et al. (2001), included: (1) population size of the community, (2) a perceived crisis in terms of reduced fish populations, (3) successful alternative income projects, (4) high levels of participation in community decision making, and (5) continuing advice from the implementing organization along with inputs from local government. In Kimbe Bay, West New Britain province, Papua New Guinea, the Mahonia Na Dari (Guardians of the Sea) conservation and research center has implemented a network of locally managed marine areas (LMMAs) that are managed by the community for the community (see **Figure 8.1**). This has been an effective grassroots approach that has contrasted with the failure of previous efforts, which failed to maintain local solutions and control.

However, it is not as easy as declaring that one management type is better than another. Mascia (2003) suggests that both locally and privately administered MPAs are particularly vulnerable to changes in leadership that diminish their ability or willingness to manage sites. Collaborative management systems are therefore advocated as a means of overcoming many of the weaknesses of community-based and centrally managed MPAs because they can merge national capacity with local interest and knowledge. Such collaboration, however, must extend beyond vertical integration to embrace cross-sector interests. Kelleher et al. (1995, p. 19) call for the integrated management of all uses of sea and land areas adjacent to MPAs, identifying land-based activities such as forest clearance, agriculture, and urban development as particular threats to marine biodiversity through marine pollution. As they argue, MPAs cannot tackle such issues in isolation and therefore must be linked with wider coastal zone management programs. The need for a holistic, integrative approach to biodiversity protection has been

Figure 8.1   Locally managed marine area (LMMA) in Kimbe Bay, Papua New Guinea.

recognized for some time, but integrated coastal zone management (ICZM) as a tool for achieving sustainable levels of economic and social activity in coastal areas, although protecting the coastal environment, has recently been the focus of an unprecedented level of interest from multilateral agencies as well as from intergovernmental and individual governments, and it links to the goal of integrating sustainability.

Integrating Sustainability

The second MDG target of most relevance to the marine realm is that of integrating sustainable principles into policies and programs and to bolster environmental quality. However, the marine environment offers significant challenges for integrating sustainability goals. In particular, the open nature of the marine environment brings with it considerable problems of management. Marine systems differ from terrestrial systems in terms of a much higher degree of connectivity attributable to "the sea's large size, enormous volume, continuity of habitats and ubiquitous currents" (Lourie & Vincent, 2004, p. 1005). The high degree of connectivity in the seas facilitates the transmission of substances and effects (Kelleher, 1999). Sea currents carry sediments, nutrients, pollutants, and organisms through, and beyond, a specific location.

Consequently, actions taken in one locality, by whatever form of activity, tourism, or otherwise, marine or terrestrial, may affect another hundreds of miles distant and often nations apart. The issue of connectivity is not confined to the seas and oceans themselves but is as vital a consideration at both the air/sea and the land/sea interfaces. Air pollution and run-off and point discharges from the land and rivers are estimated to account for around three-quarters of the pollutants entering marine ecosystems (World Resources Institute, 1996). The White Water to Blue Water Partnership (WW2BW), launched at the World Summit on Sustainable Development in 2002, recognizes the significance of land-based sources of marine pollution such as sewage, industrial pollution, and agricultural run-off and aims to promote integrated watershed and marine ecosystem-based management.

In development terms, it is interesting to note that traditional societies often recognize the inextricability of the land and sea. The indigenous people of South Pacific islands regard "the land, its adjacent reefs and lagoons, and the resources therein, together with the people [as] . . . a single integrated unity" (Sofield, 1996). Traditional clan territories in the Torres Strait islands, Australia, by custom if not by law, comprise both land and sea territories that include adjacent home reefs as well as extended sea tenure over the waters, submerged reefs, and sandbanks beyond (Zann, 2005). The residents of Mafia Island, Tanzania, view the "ownership" and use of both land and sea in related terms and fail to make an artificial distinction between the two, regarding terrestrial and marine activities as complementary. Walley (2004, pp. 153–156) describes how residents sometimes describe the work they do on both land and sea as "farming," as well as their view that the communal "proprietorship" or *wenjeyi* over the land extends to the sea.

This notion of communal proprietorship leads us to consider the whole question of ownership and access to marine resources. Whereas the seas and oceans have frequently been described as common property, and consequently subject to Hardin's "tragedy of the commons," (1968) it is more accurate to describe them as a common-pool resource. A common property resource is one in which the members of a clearly defined group have the legal right to exclude nonmembers from using that resource and, thus, it has been argued, there may be important social institutions that can effectively manage the commons. In the permeable situation of marine resources, this exclusion is much more complex, leading to a common-pool scenario. Interestingly, Young (1999, p. 586) describes how "many of the same problems of managing common-pool resources encountered in fishing are now emerging in ecotourism." We can see, therefore, in these instances, and especially on the high seas, how marine resources can effectively be viewed as open access and that it is the "tragedy of open access" (Lynch, 1999) that we are concerned with, there being a positive incentive for individual users to exploit the resource to the maximum, even if destruction of marine resources is the inevitable result.

Sustainable Marine Livelihoods

The sustainable livelihoods approach (SLA) offers a useful integrative framework for examining the impacts of tourism, both positive and negative, on people's assets (Ashley, 2000). Although the SLA was developed during the 1990s as a new approach to poverty reduction (Carney, 1999), it has been central to the emphasis on pro-poor tourism in recent years (Ashley, Roe, & Goodwin, 2001). It will be seen that it facilitates a systematic appraisal of the various ways in which tourism in general, and marine ecotourism in particular, impacts coastal livelihoods. The approach is people-centered, designed to be participatory, and has an emphasis on sustainability. Also, as Cahn (2002, p. 3) suggests, it "is positive in that it first identifies what people have rather than focusing on what people do not have. The SLA approach recognizes diverse livelihood strategies, it can be multi-level, household, community, regional or national, and can be dynamic."

At the heart of the SLA lies an analysis of five types of assets upon which people draw to build their livelihoods (Tamasane, 2002). These are:

1. *Natural capital:* The natural resources stocks upon which people draw for livelihoods
2. *Human capital:* The skills, knowledge, ability to work, and good health important to be able to pursue different livelihood strategies
3. *Physical capital:* The basic enabling infrastructure such as transport, shelter, water, energy, and communications
4. *Financial capital:* The financial resources available to people, such as savings, credit, remittances, or pensions, that provide them with different livelihood options
5. *Social capital:* The social resources such as networks, membership in groups, and relationships of trust upon which people draw in pursuit of their livelihoods

It has been suggested, however, that to this classic pentagon should be added cultural capital, which can be defined as the cultural resources (heritage, customs, traditions) that are very much a feature of local livelihoods (Glavovic, Scheyvens, & Overton, 2002; Tamasane, 2002).

Notably, there is considerable overlap between the MDGs and the SLA. For example, *achieving universal primary education* is a cornerstone of human capital. Of relevance to this chapter, the goal of *ensuring environmental sustainability* contributes directly towards both natural and physical (especially water) assets. The SLA is also important if represented

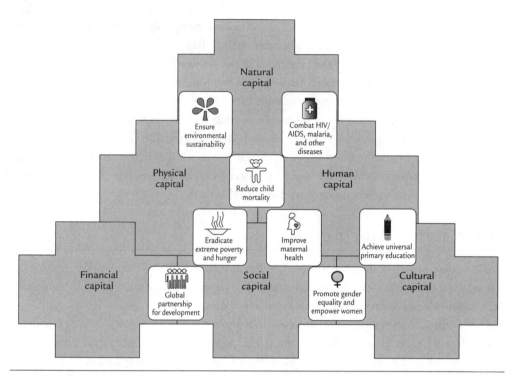

Figure 8.2 The building blocks of the sustainable livelihoods approach with corresponding MDGs.

diagrammatically whereby natural capital can be seen as the top of a pyramid of livelihood assets (see **Figure 8.2**). In this sense, ensuring environmental sustainability both rests on and is crucial to the foundations of all of the other community assets. This building blocks approach is particularly relevant to the marine environment in which all stakeholders, including tourism, are so interdependent.

Marine Tourism's Contribution to Environmental Sustainability on the Great Barrier Reef

Tourism on the Great Barrier Reef

As the largest biological feature on earth, the Great Barrier Reef is arguably the world's most famous marine tourism attraction, stretching more than 2,300 km along the northeast coast of Australia from the northern tip of Queensland to just north of Bundaberg. Aside from the coral reefs, the region also contains a wide variety of other habitats and an extraordinary diversity of plant and animal species. Its popularity as a destination has been somewhat in parallel to increased political and scientific interest in the marine environment felt since the 1950s. Technological advances that enabled access to this environment, particularly the invention of scuba equipment, had no small part to play in significant increases in visitation through the 1970s and 1980s. At this time, forecasts were being made of continued growth for the foreseeable future, and thus a concern with the potential impacts of these tourists led to the founding of the Great Barrier Reef Marine Park Authority (GBRMPA) in 1975 and World Heritage listing in 1981. The rapid increase in the number of tourists and the development of tourism infrastructure on the reef, which caused great concern in the 1980s, has stabilized since 1995, but the reef's global reputation and the emergence of new inbound markets may bring increased pressure.

As befits a destination such as the Great Barrier Reef, the scope and range of tourism activity within its boundaries is truly diverse. Figures suggest that tourism is the largest commercial activity in the Great Barrier Reef region, generating over AU$4.228 billion per annum (Bureau of Tourism Research [BTR], 2003). As a consequence, the marine tourism industry is a major contributor to the local and Australian economies. In 2010 there were approximately 840 permitted tourism operators and 1,700 vessels and aircraft permitted to operate in the park (GBRMPA, 2011). Tourism attracts approximately 1.9 million tourist visitors each year (GBRMPA, 2011). Recreational use of the Great Barrier Reef region by coastal residents is also high, with almost 5 million visits per year, and in many circumstances, the impacts of recreational users can be impossible to separate from those of commercial tourism activities (Harriot, 2002). Some of the principal tourist activities that take place within the marine park include boat trips, snorkeling, scuba diving, fishing, whale watching, island resorts, and cruise ships. However, it is important to note that this tourism activity is highly concentrated. Some 85% of all visits take place within the Cairns and Whitsunday sections of the park, which represent less than 7% of the total area (CRC Reef, 2003).

Environmental Threats

The two principal environmental threats to the Great Barrier Reef are those of crown-of-thorns starfish and coral bleaching. Both are clearly a threat to the reef as a tourist resource because they have the potential to destroy the very thing that tourists come to see. Indeed, much travel media reporting has taken a "see it while you can" tone in recent years. The diversity and beauty of the corals themselves, and their central role in reef ecosystems, make them the keystone species in the tourist–marine interface. The threat that these pose is taken very seriously. Overfishing is less of an issue in the Great Barrier Reef than in other coral reefs, as a result of an effective and adaptive protection strategy, described later in this chapter. However, marine tourists play an important part in the justification for, and sometimes implementation of, many of these environmental protection strategies.

Crown-of-thorns starfish are a threat to the reef because once the starfish reach maturity, at about 6 months, their primary diet is live coral, and they may live up to 7 years. During a severe outbreak, there can be several crown-of-thorns starfish per square meter, and they can kill most of the living coral in an area of reef, reducing coral cover from the usual 25–40% of the reef surface to less than 1%. Such a reef can take 10 years or more to recover its coral cover (CRC Reef, 2001). Outbreaks of the starfish have been observed with some regularity since the advent of scuba equipment, and underwater observation has been made possible.

An outbreak in 1962 on Green Island swept throughout the reef during the next decade, as the larvae from this colony were carried by ocean currents to the southern areas. This southward

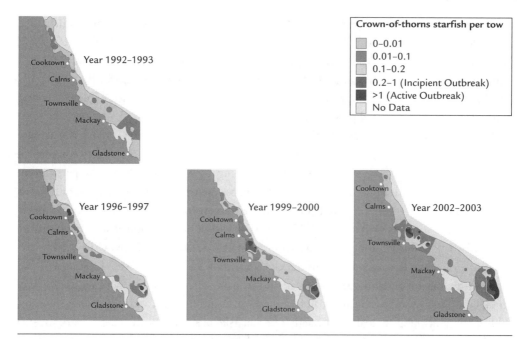

Figure 8.3   Changes in density of crown-of-thorns starfish on the Great Barrier Reef.
Source: © Australian Institute of Marine Sciences, 2011.

progression of outbreaks has been a consistent pattern in subsequent events in the central Great Barrier Reef. A much larger outbreak occurred in 1979, and an estimated 17% of the total reef area was affected by this over the next few years. Further outbreaks occurred in the years following 1994, and by 2000, the greatest concentrations were to be found in the region between Cairns and Townsville (see **Figure 8.3**). Controlling the starfish is extremely difficult, given the size and variability of the underwater environment. Although the GBRMPA does not support the widespread eradication of the crown-of-thorns starfish, the GBRMPA grants permits for localized, small-scale crown-of-thorns starfish control programs at key tourism or research sites (Hoey & Chin, 2004). A selective method of control is to inject individual starfish with a poison that kills them within a few days.

Earlier research suggests that some tourism operators in the Cairns region were spending up to AU$300,000 each per year in crown-of-thorns starfish control (CRC Reef, 2001). The federal government committed a total of AU$2.4 million to starfish control from 2002 to 2007 for distribution to operators through the Association of Marine Park Tourism Operators. By December 2003, divers involved in the program had removed some 48,000 starfish across 51 reefs and had helped to significantly reduce starfish numbers at key sites. It has recently been suggested, from work conducted in Fiji (*Diver*, 2004), that more comprehensive controls on fishing and a strong network of sanctuary zones could reduce the number of starfish outbreaks.

Rising sea temperatures, caused by global climate change, may also have a significant impact on the Great Barrier Reef. Coral polyps are extremely sensitive to even minor changes in sea temperature. It is estimated that corals on the Great Barrier Reef will experience between 2 and

6 degrees Celsius increases in sea temperature by 2100. Such a rise causes the coral polyps to eject the algae that give the coral structures their color, leading to so-called bleaching. The coral polyps can continue to survive for a period without the algae, but, unless they return, and their nutrient provision is regained, the polyps and hence the coral colony itself will die. Significant warming, and hence major bleaching events, occurred in the Great Barrier Reef in 1998, and 4 years later, in 2002. In the more recent event, of all the reefs surveyed across the whole marine park, 60–95% were bleached to some extent. Around 5% of reefs have been severely damaged, and between 50% and 90% of corals on these reefs were dead (WWF, 2003a). In relation to the Great Barrier Reef specifically, the Intergovernmental Panel on Climate Change stated that the Great Barrier Reef faces significant death or damage from coral bleaching of medium to high certainty over the next 20–50 years (WWF, 2003b). In addition, the increase in storms and wave action as a result of climate change also pose a threat to the future stability of the reef (WWF, 2001). There is very little that can be done to control coral bleaching at a local level. Some recent work suggests that corals may be able to partially adapt to sea temperature change through altering their relationship to the algae (Buddemeier & Fautin, 1993). However, this evidence comes from areas used to greater variability in sea temperatures, and should not be relied upon as a strategy that can be employed by the Great Barrier Reef coral communities. Nevertheless, tourism operators provide an important early warning system for coral bleaching episodes, as detailed in the following section.

Managing Tourism on the Great Barrier Reef

Managing tourism activity and ensuring environmental sustainability in this huge area (the park is bigger than the area of the United Kingdom, Switzerland, and Holland combined) is far from simple. Under the World Heritage listing the Australian government is responsible for ensuring a delicate balance between reasonable human use and the maintenance of the area's natural and cultural integrity. As a United Nations Educational, Scientific, and Cultural (UNESCO) report in 2002 stated:

> The enormity of this task is compounded by the sheer size of the GBRWHA, its economic importance, the political and the jurisdictional complexities determined by Australia's system of Federalism, the close proximity of rural and urban populations to the coast, the range of users and interest groups whose use patterns frequently compete and displace each other, the need for equity and fairness in access to resources, and the ecological diversity of the region. (p. 10)

Management has been achieved primarily by using a spectrum of multiple use zones ranging from general use zones, where most reasonable activities can occur, through to national park zones (no-take zones that provide opportunities to see and enjoy the diversity of the reef but where no fishing or collecting are allowed), to preservation zones (reference areas that are off limits to virtually everyone except for limited scientific research).

In 2003–2004, the Great Barrier Reef Marine Park was rezoned as a result of implementing the Representative Areas Program. This was instigated as recognition that the previous zoning of no-take or green zones, which made up less than 5% of the park, did not adequately protect the entire range of plants and animals and should be revised. In addition, there were a number of inconsistencies between the management of state waters, extending to 3 nautical miles offshore, and the federal zone beyond. As a result, a selection of 70 bioregions was identified, being representative examples of all of the different habitats and communities in the GBRWHA. Each bioregion contains plant and animal communities, together with physical features, that are significantly different from the surrounding areas and the rest of the GBRWHA (GBRMPA, 2003). A high degree of public consultation was encouraged throughout the planning process. These representative areas join the existing network of green zones in forming a greater area that restricts extractive activity. Approximately a third of the total area of the park is now afforded this higher level of protection. Many nonconsumptive tourism activities, such as swimming and snorkeling, are still permitted within these zones.

The Great Barrier Reef Marine Park Authority takes the lead role in day-to-day management of the region in conjunction with Queensland Parks and Wildlife Service. This activity is funded by both the commonwealth and state governments, who provide matching funds primarily for enforcement, surveillance, monitoring, and education/interpretation. In order to provide additional funds for these activities, an environmental management charge (EMC) was introduced in mid-1993, payable by all visitors to the reef on commercial operations. At present the charge for individual visitors is AU$5.50. EMC logbooks and charging returns are provided by the GBRMPA to all commercial operators at the beginning of each calendar year or when a new permit is granted. Operators are required to keep a logbook of operations and supply charging returns on a quarterly basis. Penalties exist for commercial operators who do not maintain records or pay the required EMC. EMC data from the logbooks are used for the purposes of charging but also provide valuable information to the GBRMPA relating to tourism use of the marine park.

From Sticks to Carrots

The GBRMPA is advised on management issues about the marine park at a local level by voluntary community-based committees called local marine advisory committees (LMACs). The committees were established in 1999 to enable local communities to have effective input into the management of the Great Barrier Reef Marine Park. They provide a community forum for representative interest groups, government representatives such as the Queensland Parks and Wildlife and Queensland Department of Primary Industries and Fisheries, and the local community to come together to discuss issues about marine resources and their concerns. This helps the GBRMPA and other management agencies to keep in touch with marine and coastal issues at a local level and understand the use of the marine park. LMACs provide both an advisory and a communication role between the community and the GBRMPA.

The GBRMPA has also moved from a regulatory to a collaborative approach with tourism operators working in this environment. Recognizing that tourism operators are the ones who have perhaps the greatest stake in ensuring the long-term sustainability of the tourist resource (the reef itself), a number of initiatives have been put in place through the Tourism and Recreation Reef Advisory Committee (TRRAC). The Eye on the Reef is a partnership among the tourism industry, the GBRMPA, and the reef research community that makes use of the fact that tourism operators are the most regular visitors to the reef. Being in an ideal position to observe changes to the reef, selected tourism operators collect a range of biological information at frequently visited reef and island sites. The data are then stored in a database available to reef managers and reef researchers, and site reports are prepared for tourism operators and crew. Moving towards a more interactive approach that suits the contemporary business environment and high staff turnover, GBRMPA now has an online tourism operators' handbook called *Onboard*, which covers all aspects of operating in the marine park. The website helps operators to keep up-to-date about changing management arrangements for the marine park, and also provides interpretive and educational resources.

Perhaps the most significant push towards collaborating for environmental sustainability has come through the High Standard Tourism Program (HSTP), which rewards operators with longer permit terms for achieving eco-certification. This initiative encourages best practices tourism operations and offers benefits to operators who are certified to a high standard. Currently, GBRMPA recognizes the comprehensive ECO Certification Program operated by Ecotourism Australia, at the Ecotourism and Advanced Ecotourism levels of certification. Initially the GBRMPA is offering high-standard operators achieving Advanced Ecotourism certification an extended permit term of 15 years. Certified operators are also showcased on the GBRMPA website and at trade events such as the Australian Tourism Exchange.

Policy Context

The policy context in which the Great Barrier Reef exists is almost as diverse as the reef itself. In addition to the World Heritage Convention, a number of other international conventions discussed in this chapter apply to the GBRWHA or parts of it, such as the 1971 Ramsar Convention, the 1973 Convention on International Trade in Endangered Species of Wild Fauna and Flora (CITES), the 1979 Convention on Conservation of Migratory Species of Wild Animals (Bonn Convention), the 1982 U.N. Convention on the Law of the Sea (UNCLOS), the 1973 International Convention for the Prevention of Pollution at Sea (MARPOL), and the 1992 Convention on Biological Diversity (CBD) (UNESCO, 2002).

At a national level, the most important legislation is the Great Barrier Reef Marine Park Act (GBRMPA), which was enacted in 1975 "to provide for the protection, wise use, understanding and enjoyment of the Great Barrier Reef in perpetuity . . ." (GBRMPA, 2011); in other words, to protect the area's outstanding biodiversity while providing for reasonable use. However, a plethora of other commonwealth acts are also relevant to its management, such as the Environment Protection and Biodiversity Conservation Act (1999) and the Environment Protection (Sea Dumping) Act (1981). Within the Australian federal system, Queensland state legislation is also relevant. For example, almost 50% of the state islands within the GBRWHA are national parks under the (Queensland) Nature Conservation Act of 1992. In some areas within the GBRWHA, the tidal lands and tidal waters are declared as state marine parks under the Marine Parks Act (1982) to complement the provisions of the adjoining commonwealth marine park.

By and large, the planning and management of tourism to the Great Barrier Reef has been very successful in ensuring environmental sustainability and demonstrates clear integration of sustainability principles into policies and programs (MDG Goal 7a). In many cases the region is upheld as an example of world-class planning practice, with significant recognition of the issues of connectivity and consultation relevant to such a large natural area. It is important that this planning is adaptive to future threats and opportunities, especially that of global warming and resultant coral bleaching, which occurred on a significant scale in 1998 and 2002. In addition, certain commentators have suggested that federal and state governments see the Great Barrier Reef as a tourism cash cow (Mules, 2004). Without fair reinvestment of the significant returns from tourism to the region, adequate planning for the future may be jeopardized.

Conclusion

This chapter has shown the central position of environmental sustainability in achieving all other MDG outcomes in a marine setting. Our oceans are so interconnected, and the users of this resource so diverse that solutions for environmental sustainability must engage all stakeholders, including the tourism industry. The sustainable livelihoods approach helps us assess community assets, with natural capital at its core. Indeed, protection of biodiversity is fundamental, but this can only come with effective and adaptive management regimes, which itself requires high degrees of community support and long-term vision. This is the approach taken by the Great Barrier Reef Marine Park Authority, with a highly adaptive and consultative management regime. Furthermore, ensuring environmental sustainability of ecotourism operators through rewarding eco-certification encourages best practices in the industry. Additionally, by engaging the main users of the resource in various initiatives, environmental sustainability becomes embedded in policies and programs, not just in the tourism industry but in management of the marine environment as a whole.

References

Ashley, C. (2000). *The impacts of tourism on rural livelihoods: Namibia's experience*. Working paper 128. London: Overseas Development Institute.

Ashley, C., Roe, D., & Goodwin, H. (2001). *Pro-poor tourism strategies: Making tourism work for the poor*. Pro-Poor Tourism Report No. 1. London: Overseas Development Institute, International Institute for Environment and Development.

Buddemeier, A., & Fautin, B. (1993). Coral bleaching as an adaptive mechanism: A testable hypothesis. *BioScience, 43*, 320–326.

Bureau of Tourism Research (BTR). (2003). *Assessment of tourism activity in the Great Barrier Reef Marine Park region*. Canberra, Australia: Bureau of Tourism Research.

Burke, L., & Maidens, J. (2004). *Reefs at risk in the Caribbean*. Washington, DC: World Resources Institute.

Cahn, M. (2002). *Sustainable livelihoods approach: Concept and practice*. Paper given at Development Studies of New Zealand Conference, Massey University.

Carney, D. (1999). *Livelihood approaches compared*. London: Department for International Development.

Cordell, K. (2004). *Outdoor recreation for 21st century America. A report to the nation: The national survey on recreation and the environment*. State College, PA: Venture.

CRC Reef. (2001, April). *Crown-of-thorns starfish on the Great Barrier Reef. Current state of knowledge.* Townsville, Australia: CRC Reef.

CRC Reef. (2003, June). *Marine tourism on the Great Barrier Reef: Current state of knowledge.* Townsville, Australia: CRC Reef.

Diver. (2004). Fishing good news for starfish. *49*(7), 18.

End of the Line. (2009). Retrieved April 12, 2012, from http://endoftheline.com

Glavovic, B., Scheyvens, R., & Overton, J. (2002). *Waves of adversity, layers of resilience: Exploring the sustainable livelihoods approach.* Paper given at Development Studies of New Zealand Conference, Massey University.

Great Barrier Reef Marine Park Authority (GBRMPA). (2003). Representative areas program. Retrieved April 12, 2012, from http://kurrawa.gbrmpa.gov.au/corp_site/management/zoning/rap/rap/index.html

Great Barrier Reef Marine Park Authority (GBRMPA). (2011). Tourism and recreation GBRMPA, Townsville. Retrieved April 12, 2012, from http://www.gbrmpa.gov.au

Hall, C. M. (2001). Trends in ocean and coastal tourism: The end of the last frontier? *Ocean and Coastal Management, 44*, 601–618.

Hardin, G. (1968). The tragedy of the commons. *Science, 162*, 1243–1248.

Harriott, V. J. (2002). *Marine tourism impacts and their management on the Great Barrier Reef.* CRC Reef Research Centre Technical Report No 46. Townsville, Australia: CRC Reef Research Centre.

Hoey, J., & Chin, A. (2004, August). Crown-of-thorns starfish. In: A. Chin (Ed.). *The state of the Great Barrier Reef.* Townsville, Australia: Great Barrier Reef Marine Park Authority.

International Union for Conservation of Nature & World Wide Fund for Wildlife (IUCN/WWF). (1998). Creating a sea change: A WWF/IUCN vision for our blue planet. Retrieved April 12, 2012, from http://cmsdata.iucn.org/downloads/seachang_1.pdf

Kelleher, G. (1999). *Guidelines for marine protected areas.* Gland, Switzerland: International Union for Conservation of Nature.

Kelleher, G., Bleakley, C., & Wells, S. (1995). *A global representative system of marine protected areas.* Washington, DC: Great Barrier Reef Marine Park Authority, World Bank, and World Conservation Union (IUCN).

Lourie, S .A., & Vincent, A. C. J. (2004). Using biogeography to help set priorities in marine conservation. *Conservation Biology, 18*(4), 1004–1020.

Lynch, O. J. (1999). Promoting legal recognition of community-based property rights, including the commons: Some theoretical considerations. Retrieved April 12, 2012, from http://www.ciel.org/Publications/promotinglegalrecog.pdf

Mascia, M. B. (2003). The human dimension of coral reef marine protected areas: Recent social science research and its policy implications. *Journal of the Society for Conservation Biology, 17*(2), 630–632.

Mules, T. (2004). *The economic contribution of tourism to the management of the Great Barrier Reef Marine Park: A review.* Queensland, Australia: Queensland Tourism Industry Council.

Pollnac, R. B., Crawford, B. R., & Gorospe, M. L. G. (2001). Discovering factors that influence the success of community-based marine protected areas in the Philippines. *Ocean and Coastal Management, 44*(11–12), 683–710.

Sofield, T. (1996). Anuha Island Resort: A case study of failure. In: R. Butler & T. Hinch (Eds.), *Tourism and indigenous peoples* (pp. 176–202). London: Thomson.

Tamasane, T. (Ed.). (2002, March). Social capital and sustainable livelihoods. *Sustaining Livelihoods in Southern Africa, 5*. Retrieved April 12, 2012, from http://www.cbnrm.net/pdf/khanya_002_slsa_issue05_sc.pdf

United Nations (UN). (2008). *The Millennium Development Goals report 2008.* New York: Author.

United Nations Educational, Scientific, and Cultural Organization (UNESCO). (2002). *Australian national periodic report section II: Report on the state of conservation of Great Barrier Reef.* Paris: Author.

Walley, C. J. (2004). *Rough waters: Nature and development in an East African marine park.* Princeton, NJ: Princeton University Press.

World Resources Institute. (1996). Pressures on marine biodiversity. Retrieved December 1, 2011, from http://www.wri.org

World Wide Fund for Wildlife (WWF). (2001, June). *Clear? . . . or present danger? Great Barrier Reef pollution report card.* Sydney, Australia: WWF Australia.

World Wide Fund for Wildlife (WWF). (2003a). *The implications of climate change for Australia's Great Barrier Reef.* Sydney, Australia: WWF Australia.

World Wide Fund for Wildlife (WWF). (2003b). *Securing Australia's Great Barrier Reef. WWF Australia's proposal: World class protection for special, unique and representative areas.* Sydney, Australia: WWF Australia.

Young, E. (1999). Balancing conservation with development in small-scale fisheries: Is ecotourism an empty promise? *Human Ecology, 27*(4), 581–620.

Zann, L. P. (2005). The social value of the coastal and marine environment to Australians. In: *Our sea, our future: Major findings of the state of marine environment report for Australia.* Retrieved April 12, 2012, from http://www.deh.gov.au/coasts/publications/somer/chapter2.html

Sea Turtle Conservation Travel Case Study

Brad Nahill and Chris Pesenti

LEARNING OBJECTIVES

- To understand the pros and cons of turtle watching as an ecotourism activity
- To learn about different types of turtle conservation tourism happening around the world
- To compare how different organizations manage tourism to turtle habitats
- To comprehend the various challenges that have to be overcome to successfully incorporate sea turtle conservation

Six out of seven species of sea turtles around the world are in danger of extinction, due primarily to poaching (meat, eggs, and shells) and entanglement in fishing gear. With slow growth rates and long maturation periods, sea turtles are especially susceptible to these threats. In many places, people earn income from these activities, including from the sale of meat and eggs or fishing in turtle hotspots. Ecotourism has long been touted as a win–win solution for reducing these threats; however, despite the success of a handful of projects, the full potential of this large and growing tourism market has yet to be effectively harnessed on a wide scale. This case study illustrates the role that sea turtle conservation tourism can have for environmental sustainability (Millennium Development Goal 7).

Conservation tourism (often considered synonymous with ecotourism) has been advocated in most major international sea turtle conservation strategies, including the following:

- *A Global Strategy for the Conservation of Marine Turtles* (International Union for Conservation of Nature Marine Turtle Specialist Group [IUCN MTSG], 1995): Identify and promote economic alternatives to exploitation and economic incentives to conserve marine turtles (e.g., ecotourism, handicrafts).
- *Marine Turtle Conservation in the Wider Caribbean Region: A Dialogue for Effective Regional Management* (Wider Caribbean Sea Turtle Network [WIDECAST], IUCN MTSG, 2001): Work with stakeholders to develop and encourage economic alternatives to eliminate illegal poaching of eggs and nesting females.
- *Manual for the Best Practices of Conservation of Marine Turtles in Central America* (Asociación ANAI, 2000): Ecotourism based in community participation is an excellent way to alter the direct exploitation of turtles and their eggs.

Sea turtles, based on their behavioral habits, are especially advantageous to conservation travel because most species return to the same beaches to nest every year during the same time period, making their nesting predictable. When they begin the process of egg laying, they go into a trance-like state in which all of their focus is on digging and laying the eggs, so they have little to no awareness of what is going on around them. Where guided tours are managed to approach during this part of the nesting process, the impact and stress on the turtle is minimized.

Researchers have studied the effects of having people in close proximity to turtles and have recorded no change in the behavior of the turtles (Tisdell & Wilson, 2005). Other reasons that turtles are appropriate for conservation tourism is that they do not pose a danger to tourists and that viewing them does not require people to enter the water. For volunteer tourism programs, minimal training is required to have people participate in measuring turtles, collecting data, and moving eggs to a safe place.

In a few isolated places, conservation tourism has benefited local sea turtle protection programs and local communities. Unfortunately, tourism remains a relatively untapped resource for sea turtle conservation. Although an estimated 10 million people spend more than US$1.25 billion every year to see whales and dolphins, a recent World Wildlife Fund (WWF) study (Troeng & Drews, 2004) estimated fewer than 200,000 tourists visit turtle sites annually worldwide, with roughly half of those visits to only five sites around the world. There are more than 2,800 sea turtle nesting beaches recorded around the world, and hundreds if not thousands more foraging areas and other places where turtles congregate.

When conducted sensitively, tourism can have many benefits to local communities, such as:

- Providing revenue for conservation and scientific research programs through visitor fees and donations.
- Providing alternative sources of income for local residents as guides, many of whom are former poachers.
- Increased community support for conservation due to indirect income spent in local businesses by travelers.
- Volunteers provide crucial manpower needed to cover long nesting beaches, and in many places directly benefit local families through homestays.
- Recent studies show that marine wildlife watching can move people toward more sustainable lifestyles and involvement in conservation efforts (Ballantyne, Packer, & Hughes, 2009).

A landmark 2004 WWF study called *Money Talks: Economic Aspects of Marine Turtle Use and Consumption* compared non-consumptive use (primarily ecotourism) to consumptive use (i.e., consumption and/or sale of turtle meat, eggs, and shells) of turtles. The study found that, "[n]on-consumptive use generates more revenue, has greater economic multiplying effects, greater potential for economic growth, creates more support for management, and generates proportionally more jobs, social development and employment opportunities for women than consumptive use" (Troeng & Drews, 2004, p. 7).

As the study also noted, turtle-based tourism can have negative impacts on the animals if not properly controlled. These impacts include (but are not limited to) tourism development on turtle nesting beaches, an increase in trash (particularly plastic bags) in turtle habitats, boat strikes from marine-based tours, and harassment of nesting and basking turtles resulting in behavioral changes. Tourism in turtle habitats can generate relatively little financial support for conservation programs in places where legal protections are lacking (Troeng & Drews, 2004).

Building a Model for Sea Turtle Conservation Tourism

SEE Turtles, a project of the Ocean Foundation, links people with turtle sites in ways that directly support protection efforts, while increasing resources in communities to help residents thrive and value sea turtles in their environment. SEE Turtles works with community-based organizations at key turtle sites to promote responsible tourism that will allow the organizations to expand their work and bring alternative sources of income to communities where poaching and fishing are common practices.

SEE Turtles aims to strengthen the international network of sea turtle conservation organizations by filling gaps in tourism market access and capacity building. To enhance market access, SEE Turtles develops relationships with international tour operators to include sea turtle conservation activities and educate key constituencies through its website, media outreach, and other outlets. It also builds capacity in turtle communities by providing mini-grants to partners, sharing knowledge on the necessary components of a tourism strategy, and training community members to run small tourism businesses and earn income as guides. In addition, SEE Turtles has worked with representatives of more than 20 conservation organizations and government agencies to create and disseminate a turtle watching best practices guide for travelers, tour operators, and turtle communities.

The primary goal of SEE Turtles is to encourage a transition away from destructive and consumptive uses of sea turtles by providing alternative sources of income for local communities. Secondary goals are to support field conservation efforts through increased income and technical support, to set the standard for turtle-friendly ecotourism and elevate sea turtles into a top wildlife attraction, and to inspire life-long conservationists for marine wildlife and the ocean.

Case Studies of Sea Turtle Conservation Tourism in Action

Voluntourism in Gandoca, Costa Rica

WIDECAST Costa Rica (and its predecessor Asociación ANAI) have protected the nesting beach of the leatherback sea turtle (*Dermochelys coriacea*) along the southernmost stretch of beach on Costa Rica's Caribbean coast since 1986. ANAI established a volunteer program in 1990 to provide support for research staff to cover the approximately 5-mile-long stretch of beach and to help generate income for the local community. In 2007, the ANAI turtle research staff moved the project management to WIDECAST, the Wider Caribbean Sea Turtle Network.

From 1996 to 2010, the number of annual volunteers grew to more than 500 people per year with a gross income in 2010 of US$273,000. Approximately 10% of those funds went to sustain the conservation work, and the rest was spent at locally owned cabins, shops, and bars or for services such as taxis and nature guides. The volunteer program provided about 15–20% of the project's total budget, with the balance coming primarily from grants and donations.

According to ANAI/WIDECAST data, the volunteer program has had a significant impact on conservation efforts. In 1985, 100% of the nests were poached; since 1996, the percentage of nests that were illegally poached declined from nearly 40% to less than 5% in 2003 to 1% during the last 3 years. Actual income from volunteers has exceeded the potential value of the turtle eggs on the black market every year from 1996 to 2010. From 2000 to 2010, volunteer income averaged about US$60,000 whereas the total black market value of the turtle eggs averaged just US$10,000, meaning that volunteer tourism has generated more than six times the black market value of the eggs. During 2010, the gross income produced by ecotourism at Gandoca Beach was eight times more than the total value of the eggs in the black market.

Tortuguero, Costa Rica: Managing Tourism at the World's Most Popular Turtle Destination

Located along Costa Rica's northern Caribbean coast, Tortuguero was established in 1955 as the world's first sea turtle conservation project. The Sea Turtle Conservancy (formerly the Caribbean Conservation Corporation) has managed the annual conservation and research program since 1955. The 18-mile-long beach hosts the largest nesting population of green turtles (*Chelonia mydas*) in the Western Hemisphere, with up to 180,000 nests per season, as well as significant nesting of leatherback turtles. The Sea Turtle Conservancy helped the

Costa Rican government to establish Tortuguero National Park to both protect the turtles and encourage tourism. Tourism to Tortuguero became significant in the early 1990s and quickly rose to more than 100,000 people in 2007. With the growth in tourism, about 25 hotels and small cabins have been built in the town of Tortuguero to accommodate this increased visitation. To the benefit of the turtles, however, this growth has mostly been limited to a very small proportion of the coast (i.e., only 1 mile of the 18 miles undeveloped). The number of tourists to the park who take turtle tours has nearly doubled from approximately 20,000 in 1999 to nearly 40,000 in 2007 (RED Sustainable Travel, 2011).

This increase in both visitors to the town and people going out on the beach to see the nesting of the turtles has caused significant logistical challenges for both the staff of the conservancy and park management. To effectively prevent negative impacts on the turtles while allowing the community to benefit from tourism, a number of regulations have been established, including restriction of tours to two areas of the beach; limits on the number of people per guide (10), the number of people per turtle (20), and the hours that tourists are allowed on the beach (2 hours per group); and a requirement that tourists be accompanied by a trained and licensed local guide.

In 2004, a group including representatives from the park, the conservancy, and others initiated a new system for managing tourists called the Turtle Spotter Program. Prior to 2004, tourists would walk on the beach with their tour guide, searching for a nesting turtle to observe. Due to the increasing number of tourists on the beach there was concern from conservancy staff and park managers that sea turtles coming ashore to nest were being disturbed. The innovative new system uses trained spotters to search for turtles on the beach, while the tour groups stay with their guides in special waiting areas off the beach. Once a turtle has been located, the groups walk behind the beach to the closest entrance to the turtle. The spotter notifies the guide when the turtle can be approached, minimizing the time tourists are on the beach and helping to prevent disturbance to turtles before they lay their eggs. The success of these tourism management initiatives is apparent. Since 1970 the average annual number of nesting green turtles has increased more than 500% despite more than 100,000 annual visitors that currently come to this beach (RED Sustainable Travel, 2011).

Magdalena Bay, Baja California Sur, Mexico: Building a Community-Based Model for Turtle Conservation Tourism

Magdalena Bay on the Pacific coast of Baja California Sur, Mexico, represents one of the most important wetland ecosystems on the west coast of North America. Its waters provide protection to calving gray whales, migratory and marine birds, and numerous species of marine mammals, and are important feeding grounds for endangered black sea turtles. Additionally, Magdalena Bay is one of the most productive fisheries in Mexico. Unfortunately all of these resources are threatened by overfishing, poaching, bycatch (entanglement in fishing gear), and poorly regulated coastal development. Lax fisheries regulation and enforcement, together with rapid population growth resulting from migration from states throughout Mexico, have formented a tragedy of the commons, with little regard for the natural resources that sustain the communities of the bay.

Figure CS 7.1   Turtle conservation is a win-win for communities.

Sea turtles, principally endangered black turtles (a subspecies of green turtles), suffer both from entanglement in fishing nets and longlines and from active poaching for consumption and sale on the black market. Although sea turtle research and conservation projects have taken hold in this area, and education efforts have been effective in reaching youth, the majority of the adult population has remained a challenging target because their daily decisions may include participation in poaching or including sea turtle in the family diet, both of which have the greatest impact on sea turtle populations in Magdalena Bay.

Grupo Ecotortugueros de Puerto San Carlos (GET) is an ecotourism cooperative operating in Magdalena Bay (see **Figure CS 7.1**). The cooperative was launched as part of the RED[1] Sustainable Tourism Project in an effort to create alternative incomes linked directly to conservation—specifically sea turtle research and conservation. The launch of the cooperative is the product of collaboration among RED, Vigilantes de Bahía Magdalena (VBM), Grupo Tortuguero de las Californias (GTC), and members of the local fishing community.

In late 2009, the RED project, together with its partners, worked with local community members to launch GET, in an effort to generate sustainable employment opportunities to compliment fishing, and as an alternative to illegal poaching. As a result, using the Grupo Tortuguero turtle monitoring as the core product offering, the project has generated part-time employment for 13 individuals, including key elements in the community such as active (now former) sea turtle poachers. As part of the business incubation process, the cooperative has incorporated environmental sustainability as one of its main tenets, and has worked with RED to specifically define strategies to benefit conservation and community development. The tours benefit turtle conservation in a variety of ways, including promoting complementary sources

---

[1] The name *RED* comes from the Spanish word *red*, which means "net," as in fishing net or network. The name symbolizes the network of fishing communities where the RED project was born.

of income for fishermen, generating funding for local environmental education campaigns, covering the costs of research and monitoring programs, engendering stewardship, and informing national and international visitors. RED's ultimate goal is to bring this model of community-based conservation tourism to other wildlife hotspots across the peninsula and Mexico.

Discover Grenada Turtle Tours: Linking Community-Based Ecotourism and Sea Turtle Conservation

Grenada is a small Caribbean island that has one of the most important leatherback sea turtle nesting beaches in the region (Levera Beach). Turtle eggs are considered by many residents to be an aphrodisiac (which is common in the region and many other places around the world) and are sold on the black market. Ocean Spirits, a locally based organization that has worked to protect the island's sea turtles since 1999, partnered with RARE, an international conservation organization, to create a new business with the primary goal of generating income to expand turtle conservation efforts to new beaches on the island. Other goals for the enterprise include creating a new source of income for local residents, developing a presence on previously unprotected beaches as a deterrent to poachers, and supporting environmental education programs.

Tourism is one of the key industries in Grenada, with an average of approximately 120,000 visitors per year. Prior to this partnership, several tour operators brought clients to see the leatherback turtles, but little if any of the income went toward conservation programs. Ocean Spirits had previously attempted to develop turtle tours but abandoned the effort once it determined that it did not have adequate staff time and capacity (Ocean Spirits, 2011).

In 2008, the partnership with RARE's Enterprises program (now part of Solimar International) launched Discover Grenada Turtle Tours. The tours were sold through local hotels and tour operators, and a local outlet in St. George's, the primary tourist venue on the island. The tours are managed entirely by local residents who were trained by RARE staff in business management, logistics, and marketing. In the company's first season in 2008, there were 233 tourists worth nearly US$17,000 in gross sales, with a large portion of the profits going to expand a previously unprotected nesting beach (Bathway Beach). Ocean Spirits calculated the value of a live turtle was more than US$3,000, whereas the turtle meat would have been worth less than US$100. Unfortunately, due to budget constraints and changing organizational priorities, RARE was not able to continue its capacity-building support to Ocean Spirits. After two seasons, the business was discontinued and to date has not been revived. One key lesson in this case study is that in developing partnerships, ensuring the ability of organizations to follow through until the work is complete is critical. Starting new companies can require an investment of several years by partners before the business can function on its own.

Conclusion

No magic formula exists when it comes to species conservation and protection. However, there are strategies that have proven successful. Voluntourism has the potential to earn income that exceeds that of black market sales—in the case of Magdalena Bay, the income ratio was 6 to 1. Education is critical for long-term sustainability, including developing youth programs as well as educating community members and local fisherman. Voluntourism supports many of these initiatives. As with all cases, it is critical to build partnerships that enable new businesses or organizations over time, often several years. Having partners that are involved for the long haul appears crucial to ensuring success. Communicating the value of live species is important as part of the educational process as well. In all locations identified in this case, the protection of turtles demonstrated higher income and value to society than did simply consuming the turtles. Often this is not communicated or known and does provide a case to all stakeholders for conservation efforts.

References

Ballantyne, R., Packer, J., & Hughes, K. (2009). Tourists' support for conservation messages and sustainable management practices in wildlife tourism experiences. *Tourism Management, 30*(5), 658–664.

Ocean Spirits (Grenada). (2011). About us. Retrieved April 5, 2012, from http://www.oceanspirits.org

RED Sustainable Travel. (2011). Homepage. Retrieved April 5, 2012, from http://www.redtravelmexico.com

Tisdell, C., & Wilson, C. (2005). Perceived impacts of ecotourism on environmental learning and conservation: Turtle watching as a case study. *Environment, Development and Sustainability, 7*, 291–302.

Troeng, S., & Drews, C. (2004). *Money talks: Economic aspects of marine turtle use and conservation.* Gland, Switzerland: WWF International.

Ecotourism and the Challenge of Climate Change: Vulnerability, Responsibility, and Mitigation Strategies

Wolfgang Strasdas

LEARNING OBJECTIVES

- To demonstrate how nature-based tourism is contributing to climate change mediation through energy consumption
- To understand how nature-based tourism is and will be affected by global warming
- To understand existing mitigation strategies in the industry and develop an encompassing framework for carbon management and climate protection as part of an extended ecotourism concept
- To be familiar with climate adaptation strategies (including risk management) for nature tourism companies and destinations
- To be able to consider the future of ecotourism—ways of responding to the challenge of global warming

The concept of ecotourism was developed in the 1980s when the conservation of biodiversity was one of the most prominent environmental concerns globally. Although this problem has by no means been resolved, an even more encompassing environmental threat has taken center stage in the new millennium: climate change. How to respond to the challenges posed by global warming[1] has become a key issue for the sustainable development and ultimate viability of tourism. Nevertheless, the tourism industry has been rather slow in addressing both adaption to and mitigation of climate change. It could be argued that ecotourism, with its long-standing tradition of resource conservation and sustainable development, should play a significant role in this endeavor. So far, however, ecotourism has largely focused on local sustainability issues, neglecting the important impact that transportation has on world climate. In the spirit of Millennium Development Goal 7, with its focus on environmental sustainability, this chapter highlights implications of climate change and interventions to consider in sustainable tourism development to mediate the environmental impacts of tourism.

First, this chapter briefly describes the interrelationship between climate change and tourism in general, showing that tourism is both affected by global warming and a significant source of man-made greenhouse gases. This is followed by an outline of the principles of carbon management as a mitigation strategy. Second, an analysis of how nature-based tourism in particular fits into the overall picture is provided. Apart from a few case studies, this segment of the tourism industry has not been systematically researched. However, the scant evidence and plausibility show that nature-based tourism is particularly vulnerable to the consequences of climate change due to its reliance on intact natural resources. On the other hand, it is likely that nature tourism's role as a "co-perpetrator" is enhanced because pristine natural areas tend to be remote, thus increasing transport-related emissions. Third, to shed more light on these complex interrelationships, recent research conducted by the author in Namibia will be presented, focusing on the climate impact of safari and wilderness tourism in that country and discussing possible mitigation strategies.

Based on the results of the analyses, ecotourism's present state in relation to the challenge of climate change will be assessed. With a focus on mitigating its impacts, recommendations will be given on how ecotourism could once again assume its pioneering role in terms of sustainable development in the new millennium by more vigorously incorporating climate protection as one of its strategies. A key message is there are synergies between climate protection and other goals of sustainable development, and mitigation is also a way to adapt to the indirect, societal changes brought about by global warming.

---

[1] Although the terms *climate change* and *global warming* describe slightly different phenomena, in that global warming is the underlying cause of climate change, which is characterized by rising temperatures, in this chapter the terms often are used interchangeably, where appropriate.

The Interrelationship Between Tourism and Climate Change

There is ample evidence and a large body of literature showing that tourism in general is both vulnerable to and contributes to global warming. In this chapter, both forms of this interrelationship will be briefly outlined.[2]

Impacts of Climate Change on Tourism

Although some tourism segments such as business travel or cultural tourism are largely independent of climate as a factor in selecting a holiday destination, most forms of holiday tourism clearly rely on climatic conditions. In fact, the main reason behind the world's most significant tourism flows from Northern Europe to the Mediterranean and from North America to the Caribbean is a warmer, sunny climate and warm water temperatures in southern latitudes. Winter tourism is another important tourism segment that is entirely dependent on climate, in this case on a single climate-related resource: snow. It is therefore clear that rising temperatures, less predictable rainfall patterns, increased climate variability, and extreme weather events in the wake of global warming will have a significant impact on tourism ranging from infrastructure damage to modified travel behavior. Whereas northern latitudes may actually benefit from these changes, southern tourism destinations, some of which are already hot and drought-stricken in the summer season, are more likely to lose out (Deutsche Bank Research, 2008). In low-lying ski resorts the negative impacts of climate change can already be felt.

Apart from the more obvious direct physical impacts of global warming, a number of indirect effects also may have an influence on tourism:

- *Indirect physical impacts* affect tourism's nonclimatic natural resource base, such as water, forests, biodiversity, or scenery. Throughout the world, most of these resources are expected to be negatively affected if no countermeasures are taken. Rising sea levels put tourism infrastructure at risk. In addition, the natural or traditional cultural landscape will be transformed by adaptation measures taken by other sectors, such as flood control or increased irrigation in agriculture. Vector-borne diseases will probably spread, thus increasing health risks for tourists and tourism staff.

- *Mitigation policies*, with the aim of lowering man-made greenhouse gas emissions (e.g., the European Union's emissions trading scheme for aviation that was enacted in 2012), will make the use of fossil energy sources more expensive. This is of particular concern to tourism destinations dependent on long-haul air transport.

- Worldwide there is an increasing *public awareness* about the negative impact people's travel may have on the world climate, possibly leading to more climate-friendly travel behavior (see Eijgelaar, 2007; McKercher, Prideaux, Cheung, & Law, 2010; Strasdas, 2010a).

---

[2] This is based on the extensive report by the United Nations World Tourism Organization and United Nations Environment Programme (2008), if not noted otherwise.

- There could be *destabilization of economies and societies* as a result of severe impacts of climate change, if global temperatures continue to rise unabated. Obviously, this would greatly decrease disposable income for traveling and have dramatic consequences for the attractiveness of tourism destinations.

Even though the general trends are clear, there are some important challenges in determining global warming impacts and designing appropriate adaptation strategies (see Hall, 2009; Strasdas & Zeppenfeld, 2010). First, the extreme complexity of both physical and societal factors that influence the extent of global warming and its impact on tourism make it impossible to forecast any future developments. Instead, scenarios and probabilities must be used. Second, although there is a fair degree of certainty about global warming trends and generally increasing climate variability, impacts on the local level may significantly differ from the global average. In addition, the effects of climate change in a given tourism destination are also influenced by how source markets and competing destinations are affected. Third, time frames vary as well. Although some impacts of climate change can already be felt in certain regions, the more severe effects are not likely to become evident before the second half of the century. Therefore, core elements of proper adaptation strategies, including constructing likely scenarios, handling uncertainties, and managing risks, may not be exactly determined. Long-term tourism policies and planning processes must become more flexible to account for unforeseen climatic impacts, and more rigorous risk assessment must be applied when planning larger investments, such as in tourism infrastructure.

Tourism's Contribution to Climate Change

Worldwide, tourism is estimated to be directly responsible for about 5% of energy-related CO_2 emissions (United Nations World Tourism Organization & United Nations Environment Programme [UNWTO/UNEP], 2008). Although this share may appear to be relatively small at first glance, it becomes more significant when comparing it with other sectors. Roughly, tourism's share of global CO_2 emissions equals those of the chemical industry (World Resources Institute [WRI], 2005). Within the tourism industry, emissions are unevenly distributed: 75% are attributed to transportation, of which air transport accounts for 40% and automobile traffic 32%; the share from accommodations is 21% (see **Figure 9.1**) (WRI, 2005). This means that emissions of aviation-dependent long-haul tourism are substantially higher per travel day than the average tourism trip. In Germany, for example, domestic tourism represents only 1.6% of national emissions (with transportation's share of this being 62%); however, for intercontinental trips taken by Germans, their flights alone account for about 90% of the overall trip emissions (German Federal Agency of the Environment & Öko-Institut, 2002).

The problematic role of air travel is further aggravated by scientific evidence that non-CO_2 emissions from aircraft at high cruising altitudes increase the overall warming effect (or "radiative forcing") of aviation. However, due to the high complexity of the various factors involved, scientific knowledge of the exact interactions and impacts is still sketchy. It is now believed the overall warming effect from aircraft may be twice as high as if CO_2 alone was taken into account. In its 2007 report, the Intergovernmental Panel on Climate Change used a multiplier of 2.7 because some studies suggest that radiative forcing from

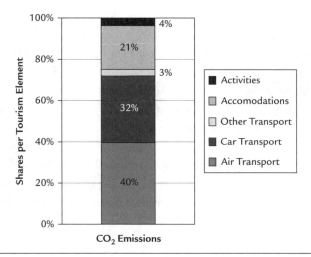

Figure 9.1   Shares of CO_2 emissions per tourism subsector.
Source: UNWTO (United Nations World Tourism Organization) & UNEP (United Nations Environment Programme). (2008). *Climate change and tourism: Responding to global challenges.* Madrid/Paris. © UNWTO (9284402012)

aircraft may be substantially higher due to the formation of cirrus clouds from contrails (see Strasdas, 2009).

At the individual consumer level, a lifestyle of frequent flying and long-haul holidays affects reasonable personal climate budgets. A single round-trip flight from Frankfurt to Sydney emits about 11 tons of greenhouse gases (calculated as CO_2 equivalents), about the same as an average German citizen emits in one year. Three tons per year per individual are considered to be climate-compatible, assuming that each global citizen has the same emission rights.[3]

Most national governments around the world have now officially accepted that global warming should be kept within a limit of +2°C (compared to preindustrial levels), if unmanageable impacts and severe consequences to humanity are to be avoided. This means that substantial reductions in greenhouse gas emissions need to be achieved, in particular by industrialized countries but increasingly by emerging economies as well, decoupling their economic growth from a further increase of emissions. It now is widely believed that global emissions must decrease in absolute terms no later than 2020, and industrialized countries need to reduce their current emissions by 80% by 2050 (Gössling, 2011). There is pressure on the tourism industry to contribute to climate protection like all other sectors. However, business-as-usual scenarios for global tourism forecast an emissions increase of about 250% by 2035 (compared to 2005 levels), even with modest energy-efficiency gains already taken into account (Gössling, 2011).

It is clear from the evidence that such a development is entirely unacceptable. If tourism is to continue to thrive as an economic activity, substantial savings in emissions need to be made

[3] Calculation based on the climate calculators of atmosfair (http://www.atmosfair.de), a carbon offset provider, and the German Federal Agency for the Environment (http://uba.klima-aktiv.de).

(see Scott & Becken, 2010; Weaver, 2011). Leading global tourism organizations such as the World Travel and Tourism Council (WTTC) have responded to public and political pressure by pledging to reduce the sector's emissions by 50% by 2035 (compared to 2005 levels) (WTTC, 2010). Similar intentions have been announced by the International Civil Aviation Organization (ICAO) and the International Air Transport Association (IATA), although their reduction targets (–50% by 2050) are less ambitious. Unfortunately, there are no concrete strategies on how these targets can actually be achieved, especially in relation to air transport (Gössling, 2011).

A systematic approach to reduce a company's, organization's, or destination's greenhouse gas emissions as much as possible—ideally to zero—is usually described by using the term *carbon management*.[4] Carbon management is implemented through the following steps (Gössling, 2011; Strasdas, 2010b):

1. *Measure* and analyze emissions.
2. *Eliminate* or avoid emissions by foregoing energy-intensive travel products or activities.
3. *Reduce* energy consumption by increasing energy efficiency.
4. *Substitute* fossil energy sources with renewable energy sources.
5. *Offset* remaining emissions by investing in certified, high-quality compensation projects.
6. *Communicate* about carbon management with customers, employees, suppliers, and other stakeholders.

Carbon management can be implemented by a combination of strategies or tools (Gössling, 2011; Strasdas, 2010b):

- *Technological:* Increased use of renewable energies as well as energy efficiency in aircraft, vehicles, and accommodation businesses
- *Managerial:* For example, optimizing long-haul flight routes, improving transport logistics, or procuring food more locally
- *Modal shift:* Shifting tourist mobility from more energy-intensive to less energy-intensive modes of transport, that is from air to ground transport and from individual to collective forms of transportation
- *Behavioral changes:* Changing individuals' behavior and developing corresponding travel products that are less energy-intensive per day of travel (especially increased length of stay in exchange for fewer trips); spending more quality time at fewer, selected locations; and showing a preference for nearby destinations

How carbon management as a mitigation strategy can be implemented in relation to nature-based tourism will be discussed in the final section of this chapter.

---

[4] The use of the term *carbon* in this case is actually quite narrow in that in its strictest sense it would only include CO_2 emissions. However, as already discussed, it is imperative to include other greenhouse gases as well, especially for aviation. Therefore, the more correct term would be *greenhouse gas management*. Nevertheless, the term *carbon management* is preferred for its greater ease of use but shall be understood in a more comprehensive way. The overall warming potential of emissions would then be measured in CO_2 equivalents (CO_2-e).

The Specific Situation of Nature-Based Tourism

In the context of this article "nature (-based) tourism" is defined as any type of tourism that takes place in natural or semi-natural settings where experiencing nature is the main motivation of visitors regardless of impact (Strasdas, 2001). The term *ecotourism* (as defined by The International Ecotourism Society [TIES]) is "responsible travel to natural areas that conserves the environment and improves the well-being of local people" (TIES, 2012, p. 1) and is used for forms of nature-based tourism that explicitly strive to achieve positive impacts.

Climate-Induced Impacts on Nature-Based Tourism

As mentioned earlier, it is not possible to draw generally valid conclusions as to how nature-based tourism will be affected by climate change because impacts are highly dependent on specific regional circumstances and demand segments. Nevertheless, it is quite plausible to assume that the tourism industry is particularly vulnerable to the consequences of global warming for the following reasons:

- Nature tourism usually takes place outdoors, so infrastructure, equipment, staff, and tourists themselves are directly exposed to rising temperatures, precipitation, and extreme weather phenomena, possibly leading to deteriorating levels of comfort, safety, and health (Piotrowski & Xola Consulting, 2010).
- Nature tourism's natural resource base (biodiversity, scenic values, mountains, rivers and other bodies of water) also is directly affected by climate change, predominantly in a negative way (UNWTO/UNEP, 2008).
- Nature-based tourism often takes place in remote areas, many of them in developing countries. This leads to two types of consequences: First, in case of emergencies help may be far away, thus producing higher physical risks and safety issues (Piotrowski & Xola Consulting, 2010). Second, remote areas require covering greater distances and more transportation challenges, usually entailing higher fuel use, which in turn makes nature tourism more susceptible to market- and climate policy–induced increases in transport costs. On the other hand, such trips tend to be upscale products where price sensitivity may be lower than in other tourism segments.
- As a rule, people participating in nature-based tourism have above-average levels of education and awareness of environmental issues, which includes climate change. Even though this has not yet significantly influenced travel decisions, it may do so in the future (e.g., by giving a competitive advantage to businesses engaged in climate protection [Strasdas, 2010a]).

These general trends need to be differentiated in relation to specific tourism destinations, ecosystems, and species. Only a few studies have specifically analyzed the impact of global warming on nature-based tourism, but there is more scientific evidence on the vulnerability of its natural resource base. Quite often, ecosystems have already been weakened by other factors, but this is usually exacerbated by climate change. Some examples are the following:

- Nature-based tourism in marine and coastal environments is vulnerable to various climate-induced impacts ranging from sea level rise and higher water temperatures to more frequent

Figure 9.2 Hippos in a mud pool (rather than water) during an extended dry season in Tanzania.

and intense storms. This, in combination with current stress factors, may endanger coastal ecosystems, especially coral reefs, and charismatic marine animals, such as whales or sea turtles. Diving tourism in particular is expected to be severely affected as a result (Plume, 2009; UNWTO/UNEP, 2008).

- Endemic and rare species living in isolated habitats and usually dependent on very specific ecological conditions are vulnerable to destabilization brought about by climate change. Some of these species are tourism attractions, such as orangutans in Indonesia or tropical frogs in Central America (Plume, 2009; UNWTO/UNEP, 2008).

- Increasing drought conditions in Southern and Eastern Africa may endanger large mammal populations, the region's major tourism asset (Reid, Sahlén, MacGregor, & Stage, 2007) (see **Figure 9.2**).

- Nature-based mountain tourism is susceptible to receding glaciers, increased erosion, forest insect infestations, and the so-called "summit trap," where isolated plant communities specifically adapted to an alpine climate cannot migrate further upwards to escape rising temperatures (Strasdas & Gössling, 2008).

- Temperature rise has been particularly significant in polar regions, leading to decreasing ice cover and thawing permafrost soils. This poses a threat to charismatic species such as polar bears, among others (Dawson, Stewart, Lemelin, & Scott, 2010). On the other hand, increased public attention to climate change also may trigger "last chance tourism" to Antarctica and the Arctic (Eijgelaar, Thaper, & Peeters, 2010), with the polar bear having become an icon of global warming threats and disappearing species.

Currently, systematic adaptation strategies to climate change that are specific to nature-based tourism do not seem to exist. In general, adaptation of tourism to climate change is incipient at best (see KPMG International, 2008; Scott & Becken, 2010). In some tourism destinations, more or less extensive research has been done on their vulnerability to climate change and initial adaptation strategies have been drafted. An example of a relatively well studied destination in this regard is Australia, where a sizeable portion of the tourism industry is nature-based and the impacts of global warming are already being felt (Sustainable Tourism Cooperative Research Centre [STCRC], 2009). Another more limited study was conducted on the climate vulnerability of small businesses in the adventure tourism sector. It analyzed risks and opportunities for three companies in the Amazon, the Himalayas, and the Arctic/Antarctic. Although these regions are believed to be particularly sensitive to global warming, adaptation so far has remained limited (Piotrowski & Xola Consulting, 2010).

Nature-Based Tourism and Its Contribution to Global Warming

Even though only a handful of studies have empirically analyzed the energy use and the climate impact of nature-based tourism in comparison to other segments of the tourism industry, nature tourism has some inherent characteristics that lead the following general conclusions:

- Typical nature tourism destinations such as Costa Rica, Ecuador, Tanzania, Namibia, Nepal, New Zealand, and virtually all small island states have relatively small or less affluent populations, making them largely dependent on long-haul source markets, mostly in North America and Europe. This is even more pronounced in the cases of the Arctic and Antarctica, thus causing a relatively high level of emissions caused by air transport.
- The remoteness of nature tourism destinations also applies at the domestic level, particularly in large countries, such as Canada, the United States, Russia, China, Australia, and Brazil, where natural attractions visited by tourists often are far away from the metropolitan areas or international airports. This leads to the necessity to transport tourists, staff, construction materials, fuels, and other provisions over long distances. In destinations with a good road or rail network this may be done by using ground transport; in its absence, aircraft have to be used for this purpose, particularly in developing countries.
- Most nature-based holidays are not stationary like the typical beach vacation, where guests spend most of their time in a single resort. Instead, on nature tours several sites are usually visited, thus further increasing distances covered. This is partially due to the once-in-a-lifetime character of many nature or adventure tours where travelers would like to see as much as possible of a far-away destination during a limited period of time.
- Accommodations in nature-based tourism tend to be simpler than in mainstream tourism as far as physical comfort and electric appliances (e.g., air conditioning, television) are concerned. The use of rustic cabins or camping is more widespread and part of the tourist's experience. Although more effort is made in this segment to use renewable energies and encourage energy efficiency as a result of a broader environmental management approach, on the other hand, remoteness and the absence of public utilities lead to greater logistical effort and transport, as mentioned previously. Relatively low occupancy rates (due to often marked seasonality) and short stays (requiring more frequent room cleaning) also tend to increase energy use per guest night.
- Nature-based leisure activities can be simple and self-reliant. Hiking, cycling, and canoeing are popular activities with a low climate impact. However, with the increasing average age of many travelers, support vehicles are often provided. In addition, many on-site activities in nature tourism are motorized, such as scenic flights, game drives, or whale watching.

The assumption that nature-based tourism is likely to be more energy-intensive per day of travel, and thus have a greater climate impact than average tourism, was first substantiated by a study from New Zealand. Simmons and Becken (2004) showed that, because of remoteness and motorized leisure activities (in New Zealand, often marine wildlife observation by boat), nature tourism's climate impact is substantially higher than for urban-based tourism. They also compared an average holiday in New Zealand—which is usually nature-based and covers more or less the entire country—to a beach resort holiday in the Caribbean (St. Lucia) and found the former to be about three times as energy-intensive (on a per day/per person basis, considering only emissions within the destination). Two more recent studies (Dawson et al., 2010; Eijgelaar et al., 2010) compared the climate impact of polar bear watching in Northern Canada and of cruises to Antarctica with the average international tourist trip and found them several times more carbon-intensive. This is not just due to the emissions incurred by the flights but also due to the high energy consumption of cruise ships in the case of Antarctica and to motorized leisure activities in the Arctic.

One may argue the two latter examples are extreme and cannot be applied to nature-based tourism in general. More empirical evidence is certainly needed, some of which will be provided in the later section on safari tourism in Namibia. Nevertheless, it is clear that mitigation strategies are urgently needed in the nature-based tourism segment. Whether and to what degree this has actually happened is very difficult to judge due to the dispersed nature of this segment. An international survey of nature-based tour operators conducted by this author in 2007 in cooperation with the International Ecotourism Society, Sustainable Travel International, and the Adventure Travel Trade Association revealed a high awareness of the problem but only limited action. Inbound operators tried to reduce emissions from accommodations and local transport mostly by efficiency measures and the use of renewable energy sources. Outbound operators had begun to contemplate carbon-offsetting, but almost none of them considered modifying their travel products, for instance by favoring nearby destinations, increasing length of stay, using public transport, or reducing motorized activities (Strasdas, 2009). More recent studies (Gössling, 2011; Rumpelt, 2009; University of Colorado et al., 2008) show there are a number of individual tourism operators around the world, many of them nature-based and mostly accommodation businesses, that are dedicated to climate protection or have achieved climate neutrality. On the other hand, generally, voluntary carbon offsetting, both by tourism companies and individual travelers, has remained limited (McKercher et al., 2010; Strasdas, 2010a).

In terms of recognizing, supporting, and rewarding climate change action in the nature-based tourism industry, the most advanced program is Ecotourism Australia's Climate Action Certification, which measures participating businesses' climate impact and evaluates their efforts in terms of climate change adaptation and mitigation (Ecotourism Australia, n.d.). The program's criteria cover energy efficiency, the use of renewable energies, and carbon-offsetting but do not require the modification of products or activities offered.

Some countries have pledged to become carbon-neutral tourism destinations over a period of 15 years or more. For most of them, such as Norway, Scotland, Costa Rica, or the Maldives, nature tourism is a major tourism segment. However, until recently there has been little substance to this commitment that would require a radical restructuring of a country's tourism system (Gössling, 2009; Gössling & Schumacher, 2010).

Climate Impact[5] Assessment
of Safari Tourism in Namibia

Namibia is a mostly arid, thinly populated country (2.2 million inhabitants) in the southwest of Africa. Its overwhelming desert landscapes and rich wildlife make it a prime destination for nature-based tourism. A fairly large proportion of the country has been declared as national parks, and environmental protection is part of Namibia's constitution. In addition, much privately owned land (former farms that are no longer profitable because of frequent drought conditions) has been converted into conservation areas. An internationally renowned specialty of Namibia is its third pillar of nature conservation: communal conservancies that have been put under the management of local communities under a government contract (Namibian Association of CBNRM Support Organisations [NACSO], 2010).

Since independence in 1990, tourism has grown steadily and is now one of Namibia's main economic sectors, with about 1 million international arrivals in 2009. Vacationing tourists are mostly from Europe, with Germany as the main source market. Intraregional tourism is mostly related to business, shopping, and visiting friends and relatives; only a limited number of tourists, mainly from South Africa, visit Namibia for leisure purposes (Namibia Tourist Board [NTB], 2010). Domestic tourism is underdeveloped due to the country's small population and low average income. These factors make Namibia a predominantly long-haul destination.

According to the World Bank classification, Namibia is a middle-income developing country, albeit with extremely high unemployment and poverty rates of almost 50% and one of the world's highest income inequalities (WTTC, 2006). Tourism is now among Namibia's key industries in terms of revenue generation, employment, and foreign exchange earnings (WTTC, 2006). The country's primary resources are based on landscape and wildlife. That provides economic benefits, as well as benefits to biodiversity conservation and rural communities. Communal conservancies tourism is the most significant source of income and gives economic value to the state-protected areas (NACSO, 2010; WTTC, 2006).

However, tourism in Namibia is not prepared for the challenges of climate change. With its dependence on natural resources and frequent operations in remote, undeveloped areas, it is particularly vulnerable to the physical impacts of climate change, namely heat waves, prolonged droughts, biodiversity loss, and extreme weather events such as floods. Even though tourism operators in Namibia have always had to deal with adverse climatic phenomena, their projected increased frequency and intensity will pose new risks. Furthermore, being a long-haul destination at approximately 8,000 kilometers or 10 flight hours from its main source markets, Namibia is reliant on affordable airfares and thus at risk from increasing energy costs. In addition, because of large distances, low population density, and a high import rate of electric energy, fuels, and vehicles, it is also vulnerable in terms of domestic transportation needs. Finally, climate awareness and criticism of frequent flying are particularly high in Namibia's major source markets: Germany and the United Kingdom (Strasdas, 2010a).

---

[5] The term *climate impact* is generally preferred over the more popular "carbon footprint" because it also takes into account greenhouse gases other than CO_2 and the metric is in tons of CO_2 equivalents rather than m².

A 2-month research project carried out by the author in early 2011 analyzed the climate impact of five representative package tours offered by three different inbound tour operators for European tourists, all of which are nature-based and can be categorized as scenery and wildlife tourism, usually called "safari tourism" in Southern and Eastern Africa. The tours can be described as follows:

1. *Great Namibian Journey:* Upscale, small group tour with a strong focus on natural, partially remote settings and nature interpretation; distance covered: ca. 1,500 kilometers by road, ca. 1,100 kilometers by air; duration: 16 days (this and the following packages include 2 days for the international flights); transport by four-wheel-drive vehicles and small aircraft

2. *Best of Namibia Circuit:* Luxury, customized tour covering Namibia's natural tourism highlights with a strong focus on nature interpretation; distance covered: ca. 1,750 kilometers; duration: 10 days; transport exclusively by small aircraft

3. *Etosha group tour:* Mainstream, medium-sized group tour covering Namibia in depth; distance covered: 4,995 kilometers; duration: 20 days; transport by all-terrain bus

4. *Mopane self-drive tour:* Mainstream, customized tour covering Namibia's tourism highlights; distance covered: 3,170 kilometers; duration: 15 days; transport by automobile (all-terrain or four-wheel-drive)

5. *On Foot in Namibia's Canyons, Deserts and Mountains:* Medium-sized trekking tour covering several hiking destinations within Namibia; distance covered: 2,780 kilometers; accommodation in tents or mid-range hotels; duration: 20 days; transport by all-terrain van

Methodology

The climate impact of an individual's entire journey was calculated from a consumption point of view on a per-person/per-trip and a per-person/per-day-of-travel basis, covering the trip from home to the airport, the international flight(s), accommodations, catering, transport, and activities at the destination as well as the operators' office operations. Only direct emissions were considered; emissions incurred by the manufacturing of vehicles or appliances, the construction of buildings, or the production and transport of food and fuels were disregarded because there were no available data. For the international flights, the emissions calculator of the German offset provider atmosfair was used. Atmosfair takes non-CO_2 emissions into account by applying a multiplier of 2.7. For all other trip elements, only CO_2 was measured. The calculations for the office, accommodation, and domestic transport emissions were based on fuel types and quantities, which were then converted into kilograms of CO_2 emissions. The conversion factors were taken from a study conducted for one of the companies, Wilderness Safaris (Carlyon, 2009).

All figures (fuel consumption, distances covered, occupancy, party size, and trip duration) were provided by the participating tour operators. However, regarding accommodations, Wilderness Safaris was the only company that could provide figures because it uses its own facilities, whereas the two other companies mostly rely on lodges or guesthouses they do not own. In these cases, default values were used. The global average value for hotels (including catering) of 20.6 kilograms CO_2 per guest night given by the UNWTO/UNEP 2008 study

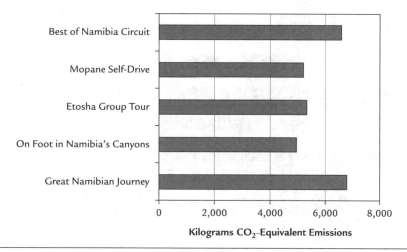

Figure 9.3   Climate impact of safari tourism in Namibia, per person per trip.

was used as a basis for calculations. Accommodations used on the five tours are mid-range to up-market, sometimes with air conditioning but rarely in the luxurious segment. Hotels supplied with electricity from the public grid tend to be more upscale, but off-grid locations usually rely on more emission-intensive diesel generators. Thus, depending on the physical standard and the degree to which renewable energies are used, values between 20 and 30 kilograms of CO_2 per guest night were assumed.

The results show that a safari trip from Europe to Namibia has a very high climate impact, ranging from 4.9 to 6.8 tons of CO_2-e per person (see **Figure 9.3**). The daily emissions per person range between 247 and 659 kilograms (see **Figure 9.4**). This is substantially higher than the average international trip (around 0.5 tons/person/trip and 60 kilograms/person/day, respectively [UNWTO/UNEP, 2008]), even considering that the UNWTO/UNEP figures relate to CO_2 emissions only. A trip to Namibia is equal to about 50% of the average annual emissions of a

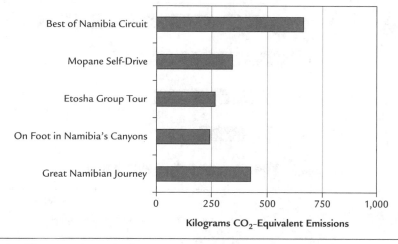

Figure 9.4   Climate impact of safari tourism in Namibia, per person per day.

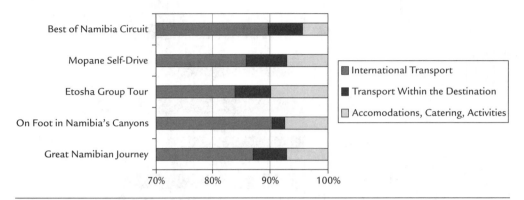

Figure 9.5   Share of trip components contributing to CO_2 emissions.

German citizen, and 84–90% is accounted for by the international flight (see **Figure 9.5**). The daily emissions are high despite the fact the five packages have an average duration of 16 days, about twice as long as the global average for international trips. However, the high per-day emissions of the Best of Namibia Circuit are mostly due to its short overall duration.

To gain a clearer picture of the in-country emissions, the five tours were also analyzed excluding the long-haul flight, and major differences became evident. Not surprisingly, the two upscale packages offered by Wilderness Safaris (Best of Namibia Circuit and Great Namibian Journey) have the highest emissions per person per day, followed by the self-drive tour, whereas the trekking tour has the lowest climate impact (see **Figure 9.6**). This is largely due to the different means of domestic transport that are used. Best of Namibia Circuit is an exclusive fly-in safari and the Great Namibian Journey uses a combination of small aircraft and converted Land Rovers. Interestingly, the transport component of the self-drive tour (an average party size of two using a small 4×4 vehicle—a very popular way of tourist travel in Namibia) is as energy-intensive per person as the former tour. The trekking tour (On Foot in Namibia's Canyons) has the most

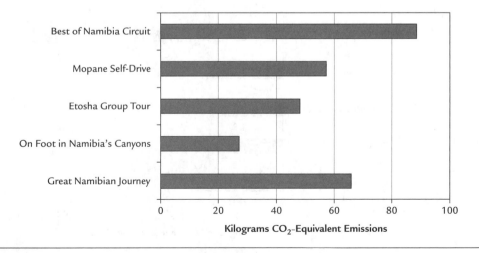

Figure 9.6   In-country emissions per person per day.

Table 9.1   Emissions as a Function of Transport Mode and Occupancy

Type of Vehicle	Fuel (per 100 km)	CO$_2$ Emissions (per 100 km)[a]	Average/Full Occupancy	Per Capita Emissions (per 100 km)
All-terrain van (Toyota Quantum)	12 l (diesel)	31.56 kg	8 passengers (9 passengers)	3.95 kg (3.51 kg)
Small all-terrain bus (Oryx Midi)	25 l (diesel)	65.75 kg	10 passengers (16 passengers)	6.58 kg (4.11 kg)
Small 4×4 vehicle (Daihatsu Terios)	10 l (petrol)	23.27 kg	2 passengers (4 passengers)	11.63 kg (5.82 kg)
Small aircraft (Cessna caravan)	64 l (aviation gasoline)[b]	148.80 kg	8 passengers (12 passengers)	18.60 kg (12.40 kg)

[a] Conversion factors taken from Carlyon (2009).
[b] Fuel consumption was given as 200 liters per flight hour; the average speed was estimated to be 250 km/h (including take-off and landing). In order to take into account that flights in Namibia go directly from A to B, whereas roads must take detours, a correction factor of 25% was added, resulting in an equivalent of 312.5 km/h.

favorable climate performance because of both the more modest accommodations used and lower transport emissions. This is because the trekking tour covers about 140 kilometers per day of travel whereas the other trips cover between 200 and 250 kilometers. In addition, the trekking group uses a small bus with a relatively high occupancy. **Table 9.1** shows the CO$_2$ emissions per transport mode per 100 kilometers, with average and full occupancy, and confirms the high fuel consumption of all-terrain vehicles and the relative climate-friendliness of tour buses compared to the automobile at full occupancy. Travel by small aircraft is about 2 to 3 times as carbon-intensive, even though aircrafts' ability to fly straight from A to B has been taken into account. It also becomes apparent that there is a trade-off between environmental sustainability and comfort levels. Tour groups often complain about lack of space, especially on long trips (based on verbal communication by all three tour operators). In addition, travel in Namibia is becoming more individualistic with smaller group sizes and higher flexibility requirements—all of which leads to an average occupancy that is below full capacities.

A surprising result of the study is that the average amount of accommodation-related emissions (in combination with catering and local leisure activities) is slightly higher than the emissions produced by domestic transport (see Table 9.1). This is because Namibia's hospitality industry makes only limited use of the country's ample potential for renewable energies (especially solar and wind) and of energy-efficiency measures. Due to the remoteness of many lodges, their use of diesel generators as the main power source, the import of food, and a focus on vehicle-based leisure activities, the energy needs of these lodges are quite high.

It is interesting to note the emissions per guest night are the highest with Wilderness Safaris, a company with an environmental management program and several lodges certified by Eco-awards Namibia (a national environmental certification scheme for tourism accommodations) and a high, demonstrated commitment to biodiversity protection, water conservation, and community involvement (Wilderness Safaris Namibia [WSN], n.d.). Its top environmental lodge, Skeleton Coast Camp, has received the highest certification level by Eco-awards Namibia but has substantial CO$_2$ emissions per guest night (60 kilograms) in spite of its exclusive use of

Table 9.2 Eco-Efficiency of Safari Tourism in Namibia

Tour Package	CO_2-Equivalent Emissions (in kg) ÷ Package Price (in Euros) (with long-haul flight)	CO_2 Emissions (in kg) ÷ Package Price (in Euros) (in-country only)
Great Namibian Journey	0.97	0.17
On Foot in Namibia's Canyons	1.25	0.20
Best of Namibia Circuit	1.34	0.20
Etosha group tour	1.33	0.32
Mopane self-drive	1.96	0.44
Tok Tokkie Trails	–	0.10
Skeleton Coast Camp	–	0.22

solar energy for guest rooms and staff sleeping quarters. The high emissions are due to the lodge's remoteness with high logistics requirements (including flying in staff, provisions, and even laundry), a low number of beds (12), and a below-average occupancy rate. In addition, extended day excursions (400 kilometers on average per person per stay) by Land Rover with a low occupancy are offered. Clearly, the company's otherwise excellent environmental performance is offset by the luxurious nature of its product in terms of comfort, reduced travel times, exclusiveness, high-quality food, and personnel-intensive services. On the other end of the spectrum, trekking tourism that uses a combination of wilderness camping and medium-range guesthouses only emits about 18 kilograms of CO_2 per guest night.

Finally, in order to broaden the analysis and take economic sustainability into account, the eco-efficiency of the different tour packages, calculated as the ratio between each one's direct greenhouse gas emissions per person and the average price charged per trip (direct revenue generation in Euros) was computed. This means that the lower the value, the higher the eco-efficiency. The results can be seen in **Table 9.2**.

The results first show that eco-efficiency is much lower when the international flight is included, even though that figure includes the airfare and also the mark-up paid to the outbound operator or travel agency in the source countries. Secondly, the Great Namibian Journey, in spite of its high absolute emissions, has the highest eco-efficiency due to the high revenue it generates. The retail price for this exclusive 16-day trip is approximately 7,000 Euros per person, including the international flight and out-of-pocket expenditure. Wilderness Safaris' other upscale product, the Best of Namibia fly-in safari, fares less well because it is relatively short and relies on air transport only. However, when only in-country emissions are considered, both packages have a similar eco-efficiency. At the other end of the spectrum, the self-drive tour has the lowest eco-efficiency due to its unfavorable combination of automobile-related emissions and minimal services purchased from the tour operator.

The trekking tour fares second best, generating a fair amount of revenue in spite of relatively low comfort levels. A specialty product of the same operator (named Tok Tokkie Trails) has the highest eco-efficiency if only in-country emissions are considered. It is a guided 2-day nature walk with accommodation in simple but fully serviced camps (see **Figure 9.7**), and partial use of renewable energies, that is sold at a relatively high price. Tok Tokkie Trails also has the

Figure 9.7   Desert hiking with style: Tok Tokkie Trails camp, Namibia.

advantage of being located in a nature reserve near one of Namibia's main tourist attractions, thus minimizing transport to get to the trail.

A similar, more encompassing study was conducted by Gössling et al. (2005), which analyzed the eco-efficiency of various tourism destinations around the world. Congruent with the findings in Namibia, Gössling et al. identified travel distance, means of transport, length of stay, and expenditure as the main variables influencing the eco-efficiency of a trip or travel product. A direct comparison of the results in quantitative terms, however, is difficult because revenue would have to be adjusted according to exchange and inflation rates. Furthermore, revenue generated by transport was not always taken into account. Therefore, the following statements need to be interpreted with some caution.

In the case of tourism in the rural Italian Val di Merse (where transport-related revenue was accounted for) the average eco-efficiency value was 0.9, with a range between 0.4 (for the predominant domestic arrivals) and 4.0 (for long-haul tourism from Oceania). Most of the analyzed packages to Namibia are clearly less eco-efficient but fare quite well in comparison to long-haul tours to Val di Merse. With the exception of the self-drive tour, safari tourism in Namibia also achieves a slightly better result than tourism to Rocky Mountain National Park in the United States (eco-efficiency ratio of 1.56). The most likely explanation for this is that the Namibian tours are guided group activities offered by tour operators in the middle to upper price (even luxury) segment that generate significantly more revenue than trips that are individually organized—the predominant types of travel analyzed by Gössling et al. (2005). In addition, the prevalent mode of transport in Val di Merse and Rocky Mountain National Park is the carbon-intensive automobile, which generates relatively little revenue. However, the example of the Mopane self-drive tour, which also is quite typical for Namibian tourism, shows this is also the case in Namibia.

To summarize, safari tourism in Namibia in absolute terms has a high climate impact and low eco-efficiency, but, in comparison to other long-haul destinations, this is partially mitigated by the fact that organized group tours tend to be in the upper market segment. On the other hand, nature-based tourism in Namibia clearly has demonstrated positive effects on biodiversity conservation and rural community welfare (NACSO, 2010). Tourism-related mitigation strategies have hardly been discussed in Namibia, but there is an incipient awareness of the climate change problem.

Conclusions and Recommendations: Mitigation Strategies to Make Ecotourism More Climate-Friendly

The literature analysis and the research on Namibia have shown that nature-based tourism, more than most other tourism segments, is both affected by and contributes to climate change. On the one hand, nature tourism is more exposed to the physical impacts of global warming; on the other hand, it also tends to be more energy-intensive, largely due to its transportation needs to remote destinations and more mobile travel patterns. Apart from negative impacts on the world climate, this leads to a higher vulnerability with respect to rising energy and transportation costs. In addition, travelers interested in experiencing pristine nature show an above-average level of awareness of environmental issues, including climate change, and expect nature tourism operators to act accordingly.

Ecotourism, understood as a concept that strives to turn nature-based tourism into a positive force for conservation and local communities, so far has largely focused on local sustainability issues at destinations. Undoubtedly, there are many examples where ecotourism has contributed to biodiversity and resource conservation, as well as improved local livelihoods. Namibia is one such case. Other inspiring examples have been provided by individual eco-lodge designers and operators from around the world (see Mehta, 2010); however, apart from general statements and a few exceptions, transport between the destination and the source markets and altered travel patterns remain absent from the ecotourism debate. Thus, ecotourism's local benefits are at least partially offset by the segment's greenhouse gas emissions, which in turn endanger the communities and biodiversity it claims or has helped to sustain.

The case of Namibia is typical of this conflict. For ecotourism to continue its pioneering role in the sustainable development of tourism in the 1990s and early 2000s, an encompassing and vigorous strategy for the mitigation of its climate impact is needed. The concept of carbon management, as discussed in this chapter, can serve as a general guideline for this endeavor. Anecdotal evidence as well as environmental certification schemes in some nature tourism destinations (such as Costa Rica and Australia) suggest that climate protection is an important issue in the ecotourism accommodations subsector. Innovative energy-efficiency measures and renewable energy sources have been developed by many eco-lodges (Gössling, 2011; Mehta, 2010; University of Colorado et al., 2008). However, the case of Namibia shows these initiatives do not represent the whole nature tourism industry.

Carbon management in ecotourism needs to encompass the entire travel chain. As well as technological and managerial measures at the company level, sustainable transport and behavioral mitigation measures need to be targeted. Such a strategy should aim to include the following eight elements:

1. Preferring/offering *nearby destinations* when holidays are short (Gössling, 2011; Strasdas, 2009). Attractive natural areas, such as national parks, can be found in almost all countries of origin of international tourists, including densely populated Europe.

2. Long-haul trips should be reduced and involve *extended lengths of stay* to reduce emissions per day of travel. This would not decrease the overall number of days spent abroad, but

the amount of travel needed to get there and back. As an incentive, tour operators could offer add-on packages to extend stays in a destination and indicate prices per day of travel, which would be lower than for shorter trips (Peeters, Gössling, & Lane, 2009). Apart from preferring nearby destinations, extending the average length of stay has been identified as one of the most effective ways to reduce overall travel emissions (UNWTO/UNEP, 2008).

3. *Modal shift:* Using or (re-)developing effective mass transit rail or bus systems with attractive fares to replace aircraft or the automobile for short- to medium-haul holiday destinations (for example Destination Nature in Germany, a marketing campaign of Deutsche Bahn to visit protected areas by train; Strasdas, 2009) or within heavily visited protected areas (e.g., bus shuttles in Grand Canyon National Park; TIES, 2007) is another option that would substantially reduce transport-related tourism emissions (World Economic Forum, 2009). In general, using tour buses within a destination is more climate-friendly than individual travel by automobile, as demonstrated by the Namibian research.

4. *Optimizing flight routes* by using mass transit to get to international airport hubs, preferring direct flights, and selecting airlines with relatively high fuel efficiency per passenger mile would all improve emissions. (See atmosfair [2011] and Brighter Planet [2011] for airline rankings.) When a developing country is the selected destination, using a national carrier may increase revenue.

5. *Slow travel:* On a tour, spending more quality time at selected attractions rather than travelling to another tourist site every day not only reduces a trip's climate impact but also allows for in-depth nature experiences and meaningful social and cultural encounters with host communities. Furthermore, the principle of slow travel—which was derived from the Slow Food movement in Italy—implies a preference for ground and nonmotorized transport wherever possible (Dickinson, Lumsdon, & Robbins, 2011).

6. *Nonmotorized outdoor activities:* Although comparatively insignificant in relation to the overall climate impact of a long-haul trip, replacing motorized sightseeing or wildlife watching activities with hiking, cycling, or canoeing also reduces local impacts and may enhance guests' health as a side benefit. When animals are used for transport, local revenue is often generated (Strasdas, 2009).

7. *Carbon-offsetting* is an important measure to compensate the remaining emissions of a trip, especially where the previously suggested strategies are difficult to implement. In Namibia, for instance, targeting long-haul source markets for tourism is virtually indispensable, and length of stay is already relatively high. If appropriate and feasible, using high-quality, certified offset projects[6] in nature tourism destinations may increase guests' willingness to voluntarily pay for them and support biodiversity conservation or the development of renewable energies.

8. *Increasing eco-efficiency* with regards to greenhouse gas emissions should be an important goal of any tourism destination because it reduces environmental impact in relation to

---

[6] It is not possible in the limited framework of this chapter to further discuss the complexities of carbon offsetting. For more information, see the David Suzuki Foundation (2009), among others.

the revenue generated by an economic activity. For long-haul destinations this means that upscale tourism segments should be given preference in marketing. Eco-efficiency is also higher when added value is generated through services such as guided tours. In contrast, renting automobiles to individual travelers generally has a low eco-efficiency, as the case of Namibia has shown. Like many other developing countries, Namibia also has a high degree of transport-related leakage from its national economy because it needs to import vehicles and fuels.

Making ecotourism more climate-friendly remains more than a matter of vague responsibility for the global climate. Many of the proposed mitigation measures create cobenefits for the stakeholders involved—for instance, for companies these include cost savings, minimizing regulatory risks, or a better reputation among increasingly discriminating consumers. Thus, voluntary mitigation can be seen as an adaptation strategy to the societal consequences of climate change. For consumers, changed travel patterns might result in health benefits or enhanced travel experiences. Furthermore, global warming endangers the welfare of communities, the availability of natural resources, and biodiversity around the world, especially in developing countries. Helping to conserve and support these assets is at the core of ecotourism's environmental, social, and cultural principles and part of the Millennium Development Goals. Thriving local communities and intact natural landscapes are also the economic foundation of the nature-based tourism industry, and thus are essential for its own long-term viability.

References

Atmosfair. (2011). atmosfair airline index 2011. Retrieved April 14, 2012, from http://www.atmosfair.de/fileadmin/user_upload/Airline_Index/Atmosfair_Airline_Index2011.pdf

Brighter Planet. (2011). Air travel, carbon and energy efficiency. Retrieved April 14, 2012, from http://brighterplanet.com/research

Carlyon, K. (2009, October). *A carbon neutrality plan for Wilderness Safaris, Namibia* (student project report). Stellenbosch University, Department of Conservation Ecology & Entomology.

David Suzuki Foundation. (2009). Purchasing carbon offsets. A guide for Canadian consumers, businesses, and organizations. Retrieved April 14, 2012, from http://www.davidsuzuki.org/publications/resources/2009/purchasing-carbon-offsets

Dawson, J., Stewart, E., Lemelin, H., & Scott, D. (2010). The carbon cost of polar bear viewing tourism in Churchill, Canada. *Journal of Sustainable Tourism, 18*(3), 319–336.

Deutsche Bank Research. (2008, April). *Climate change and tourism: Where will the journey lead?* Frankfurt: Author.

Dickinson, J., Lumsdon, L., & Robbins, D. (2011). Slow travel: Issues for tourism and climate change. *Journal of Sustainable Tourism, 19*(3), 281–300.

Ecotourism Australia. (n.d.). Climate action certification overview.

Eijgelaar, E. (2007). *Voluntary carbon-offset schemes and tourism emissions*. Master's thesis, Eberswalde University for Sustainable Development, Eberswalde, Germany.

Eijgelaar, E., Thaper, C., & Peeters, P. (2010). Antarctic cruise tourism: The paradoxes of ambassadorship, "last chance tourism" and greenhouse gas emissions. *Journal of Sustainable Tourism, 18*(3), 337–354.

German Federal Agency of the Environment (UBA) & Öko-Institut. (2002). *Environment and tourism: Data, facts, perspectives.* Berlin: Erich Schmidt Verlag.

Gössling, S. (2009). Carbon-neutral destinations: A conceptual analysis. *Journal of Sustainable Tourism, 17*(1), 17–37.

Gössling, S. (2011). *Carbon management in tourism—Mitigating the impacts on climate change.* New York: Routledge.

Gössling, S., Peeters, P., Ceron, J. P., Dubois, G., Patterson, T., & Richardson, R. (2005). The eco-efficiency of tourism. *Ecological Economics, 54*(4), 417–434.

Gössling, S., & Schumacher, K. P. (2010). Implementing carbon neutral destination policies: Issues from the Seychelles. *Journal of Sustainable Tourism, 18*(3), 377–391.

Hall, M. (2009, July). *Gaps in knowledge on tourism and climate change.* Paper presented at the 7th International Symposium on Tourism and Sustainability, Travel and Tourism in the Age of Climate Change: Robust Findings, Key Uncertainties, CENTOPS, University of Brighton, England.

KPMG International. (2008). Climate changes your business: KPMG's review of the business risks and economic impacts at sector level. Retrieved December 1, 2011, from http://www.kpmg.com/Global/en/IssuesAndInsights/ArticlesPublications/Documents/Climate-changes-your-business.pdf

McKercher, B., Prideaux, B., Cheung, C., & Law, R. (2010). Achieving voluntary reductions in the carbon footprint of tourism and climate change. *Journal of Sustainable Tourism, 18*(3), 1–21.

Mehta, H. (2010). *Authentic ecolodges.* New York: HarperCollins.

Namibian Association of CBNRM Support Organisations. (2010). *Namibia's communal conservancies: A review of progress and challenges in 2009.* Windhoek, Namibia: Author.

Namibia Tourist Board. (2010). *Number of tourist arrivals 2005–2009.* Windhoek, Namibia: Author.

Peeters, P., Gössling, S., & Lane, B. (2009). Moving towards low-carbon tourism: New opportunities for destinations and tour operators. In: S. Gössling, M. Hall, & D. Weaver (Eds.), *Sustainable tourism futures: Perspectives on systems, restructuring and innovations* (pp. 240–257). London: Routledge.

Piotrowski, R., & Xola Consulting. (2010). Adventure tourism companies and climate change. Retrieved April 14, 2012, from http://www.xolaconsulting.com/Climate-exec-summary.pdf

Plume, K. (2009, November). Climate change and nature-related tourism: Vulnerability, mitigation and adaptation. The example of Mu Koh Chang designated area in Thailand. Master's thesis, Eberswalde University for Sustainable Development, Eberswalde, Germany.

Reid, H., Sahlén, L., MacGregor, J., & Stage, J. (2007, November). *The economic impact of climate change in Namibia: How climate change will affect the contribution of Namibia's natural resources to tourism.* IIED Discussion paper 07-02. London: International Institute for Environment and Development.

Rumpelt, S. (2009, October). *Climate-friendly holidays in Germany: Evaluation of climate-neutral tourism offers.* Master's thesis, Eberswalde University for Sustainable Development, Eberswalde, Germany.

Scott, D., & Becken, S. (2010). Adapting to climate change and climate policy: Progress, problems and potentials (Editorial introduction). *Journal of Sustainable Tourism, 18*(3), 283–295.

Simmons, D., & Becken, S. (2004). The cost of getting there: Impacts of travel to ecotourism destinations. In: R. Buckley (Ed.), *Environmental impacts of ecotourism* (pp. 15–24). Wallingford, United Kingdom: CABI Publishing.

Strasdas, W. (2001). *Ecotourism in practice: The implementation of an ambitious tourism concept in developing countries.* PhD dissertation, Technical University of Berlin, Ammerland: Studienkreis für Tourismus.

Strasdas, W. (2009). Sustainable transportation guidelines for nature-based tour operators. In: S. Gössling, M. Hall, & D. Weaver (Eds.), *Sustainable tourism futures: Perspectives on systems, restructuring and innovations* (pp. 258–281). London: Routledge.

Strasdas, W. (2010a). *Attitudes and actual behaviour in relation to the voluntary compensation of greenhouse gas emissions. Results of a literature analysis.* Internal report to the German Consumer Association (vzbv), Berlin.

Strasdas, W. (2010b). Carbon management in tourism: A smart strategy in response to climate change. In: R. Conrady & M. Buck (Eds.), *Trends and issues in global tourism 2010* (pp. 57–70). Berlin, Germany: ITB Convention Market Trends and Innovations.

Strasdas, W., & Gössling, S. (Eds.). (2008, November). *Climate change requires tourism change—Risks and opportunities for biological diversity and tourism in Germany.* Conference reader on behalf of the German Federal Agency for Nature Conservation (BfN) and the German Tourism Federation (DTV). Retrieved December 1, 2011, from http://www.tourismus-klima.de

Strasdas, W., & Zeppenfeld, R. (2010). *Berlin-Brandenburg innovation network for adaptation to climate change, tourism sub-project. Literature analysis.* Unpublished internal report. Eberswalde University for Sustainable Development, Eberswalde, Germany.

Sustainable Tourism Cooperative Research Centre. (2009). The impacts of climate change on Australian tourism destinations—Developing adaptation and response strategies. Retrieved April 14, 2012, from http://www.crctourism.com.au/Page/Research/Innovations/Climate+Change+Project.aspx

The International Ecotourism Society (TIES). (2007, first quarter). Sustainable transportation. *Eco Currents*, 1-7.

The International Ecotourism Society (TIES). (2012). What Is Ecotourism? Retrieved March 27, 2012, from http://www.ecotourism.org/what-is-ecotourism

United Nations World Tourism Organization & United Nations Environment Programme. (2008). *Climate change and tourism: Responding to global challenges*. Madrid/Paris: Author.

University of Colorado, National Renewable Energy Laboratory & East Carolina University. (2008). Renewable energy in tourism initiative. Best practices in the accommodation/airline/cruise line/tour operator sector. Retrieved April 12, 2012, from http://www.renewabletourism.org

Weaver, D. (2011). Can sustainable tourism survive climate change? *Journal of Sustainable Tourism, 19*(1), 5–15.

Wilderness Safaris Namibia. (n.d.). We are wilderness. Retrieved April 14, 2012, from http://www.wilderness-safaris.com/download/12972/We%20are%20Wilderness%20Namibia.pdf

World Economic Forum. (2009, May). *Towards a low-carbon travel and tourism sector*. Geneva, Switzerland: Author.

World Resources Institute. (2005). Navigating the numbers: Greenhouse gas data and international climate policy. Retrieved April 14, 2012, from http://pdf.wri.org/navigating_numbers.pdf

World Travel and Tourism Council. (2006, August). *Namibia: The impact of travel and tourism on jobs and the economy*. London: Author.

World Travel and Tourism Council. (2010, October). *Climate change: A joint approach to addressing the challenge*. London: Author.

Small Island Protected Area Planning: A Case for West Caicos

Hitesh Mehta

LEARNING OBJECTIVES

- To understand the environmental and social implications of a tourism planning process
- To learn about techniques used to protect and conserve biodiversity when planning for tourism development
- To learn about the benefits of public–private partnerships in protected area planning
- To understand the importance of integrated master planning in sustainable tourism development
- To become familiar with the standards and norms for low-impact development for tourist destinations

This text describes the protected area planning and sustainable development strategy for the small island of West Caicos, Turks and Caicos, West Indies, an area of 810 hectares. The strategy incorporates the Millennium Development Goals (MDGs) of environmental and social sustainability, designed to ensure there will be minimal negative impacts on the natural environment by tourism activities and that potential social and economic benefits will be derived for local communities.

The aim of this text is to demonstrate through one case study, the West Caicos Sustainable Tourism Master Plan, the positive benefits of public–private partnerships in protected area planning, the importance of integrated master planning in sustainable tourism development, and how ecotourism and sustainable tourism can assist in supporting and meeting the MDGs of ensuring environmental and social sustainability and developing a global partnership for development.

In the last decade, sustainable tourism has heightened local people's awareness of the importance of conservation and provided new incentives for governments and local communities to preserve protected areas. It has also generated revenue for local and regional economies. Unfortunately, although sustainable tourism has brought some financial gains, it has also led to problems in protected areas, including undue pressures and threats on the very natural resources that sustain it.

The sustainable tourism industry is at a crossroads in its development. It is increasingly confronted with arguments about its sustainability and compatibility with environmental protection and community development, and is facing serious and difficult choices about its future. If we are to move positively from these crossroads, governments, NGOs, and private developers will be required to rise to the challenges and demands of sustainable tourism in or near protected areas by offering facilities and activities that give visitors an intact natural and cultural experience while affording them an unpolluted environment.

In recent years, the conservation community has become interested in developing various ways to use sustainable tourism as a positive force while controlling its potentially negative environmental and cultural impacts. One mechanism is through sensitive master planning and ecologically conscious landscape design that protects the environment, empowers local cultures, and creates areas for the enjoyment of visitors.

Objectives and Background

As governments and conservation organizations struggle to cover the cost of protecting wilderness and culturally rich areas, increasing numbers of tourists are travelling to island destinations to enjoy nature and experience different cultures (United Nations World Tourism Organization [UNWTO], 2002). Sustainable tourism currently represents a small but rapidly growing tourism niche in the global tourism marketplace with strong growth. In 2010 there were over 940 million international tourist arrivals, and in the first 2 months of 2011 arrivals surpassed 124 million (UNWTO, 2011).

The rapid growth of tourism within the last decade has resulted in the development of numerous tourism facilities in and around protected areas in small islands. Unfortunately, such developments often have had detrimental ecological and social impacts, such as the loss of habitat, water and soil pollution, damage of geological and marine life features, disruption of natural animal behavior such as the blockage of migration routes, isolation of local communities, and impacts on the natural environment through obtrusive structures.

The Turks and Caicos Islands' (TCI's) economic future depends on a continuing ability to develop its tourist and investment industry, thereby stimulating other sectors of the country's economy. The ability to sustain tourism growth is dependent upon the island retaining its pristine natural character. The 15-year West Caicos Sustainable Tourism Master Plan places a strong emphasis on economic development and environmental conservation in protected areas. The main objective of the Master Plan is to provide a strong basis for residential, retail, resort, and recreation development in West Caicos. More specifically, the objectives are to:

- Expand and enhance existing protected areas
- Articulate standards and norms for low-impact development for tourist destinations
- Make the case for West Caicos as a model for island sustainable development, for the benefit of neighboring islands
- Recommend "themes and missions" that will distinguish West Caicos from other tourist destinations
- Commit to support local development, training, and Belongers (local people who have close ties to TCI, normally by birth and/or ancestry)

The sustainable development strategy focuses on the following areas:

- Protected areas (national parks and reserves, historic and archaeological sites)
- Crown Land Reserve (reserved lands not to be sold, leased, or licensed) for future development
- Beach and shoreline parks and beach accesses
- Open spaces and buffer areas
- 120 hectares currently under a development agreement between the government and Logwood Development Company Ltd., a privately owned company
- A road network
- Airport development and buffer areas
- Utilities (e.g., water, electricity, solid waste)

The West Caicos Sustainable Tourism Master Plan falls within the Sustainable Development Planning Initiative (SDPI), which is a cutting-edge effort begun by the TCI Department of Planning in 2002. SDPI provides a framework for the overall development of TCI, emphasizing the unique character of each island. This framework establishes complementary relationships among the economic sectors, communities, and natural resources of each island.

Taking into consideration the current demand for tourism destinations (UNWTO, 2011), it was crucial that the planning and development of tourism-related facilities in and around protected areas place the integrity of the existing ecosystem as a high priority. Therefore, the site planning for a site must be an instrument that safeguards the sustainability and conservation of its natural and cultural heritage. It should not only conserve the natural ecosystems in the long term but also contribute to repairing any ecological damage that may exist.

Sensitive master planning and ecologically and socially sensitive designs are crucial to creating harmony between tourism developments and environmental/cultural protection of the area. Without careful and well-researched master planning and landscaping, tourism facilities cannot contribute to solving the negative impacts of mass tourism. Preserving the special characteristics of a site requires an in-depth understanding of the site's natural systems and an immersion into the cultural responses to that environment's opportunities and constraints. Good planning and design require hard work, advanced planning, and a team of professionals with proven experience in the conceptualization and creation of such projects, especially if future sustainable tourism facilities and destinations are to succeed in the competitive world of international travel and tourism.

Methodology

Five data collection methods were used to prepare the West Caicos Sustainable Tourism Master Plan:

1. *Stakeholder meetings and open discussion* with a wide cross-section of residents
2. *On-site visits* to accessible areas of the island
3. *Participatory planning workshops* that were held in Providenciales and Ft. Lauderdale and attended by a wide cross-section of the residents of Providenciales, local and visiting professionals, staff of the Department of Planning, and officials from various governmental and nongovernmental utility and environmental offices
4. *Research* into the history, culture, flora, and fauna of the island
5. *Analysis* of aerial photographs and other base information

The 15-year master plan for West Caicos, which contains two protected areas that have rich terrestrial and marine biodiversity, was contracted to a planning and landscape architecture firm (EDSA, 2002).

Context

The Turks and Caicos Islands are currently under British rule. West Caicos covers approximately 2,430 hectares and is the most westerly island in the Turks and Caicos archipelago. Its northern and eastern shores consist mainly of beaches, bounded by sand dunes. The western and southern shores are rugged iron-shore limestone weathered into jagged rock. West Caicos is 920 kilometers south of Miami and 62 kilometers from the easternmost island of the Bahamas, Mayaguana (see **Figure CS 8.1**).

The geographical position of West Caicos, at the most western extreme of the Turks and Caicos Islands, places it outside the normal path of tourists and development. Special consideration has been given in the West Caicos Sustainable Tourism Master Plan to promote a self-sustaining economic base and infrastructure, while integrating West Caicos into a social and economic network that will benefit the entire chain of islands. For the first phase of developments, installation of an environmentally sensitive infrastructure required to service the residential development areas has

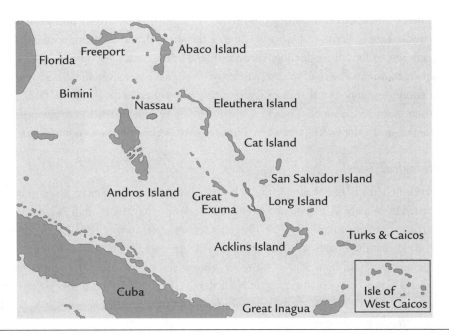

Figure CS 8.1 The Turks and Caicos Islands.

included roadways and electric-cart paths, underground power, television, telephone cable, and Internet connections as well as a potable water system for each site.

During this first phase, Belongers and non-permanent residents of the Turks and Caicos Islands have derived direct benefits. The labor force was drawn from existing resources throughout the islands and, as necessary, supplemental labor was sought from offshore.

History

In 1857, Belle Isle Salt Manufacturing Company was given a lease for 100 acres of Salina ground on West Caicos. The company existed for about 3 years. The site was then reoccupied about 30 years later, and from 1890 to 1903 about 400 hectares were planted in sisal, a plant that produces a fiber for making rope. Yankee Town, as it was then known, is now a ghost town on the west coast near the shores of Lake Catherine, a saline body of water that rises and falls with the tides. The lake is now a national park and home to flocks of pink roseate flamingos. This abandoned settlement still contains a sisal press, the ruins of railroad tracks, engines, and old stone buildings, and is crested by an osprey's nest. Except for settlements developed in the 1950s and 1970s and some tourism developments, West Caicos has been uninhabited and, thus, has retained its natural beauty and biodiversity. On the west side of the island coral reefs provide prime dive sites (Hall Tech, 2002).

Natural Environment

An understanding of the vegetation history of West Caicos is important to identify trees and plants that require protection. West Caicos has been subjected to settlement events of varying intensity over the last 300 years. During this period, vegetation was cleared for housing in localized areas such as at Yankee Town, and for cultivation of cotton, sisal, and food crops. Inland wetlands were greatly altered for salt production, particularly the Salinas and Lake Catherine. To date, the disturbed vegetation has not had time to return to its original state, given the very dry and saline ambient conditions and disturbance of the original thin soil cover (Hall Tech, 2002). Human influences are seen on the modern beaches, where long shore drift patterns have been affected by canal dredging and a shipwreck, and where human debris is a major water contaminant.

Archaeological Sites

The Turks and Caicos Islands were one of the last areas of the Caribbean archipelago to be visited and inhabited by humans. Although people entered the Antilles as early as 4000 BC, the Turks and Caicos were not exploited until AD 700 (Keegan, Carlson, & Torrence, 1994). Some researchers have suggested that the islands were too dry and contained insufficient surface water to support human populations (Sullivan, 1981). However, recent surveys of the dry tropical islands of the Turks and Caicos[1] suggest that most of the habitable coastline contains sites dating back to prehistory (post AD 1000). Currently, over 60 prehistoric sites have been recorded in the Turks and Caicos Islands, but these sites are being affected by development.

The island's first known dwellers were the Taino, a tribe of Arawak native Americans who named the island Makobisa. They were the inhabitants that Columbus, in 1492, or Ponce de Leon, in 1512, may have encountered.

Integrated Planning Process

What is innovative about this project is the process used to develop the Sustainable Tourism Master Plan to ensure that all additions to the existing built environment and island infrastructure were at a scale appropriate to the local ecological and cultural carrying capacity of West Caicos. The integrated approach utilized during this project takes into account the various parts that make a whole (i.e., the social, environmental, political, development, and tourism elements).

Through stakeholder meetings, members of the local professional community and citizens made valuable contributions to the planning and first-phase implementation process. Once the analysis of the stakeholders' meetings was completed, several local citizens were invited to participate in a planning workshop. The West Caicos Sustainable Tourism Master Plan is the result of extensive consultation and contributions from residents of Turks and Caicos.

Site Analysis

An intensive site analysis was carried out to understand both the natural and cultural factors of the site. High-resolution aerial photographs and base data were interpreted to evaluate slopes, elevations, landforms, and existing vegetation for all sites identified in the process.

---

[1] Riggs, B. (2002). Turks and Caicos National Museum, Grand Turk, Turks and Caicos, personal communication.

Using Arcview GIS Spatial Analyst software, slope analysis, elevation analysis, and slope aspects plans were generated to understand the site. An elevation study was conducted to show high points to use to maximize optimal views and minimize undesirable views. By using these studies in the early stages of the design process, two things could be accomplished: a realistic development program and a protected area plan to minimize impacts on pristine areas.

Using the 3-D Analyst extension of Arcview, the master planners generated several terrain models to understand the island's topography, ridgelines, view sheds, water sheds, and drainage. Understanding the natural drainage systems within the site is another important issue. These natural drainage lines need to be preserved wherever possible and can provide undisturbed vegetation corridors. Additionally, if maintained, they can aid in site drainage and minimize the need for costly storm sewers. Research also was completed on previous studies related to water and sanitation (Stanley Associates & D. K. Todd Consulting Engineers, 1981).

The detailed site analysis that was developed helped identify the opportunities and constraints to development and allowed a design responsive to the natural and cultural environments. By using all site analysis information, the planners assured maximizing low-impact development opportunities while minimizing disturbances to protected areas.

Zoning and Land Use Plans

There are currently eight planning zones in West Caicos:

1. Sustainable Tourism Zone (small hotels and villas)
2. Residential Zone (low density and high density)
3. Conservation Zone (national park and reserve)
4. Crown Land Reserve Zone (for future generations)
5. Buffer Zone (between residential areas and open space)
6. Recreation Zone (e.g., beach, parks)
7. Retail Zone (marina village)
8. Coastal Zone (allowing pedestrian travel around the entire perimeter of the island)

The Land Use Plan allows for a range of land uses. Buffer zones also can be created, consisting of natural vegetation between the various land uses. Recreation areas are composed of the shoreline and beach parks and a sports area adjacent to the marina.

Sustainable Tourism Master Plan

The Sustainable Tourism Master Plan has already promoted the cultivation and application of innovative, world-class tourism infrastructure development solutions for the long-term economic benefit and participation of the Belonger population. Construction of the boutique Ritz-Carlton Reserve Lodge was 90% completed in 2008 before the global financial crisis caused its abandonment and is now scheduled to open in 2013. The Master Plan provided a planning environment that has attracted quality development while concurrently fostering protection of the culture and heritage of West Caicos residents (see **Figure CS 8.2**).

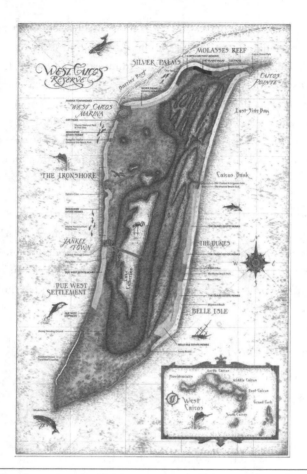

Figure CS 8.2   West Caicos Sustainable Tourism Master Plan.
Source: EDSA (Ed Stone Jr. and Associates). (2003). West Caicos Sustainable Tourism Master Plan.

The premise of development on this island is based on its compatibility with nature and culture. Guiding principles for development in the West Caicos are:

- Protect and expand Lake Catherine and West Caicos Marine National Park.
- Enhance the environmental quality of existing natural reserves and parks by creating corridor linkages and development-restricted zones.
- Preserve and enhance archaeological and cultural sites.
- Low-impact infrastructure and self-sustaining technology.
- No development on ridgelines.
- No development on slopes over 20%.
- No development within critical view corridors.
- No development adjacent to the national parks or nature reserves, which could degrade the physical and visual aesthetics of the area.
- Balance economic, social, and environmental issues to achieve ongoing benefit to residents, visitors, and future generations.

- Preserve and enhance public beach access.
- Maintain the essence of the unspoiled ambience of West Caicos.
- Identify areas for permanent resident neighborhoods, including land bank reserve for future generations.
- Incorporate NE Salina Complex into the Lake Catherine Marine National Park.
- Maintain sustainability; 93% of island to remain undeveloped.
- Create a 790-meter airstrip for day-use only.

It is interesting to note that most of these guiding principles were created, agreed upon, and accepted as appropriate at the first stakeholder meeting.

Protected Area Conservation

Flora

The island can be divided into three main vegetation communities: the strand dune community, the coastal coppice plant community, and the silver palm community.

Strand Dune Community

These back-beach areas above high tide level are loosely vegetated with a community of herbs and shrubs (see **Figure CS 8.3**). The dune vegetation is dominated by salt-tolerant and frequently succulent plants, such as island sea blite (*Suaeda conferta*), bay cedar (*Suriana maritima*), the aromatic sweet bay (*Ambrosia hispida*), and bay lavender (*Mallotonia gnaphalodes*). The broad dune habitat at Logwood Point, like a few other patches along the east coast, is dominated by stands of the tall sea oats (*Uniola paniculata*) (see **Figure CS 8.4**).

The strand dune plant community plays an important ecological role in stabilizing wind-blown sand, thus leading to its accumulation and dune formation. The presence of rooted vegetation serves to reduce sand transport and dune migration to leeward. Care has been taken to protect these strand communities during development. No development will be allowed within the dune communities.

Figure CS 8.3   Strand dune vegetation.

Figure CS 8.4   Sea oats on the eastern coast.

Figure CS 8.5   Coastal coppice on the western part of the island.

Coastal Coppice Plant Community

Where the substratum is more consolidated but is still largely sand, a zone of shrubs and low trees has developed landward of the beaches. This community was assigned to the "coastal coppice" category by Correll and Correll (1982). These back-beach areas along the north and east coasts of West Caicos are dominated by a low scrub containing predominantly blacktorch (*Erithalis fruticosa*), darlinplum (*Reynosia septentrionalis*), sevenyear apple (*Casasia clusiifolia)*, and black-bead (*Pithecellobium keyense*), with frequent palms. This forms an open canopy between which are scattered herbs, such as jackswitch (*Corchorus hirsutus*), coastal ragweed (*Ambrosia hispida*), and pridè of big pine (*Strumpfia maritima*) (see **Figure CS 8.5**).

Silver Palm Community

In some areas, silver thatch palms are numerically and structurally dominant, producing vegetative cover similar to what Correll and Correll (1982) called the "sand *Coccothrinax* community/ silver palm association" in other parts of the Bahamas/Turks and Caicos archipelago. This community occurs on landward-facing slopes of coastal coppice ridges behind the northern beaches,

Figure CS 8.6   Dense groves of the silver thatch palm on the eastern side of the island.

and is particularly well developed along the eastern side of the island. Between North Canal and South Canal, in depressions, and on the westward facing (sheltered) slopes of the coastal sand ridge overlooking Eastside Salina, dense groves of *Coccothrinax* produce a very distinctive vegetation, as well as spectacular scenery (see **Figure CS 8.6**).

Coccothrinax inaguensis is the most common species of palm on the island. These palms reach heights of over 3 meters and widths of 12.7 centimeters, and dominate a community of only three to four other species. Throughout the areas dominated by palms, there are large patches of white sand and accumulations of leaf litter and fallen fruits. The palm communities merge into the strand-dune and terrestrial scrub areas that surround them. It is unlikely that the eastern dune ridge and coppice area would have been cleared for cultivation by early settlers because of the almost pure sand "soils," so these silver thatch palm stands may be the only natural (primary) plant communities remaining on West Caicos.

The West Caicos Sustainable Tourism Master Plan calls for the protection and enhancement of this valuable silver thatch palm community. Under the Development Manual, the specified building footprints and setbacks will help protect the silver palm trees. Additionally, the manual will require transplantation of those species that fall within the footprints.

Logwood Development Company Ltd. also will be developing an on-island plant nursery to begin propagation of *Coccothrinax inaguensis*. This approach will not only maintain the existing silver palm population but also expand it through additional planting.

Fauna

Fauna on the island are limited, and consist of occasional ghost crabs (*Ocypode quadrata*) and small benthic invertebrates, the latter supporting some shorebirds. Birds recorded feeding at the strand-line on north and east coast beaches include Wilson's plover (*Charadrius wilsonia*), the ruddy turnstone (*Arenaria interpres*), sanderlings (*Crocethia alba*), and the American oyster-catcher (*Haematopus palliatus*).

Sea turtles have been recorded on West Caicos beaches. Fletemeyer (in Bacon, 1999) and Groombridge and Luxmore (1987) list West Caicos as a nesting site for green and hawksbill turtles (*Chelonia mydas* and *Eretmochelys imbricata*) during a season from April through August. Although there are no recent data on turtle numbers, they appear to be uncommon.

The most abundant invertebrates in terrestrial habitats appear to be land snails, which feed on green leaves and fallen plant debris. *Cerion lewisi*, *Hemitrochus gallopavonis*, and *Plagioptycha bahamensis* were commonly found feeding in silver thatch palm stands.

The land crab (*Gecarcinus lateralis*) is found occasionally in the dry scrub areas, although it appears to prefer the wetter coastal coppice habitat (see **Figure CS 8.7**). Three species of butterflies were observed closely enough for identification; these were the small lace-wing, which was frequent; the monarch, which was seen occasionally; and the swallowtail, which was recorded once during two field days in April 2001. The sand wasp (*Stictia signata*) was encountered frequently in open, sandy patches and in the cuts through the Central Ridge.

Two ground lizards were common throughout Whiteland habitats, *Anolis scriptus* and *Sphaerodactylus caicosensis*, the former being more active during daylight hours. The presence of so many lizards suggests that a range of insect food is available, such as ground beetles, crickets, and ants. However, potential prey organisms have not been collected to date (see **Figure CS 8.8**).

Figure CS 8.7   Land crab.

Figure CS 8.8   Grasshopper in the strand dune vegetation.

Sixteen species of terrestrial scrub-living birds, all of which were fairly common, were recorded by Clarke and Norton (1988) during surveys over several years. Bacon (1999) reported a further five species, making a total of only 21 for the island of West Caicos. These included a pigeon, two doves, a nightjar, a hummingbird, a swallow, both the Northern and Bahama mockingbirds, two vireos, and the blue-gray gnatcatcher, plus the bananaquit and six other warblers. All the terrestrial birds observed are common to the Caicos Islands, no species being rare or endangered. The terrestrial avifauna is not of particular conservation interest (Ground, 2001).

The West Caicos Sustainable Tourism Master Plan respects the fauna in West Caicos, and the proposed development will not impact the faunal populations. A beach for turtle egg laying has been placed under protection status.

Biodiversity Conservation

Conservation International, the U.S.-based NGO, has identified 27 worldwide areas of high biodiversity value that are rich in species but are under particular threat. These are known as Biodiversity Hotspots; the Caribbean Hotspot ranks eighth in the world for the diversity of its species. Only 11.4% of the natural vegetation in the region remains, and almost half of the plant species of the region are unique. Shrub-land and dwarf forest are underrepresented in the national protected area systems.

In this context, West Caicos, which has been uninhabited and undisturbed for approximately 100 years with a high proportion of undisturbed natural habitats, is a unique situation and of high regional conservation significance. Habitats on the island include coral reefs, sea grass beds and other marine habitats, fish breeding areas, salinas, wetlands and sink holes, strand dunes, coastal coppice and silver palm sand communities, beaches and turtle nesting sites, and limestone and cave systems.

Biodiversity conservation and protection is a primary consideration in any developments, and this commitment applies to the aesthetic as well as physical aspects of development on West Caicos. The objective for ecosystem conservation is to protect representative samples of all major ecosystem habitat and vegetation types for biodiversity conservation, ecosystem services, and productive capacity. Unique examples of ecosystems and rare and vulnerable species will also be protected. The maintenance of biodiversity is being increasingly recognized as an indicator of sustainable development as well as of quality of life. The biodiversity of the island will be maintained as an integral part of the island's development.

To improve existing knowledge, a Biodiversity Assessment and Management Plan for the island will be carried out in the early part of the West Caicos Sustainable Tourism Master Plan. This plan will be coordinated between Logwood Development Company Ltd. and Turks and Caicos Government (TCIG) and will more effectively inform both the development proposed within the 15-year plan and the follow-up plan which will be prepared after the 15-year plan (EDSA, 2002). The Biodiversity Assessment and Management Plan will identify in detail the location and management of key species and habitats for conservation, list species that should not be introduced, and assess the possibility of reintroducing the Turks and Caicos rock iguana to part of the island.

National Protected Areas

Two areas of West Caicos have been established as protected areas under the National Parks Order (1992). These are Lake Catherine Nature Reserve, a land area comprising 390 hectares of surface water and a designated buffer zone, and West Caicos Marine National Park, a marine area comprising 396 hectares (see **Figure CS 8.9**).

The West Caicos Sustainable Tourism Master Plan proposes an enlargement of Lake Catherine Nature Reserve to include the Northeast Salina complex and the wetlands and sinkholes area south of the lake (see **Figure CS 8.10**). The plan also calls for the creation of wildlife and bird corridors connecting the lake to both the Marine Park and the Northeast Salina Complex.

Logwood Development Company is committed to providing office accommodation for a resident park warden, who will monitor and enforce activities in the Marine National Park and Lake Catherine Nature Reserve.

Figure CS 8.9   Lake Catherine Nature Reserve with West Caicos Marine National Park in the background.

Figure CS 8.10   The Northeast Salina Complex will be incorporated into the Lake Catherine Marine National Park.

Key Resources

Resources will be protected, including the silver thatch palm areas not located within the national protected areas; natural vegetation will be protected through the development manual; and animal and plant invasive species will be controlled through Planning and Environmental Health Ordinances (see **Figure CS 8.11**).

The West Caicos Sustainable Tourism Master Plan is based on the premise that the Turks and Caicos government wants an increase in quality sustainable tourism with its related employment opportunities.

> Sustainability and tourism has much broader implications. It means complementary relationships between the tourism and the overall economy of the community. Sustainable tourist activity makes use of local businesses, which broadens and strengthens the local economy. Land use regulations and investment policies that allow segregated all-inclusive resorts defeat these complementary relationships. A common centralized district generates far greater economic interaction. (Village Habitat Design, 2002)

From a cultural perspective, the Sustainable Tourism Master Plan creates a place for local artists to exhibit their artwork in resorts and art galleries. Classes on local history and culture will be taught by and for local residents in order to encourage an interest in and to create pride for their island.

The Sustainable Tourism Master Plan has been designed to ensure there will be minimal negative impacts on the natural environment, and it will act as a catalyst for social development and island conservation. The overall master land use plan proposes the development of two ecoresorts, an ecolodge, an interpretive center, boardwalks, and a ranger station.

The vision of the Sustainable Tourism Master Plan is to create a balance between protecting the natural environment and creating acceptable built structures that minimize the visual and physical pollution to this predominantly pristine site. The plan is already promoting the development and application of innovative, world-class tourism infrastructure development solutions, for the long-term economic benefit and participation of the Belonger population.

Figure CS 8.11   Cove Anchorage is an area of outstanding natural beauty and will be protected.

It also provides a planning environment that will attract quality development while concurrently fostering protection of the culture and heritage of the residents of West Caicos.

Development Credo

The planners have proposed the establishment of a development "credo" for West Caicos that will give it a distinct island identity. The credo includes concepts such as:

- Celebrating family and heritage
- Honoring local fishing rights
- Sharing customs, food, and traditions
- Educating guests on the island
- Cooperating with nature and creating sound, environmentally friendly water, waste, and energy systems (see **Figure CS 8.12**)

Development Control Policies

The Development Manual for West Caicos has been drafted to reflect the low-density, low-impact, environmentally sensitive, and architecturally coordinated theme of the West Caicos Sustainable Tourism Development Plan. Chapter 3 of the manual addresses critical issues such as site clearance, setbacks, densities, building heights, site coverage, landscaping, and sewage disposal.

Plans for all buildings within the development areas will be subject to the scrutiny of the planning department and then of the developer for conformance to architectural and aesthetic standards, including building profiles and color finishes. The maximum height of any building on the island will be three stories, up to a maximum of 15 meters.

Both the government and the developers anticipate the planning and construction of sustainable development. The purpose of the dynamic and consultative planning process employed for this project is to establish the direction for future development of West Caicos as a major low-impact, sustainable tourist destination and residential area. Coastal resources, areas of high landscape value, and areas of special ecological or scientific value will be protected as part of the plan.

Figure CS 8.12   Coastal vegetation (sea grapes) on the eastern side of the island.

Implementation

It is anticipated that with the sustainable development guidelines and regulations, West Caicos can be crafted into a niche market that can distinguish itself in the Caribbean basin. Sustainable tourism policies will increase TCI's competitiveness while at the same time strengthening the economy and cohesiveness of the community. Regulations should be more specific in order for them to be converted into law. This would be a follow-up by the Department of Planning after the master plan has been approved by the government. The plan recommends that the government of Turks and Caicos create an independent body responsible for all land conveyance, leasing, zoning, architectural approvals, development, construction, and maintenance of the lands situated within the West Caicos Sustainable Tourism project area. Provisionally, this will cover a 15-year build-out program that could include two boutique ecoresorts, one ecolodge, and one ranger station, together with roads, trails, utilities, water and waste management, and telecommunications to support low-impact, low-density tourism development.

The mandate of this proposed body will be to ensure all tourism development in West Caicos follows the above-mentioned laws and guidelines. This body will partner with the National Trust, universities, conservation organizations, research institutions, and government agencies interested in sustainable development for small island states. The body will develop programs for guests and island residents that ensure the values of sustainable tourism and preserve the natural and cultural heritage of West Caicos. Environmental assessment and monitoring will ensure no net loss of biodiversity occurs and that residents and guests become stewards of West Caicos.

Conclusion

The West Caicos Sustainable Tourism Plan demonstrates how sustainable master planning of small island destinations can help protect fragile ecosystems, support biological diversity, and make a significant contribution to local communities. The economic future of Turks and Caicos depends on a continuing ability to develop its tourist and investment industry, thereby stimulating other sectors of the country's economy. The West Caicos Sustainable Tourism Master Plan aims to:

- Strengthen the existing national protected area system and link ecosystems via corridors
- Protect key resources outside of the national protected area system through designation of conservation areas under the Planning Ordinance, provisions and covenants within the West Caicos Development Manual, stabilizing Heritage Coastline, and establishing open spaces

Sustainable development is neither well understood nor well practiced. However bold, it is the right choice for this area. Protecting the natural and cultural values of island states is a high priority throughout the world. Ensuring these fragile, isolated communities have a right to develop and prosper is vital for the cultural, aesthetic, and spiritual health of local communities. Stewardship for the island's planning, development, and infrastructure will require close cooperation in a public/private venture. Development will begin with low-impact resorts with a view towards development partnerships whose high standards and values are compatible with the credo established with and for West Caicos.

References

Bacon, P. (1999). *Environmental assessment report for proposed Aman Resort development at North West Point.* Trinidad: University of the West Indies.

Correl, D. S., & Correl, H. B. (1982). *Flora of the Bahama archipelago.* Hirschberg, Germany: J. Cramer.

Clarke, N. V., & Norton, R. L. (1988). *A Ramsar site proposal: The Turks and Caicos Islands, final report.* London: WWF-UK Department of the Environment/Overseas Development Administration.

EDSA. (2002). *15-year West Caicos sustainable tourism master plan.* Providenciales, Turks and Caicos: Government of Turks and Caicos.

Groombridge, B., & Luxmoore, R. (1987). *The green turtle and hawksbill (Reptilia: Cheloniidae) world status, exploitation and trade.* Lausanne, Switzerland: CITES.

Ground, R. (2001). *The birds of the Turks and Caicos Islands.* Providenciales, Turks and Caicos: Turks and Caicos National Trust.

Hall Tech. (2002). *Environmental impact study for West Caicos.* Providenciales, Turks and Caicos: Author.

Keegan, W., Carlson, B., & Torrence, G. (1994). *The archaeological history of Providenciales.* Gainesville, FL: Florida Museum of Natural History.

Stanley Associates Engineering, & D. K. Todd Consulting Engineers. (1981). *Final report for development of water supply and environmental sanitation services, May 1980–March 1981.* Vol. 1. Edmonton, Canada: Authors.

Sullivan, R. (1981). *A short history of the Arawak Indians.* Providenciales, Turks and Caicos: Turks and Caicos National Trust.

United Nations World Tourism Organization (UNWTO). (2002). *Projected average yearly growth 1995–2020 study.* Madrid, Spain: Author.

United Nations World Tourism Organization (UNWTO). (2011). *World tourism barometer.* Madrid, Spain: Author.

Village Habitat Design. (2002, March 25–27). *Sustainable development planning workshop.* Atlanta, Georgia.

Developing Partnerships

Bridging the Gap: Volunteer Tourism's Role in Global Partnership Development

Emily Eddins

LEARNING OBJECTIVES

- To understand volunteer tourism and volunteering in ecotourism as an increasingly important, multifaceted, and useful development tool
- To understand how volunteer tourism connects essential multiscale global partnerships for development
- To explore capacity building, relationship development, and increased understanding resulting from volunteer tourism–related multiscale partnerships
- To understand the critiques and challenges of volunteer tourism and the eighth Millennium Development Goal of developing global partnerships
- To learn about specific examples of how volunteer tourism's global partnerships address and aid in the achievement of other Millennium Development Goals

As human and natural communities become increasingly interrelated and complex, so do the ways in which global partnerships are formed and operate at the local level (Lamoureux, 2009). Tourism has been heavily criticized for its negative impacts, particularly in international development discourse regarding sustainable tourism development in developing countries (Mowforth & Munt, 2008). The highly fragmented tourism industry also is well-known for its lack of cohesion and coordination (Jamal & Getz, 1995). It is necessary to increase understanding of the dynamic relationships within ecotourism and sustainable tourism partnerships, both locally and globally, in order to make better decisions and to better understand the key players involved and how they relate to each other. This chapter draws particular attention to volunteer tourism as a force for achieving global sustainable development and a means of connecting global and local scales through multistakeholder partnerships. Volunteer tourism is "a development strategy leading to sustainable development and centering on the convergence of natural resource qualities, local people and the visitors that all benefit from tourism activity" (Wearing, 2001, p. 12). This definition of volunteer tourism inherently connects global processes of development with local people; for volunteer tourism to be able to attain sustainable development requires a vastly complex system of these connections.

In the face of global climate change, devastating natural disasters from Thailand to Haiti to Chile to Pakistan, and persistent silent crises of poverty and disease, volunteers are said to be the unsung heroes of development, particularly in their role in helping to achieve the Millennium Development Goals (MDGs) (United Nations Volunteers [UNV], 2005). The range of volunteer projects is vast and varied, ranging from the Caribbean Conservation Corporation's sea turtle conservation in Costa Rica (Campbell & Smith, 2005) to Habitat for Humanity's construction of shelter in South Africa (Stoddart & Rogerson, 2004) to WorldPULSE's Youth Ambassador Program, which provides a cross-cultural leadership training program for underprivileged young adults (McGehee & Santos, 2005). Volunteer tourism is an increasingly important, multifaceted, and useful development tool connecting developing and developed economies from global to local scales. Within the volunteer tourism industry, as well as within other forms of sustainable tourism, local community participation, empowerment, and participatory learning approaches have become recognized as central to obtaining community support of tourism; the benefits of tourism and volunteer tourism directly align with the community's needs (Brocklesby & Fisher, 2003; Cole, 2006). Partnerships with and relationships among local communities, volunteer tourism organizations, host organizations, and volunteer tourists are vital to successful and sustainable development-based volunteer projects.

Cohesive, well-formed, multiscale partnerships are best achieved through collaboration and are vital to the identification, implementation, and management of development-based volunteer projects at the local level. Collaborative partnerships are vital not only to successful development and the achievement of the MDGs but also to the sustainability of the daily lives of local communities and their surrounding ecosystems; yet only recently have cross-sector partnerships been explored in a volunteer tourism context (Lamoureux, 2009). Partnerships formed for the purpose of international development have been contested and problematic, and mostly descriptive in nature (Biermann, Chan, Mert, & Pattberg, 2007; Selin, 1999). "Concentration of power in multinational firms may be efficient in monetary terms but may marginalize national social justice and environmental laws" (Selin, 1999, p. 260). Due to the increasing importance of volunteer tourism as a global industry and a mechanism for sustainable development, particularly regarding the environmental sustainability of developing countries, an exploration of these dynamics will help inform how volunteer tourism contributes to achieving the eighth and final, and perhaps most important, MDG of developing global partnerships for development, hereafter referred to as MDG 8.

This chapter outlines the premise of MDG 8 and its associated targets put forth by the United Nations (UN) in 2000 and discusses key critiques of and challenges for attaining this goal in a global context. Volunteer tourism is then situated within the development discourse, and how volunteer tourism may be a force for achieving development is discussed. This discussion continues with an analysis of global partnerships for development within volunteer tourism and outlines how cross-sector, multistakeholder partnerships in volunteer tourism connect global and local scales. Focus is given to capacity development and building relationships within these partnerships in response to failures, and critiques of volunteer tourism as a force for development. The chapter concludes with a discussion of the future potential of volunteer tourism partnerships.

MDG 8: Develop a Global Partnership for Development

The achievement of MDG 8 is essential to operationalize the other MDGs. Without global partnerships, community level interests and needs could become neglected, resulting in miscommunication or misplaced aid (Lamoreux, 2009). In order for the MDGs to have a successful and sustainable implementation, "the amount of planning is much more complex than for any one project, and requires a working partnership between government, the private sector, nongovernmental organizations, and civil society" (Sachs & McArthur, 2005, p. 351). Due to the complexity and magnitude of social forces surrounding globalization, the relationship between global change and local community viability remains unclear and not fully understood (Almas & Lawrence, 2003). What we do know is that global/local interactions are changing.

Partnerships for development, although vital for the achievement of development initiatives, are difficult to measure, with their success resting on the intangible qualities of trust, commitment, and reciprocity (Eade, 2007; Lamoureux, 2009). The targets the UN has established for measuring partnerships for development discuss debt relief in the poorest countries and developing countries' access to resources, specifically technology and pharmaceutical drugs, predominantly through open financial trade systems. The targets stress partnerships with the private sector, which has stirred much debate and critique of the goals of these partnerships, the collaborative nature of the players involved, who they are composed of, and their associated aid, ideological, and development goals. Whose interests do the partnerships serve? Who is included, and perhaps more importantly, who is left out? In a critique of the MDGs from developing countries' perspectives, Amin (2006) asserts, "the partnership thus becomes synonymous with submission to the demands of the imperialist powers" (p. 4). A key critique and challenge of MDG 8 is its failure to challenge existing neoliberal economic systems because of the proposed targets' inclusion of open markets and financial systems. Because of this, MDG 8 also fails to

Table 10.1   MDG 8: Develop a Global Partnership for Development Targets

Finance and trading system	• Open, rule-based, non-discriminatory, predictable • Developing countries benefit from access to developed countries' markets • Poorest countries gain from reduced tariffs
Special needs of the poorest countries	• Specifically needs of landlocked countries and small island developing states
Debt issues	• Deal with comprehensively • Implement national and international measures
Access to pharmaceuticals	• Affordable drugs • Essential drugs • Cooperation with pharmaceutical companies
Availability of new technologies	• Access to new information technologies • Access to new communication technologies • Cooperation with private sector • Specifically access to World Wide Web

Source: Adapted from United Nations Development Programme. (2011). Goal 8: Develop a global partnership for development. Retrieved April 13, 2011, from http://www.un.org/millenniumgoals/global.shtml.

include social, environmental, and institutional progress in market value, as well as the clear, measurable goals put forth by other MDGs.

The reluctance of major bilateral global institutions like the World Bank and United Nations to divorce themselves from neoliberal economic growth and globalization as a form of development is reflected, yet seemingly masked, in their support of the oxymoron of sustainable development and other pro-poor alternative forms of development (Kiely, 1998; Mowforth & Munt, 2008), perhaps most readily witnessed in the MDG 8 targets listed in **Table 10.1**. When discussing the UN and World Bank's role in development, Lewis (2006) asserts, "for some observers, a neo-liberal consensus around economic globalization and a belief in the transformative power of markets to reduce poverty has now begun to replace development as the dominant idea that informs change" (p. 16). Volunteer tourism can potentially help to subdue the critique of MDG 8 of failing to challenge existing neoliberal financial and economic systems that minimize the importance of social (e.g., quality of life) and environmental (e.g., biodiversity) factors when assessing the value of development projects.

Volunteer Tourism in Development

The current trend of volunteer tourism as a means of achieving development through the traditionally leisure-based activity of tourism has added a complex dimension to tourism theory and practice. Tourism in all its forms has been discussed at length as a mechanism for development. Volunteer tourism, in contrast to other forms of tourism, exists for the fundamental purpose of development in various forms, whether community development, conservation, or scientific research projects (Wearing, 2001). However, volunteer tourism is distinguished from ecotourism and sustainable tourism, in which tourists learn about and experience culture and nature. These types of tourists are fundamentally still touring a destination, whereas volunteer tourists *do* development in addition to learning about and experiencing nature and culture and touring the place.

The mantra of the volunteer tourism industry has become "make a difference," urging potential volunteer tourists to embark on a journey that will simultaneously aid in development practice and promote intercultural learning and international understanding in the form of a meaningful experience (Fee & Mdee, 2011; Ingram, 2011; Lewis, 2006; Palacios, 2010; Raymond, 2008;

Wearing, 2001). Development has become fashionable thanks to volunteer tourism, as well as its trendy counterparts such as fair trade, benefit concerts, and many other development-based alternative, yet increasingly mainstream, activities (Ingram, 2011). This trend can be explained, in part, by the creation of a global community sentiment, with individuals feeling simultaneously increasingly interconnected and disconnected from the rest of the world. Global partnerships for development within volunteer tourism help individuals respond to potential identity confusion as a result of globalization, connecting people from different cultures, backgrounds, and values in a united cause-based partnership for development.

The key aspect that sets volunteer tourism apart from other forms of tourism is the bilateral benefits derived by the host communities and the volunteer tourist. Volunteer tourism provides a more in-depth, authentic tourism experience characterized by highly integrated cross-cultural interaction, educational components, community development, conservation or nature-based projects, and research (Wearing, 2001). Volunteer tourism bridges geographic and ideological gaps and can be a realistic, creative, empowering, and powerful global development tool. As an industry, it has the potential not only to reach beyond current economic systems as a nonmarket mechanism based on trust, international understanding, capacity building, and relationship development but also to help to achieve direct and tangible benefits through project work on the ground (Devereux, 2008).

Volunteer tourists primarily travel from developed, rich countries to developing, poor countries (Wearing, 2002), which inherently establishes power issues between host (typically residents of rural communities where volunteer projects take place) and guest (volunteer tourists). However, highly integrated experiences between volunteers and host communities are said to create relationships and greater cross-cultural understanding (Wearing, 2001). According to Lewis (2006), volunteer tourism can not only provide tangible contributions to development but also promote international understanding and solidarity. Volunteers can therefore raise awareness of the underlying causes of poverty, injustice, and unsustainable development when they return home (Devereux, 2008). Through volunteer tourism, the causes of (under)development can be challenged with enhanced collaboration and action aiding in increased global–local communication and understanding and through developing more equal relationships (Devereux, 2008).

Global Partnerships in Volunteer Tourism

Volunteer tourism partnerships are dynamic, involving multiscale parties representing multiple geographic regions, ideologies, and goals. A large number of collaborative relationships exist in order to structure, operate, fund, manage, and implement volunteer tourism projects. Governmental agencies, nongovernmental organizations (NGOs), private businesses, and civil society comprise cross-sector partnerships for volunteer tourism management (Lamoureux, 2009). Additionally, private, nonprofit, and public sectors within the volunteer tourism industry are becoming increasingly blurred as private tourism businesses are incorporating volunteering into the services they offer and nonprofit agencies and organizations are utilizing volunteers to achieve their humanitarian and/or environmental goals. Lamoureux found intangible partner behaviors such as trust, commitment, management involvement, meaningful communication, and open sharing of information to be key components to more successful volunteer tourism projects. Further, research shows that collaboration is necessary to address issues beyond the capacity of a single organization's efforts, such as environmental management, poverty alleviation, or education (Buckley, 2004; Jamal & Getz, 1995; Selin, 1999; Selin & Chavez, 1995).

Much of the research conducted regarding collaborative processes and partnerships in tourism has focused on community-based tourism planning and collaboration to utilize tourism or ecotourism as a mechanism for development (see, e.g., Jamal & Getz, 1995; Jamal & Stronza, 2009; Reed, 1999; Stronza, 2008). Volunteer work in or around the community, however, conceptually and realistically segregates ecotourism partnerships from volunteer tourism partnerships. Volunteer tourism is not just implemented into the dynamics of the community as a form of tourism—the tourists are actually *doing* development in and around the community and working on projects that affect the daily lives of local people beyond being toured. Volunteer tourism partnerships are complex because of the integrated dynamic of interaction between hosts and volunteer tourists as well as the physical work being done rather than solely touring the place.

Global cross-sector collaboration among a single volunteer tourism organization, a group of volunteer tourists, a host organization, a local government, and a host community to achieve a specific community development or conservation project is the most common organizational structure represented in volunteer tourism literature, and is frequently represented through case studies. Volunteer tourism organizations are generally large NGOs, based in developed countries, and have missions similar to international development agencies. Volunteer tourists are typically young travelers from developed countries, and have been found to have wide-ranging motivations for their trip (see, e.g., Brown & Lehto, 2005; Campbell & Smith, 2005; Mustonen, 2007). Host organizations typically act as an intermediary between the host community and the volunteer tourism organization and work most closely in the field with volunteer tourists. These organizations can take a variety of forms, including local government agencies or local grassroots organizations, and are generally considered the volunteer-receiving organization. Host communities are generally situated in rural areas in developing countries, and their residents have limited access to resources (Sin, 2010). Sammy (2008) notes, "The simplicity of the host-guest relationship that is frequently used as an analogy when explaining the community-tourist relationship does not adequately capture the complexity of the interactions that occur" (p. 76). This is especially accurate in volunteer tourism because cross-cultural interaction is present and even necessary to accomplish volunteer projects. Joyce (2009) asserts that volunteer tourists must undergo an intensive cross-cultural learning process before their arrival to mitigate intercultural tensions, imperialist value judgments, and designation of the hosts as "other," and to facilitate relationships. In her study of cross-sector partnerships in volunteer tourism, Lamoureux (2009) states that, "Because of the proximity of volunteer tourists to the natural and cultural resources of a destination, it is critical that interested parties collaborate to create relationships that are financially viable and that serve to improve the environmental or cultural situation that is directly impacted by the volunteers" (p. 10).

The global impact of volunteer tourism on local, predominantly rural communities in biodiverse and ecologically sensitive areas is growing. Tourism Research and Marketing (TRAM; 2008) estimated a total of 1.6 million volunteer tourists traveling per year, with this number expected to continue to grow. The voluntary sector as a whole accounts for an equivalent of

10 million full-time employees, excluding volunteers with religious-affiliated organizations. The local human and environmental implications of these impacts, however, are less understood and tend to be described by case studies isolated in space and time. Volunteer tourism activities, although carrying with them a global impact, operate at the local level. The process in which community members are involved is less understood in volunteer tourism (Sin, 2009, 2010); however, it is clear their role in operationalizing volunteer tourism on the ground is necessary to create and manage projects that suit their daily livelihoods. The connection to the local level, most commonly in developing countries, is mediated by multiple complex organizations, including governments, nonprofit organizations, private corporations, and civil society, creating a disconnect between global development goals and local results. It is difficult for local governments and people to see how the MDGs are relevant to their daily lives (Mowforth & Munt, 2008). Volunteers have the potential to close this gap twofold. First, they can create dialogue and rapport between developed countries' interests and goals and developing countries' local livelihoods and knowledge. Second, they can develop relationships creating a medium for strengthening networks beyond the traditional giver and receiver, providing developing countries an opportunity for better representation and voice (Devereux, 2008; Smith & Yanacopoulos, 2004). The potential of volunteer tourism as a mechanism and driver of development exists but not without associated critiques and challenges.

Volunteers Make a Difference: What Kind of Difference Is Being Made?

Critical theory questions the benevolence of volunteer tourism, referring to power, domination, and class exploitation issues in the interactions of the economically and socially powerful tourists volunteering in a less powerful, remote host community in the developing world (Guttentag, 2009; Mowforth & Munt, 2008; Raymond & Hall, 2008; Sin, 2009). This refers to potential negative impacts caused by the presence of volunteer tourists, particularly those volunteering for a short period of time. These negative impacts include neglect of local interests due to little local involvement, insufficient or incomplete project work due to short-term stays of low-skilled volunteers, reinforcement of the concept of the "other" due to instigated interactions of less educated volunteers with local cultures, and dependency on volunteer projects resulting in decreased employment opportunities for locals (Guttentag, 2009). Short-term volunteering is becoming more popular within the volunteer tourism industry (Halpenny & Caissie, 2003), making the heralded integrated cross-cultural connection between volunteer tourists and host communities more fragmented and difficult to achieve (Raymond, 2008). It has become increasingly important for volunteer tourism organizations and their staff to maintain positive, trusting, and long-standing relationships with the host communities in which volunteer tourism projects are conducted.

Volunteer tourism is described as a mechanism for sustainable development and a form of pro-poor tourism (Wearing, 2001). Within the literature, an overriding power structure exists that assumes that volunteer tourists and volunteer tourism organizations hold similar, altruistic motivations and values (Sin, 2010). Especially in this context, tourism occurs in places with great inequality in wealth and power, as well as an element of unsustainability in development processes, which is an issue that has been played down in the literature (Gonsalves, 1993; Mowforth & Munt, 2008). The issue of power tends to be addressed in passing, with references to ideology, discourse, colonialism, or imperialism (Mowforth & Munt, 2008). The issue of power can be linked back to a structural flaw in the concept of sustainable development and how volunteer tourism is understood as a mechanism for sustainable development. Both volunteer tourism and sustainable development are constructs of the developed world and are inherently products of developed countries' methods of development. "Yet in order for a collaboration to be true to the public interest, and to succeed, there has to be a roughly equal power equation among the stakeholders, within the context of the issues at hand" (Snow, 2001, p. 10). The manner in which collaborative partnerships are approached and framed, considering the inherent power structures in volunteer tourism and sustainable development, is critical to successful development and achievement of the MDGs.

Building Capacity, Working Together

Integration of local livelihoods interests is increasingly recognized as a keystone to successful and effective development projects. Volunteer tourism provides the opportunity to turn local interests into realistic and creative projects on the ground through capacity building, relationship development, and increased cross-cultural understanding. The causes of (under)development, rather than the symptoms, are challenged through individual action, not only while the volunteers are abroad but also when they return home, aiding in increased global–local connection (Devereux, 2008; Wearing, 2001).

Capacity development is a set of "development approaches that stress facilitation and fostering the growth of social capital rather than the transfer of technical expertise" (Pratt, 2002, p. 95). This concept is particularly important for volunteer tourism researchers and practitioners. In order for volunteer tourism to distance itself from neo-colonial criticism of creating dependency of the communities on volunteer projects, communities must be the central participatory structure in defining what projects are to be completed, in what way, and how these projects may affect their daily livelihood needs (Sin, 2009). Capacity building is the ability to build on the existing strengths of the community, bring forth strengths that may not have been recognized previously, and allow for the community to take control of those capabilities with a more robust sense of agency in their everyday lives and broader social context (Moscardo, 2008). In volunteer tourism, this must be achieved through a collaborative and participatory process in order to address the sustainable livelihood needs of the community and actually build community capacity (Devereux, 2008). Volunteer tourism organizations have experience implementing volunteer tourism projects in a multitude of settings and contexts, whereas host communities have knowledge of their particular differentiated situation and local context, and volunteer tourists provide labor for projects that increase community capacity and affect the daily lives of the community members. If collaboration is used in volunteer tourism processes, real positive change could occur. If not, how do we know the impact of volunteer tourism activities is a good one? Because of the increase in reported negative impacts of volunteer tourism to the detriment of local communities over the past few years (Guttentag, 2009; Raymond & Hall, 2008), reported increases in the participation of volunteer tourists in increasingly diverse and wide-ranging geographical and cultural contexts and their own associated complexities (Benson, 2011), and the integrated cross-cultural nature of volunteer tourism (Raymond & Hall, 2008; Wearing, 2001, 2004), the need to understand livelihoods and how volunteer tourism impacts livelihood sustainability is increasing.

Volunteer tourism must stress participation, collaboration, and negotiation with local populations, perhaps even to a greater degree than other forms of tourism due to volunteer tourists performing physical work in the community (Benson, 2011). Devereux (2008) asserts that for people in developing countries and host communities of volunteer tourism projects, there is an indication of "the importance of achieving local trust and engagement with local struggles before simply 'getting things done'" (p. 363). Community capacity should be a primary goal of volunteer tourism, alongside community development or environmental conservation projects, international understanding, and intercultural learning, in order to avoid the dependence of local populations on volunteer work. Further, long-term partnerships are essential to effective development (Eade, 2007; Ingram, 2011).

The capacities that volunteer tourism organizations seek to build are diverse and wide-ranging, including goals regarding social, political, economic, environmental, and technical aspects of local communities around the globe (Ossewaarde, Nijhof, & Heyse, 2008, in Ingram, 2011). Partnerships among volunteer tourism organizations and host communities can help hedge recent criticisms of development, as well as criticism of insufficient or incomplete projects or catering to short-term volunteer tourists, by consolidating project goals with other volunteer tourism organizations and involving the community in project decision making and management. Volunteer tourism organizations have been criticized recently for their procedural and organizational structure in local contexts and their potential responsibility for preparing volunteers for cross-cultural interaction and representation (Coghlan, 2007; Cousins, 2007; Joyce, 2009; Raymond, 2008). Enhancing and promoting partnerships with local communities will integrate volunteer tourism stakeholders into the broader global development community.

Volunteer Tourism and the Other MDGs

Many major international development schemes, such as the MDGs, are operationalized by the volunteer tourism industry through a variety of approaches and projects, and in diverse and complex geographical, social, economic, and cultural contexts. By nature, volunteer development projects are diverse, and this section will address multiple ways that demonstrate the breadth and potential of volunteers' work around the world, and how particular projects work to attain different MDG targets. NGOs are frequently called upon to help achieve the MDGs (Ingram, 2011; Sachs & McArthur, 2005), and volunteer tourism organizations' preexisting links to the local level and access to free labor via volunteers provides a structure for achievement of MDGs, particularly in the poorest countries. According to Sachs and McArthur, the poorest countries most need development assistance in order to emerge from the poverty trap, in contrast to other developing countries whose responsibility for poverty reduction is predominantly their own. Unfortunately, although volunteer tourism tends to occur in developing countries, volunteer tourism organizations tend to avoid sending volunteers to the poorest countries.

For example, U.S. Peace Corps volunteers currently are banned from entering Haiti. A colleague of mine and recent Peace Corps volunteer in the Dominican Republic noted several of his Peace Corps colleagues were relieved of their duties as volunteers after the Peace Corps learned of their help in Haiti after the devastating earthquake in 2008. Moreover, despite debates regarding power structures and self-interested volunteer tourists, volunteer tourism does much to achieve each of the other MDGs.

Bi-directional development volunteering increases relationship development between developed and developing countries through volunteer exchange programs (Joyce, 2009). Callanan and Thomas (2005) developed a breakdown of volunteer tourism activities by project activities of over 1,000 volunteer projects around the world. Each of the categories they examined could be identified as contributing to MDGs, with the most frequent category of volunteer projects being community welfare. Volunteers around the world work to reduce poverty (MDG 1) by donating time and capacity building (Devereux, 2008; Lewis, 2006). They build schools and teach children (MDG 2), which was the second most common volunteer activity found by Callanan and Thomas. In South Africa, Habitat for Humanity and other local organizations integrate women into the decision-making, design, and construction processes and are committed to their full participation in these processes (MDG 3) (Stoddart & Rogerson, 2004). Programs like Doctors and Nurses Without Borders provide medical expertise and resources to help reduce child mortality (MDG 4), improve maternal health (MDG 5), and combat HIV/AIDS, malaria, and other diseases (MDG 6). As of 2005, most countries, if not all, were failing to achieve the environmental sustainability targets (Sachs & McArthur, 2005). This goal is perhaps most easily achieved by unskilled volunteer tourists because most conservation work requires little formal skill set and training. Volunteers work to achieve environmental sustainability (MDG 7) through planting native species, eradicating invasive species, or building wildlife refuges (Halpenny & Caissie, 2003). Perhaps one of the most researched and popular conservation-related volunteer projects are sea turtle conservation efforts in Costa Rica (Campbell & Smith, 2005; Gray & Campbell, 2007).

Each study, discussion, critique, and discourse within volunteer tourism mentions the sensitivity of cross-cultural interaction and intercultural learning between volunteer tourists and host communities. Partnerships within volunteer tourism must address this aspect and work to attain a global partnership for development based on trust, commitment, and understanding in order for projects to be successful and sustainable, and aid in the achievement of the other MDGs.

Future Potential of Volunteer Tourism Partnerships for Development

Key to successful partnerships and sustainable outcomes are mutually determined goals and actions, as well as continual monitoring of those partnerships (Selin, 1999). Little is known about the collaborative processes within volunteer tourism and the manner in which these processes occur, specifically regarding power dynamics of the relationships and if, in fact, the stakeholders involved hold similar goals and values. Further research in this area has theoretical and practical value. Discourse on power structures in collaborative volunteer tourism partnerships in an idyllic, mutually beneficial volunteer tourism industry not only will help inform the extent to which volunteers can aid in the achievement of the MDGs but also provide a structure in which other development initiatives can adapt and learn. The industry holds much potential for collaboration based on cause-based partnerships and a mix of stakeholders at multiple levels with seemingly similar goals. It is important for collaboration to occur among multiscale partners for a global network but is similarly important for stakeholders with the same role in the industry to collaborate in order to attain sustainable outcomes based on mutually determined goals and actions. It also may inform volunteer tourism stakeholders of their own collaborative relationships, and may cause reflection and change in the way in which they communicate and collaborate.

How nature and the environment are framed in volunteer tourism also is important, particularly in the context of the developing world and the integrated cross-cultural experiences between volunteer tourists and host communities. And, "the ways we communicate powerfully affect our perceptions of the living world" (Milstein, 2009, p. 345). An investigation into the collaborative relationships within volunteer tourism will elicit concrete ways to improve project implementation and management of more successful and sustainable volunteer tourism projects that address the livelihoods of local people and their surrounding ecosystems.

Conclusion

Volunteer tourism has the opportunity to bridge multiscale gaps in development by creating a global dialogue and a network beyond development aid, linking the developed and developing nations by highlighting key aspects of capacity building such as local accountability, local values, and local knowledge (Lewis, 2006). Volunteer tourism is a realistic, creative, empowering, and powerful global development tool that not only reaches beyond current economic systems as a nonmarket mechanism based on trust, international understanding, capacity building, and relationship development but also helps to achieve other MDG targets through project work on the ground such as biodiversity conservation or primary education.

Better understanding of dynamic global partnerships in volunteer tourism will facilitate learning among stakeholders that will break down power constructs, foster more cohesive and realized project goals leading to more sustainably developed communities in the developing world, and better include host communities in project planning, implementation, and management. Volunteer tourism can bridge gaps through involvement of multiscale, cross-sector partnerships at individual and interorganizational levels as well as at local, regional, and global scales. Cohesive, multiscale partnerships within volunteer tourism can help promote sustainable local use of natural resources, enhance ecosystem and cultural stability and resilience for the geographic region, and help humans benefit from the global effects of conservation in biodiverse and ecologically sensitive areas.

References

Almas, R., & Lawrence, G. (2003). Introduction: The global/local problematic. In: R. Amas and G. Lawrence (Eds.), *Globalization, localization and sustainable livelihoods* (pp. 3–24). Burlington, VT: Ashgate.

Amin, S. (2006). The Millennium Development Goals: A critique from the south. *Monthly Review, 57*(10). Retrieved April 12, 2012, from http://monthlyreview.org/0306amin.htm

Benson, A. (2011). Volunteer tourism: Theory and practice. In: A. M. Benson (Ed.), *Volunteer tourism: Theory framework to practical applications* (pp. 1–6). London: Routledge.

Biermann, F., Chan, M., Mert, A., & Pattberg, P. (2007, May 24–26). *Multi-stakeholder partnerships for sustainable development: Does the promise hold?* Paper presented at the 2007 Amsterdam Conference on the Human Dimensions of Global Environmental Change, Vrije Universiteit, Amsterdam, The Netherlands.

Brocklesby, M. A., & Fisher, E. (2003). Community development in sustainable livelihoods approaches: An introduction. *Community Development Journal, 38*(3), 185–198.

Brown, S., & Lehto, X. (2005). Travelling with a purpose: Understanding the motives and benefits of volunteer vacationers. *Current Issues in Tourism, 8*(6), 470–496.

Buckley, R. (2004). Partnerships in ecotourism: Australian political frameworks. *International Journal of Tourism Research, 6,* 75–83.

Callanan, M., & Thomas, S. (2005). Volunteer tourism: Deconstructing volunteer activities within a dynamic environment. In: M. Novelli (Ed.), *Niche tourism: Contemporary issues, trends and causes* (pp. 183–201). Oxford: Butterworth-Heinemann.

Campbell, L. M., & Smith, C. (2005). Volunteering for sea turtles? Characteristics and motives of volunteers working with the Caribbean Conservation Corporation in Tortuguero, Costa Rica. *MAST, 3/4,* 169–194.

Coghlan, A. (2007). Towards an integrated image-based typology of volunteer tourism organisations. *Journal of Sustainable Tourism, 15*(3), 267–287.

Cole, S. (2006). Information and empowerment: The keys to achieving sustainable tourism. *Journal of Sustainable Tourism, 14*(6), 629–644.

Cousins, J. (2007). The role of UK-based conservation tourism operators. *Tourism Management, 13*(3), 1020–1030.

Devereux, P. (2008). International volunteering for development and sustainability: Outdated paternalism or radical response to globalisation? *Development in Practice, 18*(3), 357–370.

Eade, D. (2007). Capacity building: Who builds capacity? *Development in Practice, 17*(4), 630–639.

Fee, L., & Mdee, A. (2011). How does it make a difference? Towards "accreditation" of the development impact of volunteer tourism. In: A. M. Benson (Ed.), *Volunteer tourism: Theory framework to practical applications* (pp. 223–239). London: Routledge.

Gonsalves, P. (1993). Divergent views: Convergent paths. Towards a Third World critique of tourism. *Contours, 6*(3/4), 8–14.

Gray, N. J., & Campbell, L. M. (2007). A decommodified experience? Exploring aesthetic, economic and ethical values for volunteer tourism in Costa Rica. *Journal of Sustainable Tourism, 15*(5), 463–482.

Guttentag, D. A. (2009). The possible negative impacts of volunteer tourism. *International Journal of Tourism Research, 11,* 537–551.

Halpenny, E., & Caissie, L. (2003). Volunteering on nature conservation projects: Volunteer experience, attitudes, and values. *Tourism Recreation Research, 28*(3), 25–33.

Ingram, J. (2011). Volunteer tourism: How do we know it is "making a difference"? In: A. M. Benson (Ed.), *Volunteer tourism: Theory framework to practical applications* (pp. 211–222). London: Routledge.

Jamal, T. B., & Getz, D. (1995). Collaboration theory and community tourism planning. *Annals of Tourism Research, 22*(1), 186–204.

Jamal, T., & Stronza, A. (2009). Collaboration theory and tourism practice in protected areas: Stakeholders, structuring and sustainability. *Journal of Sustainable Tourism, 17*(2), 169–189.

Joyce, B. (2009, December 1). *Can volunteers achieve the MDGs without unintended damaging consequences?* Presented at La Trobe University, Glebe, New South Wales: Palms Australia.

Kiely, R. (1998). Neoliberalism revised? A critical account of World Bank concepts of good government and market friendly intervention. *Capital and Class, 22*(1), 63–88.

Lamoureux, K. M. (2009). Success factors of cross-sector volunteer tourism partnerships involving U.S. federal land agencies. ProQuest. UMI No. 3360151. Retrieved from the Dissertations and Theses database.

Lewis, D. (2006). Globalization and international service: A development perspective. *Voluntary Action, 7*(2), 13–26.

McGehee, N. G., & Santos, C. (2005). Social change, discourse, and volunteer tourism. *Annals of Tourism Research, 32*, 760–779.

Milstein, T. (2009). Environmental communication theories. In: S. W. Littlejohn & K. A. Foss (Eds.), *Encyclopedia of communication theory* (pp. 344–349). Los Angeles, CA: Sage.

Moscardo, G. (2008). Community capacity building: An emergent challenge for tourism development. In: G. Moscardo (Ed.), *Building community capacity for tourism development* (pp. 1–15). Wallingford, UK: CABI.

Mowforth, M., & Munt, I. (2008). *Tourism and sustainability: Development and new tourism in the Third World* (3rd ed.). London: Routledge.

Mustonen, P. (2007). Volunteer tourism: Altruism or mere tourism? *Anatolia: An International Journal of Tourism and Hospitality Research, 18*(1), 97–115.

Ossewaarde, R., Nijhof, A., & Heyse, L. (2008). Dynamics of NGO legitimacy: How organising betrays core missions of INGOs. *Public Administration and Development, 28*, 42–53.

Palacios, C. M. (2010). Volunteer tourism, development and education in a postcolonial world: Conceiving global connections beyond aid. *Journal of Sustainable Tourism, 18*(7), 861–878.

Pratt, B. (2002). Volunteerism and capacity development. *Development Policy Journal, 2*(7), 95–117.

Raymond, E. M. (2008). "Make a difference!": The role of sending organizations in volunteer tourism. In: K. D. Lyons & S. Wearing (Eds.), *Journeys of discovery in volunteer tourism* (pp. 48–60). Wallingford, UK: CABI.

Raymond, E. M., & Hall, C. M. (2008). The development of cross-cultural (mis)understanding through volunteer tourism. *Journal of Sustainable Tourism, 16*(5), 530–543.

Reed, M. G. (1999). Collaborative tourism planning as adaptive experiments in emergent tourism settings. *Journal of Sustainable Tourism, 7*(3/4), 331–355.

Sachs, J. D., & McArthur, J. W. (2005). The Millennium Project: A plan for meeting the Millennium Development Goals. *Lancet, 365*, 347–353.

Sammy, J. (2008). Examples of effective techniques for enhancing community understanding of tourism. In: G. Moscado (Ed.), *Building community capacity for tourism development* (pp. 75–85). Wallingford, UK: CABI.

Selin, S. (1999). Developing a typology of sustainable tourism partnerships. *Journal of Sustainable Tourism, 7*(3/4), 260–273.

Selin, S., & Chavez, D. (1995). Development of an evolutionary tourism partnership model. *Annals of Tourism Research, 22*, 844–856.

Sin, H. L. (2009). Volunteer tourism: "Involve me and I will learn"? *Annals of Tourism Research, 36*(3), 480–501.

Sin, H. L. (2010). Who are we responsible to? Local's tales of volunteer tourism. *Geoforum, 41*, 983–992.

Smith, M., & Yanacopoulos, H. (2004). The public faces of development: An introduction. *Journal of International Development, 16*, 657–664.

Snow, D. (2001). Coming home: An introduction to collaborative conservation. In: P. Brick, D. Snow, & S. van de Wetering (Eds.), *Across the great divide: Explorations in collaborative conservation and the American West* (pp. 1–11). Washington, DC: Island Press.

Stoddart, H., & Rogerson, C. (2004). Volunteer tourism: The case of Habitat for Humanity in South Africa. *GeoJournal, 60*, 311–318.

Stronza, A. (2008). Partnerships for tourism development. In: G. Moscado (Ed.), *Building community capacity for tourism development* (pp. 101–115). Wallingford, UK: CABI.

Tourism Research and Marketing (TRAM). (2008). *Volunteer tourism: A global analysis*. Barcelona, Spain: ATLAS.

United Nations Volunteers (UNV). (2005). Volunteers "unsung heroes" of the Millennium Development Goals: UN chief. Retrieved April 13, 2012, from http://www.unv.org/en/news-resources/news/doc/volunteers-unsung-heroes-of.html

Wearing, S. (2001). *Volunteer tourism: Experiences that make a difference*. Wallingford, UK: CABI.

Wearing, S. (2002). Re-centring the self in volunteer tourism. In: G. M. S. Dann & J. Jacobsen (Eds.), *The tourist as a metaphor for the social world* (pp. 237–262). Wallingford, UK: CABI.

Wearing, S. (2004). Examining best practice in volunteer tourism. In: R. A. Stebbins & M. Graham (Eds.), *Volunteering as leisure: Leisure as volunteering* (pp. 209–224). Wallingford, UK: CABI.

Connecting Communities to the Tourism Supply Chain

Richard G. Edwards, Kelly Galaski, and Rachel Dodds

LEARNING OBJECTIVES

- To understand the barriers to success of CBT
- To recognize the benefits of market-based supply chain intervention for CBT
- To identify various ways local partnerships in CBT can be formed
- To understand the challenges and benefits to both outbound tour operators and local CBT partners involved in such partnerships

Tour operators, travel wholesalers, and other private sector sustainable tourism practitioners have long wondered why their expertise in tourism product development, market intelligence and specific needs for product distribution have not been incorporated until the final stages of most new community tourism development projects in key travel destinations. This case study and its supporting examples will examine the work of G Adventures (formerly Gap Adventures) in community-based tourism (CBT), both directly and through the nonprofit Planeterra Foundation founded by the company in 2003, and show how G Adventures is harnessing the power of travel to develop productive partnerships in developing countries. This company, motivated by economic realities as well as concern for environmental and social well-being, is contributing to Millennium Development Goal (MDG) 8: Develop a global partnership for development. The endurance of the G Adventures projects, despite lacking significant outside public funding, illustrates how global partnerships in tourism can contribute to the sustainable development of communities and small businesses.

Through its unique partnership with Planeterra and based on relationships with local organizations, G Adventures is able to connect CBT initiatives and local organizations working toward sustainable development directly to the tourism supply chain, a process that assures the creation and maintenance of a market-ready product. Aligning the goals of CBT and its potential clients from the earliest stages of the projects is fundamental to eventual success, though this step has most often been entirely nonexistent in both small, locally driven initiatives and huge, multimillion-dollar, internationally funded tourism endeavors.

Traditional community tourism is reviewed to offer insight into the reasoning behind G Adventures' work to directly link small businesses and community tourism organizations. There are multiple barriers to successful CBT, and for that reason it often fails. G Adventures has the ability to influence the success of CBT by offering a direct market to ventures worldwide with 100,000 annual customers and the ability to guarantee flow in specific regions that CBT can benefit from directly.

Why Traditional Community-Based Tourism Often Fails

Community-based tourism has emerged out of efforts to apply tourism as a development tool in rural areas in many developing countries, responding to a niche but growing market segment of travelers who are looking for more authentic interaction with local people in developing countries. Outcomes of these projects throughout the world and the businesses that are formed as a result range from failure, and even false starts, to strong profitability. Unfortunately, most would agree there are many more examples of the former than the latter. Success is based on many aspects such as management structure, attractiveness of the destination, knowledge and skills, access to finance, ability to reach the intended consumers or tourists, quality and uniqueness of product, and, most importantly, role in a productive supply chain.

A broad definition of CBT provides context for this discussion:

> Community-based Tourism (CBT) has at its core, the aim of achieving sustainable development for communities often removed from traditional market economies, including

tourism. CBT involves increasing local peoples' contribution to the tourism value chain by providing cultural interaction experiences for domestic and foreign tourists, hospitality services including tours and accommodation, or products that complement the industry such as agriculture and handicrafts. As a sustainable development tool, its criteria for success should be based on triple bottom line thinking with a focus on environmental and social goals, and economic viability, without which the CBT initiative cannot achieve its purpose, which is to be sustainable in providing development benefits (Jamaica Social Investment Fund, 2011).

Product Development: Turning It on Its Head

The core of CBT planning has traditionally been to determine how best to use it as a development tool. From that perspective, CBT is developed based on the community's assets, the community's objectives, and the desire to achieve some form of economic development based on attracting visitors. The problem with too much focus on the supply side of the spectrum is that projects are developed based on what the area has to offer and not on what is demanded by those that are going to purchase the travel product, whether the target is direct tourists or tour operators that have a client base in their back pocket. Unfortunately, many CBT projects around the world have failed—and are doomed to fail—because of this "build it and they will come" approach.

Generally, CBT initiatives have focused on providing tourist services based on perceived need or even new unfounded perceptions of potential gaps in product offerings. Often, the fact the country itself is a popular international tourism destination is relied upon, without understanding the obstacles in reaching the international tourist from a remote community-level destination. This situation has created a number of similar tourism offerings that are not well defined in the mind of the consumer, and that compete not only within one country but also internationally with rival destinations. There is a focus on what a community has to offer, in isolation of its competition and accessibility from the main tourism highlights of the country. In countless cases, the community that develops a tour or accommodations may find itself just far enough out of the way that it is not easy to add onto a marketable tour package or established trip itinerary, or not within relatively easy access for a hotel's day-trip offering. The tourism project therefore goes unvisited, except for sporadic numbers of more adventurous travelers or domestic visitors. Both of these latter markets have the added disadvantage for the project of having a lower price point with limited revenue and margins.

Related to this issue, there tends to be a focus on accommodations and tours at the community level, targeted at international tourists. It has been shown that this focus tends to result in very low occupancy rates, making it impossible to reach economic sustainability. Research on 200 CBT initiatives in Latin America conducted by Rainforest Alliance and Conservation International indicates averages of only 5% occupancy for accommodation ventures (Mitchell & Muckosy, 2008). Many initiatives were unable to attract enough business to be viable due to unsuccessful marketing, a lack of understanding of the markets, or products that don't match market demands. These results indicate that conditions for financial sustainability are not being focused on at the outset of project plans (Mitchell & Muckosy, 2008).

Marketing to the Wrong Audience

CBT solutions invariably focus on developing fairly comprehensive direct-to-consumer marketing plans, strategies, and tactics: creating a website, and creating a collective or network that markets a whole region directly to potential tourists in main outbound countries such as the United States, Canada, and the United Kingdom. Although these tools are essential, they continue to fail because the majority of tourists do not generally buy CBT as a stand-alone product and do not often search for a CBT experience from home. They look to larger tour operators, hotels, or cruise companies that are taking them to the country to assist with this perceived higher risk purchase. Tourists who are visiting a country are more likely to participate in a CBT experience as an add-on or inclusion in their trip that visits the country's highlights.

Additionally, reaching primary tourism markets is a competitive, sophisticated, and expensive endeavor for a small, nascent business. Therefore CBT enterprises (CBTEs) are better off partnering with a regional operator, a hotel chain, or a cruise line as a primary marketing function, than to try and market their small business independently. Certainly a website that promotes the experience is an excellent supplementary marketing tool that should be exploited, but the key point is that the CBTE is not relying only on its website or a small regional marketing network's website to sell the day trip directly to the tourist.

Operations and Distribution for International Markets

Rural tourism providers involved in CBT often lack many of the skills and the knowledge required to participate in the tourism industry, especially with the demands of even fairly experienced and flexible international travelers; therefore, collaboration and partnerships are necessary. Hospitality skills may be present, but there often is a lack of awareness of the general expectations of the international traveler and the markets they represent, knowledge of product presentation at that level, and marketing networks (Bramwell & Lane, 2000; Mitchell & Hall, 2005; United Nations World Tourism Organization [UNWTO], 2003). In terms of creating a competitive market position to enhance revenue potential, rural tourism providers face "structural and product problems" due to their remote lesser-known locations, small populations with limited training, and less infrastructure and cohesiveness as destinations (Mitchell & Hall, 2005, p. 4). Such problems include lack of concern with and knowledge of demand factors, lack of skills with regard to product presentation, limited knowledge of markets they work within, and limited development of cooperation and marketing networks, which create "barriers to market access" (Forstner, 2004, p. 498; Mitchell & Hall, 2005).

Collaborations and partnerships lower the risk of failure for CBT. For example, by partnering with domestic tour companies that already work with CBTs in other areas, one initiative becomes part of a network of available activities promoted by that operator. Partnering with domestic operators lowers risk because it is easier to reach nearby markets if offering products such as day trips. This also helps to build capacity to better cater to foreign markets in the future.

Financing Sustainable CBT

There is a challenge for CBT ventures in becoming financially sustainable related to a lack of access to markets, finance, and training. Loans generally require substantiated business plans, and communities lack the ability to put appropriate plans together; therefore, they rely on external grants. Lenders normally do not have the kind of market knowledge to properly assess market feasibility and tend to rely on what they perceive as fair comparisons to other tourism products within a given region. Those comparisons are primarily based on the look and feel of the product itself. Therefore, grants may help launch initiatives, but they may be based on developing the product without the guarantee there will be buyers once the product is developed. Projects being developed that are not economically sustainable are a major and continuing issue.

Micro-finance has shown some success with community-level businesses, due to the commitment it requires on the part of the owners and managers to become profitable. However, this is linked to the capacity to produce business plans, develop quality product, and maintain financial records. Often funding schemes provide capacity-building/skills training, yet once the program is launched there is diminishing support over time, when often it is the long-term management of a project that requires capacity and skills that do not initially exist. Funding and/or loans should provide a longer-term approach to training to: (1) strengthen the ability of the owners and managers to run their businesses effectively, (2) identify opportunities for diversification and expansion, and (3) maintain financial records that can be used for additional financing in the future.

The Solution

It is difficult to clearly determine levels of success of CBT worldwide due to a lack of data on the financial sustainability of CBTEs. CBT proponents, communities interested in CBT, and funders would benefit from a wide-reaching study on profit levels. Current research provides an indication there is a high incidence of poor financial records, as well as low visitation levels (Goodwin & Santilli, 2009; Jones & EplerWood International, 2008). Combined with significant anecdotal evidence of these failures, as well as the rare success stories coming from the authors' own experience, we can easily hypothesize that many CBTEs fail and there is a more effective way of making CBT more viable and beneficial. We propose the answer is connecting these small CBTEs to the tourism supply chain through every stage of development and implementation.

How Elements of the Tourism Supply Chain Interact with Local Communities

One of the most complicated and intricate supply chain systems in any industry can be found in the adventure travel/ecotourism sector in which CBT most often finds itself. Frameworks try to illustrate how each of the actors potentially interrelates, yet none have been completely successful, due to the multiple consumer contact points up and down the supply chain and distribution channels for this type of tourism product.

For our purposes, it is simplest to say that every entity along the chain, including service providers, inbound tour operators, outbound tour operators and wholesalers, retail travel agents, and online travel agencies (OTAs), is marketing directly to consumers, while simultaneously looking for ways to access distribution through many other players throughout the supply chain. By concentrating on marketing directly to consumers, CBTEs are spending a considerable amount of time attempting to penetrate extremely competitive and distant markets with limited resources. These scenarios are happening regularly, when a close, mutually beneficial relationship with an organization within the distribution system with more marketing resources and infrastructure could potentially fulfill most or all of the marketing needs of a typical CBTE.

CBTE: A Difficult Path to Consumer Travel Markets

CBTEs are generally given advice on marketing from international and regional funders, nonprofit development organizations, and other sources that seek to assist them in launching their businesses. The often-limited private-sector tourism industry marketing and distribution expertise available through these types of organizations invariably leads to a direct-to-consumer marketing strategy. Often resource issues end up dictating a concentration on targeting in-country international travelers and local markets. An explanation for this pattern would be that consumer marketing is by far the most visible and also the easiest to understand, set up, and implement in the beginning stages. Elements of such a strategy include:

- A proprietary website or a presence on an aggregating website attempting to market a region
- A locally produced brochure outlining the product offering and project history
- Limited local print advertising (e.g., newspapers, tourist guides)
- Membership and participation in local CBT organizations and tourism fairs
- Some signage onsite or near the site to attract in-country visitors

Viable and profitable markets for CBT are fragmented as well as difficult and expensive to reach. Market intelligence is difficult to gain in any meaningful way at this level. Given this, direct-to-consumer supply chain models have proved to be frustrating for CBTEs; they are most often unsustainable, unprofitable, and short-lived, and sometimes even are damaging to future sustainable development within communities. Negative CBT experiences by locals can influence future decisions on sustainable development projects.

Accessing the Powerful Tourism Motor

In response to market demand for more authentic tourism products that allow travelers to interact with local people within the context of their traditional daily lives in destinations around the world, tour operators seek CBT partners to insert into their existing product lines. As alluded to earlier, characterizing those businesses and organizations looking to market tours that include CBT elements as "tour operators" is an oversimplification necessary to convey the primary messages. Large travel agency chains, or even online travel agents (OTAs), sometimes act as tour operators when they look to purchase certain products directly from service providers.

Tour operators are motivated by consumer demand to expand and develop their CBT product line. A typical CBTE need only develop one very strong reciprocal relationship with a tour operator from the inception of its project. There are a number of benefits to this step. By aligning with a tour operator who has demonstrated an understanding of sustainability in both theory and practice, CBTEs can take advantage of the operator's knowledge of key market demands and technical expertise to develop the product, creating what would be expected to be a market-ready CBT product from the very beginning of the project's life, or at some defining moment in the reassessment and revision of an existing CBTE.

Logically, operators focus their marketing on the product they develop. A well-defined relationship between an operator and a CBTE, in which the two parties have collaborated on business and strategic planning that defines metrics like occupancy and visitor numbers, allows the CBTE to anticipate minimal marketing expenditures. The marketing burden is naturally shifted to the tour operator. One positive aspect of these types of relationships, for all those involved, is that the relevancy and popularity of CBT in the marketplace inspires tour operators to dedicate a significant amount of focus within their marketing strategy on their CBT endeavors.

Tour operators marketing directly to consumers, or even within established distribution channels, must show their commitment to the sustainability of their markets. Their effort to accomplish this is an added benefit to their supplier partners who understand and embrace environmental and cultural sustainability, while working with them to achieve economic sustainability. Additionally, the more aspects of sustainability the partners can identify, develop, support, and foster, the more layered and relevant marketing that resonates with consumers can be developed and deployed. G Adventures works with Planeterra to gather these stories on a continuous basis, constantly communicating with its travelers about their travel experiences. The organization uses interactions between travelers and local people as the cornerstone of its successful messaging to consumers through its various web properties, social media, and print outreach. All members of distribution channels, mainly tour operators, use similar marketing strategies with their partner CBTEs.

Purchasing goods and services locally develops local supply chains, employing more local people. The nature of the goods demanded by the type of environmentally and culturally aware travelers interested in visiting CBT projects encourages environmentally sound and organic production methods for food products. There also is demonstrated demand from travelers for artisan handicrafts that reflect cultural traditions. Production of these goods not only provides employment for local people but also gives younger generations of locals an economic incentive to preserve their cultural heritage and continue living a traditional way of life, if they choose to do so.

Finally, the business drivers of having a functioning tourism enterprise that fulfills travelers' expectations motivate both the tour operator and the CBTE to work together on operational adjustments to market demands and more basic quality control. There are a number of possible scenarios that represent solvable issues; examples include:

- Finding that the product proved to be less than market-ready upon exposure to the markets by the tour operator
- Experiencing unforeseen logistical problems due to the addition of new destinations within itineraries
- Uncovering a need for increased staff training to meet international tourism standards to an acceptable level

- Realizing that visitor numbers need to be more closely monitored to maintain the integrity of the travel experience
- Discovering communication breakdowns and conflicts among community members pertaining to real or perceived benefits to certain community members

For all of these situations, it is clearly in the best interest of all parties to seek quick, effective, and lasting resolutions, which adds to the sustainability of the CBTE. There is a strong need to fully integrate any supplier into the supply chain for the product to be successful. CBT simply adds the extra layer of needing to have a successful relationship among the community, the CBTE, and the supply chain in order to function.

Case Examples: Connecting Communities to the Tourism Supply Chain

The following examples illustrate ways in which G Adventures and Planeterra connect CBT to the supply chain by directly contracting communities for their tourism services, working with community associations, developing relationships with local tour operators, and involving travel agencies in CBT programs, volunteer programs, and project funding. When studying these examples, it is worthwhile to consider how the absence of at least one interested and motivated private sector partner could have impeded or completely prevented the ongoing success of these projects and their resulting tourism products.

Example 1: Developing Local Partnerships with Indigenous Communities in the Sacred Valley of Peru

In 2005 G Adventures began operating Inca Trail trips directly with its own team of porters and local staff based in Cusco. The first porters to work for the company came from a small community called Ccaccaccollo, just outside of Cusco en route to the Sacred Valley, where all G Adventures Inca Trail groups pass through on their way to Machu Picchu. The partnership with Ccaccaccollo began with this employment relationship, and the company was instrumental in bringing about improved labor conditions by decreasing the amount of weight each porter carried, and offering training such as English, cooking lessons, and CPR/first aid.

Although grateful for the employment opportunities for the men of the community, the women of Ccaccaccollo also aspired to be involved in tourism. In 2005 they approached the company (which had formalized the nonprofit Planeterra in 2003) to take responsibility for community development projects in the destination. Planeterra worked with the women of Ccaccaccollo to develop a weaving project to bring back the culture of textiles, which had been slowly dying as the women looked for menial work in Cusco. A local NGO with capacity for training in textiles, including the spinning of the alpaca wools and the natural dying process, was brought in to train the women and help start their small business. G Adventures began bringing groups to Ccaccaccollo to visit the project and provided their travelers with an opportunity to purchase products directly from the women. Six years later, the group had grown to 40 women, and they continue to receive daily tourist groups from G Adventures.

In 2011, weekly tours including a home stay with 12 families in the community was established. The project rotated among the various families to share the benefits, and with the intention of expanding the program to include more families.

In early 2010, there was major flooding in the region, and the women's workshop was destroyed and their looms were washed away. Planeterra appealed to G Adventures travelers who had visited the community over the years and was able to raise $13,500 to rebuild the workshop, pay for fuel for road construction equipment, and deliver 1,500 kilograms of food and supplies to 80 affected families.

The relationship between the community and G Adventures continues, and both the home stay and weaving group now operate independently, still receiving capacity-building on their tourism business as well as product diversification and sales presentations. Managing this partnership has been a challenge and learning experience for G Adventures and Planeterra. Planeterra placed a staff person in Cusco to manage the partnership between the travel company and the community directly, and with the departure of that person after 2 years, Planeterra was able to hire a local Cusco resident who speaks Quechua (the local indigenous language) and is formally educated in rural community tourism development in Peru.

After several years of working directly with the community, including G Adventures operations staff coordinating events, home stay program, and daily visits, both the organizations have realized that, in order to develop this and new programs in communities to their full potential, a person with indigenous language capabilities helps to connect Planeterra and G Adventures more fully to the community and provides for more effective project management.

Additionally, Planeterra has partnered with a local NGO called Intercooperacion, facilitating the APOMIPE program (Program for the Support of Small and Micro Enterprises in Peru) for the Swiss Agency for the Development and Cooperation and the Ministry of Production of Peru (http://www.apomipe.org.pe). The program is executed by a community facilitator who regularly visits Ccaccaccollo to work directly with the women's weaving group on their planning, product diversification, and sales presentation capacity-building. This has proved effective in the progression of their weaving project.

This case example demonstrates the success that can be achieved when a project is developed based on market demand. G Adventures works closely with the community to ensure they are continually able to offer a quality experience to its travelers and to ensure the residents of Ccaccaccollo can maintain and improve their tourism businesses and expand participation in the programs.

Example 2: Involving the Wider Travel Industry in Community Projects for Local Benefits and to Improve CSR

STA Travel (http://www.statravel.co.uk), a worldwide travel agency with 500 retail locations throughout Europe, the United Kingdom, Australia, New Zealand, the United States, and South Africa, has been a long-term strong partner for G Adventures. In 2009, G Adventures committed to a new "responsible travel journey," in partnership with Planeterra Foundation and STA Travel.

STA Travel wanted to support a project that its staff and travelers, many of whom take G Adventures tours and visit Planeterra projects, could identify with, tangibly support, and follow its progress. Planeterra developed a proposal for STA Travel in conjunction with a local Thai partner, Andaman Discoveries (http://www.andamandiscoveries.com), to build a community tourism training center to support an ongoing training program in Southern Thailand where tsunami-affected communities are building small tourism businesses to supplement their meager fishing incomes. After the tsunami, many families had to relocate to a new community where there are few employment opportunities. Now, there is a promising CBT atmosphere, composed of several small businesses and enthusiastic community backing, as well as a marine conservation program. Local community members are actively engaged and participate in decision making on all aspects of their projects that are potentially under their control, including impact on the local environment, land use, resource distribution, and how individual community members may be affected by these decisions. This intimate knowledge of what works and what may not allows local leaders to share information with other communities working on CBT in the surrounding areas.

Planeterra, in close collaboration with the global STA Travel corporation, raised $80,000 for this project alone. It then selected two new projects to fund based on Planeterra's strategic plan to support social and environmental projects, destination preservation projects, emergency preparedness, and small business development. This enables Planeterra's work in other major destinations for G Adventures and STA Travel, including pressure points where tourism itself is creating negative impacts, as well as destinations that require local economic stimulation and conservation initiatives as they develop. Planeterra's role is invaluable in vetting a productive and informed local partner to support and assist, and providing the expertise necessary to select and advise the partner, while also fulfilling the goals of the funding partner.

Example 3: Long-Term Relationships: Enabling Success of Small Business on Lake Titicaca

Edgar Apaza started leading tours for G Adventures around his hometown, Puno, and Lake Titicaca in 1994 when the company was just starting. Edgar was a young man who grew up in the area and knew it well, knew the communities on Titicaca, and also knew it was a special place to share with visitors. At that time, the culture of Lake Titicaca was based on communal support and reciprocity. There were communal restaurants shared by families on Taquile Island that provided a small supplementary income to the farming and fishing families. Over the years, as tourism grew, private businesses began developing and people began selling their land; slowly the traditional cultures began to disappear.

After 2 years, Edgar and his wife, Norka Florez, established a small tour operation, Edgar Adventures (http://www.edgaradventures.com) and formed a long-term partnership to manage all of G Adventures' groups to the area. Today there are approximately 9,000 tourists per year. Edgar believed in the communities' ability to work together on projects that would benefit whole villages, and worked with two separate island villages to develop home stay businesses. He works with outbound tour operators to include these home stays in their Peru itineraries. These home stays have become very successful and well-managed and will be used for training families involved in home stays in the Ccaccaccollo community in April 2012 to provide a learning experience and exchange between the two communities facilitated by Planeterra's Peru project coordinator.

This case example illustrates the value of partnerships for development. Through G Adventures' long-term business relationships, a young entrepreneur has been able to increase his local business as well as CBT in the region, investing in community development and a more inclusive tourism industry on Titicaca.

Example 4: Connecting Small Community Business to Itineraries for Greater Impact in Guatemala

As noted earlier in the text, one of the great challenges and risks in CBT is developing accommodations in communities without knowledge of market demand and logistical feasibility. A community well-trained in tourism in the San Juan village on Lake Atitlan in Guatemala had the dream of building guest rooms on their properties for tourists, but where would the capital come from, and how could they be guaranteed visitors to support their investment?

A partnership in this scenario is crucial. Planeterra's Latin America project manager discovered this beautiful, clean, quiet, and entrepreneurial community in 2010 and proposed the project to G Adventures for its Central America itineraries, which go through the Lake Atitlan region (approximately 750 passengers per year). In 2011, home stays with the 15 families that make up the San Juan la Laguna Ecotourism Association (http://www.sanjuanlalaguna.org) are now included in tours. Presently, the rooms are part of the families' homes; they use either a vacant room or one of their children's rooms and convert it into a small guest room. The hope is that with the continual flow from G Adventures, each participating family will be able to build its own small guest room for future visitors.

The Guatemalan government provides many training courses to rural Mayan communities in the provision of tourism services. The San Juan community has developed several subassociations under the main tourism association, including artisans' and artists' workshops, a medicinal herb garden and natural soap and tea products, traditional weaving demonstrations, and Mayan tree-planting ceremonies that travelers can take part in. These types of experiences are key to enhancing the travelers' experiences, and so the partnership becomes a win–win–win. Community, traveler, and travel company all gain. This is a success story that can be replicated elsewhere, but the success hinges on many of the factors described in the CBT section earlier in this text.

This community had received and continues to receive capacity-building, supported by the government. They are in a location that is a tourism highlight; therefore, large tour operators can easily incorporate the community's product offerings into their tours without deviating from a popular itinerary. They have programs that are market-ready and well designed for half-day or full-day visits and are well-managed by a team of community members who are trained as ecotourism guides as well as family hosts.

Conclusion

A common thread among these examples is the importance of both long-term and short-term partnerships. In the case of Edgar Adventures, it has been 15 years; for Ccaccaccollo it has been 6 years. The first community G Adventures partnered with in the Ecuadorian Amazon still hosts groups several times a year after 20 years. A travel company that has an interest in showing travelers the local cultural and natural heritage has an interest in the quality and preservation of each destination. By working directly with small community operators it has the ability to offer a steady volume of travelers to small businesses that might be grasping at 5% occupancy otherwise, or trying to reach individual tourists, which has proved to be very difficult.

Barriers to success of CBT were outlined to demonstrate the necessity for market-based CBT development, most successful in partnership with a tour operator. This has been portrayed by outlining how the various elements of the supply chain interact to add and provide potential efficiencies to CBT products. Each case study provides a different viewpoint from which to see the partnership opportunities—through direct CBT development, stimulating small business for long-term partners, and buying from a CBT organization or local tour operator. Each case study offers distinct benefits and challenges and will be best suited to different operators depending on the situation.

The main lesson from this text is that the feasibility of a CBT initiative should be evaluated before going ahead. The initiative should use market-based data for the most likelihood of success, in partnership with a tour operator that can truly incorporate the program into its product line as it would any other supplier, and work with the initiative over the long term to improve and continue to provide quality cultural immersion experiences for travelers and benefits for local communities.

References

Bramwell, B., & Lane, B. (2000). Collaboration and partnerships in tourism planning. In: B. Bramwell & B. Lane (Eds.), *Tourism collaboration and partnerships: Politics, practice and sustainability* (pp. 1–19). Toronto, Canada: Channel View.

Fortstner, K. (2004). Community ventures and access to markets: The role of intermediaries in marketing rural tourism products. *Development Policy Review, 22*(5), 497–514.

Goodwin, H., & Santilli, R. (2009). *Community-based tourism: A success?* Occasional Paper 11. Leeds, United Kingdom: International Centre for Responsible Tourism (with funding from the German Development Agency [GTZ]).

Jamaica Social Investment Fund (JSIF). (2011). *Community based tourism policy.* Kingston, Jamaica: World Bank.

Jones, H., & EplerWood International. (2008). *Community based tourism enterprise in Latin America: Triple bottom line outcomes of 27 projects.* Burlington, VT: EplerWood International.

Mitchell, J., & Muckosy, P. (2008). *A misguided quest: Community-based tourism in Latin America.* London, United Kingdom: Overseas Development Institute.

Mitchell, M., & Hall, D. (2005). Rural tourism as sustainable business: Key themes and issues. In: D. Hall, I. Kirkpatrick, & M. Mitchell (Eds.), *Rural tourism and sustainable business* (pp. 3–13). Toronto, Canada: Channel View.

United Nations World Tourism Organization (UNWTO). (2003). *Sustainable development of ecotourism: A compilation of good practices in SMEs.* Madrid, Spain: Author.

Partnerships in Practice: Ecotourism and Sustainable Tourism Accreditation and Certification Programs

Rosemary Black

LEARNING OBJECTIVES

- To explore the use of partnerships and collaborative approaches in tourism
- To highlight the challenges and benefits of using partnerships in developing and implementing sustainable tourism and ecotourism accreditation and certification programs
- To discuss selected examples of ecotourism and sustainable tourism accreditation and certification programs in which partnership approaches have been used
- To discuss the potential of partnerships, especially global partnerships, in meeting the goal of sustainable tourism

Millennium Development Goal 8 (MDG 8) is to develop a global partnership for development with targets focusing on developing an open, nondiscriminatory trading and financial system dealing with developing countries' debt, cooperating with pharmaceutical companies to ensure access to essential drugs, and cooperating with the private sector to provide access to new technologies. Global partnerships are essential to meet these targets and require cooperation among government, the private sector, nongovernmental organizations (NGOs), and civil society. Tourism has a significant role to play at a range of levels in meeting MDG 8 by supporting and assisting host communities, promoting and marketing destinations, educating consumers, and delivering sustainable and high quality tourism products. Using partnerships and quality assurance mechanisms like sustainable tourism and ecotourism certification and accreditation programs can assist in meeting some of these goals.

The development of certification and accreditation programs has paralleled the growth in ecotourism and sustainable tourism. Many of these programs are a result of partnerships between organizations; however, they also offer an important mechanism for creating and enhancing local partnerships and networks, ensuring the long-term sustainability of a program.

Certification and accreditation programs ensure that products and services are genuine ecotourism and sustainable tourism and not just "green washing" or "ecotourism light" (Bien, 2004; Black & Crabtree, 2007; Honey, 2002). These programs seek to measure the tangible benefits for conservation and the local communities as well as socioeconomic and environmental criteria. Partnerships can play an important role in achieving these aims.

In 2002 there were about 260 voluntary tourism initiatives around the world, including tourism codes of conduct, labels, awards, benchmarking and "best practices." Of these initiatives, 104 were ecolabeling and certification programs offering logos, seals of approval, or awards designed to signify socially and/or environmentally superior tourism practices. Today these certification programs cover tourism professionals such as tour guides and tour operators as well as businesses, products, attractions, destinations, and services (Black, 2002; Honey, 2002).

Certification refers to a voluntary procedure that sets, assesses, monitors, and gives written assurance that a product, process, service, or management system conforms to specified requirements and norms (Black & Crabtree, 2007). To date, all the certification programs in the tourism industry are voluntary, in contrast to other industries such as the construction industry, in which there are government-required certification programs. The term *accreditation* also has been used to refer to systems for rating products, such as accommodations, tours, and attractions, particularly in Australia, New Zealand, and Canada. *Accreditation* is more commonly used to refer to a procedure by which an authoritative body formally recognizes that a certifier or certification program is competent to carry out specific tasks (i.e., it certifies the certifier or demonstrates it is doing the job properly) (Black & Crabtree, 2007).

Many others have written elsewhere about the benefits and disadvantages of certification (Bien, 2004; Black & Crabtree, 2007; Hamele, 2001; Wearing, 1995; Wearing & Neil, 2009); suffice to say these programs can benefit businesses (Font & Epler Wood, 2007), consumers, governments, the environment, and local communities (Black & Crabtree, 2007). The benefits of accreditation are that it ensures the certification process professionally, fairly, and genuinely assesses sustainability and that it has the capacity to strengthen the confidence, consistency, and performance of certification programs (Black & Crabtree, 2007).

Since the 1990s, accreditation and certification of operators and their programs has been one of the most intensely examined areas of ecotourism and sustainable tourism, including discussions and debates of the benefits, challenges, and potential of ecolabels; certification; and accreditation (Black & Crabtree, 2007). The United Nations Environment Programme (UNEP) report (1998) and Font and Buckley (2001) provide detailed lists and descriptions of this multitude of schemes or ecolabels that exist at a range of levels. Examples of international accreditation schemes include Green Globe 21 (Parsons & Grant, 2007) and the Global Sustainable Tourism Council; the majority of regional certification schemes are in Europe, such as the European Blue Flag label (Font & Buckley, 2001), PAN Parks (Font & Clark, 2007), and the Nordic Ecolabel (Font & Buckley, 2001; Hamele, 2001). National certification schemes include the Australian Eco Certification Program (Thwaites, 2007) and the Costa Rican Sustainable Tourism Certificate, and a small number of subnational certification schemes exist mainly in Europe (Font & Buckley, 2001; Hamele, 2001; Spittler & Haak, 2001), such as the Ecotourism Symbol Alcudia (in the municipality of Alcudia, Spain), and in South America, such as the Smart Voyager in the Galapagos Islands (Goodstein, 2007).

In reviewing all the existing tourism ecolabel schemes in 2001, Font and Buckley identified a number of problems and challenges: there were too many tourism ecolabels; they were not clear to the potential consumers; they were run at a small scale, frequently by environmental organizations with limited environmental management expertise; they were under pressure to increase the number of participating companies; and most were generally not self-funding, relying on external funding and support. The same trends still exist today. This text will address some of these challenges that prompt the creation of partnerships or collaborative approaches among these programs at a range of geographic levels as well as provide insight into how these programs can provide a mechanism to create and enhance local partnerships.

Partnerships in Tourism: What the Theory Says

The diffuse and fragmented nature of the tourism phenomenon within the economy and society creates problems of coordination and management in the tourism system (Bramwell & Lane, 2000; Hall, 1999). This, combined with the key forces of globalization and technology, is transforming the tourism sector (United Nations World Tourism Organization [UNWTO], 2002). Partnership and collaborative approaches in tourism offer ways to overcome the fragmented nature of tourism and have been discussed elsewhere in a range of contexts (Bramwell & Lane, 2000; Bushell & Eagles, 2007; Stronza, 2008). A variety of terms are used to describe different collaborative arrangements in tourism, including coalitions, forums, alliances, task forces, and public–private partnerships. The term *collaboration* often is used in the academic literature, whereas the term *partnership* is more common in practice (Bramwell & Lane, 2000; UNWTO, 2002).

Concepts like collaboration, coordination, and partnership are separate, though closely related, and are ideas within the emerging network paradigm. *Networks* refers to the development of linkages between actors (organizations and individuals), where linkages become more formalized towards maintaining mutual interests. Linkages occur along a continuum ranging from loose linkages to coalitions and longer-lasting structural arrangements and relationships (Mandell, 1999). According to Wood and Gray (1991, p. 146), "Collaboration occurs when a group of autonomous stakeholders of a problem domain engage in an interactive process, using shared rules, norms and structures, to act or decide on issues related to that domain." This is a useful definition because it includes the diversity of partnership forms found in practice. This definition can include partnerships at a range of levels from national to international, a broad range of issues, variation in time scale, and different objectives.

Bramwell and Lane (2000) suggest the potential of collaborative approaches is for partners to gain mutual benefits—for example, a collaborative process where the participants might learn from each other, learn from the process itself, develop innovative policies, and respond dynamically to a changing environment. Opportunities also exist for synergistic gains from sharing resources, risks, and rewards and from focusing on collaborative advantage in contrast to competitive advantage. Collaboration also can lead to the exchange of information, goals, and resources. In the case of certification and accreditation programs, the benefits can include some of the previously mentioned advantages including operational efficiency, enhanced equity, collaborative and marketing advantage, and sharing of resources and objectives.

However, there are some disadvantages of collaboration and partnerships in tourism, in terms of both principle and practice. The main problem is conceptions and misconceptions that prospective partners hold about each other, as well as the need to be cognizant of how social, economic, and political structures constrain or facilitate such collaborative processes. There are also issues of power relationships among the partners, where some groups may find it difficult to join the partnership, and variations in the degree of influence among the partners.

Over the past few decades a wealth of knowledge has developed regarding attempts to understand partnerships and collaboration and identify strategies for enhancing their capacity. As society becomes more complex and economies more interdependent, organizations are finding it more difficult to act unilaterally. This has resulted in the creation of more collaborative solutions. Gray's work (1985, 1989) sought to explore the external and internal factors that either facilitate or constrain partnership formation and growth. Gray (1989, p. 11) defines *collaboration* as "a process of joint decision making." He identifies five characteristics critical to the collaborative process:

1. Stakeholders are interdependent.
2. Solutions emerge by dealing constructively with differences.
3. Joint ownership of decisions is involved.
4. Stakeholders assume collective responsibility for the future direction of the domain.
5. Collaboration is an emergent process.

Drawing from this work, the most important lesson for the tourism system is that partnerships and collaborative arrangements are dynamic rather than static phenomena in response to a range of internal and external forces (Selin, 1999).

Tourism partnerships can be defined as situations in which there is a pooling or sharing of appreciations or resources (e.g., information, money, labor) among two or more tourism stakeholders to solve a problem or create an opportunity that neither can address individually (Selin & Chavez, 1995) or "regular, cross-sectoral interactions between two parties based on at least some agreed rules or norms, intended to address a common issue or to achieve a specific policy goal or goals" (Bramwell & Lane, 2000).

Over the past decade, the tourism literature has presented descriptive partnership case studies that typically identify the advantages of working together and recommend the model to be applied widely. However, more recently, other studies have sought to develop a deeper understanding of tourism partnerships and collaboration (Bramwell & Lane, 2000; Selin, 1999). In particular, some studies assess understanding motives for participation, identify barriers to partnership formation and growth characteristics of successful and failed partnerships, and perform outcome-based assessments of partnership successes. Selin developed a typology of sustainable tourism partnerships. Dimensions were identified by which tourism partnerships vary or are similar across time and geographic area. Tourism partnerships were plotted along five primary dimensions: geographic scale, legal basis, locus of control, organizational diversity, and size and time frame. Selin concluded that collaboration occurs in many different forms in response to a variety of societal forces, and that in the late 1990s tourism partnerships were still underdeveloped due to many geographic, organizational, and political constraints. He also indicated that tourism partnerships evolve dynamically, for example, as organizations are pressured to adopt more participatory planning and management methods. He concluded that meaningful opportunities for public involvement through the planning process are essential to enhance public ownership and support of partnership outcomes.

Partnerships are about pursuing common goals or issues. A partnership can be defined as "an on-going arrangement between two or more parties, based on satisfying specifically identified mutual needs. Such partnerships are characterized by durability over time, inclusiveness, cooperation, and flexibility" (Uhlik, 1995, p. 14). Uhlik developed the following six-stage model of partnership development that concentrates on the conditions that will lead to a successful partnership agreement:

1. Education of self and others
2. Needs assessment and resource inventory
3. Identifying prospective partners and investigating their needs and inventories
4. Comparing and contrasting needs and resources
5. Developing a partnership proposal
6. Proposing a partnership

To improve our understanding of partnerships we need to develop analytical frameworks to help us understand the processes of collaboration in tourism and tourism planning. One framework developed by Bramwell and Sharman (1999) identified three sets of issues to consider when examining the partnership relations involved in local tourism policy making prior to policy implementation. The first set of issues relates to the scope of each partnership—is there a representative group of stakeholders? The second set relates to the intensity of collaborative relations between the relevant stakeholders. How often do they meet or communicate? Finally, the third set of concerns relates to the degree to which consensus emerges among the stakeholders involved in the partnership. Opportunities exist for us to learn from these frameworks and apply them to partnership arrangements in ecotourism and sustainable tourism certification and accreditation programs.

Partnerships form for a variety of reasons that can be broadly categorized under products, research and technology, human resources, marketing and sales, infrastructure, and financing (UNWTO, 2002). For example, partnerships may be formed to create new products or services, pool resources, achieve economies of scale, and improve market efficiency. Partnerships can take a variety of forms and involve a number of partners, and according to the UNWTO there is no correct formula or model available to follow.

The KPMG Management Consulting and the Canadian Tourism Commission (1995) provided a useful list of issues that need to be covered in any partnership proposal based on clarity and transparency that are the foundations for positive outcomes:

1. Articulate the objectives for the partnership
2. Clarify the roles, responsibilities, and contribution of each of the partners
3. Select appropriate management and decision-making structures
4. Identify funding and financial arrangements
5. Develop a marketing plan
6. Clarify issues of confidentiality and ownership
7. Undertake evaluation of the objectives

Managing the day-to-day activities of the partnership is frequently where many fail. The UNWTO (2002), through interviews with tourism stakeholders involved in partnerships, identified key success factors and lessons learned from the partnering experience. The six key success factors were: clearly articulated, transparent goals and objectives; open and frequent communication; building capacity through continuous learning; indictors and measurement; adequate resources; and planning and risk management.

Partnerships in Sustainable Tourism and Ecotourism

The Brundtland Report (World Commission on Environment and Development, 1987) identified the need for partnerships between stakeholders as a key to implementing sustainable development. According to Bramwell and Lane (2000), collaborative approaches have the capacity to further the core principles of sustainable development. In the case of partnerships developed for ecotourism, according to Sproule (1996), they must also fit into systems that have been developed at regional and national levels. There are many opportunities for partnerships, including with organizations within the following spheres:

- Established tourism industry, such as tour operators
- Government tourism bureau and natural resource management agencies, especially park agencies
- NGOs

- Universities
- Other communities
- Other international organizations, public and private funding institutions, national cultural committees, and other similar groups

In the context of the UN Millennium Development Goals, in which tourism is seen as a community development tool (Bolwell & Weinz, 2008; Christie, 2002; Scheyvens, 1999), if partnerships are being considered, development must be sensitive to the requirements of many stakeholder groups, including tourism providers, public providers, and residents. According to Clements et al. (1993), partnerships must be struck to ensure that a high quality product is delivered and is based on the notion that tourism experiences rely on all aspects of the community. For developing countries where there are issues of poverty alleviation and primary health and education provision, partnerships generally offer the multitude of small ecolabels opportunities for cooperation, amalgamation, strengthening of the ecolabel "industry," marketing and promotion consolidation, economies of scale, having subsectors within a larger scheme, and extending the geographical area of the ecolabel.

According to Hamele (2001), the benefits of a joint or partnership approach between certification programs are fivefold:

1. Improved consumer recognition
2. Stimulates tour operators' use of an ecolabel
3. Makes it easier and cheaper for operators that work across a number of different countries
4. Encourages more cooperation and coordination among the range of ecolabels at national and regional levels
5. Provides a good example of best practice in tourist accommodations

In the case of Europe, for example, it has been suggested that the proliferation of subnational and national ecolabel schemes could benefit from the merging of schemes or the development of partnerships. There are two options: the first option is a merger of branding, such as two schemes that continue to run independently but then use the same label brand (e.g., Green Globe with the Danish Green Key). The second option is the takeover of a number of labeling schemes by one larger scheme (Hamele, 2001). Hamele discussed the potential of a European ecolabel for a common tourism market that calls for unified competition rules. For this to occur, prices and services should be comparable and consumers should have access to reliable information. A European-wide ecolabel could raise the profile of environmental issues among international tourism and encourage existing ecolabels to "harmonize," resulting in joint efforts.

As well as the opportunities for partnerships at a regional level, others have suggested there is potential for well-established, reliable, and well-recognized certification schemes such as Blue Flag and Australian Eco Certification to be integrated into global certification schemes such as Green Globe 21 (Buckley, 2002). Kahlenborn and Dominé (2001) suggest the future of ecolabels is the establishment of international ecolabels or certification programs that are likely to involve collaborative arrangements. They argue that globalization—with an increasing number of international tourists and the international nature of the tourism industry—warrants an international approach to ecolabels. Kahlenbom and Dominé identified a number of benefits to an international partnership approach to ecolabels. First, this approach offers economies of scale because it is easier to implement one global marketing strategy and is likely to have a greater impact on the demand side. They argue that international tourists are less likely to know about a local or national ecolabel scheme compared to an international one. A second argument for an international approach is the management and operational costs connected with ecolabeling. An international scheme is better able to cover a large number of service providers than a national or regional scheme; therefore, international schemes can offer lower fees and attract more companies. Finally, ecolabeling schemes in the tourism sector are attracting the attention of international bodies such the World Bank, UNEP, and European Union (EU) that are likely to support international schemes for the reasons just outlined. This latter trend suggests there are opportunities for supporting developing countries in establishing partnerships for developing and implementing certification and accreditation programs.

In terms of meeting the UN Millennium Development Goals, an international partnership scheme also is likely to offer more transparency and clarity in the labeling market, and thus increase consumer trust and awareness. A large scale and highly visible scheme is also able to attract more companies and have a greater impact on the tourism sector. Such schemes are also likely to create new markets by stimulating environmental awareness in national tourism markets that have not developed much sensitivity to environmental issues. From a financial viability perspective, a large scheme can be introduced into small or developing countries that could not afford to develop their own schemes. Although these schemes may be difficult to establish, this approach is likely to reduce the time and costs associated with the revision of national schemes. Larger schemes are also more able to provide ancillary services such as training, support services, joint marketing, and a lobbying voice for companies, and other advantages such as preferential use of Australian national parks by Eco Certified operators (Font & Buckley, 2001). A partnership approach also offers benefits of chains of custody; this means that companies buy from and seek out other certified companies. For example, a hotel would seek companies that are certified in other industries, such as those certified in the Forest Stewardship Council. However, this approach is not entirely new; for example, PAN Parks certification requires national parks to ensure that tourism operators located near the park comply with the park's conservation principles. Chains of custody also offer a marketing advantage because certified programs can promote each other, thus increasing exposure, strengthening their position, and reaching new markets.

However, there are some challenges associated with international partnership schemes because they are likely to involve a number of different actors. For example, the range of organizations may have different backgrounds and interests that may lead to the watering down of criteria, and, of course, close cooperation is necessary between the different organizations with appropriate structures and procedures. In addition, an international scheme needs to take into account the regional differences of environmental conditions because a large ecolabel may lose the specific features of a particular subsector of the tourism industry or geographic area. International schemes also are more likely to be misused by sectors in the tourism industry taking advantage of the geographical distances of time and space, such as misleading marketing of services.

The Partnership Model in Practice: Examples of Sustainable Tourism and Ecotourism Certification and Accreditation Programs

This section presents four certification and accreditation programs that use the partnership model at a range of levels: PAN Parks, Sustainable Tourism Certification Network of the Americas, Global Sustainable Tourism Council, and Global Partnership for Sustainable Tourism. The first program discussed is PAN Parks, a regional partnership of national parks in Europe.

PAN Parks

The Protected Area Network of Parks (PAN Parks) was developed by the World Wide Fund for Nature (WWF), various protected area authorities, and the Dutch leisure company Molecaten, which develops holiday villages across Europe. The concept of PAN Parks is to create "a network of wilderness areas with an international reputation for outstanding access to wildlife and excellent tourism facilities, combined with effective habitat protection and the minimal environmental impact possible" (WWF, 1998, p. 1). Discussed in detail elsewhere (Font & Brasser, 2002; Font & Clark, 2007), PAN Parks is an example of a certification program that offers an institutional mechanism to create and enhance partnerships at the local level. The partnership approach involves nature conservation organizations, travel agencies, the business community, and several local partners. All of these organizations have united their resources to form a network of large wilderness areas across Europe. PAN Parks' mission is to balance the protection of wilderness and tourism in Europe's protected areas. According to Font and Clark (2007, pp. 300–301), the network has four aims: to create a European network of wilderness protected areas, to improve nature protection through sustainable tourism development, to provide a reliable trademark that guarantees nature protection and that is recognized by all Europeans, and to involve local businesses in the development of a sustainable tourism strategy that forms a part of the verification process itself. In addition, PAN Parks is based on five principles:

1. Natural values
2. Habitat management
3. Visitor management
4. Sustainable tourism development
5. Tourism business partners

The first three principles apply to the protected area and its management body; it is the protected area that becomes a PAN park. Principles four and five set criteria for a suitable tourism development strategy and for participation of local partners. Tourism operators and businesses that are involved must genuinely support nature conservation; for example, a certain share of profits that tourism brings to the region is returned to the protected area, and tourism generated from the park must bring long-term benefits and jobs to the local community. The PAN Parks trademark is awarded to parks with exceptional nature and high quality tourism facilities that are balanced with wilderness protection, and to tourism business partners who contribute to meeting this aim.

The trademark also raises the awareness of visitors to the parks that their visit is contributing to the area's protection.

A partnership approach was adopted by WWF to develop the PAN Parks program as a sustainable development tool to promote conservation by emphasizing the benefits of sustainable production and consumption. "A key element of this partnership is assigning intrinsic economic value to nature preservation long term, rather than consumption of resources within protected areas" (Font & Clark, 2007, p. 301). According to Font and Clark, management tools used by the parks and their business partners are based on protection of ecosystem dynamics and systems that meet key performance indicators on visitor management, tourism strategy, and contribution of business partners. A key aspect of the partnership is that local communities located adjacent to the park benefit economically in a sustainable manner and in accordance with the natural values of the area.

The program aims to have four benefits: independent verification, strong marketing of the concept and certified parks, establishing a common communications approach towards those interested in green tourism, and creating partnerships with local communities and local/small-scale businesses to implement a sustainable tourism development strategy on a regional scale. The long-term aim is to expand the program throughout Europe to include protected areas that safeguard wilderness across the region.

In 2007, Font and Clark explored the ability of the program to deliver benefits to the PAN Parks applicants and also looked at the challenges for the organization, including the expectations and perceived benefits. A variety of program stakeholders were interviewed, and study findings provide some idea of the challenges and benefits of a locally based partnership approach for sustainable tourism certification programs. The benefits mentioned by the interviewees were two-fold. First were management benefits that help improve sustainability and quality of tourism product; second were marketing benefits, that is, additional business from increased exposure to international markets.

It appears from the study findings (Font & Clark, 2007) that this locally based partnership model has many benefits. For example, the management of PAN Parks has facilitated stakeholder relationships that reduce institutional constraints for tourism development, and increased cooperation between all partners has benefitted the natural environment and the local economies adjacent to the parks. In addition, the application process for PAN Parks has meant that the park and local businesses have worked together to develop joint plans and action programs, which did not happen in the past. More effective planning and development of local opportunities has resulted from the partnerships, creating a sound basis for the development of high quality ecotourism products. However, in some European countries challenges remain; for example, in Eastern Europe there is still suspicion of interventionist approaches and regulations. Stakeholder interviews also revealed that two-thirds of them believed there were marketing advantages to the program, in particular being part of an international quality brand.

Although many benefits were mentioned, some challenges were also identified. One of the most challenging aspects of the PAN Parks application is the need for a sustainable tourism development strategy based on a public–private dialogue and partnership. The benefits of such partnerships have been seen in other park contexts (Eagles et al., 2002;

Rainforest Alliance, 2003), where a key to successful certification of destinations is stakeholder collaboration. A key difference with the PAN Parks program is that partnerships are embedded in the certification criteria. Partnerships have been created that link PAN Parks Principle 4 (sustainable tourism development) and Principle 5 (tourism business partners). For example, in Oulanka National Park in Finland, the local PAN Parks group is responsible for formulating, implementing, and monitoring the Sustainable Tourism Development Strategy and for selecting and verifying business partners. The group encourages and monitors the selected business partners' adherence to a local set of sustainable practices that ensures authentic visitor experiences and high levels of environmental management. Importantly, the program recognizes cultural differences, and local PAN Parks groups can select their own preferred group structure. However, there are challenges of funding, participation, and limited mandates of the local groups.

Font and Clark (2007) suggest the most significant challenges relate to the management of collaboration and partnerships, especially where responsibilities for improvements are shared and where sources of impacts cannot be identified or managed. This is challenging because it involves collaboration among parks, multiple municipalities, and individual businesses. The program covers many countries across Europe, so there are also cultural, geographical, and linguistic challenges. The geographical diversity means that the standards are fairly generic and are applied at the local level by individual parks and the local verifying team; this process leads to different interpretations of the indicators (Font & Brasser, 2001).

However, PAN Parks is a good example of a locally based partnership approach to developing and implementing a sustainable development tool to promote conservation by stressing the benefits of sustainable production and consumption; however, it has problems similar to other certification programs such as its inability to be cost efficient and its reliance on external funding. To overcome the financial challenges, PAN Parks launched a new tourism model in 2009. The aim of the model is to create unique group packages by linking international tour operators with local businesses through incoming tour operators. In general, 7% of the package price is offered to PAN Parks, which invests this funding in its network. There are currently eight packages available through four international tour operators. Although it is too early to evaluate the success of the new tourism model, initial responses and support look promising, with an expected income to PAN Parks of 20,000 Euro in 2011.[1] PAN Parks is a good example of a certification program that has provided a mechanism to create and enhance local partnerships and networks, helping ensure the program's long-term sustainability.

Sustainable Tourism Certification Network of the Americas

Another example of a regional partnership is the Sustainable Tourism Certification Network of the Americas (STCNA) (Hamele, Kusters, Sanabria, & Skinner, 2007). This network was established in 2003 in response to a number of issues relating to existing nationally and locally based certification programs in the Americas. Issues included the proliferation of certification

---

[1] Z. Kun, personal communication, May 4, 2011.

programs and schemes, a lack of reciprocity and mutual recognition between programs, limited financial viability of programs, limited consumer recognition and penetration of programs, and finally the need for consolidation and harmonization of certification programs.

STCNA is a regional network of sustainable tourism stakeholders. According to Hamele et al. (2007, p. 464), "Regional networks can provide opportunities for harmonization of standards, which could lead to the development of an accreditation system for the certification programs, building consensus for developing, promoting and implementing best management practices, sharing information and building demand for an accreditation body." There also are opportunities for joint collaboration and marketing strategies.

The STCNA feasibility study consultation process with tourism stakeholders (Rainforest Alliance, 2003) identified the need for regional networks for information sharing, regional baseline standards, marketing, technical assistance, and training of small and medium-size enterprises in sustainable practices (Hamele et al., 2007). The STCNA is one of the components of the international partnership effort led by UNEP's Division of Tourism, Industry and Economics (DTIE); The International Ecotourism Society (TIES); Center on Ecotourism and Sustainable Development (CESD); and the Rainforest Alliance to promote integration of sustainability into tourism policies and improved tourism standards. The network brings together representatives from major certification programs in the region and other relevant organizations and consists of national forums that include members from each country in the Americas. Certification programs from North America, the Caribbean, and South America are included. The network aims to encourage dialogue among partners and act as a regional clearinghouse for certification information and technical assistance. The mission of the STCNA is to promote sustainable tourism in the region by strengthening tourism initiatives based on mutual respect and recognition, joint efforts, harmonizing systems, and sharing information and experience. Although the STCNA serves as a successful partnership model that can be replicated in other regions, it has challenges associated with creating common baseline standards across a wide range of ecological and geographic zones with a diversity of sustainable tourism enterprises.

Global Sustainable Tourism Council

The issues faced by the STCNA were recently addressed by the newly formed Global Sustainable Tourism Council (GSTC), a global initiative dedicated to promoting sustainable tourism practices around the world. Formed in 2010, the GSTC is a multipartnership initiative formed under the umbrella of the United Nations. More than 50 organizations from the public, private, and voluntary sectors and from the sectors of tourism, environmental management, and sustainable development have contributed to the work of the GSTC. The GSTC's mission is to improve tourism's potential to be a driver of positive conservation and economic development for communities and businesses around the world and a tool for poverty alleviation (The Tourism Company, 2011).

The GSTC has three key aims: to increase understanding of and access to sustainable tourism practices; to educate about, and advocate for, a set of universal principles that define sustainable tourism; and to generate markets for sustainable tourism. The GSTC has adopted a set of universal sustainable tourism principles and has used them to create tools and training to engage in sustainable tourism practices. It is anticipated this approach will increase the demand for sustainable tourism products and services.

Established under the leadership of the United Nations, the GSTC is part of the International Marrakech Task Force on Sustainable Tourism Development, which aims to support nations to green their economies, to help corporations develop greener business models, and to encourage consumers to adopt more sustainable lifestyles (The Tourism Company, 2011). Five priority program areas were identified: international standards, education and training, market access, destinations, and accreditation.

Core to the work of the council are the Global Sustainable Tourism Criteria, a set of 37 voluntary standards providing a framework for the sustainability of tourism businesses around the world (The Tourism Company, 2011). These criteria, launched in 2008, are the minimum requirements that any tourism business should aspire to meet to protect natural and cultural resources while ensuring tourism meets its potential as a tool for conservation and poverty alleviation. Through an extensive stakeholder consultation process involving more than 40 of the world's leading public, private, nonprofit, and academic institutions, thousands of worldwide standards were analyzed to distill the Global Sustainable Tourism Criteria (The Tourism Company, 2011).

The GSTC believes the criteria are relevant to all geographic areas around the world and many different kinds of tourism enterprises (The Tourism Company, 2011). Some of the certification schemes will be large-scale international operations or national schemes, some will have support from government agencies, and others will be small schemes covering local areas or particular types of tourism products. However, in the case of the certification standards, it is expected that they will be adapted to local and industry sector conditions to exceed minimum requirements of the accreditation program's criteria. The GSTC accreditation model involves the council engaging with certification bodies around the globe at international, national, or local levels. These certification programs will have their own sustainable tourism standards and certifying procedures, with some using national or regional standards. Once a certification scheme has been assessed and determined to comply with the GSTC standard and accreditation criteria, it will have the right to use the GSTC-Accredited mark alongside its own certification logo.

Global Partnership for Sustainable Tourism

The final example of a partnership in sustainable tourism is the Global Partnership for Sustainable Tourism (GPST). Like the GSTC, this partnership is a new arrival to the sustainable tourism field. Although it is not an accreditation or certification program per se, the GPST provides an important example of an international partnership that recognizes, promotes, and supports the development and application of quality assurance tools and mechanisms such as accreditation and certification.

The GPST owes its origins to the 2002 World Summit on Sustainable Development. Through a global effort to encourage sustainable consumption and production known as the Marrakech Process, a number of voluntary taskforces were created, including the Marrakech International Task Force on Sustainable Tourism Development. The GPST was created based on the concept and work of the taskforce. The objective of the GPST "is to mainstream sustainability into all aspects of tourism policies, development and operation" (UNEP, 2010, p. 3), and its vision is to be the leading international tourism partnership uniting the private sector, governments, academia, and NGOs to enhance sustainability within the tourism sector (UNEP, 2010).

The focus of this partnership is policy, projects, tools, and networks for all tourism stakeholders, at all levels. The creation of the partnership provides opportunities in three main areas: synergies, mainstreaming sustainability, and stakeholder engagement. The GPST aims to involve all tourism stakeholders around the globe including intergovernmental organizations, governments at all levels, destination managers, environmental and social organizations, and businesses. It is a United Nations Commission on Sustainable Development (CSD) Type II Partnership, which means it is a voluntary and multistakeholder initiative allowing all stakeholders to influence sustainable tourism policy and programs and, importantly, develop joint collaborative projects.

As of 2010 the partnership consisted of 18 national governments, 5 UN organizations, the Organisation for Economic Cooperation and Development (OECD), 17 international and business organizations, and 16 NGOs. The UN believes this partnership is a valuable means of progressing sustainable tourism globally. In the past, many initiatives were developed in isolation or duplicated, were not promoted, and lessons learned that could inform other initiatives were not transferred. Thus, the GPST aims to maximize opportunities for linking all tourism stakeholders to achieve sustainable tourism.

The partnership will engage in four main activities:

1. Implementing policy recommendations
2. Scaling up and replicating successful projects, publications, training materials, and tools in other regions
3. Developing new projects and tools that foster the implementation and monitoring of innovative management practices and technologies
4. Building networks and partnerships

It is anticipated that regional networks and resource centers also will be formed, such as the Central American Integration System, the Association of Caribbean States, and the Association of Southeast Asian Nations. Other potential networks that may become involved include the Pacific Asia Travel Association and the African Roundtable for Sustainable Production and Consumption.

The partnership's activities will support governments and tourism businesses in six key areas: policies, development and investments, capacity building, awareness and advocacy, implementation and monitoring, and delivery by 2013 (UNEP, 2010). It will seek to address problems in the tourism industry through seven thematic actions:

1. Promotion of effective policy frameworks
2. Climate change adaption and mitigation actions
3. Protection of the environment and biodiversity

4. Promotion of sustainable tourism as a means for poverty alleviation
5. Preservation of cultural and natural heritage
6. Assisting the private sector to adopt sustainable management practices
7. Integration of sustainability into finance and investment

The UNEP believes this global partnership will be successful because it takes a holistic approach, provides in-depth expertise, has a wide membership of tourism stakeholders, and focuses on tangible outcomes and that it will benefit all the stakeholders as well as the environment (UNEP, 2010). Although in its early stages, the partnership aims to mainstream sustainability into the tourism sector by enabling capacity development, implementation, and innovation to change.

Discussion

This chapter aimed to explore the role of partnerships in ecotourism and sustainable tourism certification and accreditation programs. The examples provided in the chapter demonstrate that effective partnerships can occur between organizations such as the GSTC and GPST, and programs can provide an institutional mechanism to create and enhance partnerships at a local level, such as PAN Parks. Partnerships offer many benefits as well as challenges. These types of collaborative approaches can provide opportunities and avenues for the tourism sector to address the fragmented nature of tourism, and there is now increasing interest in and use of partnerships at a range of geographic scales around the globe. Partnerships are widely endorsed by governments and public agencies in many developed and developing countries. As discussed in this chapter, partnerships between organizations such as the GSTC and STCNA offer many real and potential advantages for ecotourism and sustainable tourism certification and accreditation programs, such as cooperation, amalgamation, benefits of marketing and promoting ecolabels, economies of scale, and covering wide geographic areas. In cases where the certification program provides a mechanism for local partnerships, such as PAN Parks, the benefits also can include local and regional economic development, authentic visitor experiences, and an increased level of nature protection.

Although there are many benefits of partnership approaches, caution is needed because there are potential problems and issues associated with such arrangements. For example, it is assumed that the concepts of collaboration and partnership include notions of governance and the public interest, but in fact these may not exist (Hall, 1999). According to Hall, the predominance of narrow corporatist notions of collaboration and partnership in network structures may serve to undermine the development of the social capital required for sustainable development. He indicates that to fulfill the sustainable goal of equity, decision-making processes need to be more inclusive of the full range of values, opinions, and interests that surround tourism developments and tourism's overall contribution to development, and provide a clearer space for public argument and debate (Smyth, 1994).

Potential partners also need to be aware that although some partnership arrangements may be promoted as equal and interdependent, in reality different actors occupy different positions and hold different levels of power, and this power may be used to promote vested interests. Jamal et al. (2006) have argued that ecolabeling schemes allow strengthening of power structures and inequity, processes that should be avoided in the case of developing countries. Thus, for a successful partnership to flourish, equity of access to all stakeholders is necessary; otherwise, collaboration will be consigned to rhetoric.

In addition, any ideal collaborative or interactive approach towards the development of ecotourism or sustainable tourism accreditation and certification programs should involve as wide a set of stakeholders as possible, thereby attempting to meet the public interest rather than planning for a narrow set of interest stakeholders or private interests typical of a corporatist model (Hall, 1999). A collaborative approach should seek to balance the perspectives and opinions of nonindustry stakeholders with those of "experts" and industry stakeholders. Although this approach is more time consuming, it is more likely to provide a greater degree of ownership of the outcome and the process. In addition, this process is likely to establish greater cooperation or collaboration between various stakeholders.

The increasing use of tourism partnerships across the globe in the last 50 years suggests that quality assurance programs are benefiting from partnership approaches and can be used to assist in meeting and supporting the UN Millennium Development Goals. For example, in developing countries opportunities exist to potentially develop an internationally recognized tourism ecolabeling program that would help them on a pathway of environmentally conscious development and management (Sasidharan, Sirakaya, & Kerstetter, 2002). This could place these countries in a better position to capture the market of high-spending Western tourists; however, Sasidharan et al. outlined the following eight challenges to applying this international partnership approach to an ecolabeling program:

1. Countries vary depending on ecological, social, and economic resource conditions.
2. There is no conclusive evidence that ecolabels actually improve the environment.
3. Environmental education has not been found to stimulate environmentally responsible purchasing.
4. Ecotourists may not respond positively to ecolabel programs and those who market them.
5. The high cost incurred in running an environmentally sensitive operation, in addition to the cost of being part of an ecolabel program, may drive service providers' prices up.
6. The higher costs may dissuade ecotourists from supporting ecolabel programs and services, allowing the non-ecolabel service providers to gain at the others' expense.
7. There may be conflicts of interest among the various stakeholder groups involved in facilitating and running the ecolabel program, especially as it contrasts with the profit motive of operators.
8. The investment in technology needed to be a part of the program for service providers, while maintaining profit margins, would make it difficult for the firms to meet the high standards of the program.

According to Sasidharan et al. (2002), the foregoing would result in the emergence of large, multinational tourism enterprises as "environmental market leaders," thereby providing them with a marketing edge over small-scale enterprises of less-developed countries.

Although there has been increasing interest in and application of partnership approaches in tourism, there has been little systematic research on issues such as understanding motives for participation, identifying barriers to partnership formation and growth, characteristics of successful and failed partnerships, internal partnership processes, outcome-based assessments of partnership successes, and external impacts of these types of arrangements (Bramwell & Lane, 2000). Evaluating the success and achievements of partnerships is a difficult task because they can be evaluated on a number of different levels. Long and Arnold (1995) developed a useful framework to identify these levels to evaluate the performance of partnerships focused on environmental issues; however, we can learn from this framework and adapt it to the ecotourism and sustainable tourism field. They recommend evaluating partnerships on at least three levels: the improvement of environmental quality, the achievement of indirect benefits, and the effectiveness of the collaborative process.

Although some argue that certification and accreditation programs are politically charged and have an uncertain future, with debate over their utility, many promising partnership opportunities and initiatives exist to support effective, cooperative, and coordinated approaches to certification and accreditation and help to create and enhance locally based partnerships.

Conclusion

Partnerships at a range of levels have the capacity and potential to assist in meeting and supporting the UN Millennium Development Goals. Such arrangements have the facility to assist in creating a sustainable tourism industry, whether it is partnerships between organizations or providing a mechanism to create and enhance local partnerships. Partnerships have many benefits as well as challenges. Benefits of partnerships for certification and accreditation programs include cooperation, mergers, marketing and promoting ecolabels, economies of scale, and covering wide geographic areas; however, challenges include assurance of equity, power, transparency, and involvement of all relevant partners. Further research into the roles, processes, benefits, and challenges of partnerships is needed.

References

Bien, A. (2004). *A simple user's guide to certification for sustainable tourism and ecotourism.* Washington, DC: International Ecotourism Society.

Black, R., & Crabtree, A. (Eds.). (2007). *Quality assurance and certification in ecotourism.* Wallingford, UK: CABI.

Black, R. S. (2002). *Towards a model for tour guide certification: An analysis of the Australian EcoGuide Program.* Doctoral thesis, Department of Management, Monash University, Melbourne, Victoria, Australia.

Bolwell, D., & Weinz, W. (2008). *Reducing poverty through tourism.* Geneva, Switzerland: International Labour Organisation.

Bramwell, B., & Lane, B. (Eds.). (2000). *Tourism collaboration and partnerships: Politics, practice and sustainability.* Clevedon, UK: Channel View.

Bramwell, B., & Sharman, A. (1999). Collaboration in local tourism policy-making. *Annals of Tourism Research, 26*(2), 392–415.

Buckley, R. (2002). Tourism ecocertification in the International Year of Ecotourism. *Journal of Ecotourism, 1*(2–3), 197–203.

Bushell, R., & Eagles, P. (2007). *Tourism and protected areas: Benefits beyond boundaries.* Wallingford, UK: CABI.

Christie, I. T. (2002). Tourism, growth and poverty: Framework conditions for tourism in developing countries. *Tourism Review, 57*(1/4), 35–41.

Clements, C. J., Schultz, J. H., & Lime, D. W. (1993). Recreation, tourism and the local residents: Partnership or coexistence? *Journal of Park and Recreation Administration, 11*(4), 78–91.

Eagles, P., McCool, S. F., & Haynes, C. D. (2002). *Sustainable tourism in protected areas: Guidelines for planning and management.* Gland, Switzerland: IUCN.

Font, X., & Brasser, A. (2002). PAN Parks: WWF's sustainable tourism certification programme in Europe's national parks. In: R. Harris, T. Griffin, & P. Williams (Eds.), *Sustainable tourism: A global perspective* (pp. 103–118). Oxford, UK: Butterworth-Heinemann.

Font, X., & Buckley, R. (Eds.). (2001). *Tourism ecolabelling: Certification and promotion of sustainable management.* Wallingford, UK: CABI.

Font, X., & Clark, S. (2007). Certification of protected areas: The case of PAN Parks in Europe. In R. Black & A. Crabtree (Eds.), *Quality assurance and certification in ecotourism* (pp. 299–315). Wallingford, UK: CABI.

Font, X., & Epler Wood, M. (2007). Sustainable tourism certification marketing and its contribution to SME market access. In: R. Black & A. Crabtree (Eds.), *Quality assurance and certification in ecotourism* (pp. 147–163). Wallingford, UK: CABI.

Goodstein, C. (2007). Smart voyager: Protecting the Galápagos Islands. In: R. Black & A. Crabtree (Eds.), *Quality assurance and certification in ecotourism* (pp. 65–80). Wallingford, UK: CABI.

Gray, B. (1985). Conditions facilitating interorganizational collaborations. *Human Relations, 38*(10), 911–936.

Gray, B. (1989). *Collaborating.* San Francisco, CA: Jossey-Bass.

Hall, M. C. (1999). Rethinking collaboration and partnership: A public policy perspective. *Journal of Sustainable Tourism, 7*(3), 274–289.

Hamele, H. (2001). Ecolabels for tourism in Europe: The European ecolabel for tourism? In: X. Font & R. C. Buckley (Eds.), *Tourism ecolabelling: Certification and promotion of sustainable management* (pp. 175–188). Wallingford, UK: CABI.

Hamele, H., Kusters, N., Sanabria, R., & Skinner, E. (2007). Creating regional networks of sustainable tourism stakeholders: Europe's voluntary initiatives for sustainability in tourism (VISIT) and the Sustainable Tourism Certification Network for the Americas. In: R. Black & A. Crabtree (Eds.), *Quality assurance and certification in ecotourism* (pp. 464–488). Wallingford, UK: CABI.

Honey, M. (Ed.). (2002). *Ecotourism and certification: Setting standards in practice.* Washington, DC: Island Press.

Jamal, T., Borges, M., & Stronza, A. (2006). The institutionalisation of ecotourism: Certification, cultural equity and praxis. *Journal of Ecotourism, 5*(3), 145–175.

Kahlenborn, W., & Dominé, A. (2001). The future belongs to international ecolabelling schemes. In: X. Font & R. Buckley (Eds.), *Tourism ecolabelling: Certification and promotion of sustainable management* (pp. 247–258). Wallingford, UK: CABI.

KPMG Management Consulting & Canadian Tourism Commission. (1995). *Developing business opportunities through partnering: A handbook for Canada's tourism industry.* Ottawa, Canada: Tourism Canada.

Long, F. J., & Arnold, M. B. (1995). *The power of environmental partnerships.* Fort Worth, TX: Dryden.

Mandell, M. P. (1999). The impact of collaborative efforts: Changing the face of public policy through networks and network structures. *Policy Studies Review, 16*(1), 4–17.

Parsons, C., & Grant, J. (2007). Green Globe: A global environmental certification programme for travel and tourism. In: R. Black & A. Crabtree (Eds.), *Quality assurance and certification in ecotourism* (pp. 81–100). Wallingford, UK: CABI.

Rainforest Alliance. (2003). *Sustainable Tourism Stewardship Council: Raising the standards and benefits of sustainable tourism and ecotourism certification.* New York: Author.

Sasidharan, V., Sirakaya, E., & Kerstetter, D. (2002). Developing countries and tourism ecolabels. *Tourism Management, 23*, 161–174.

Scheyvens, R. (1999). Ecotourism and the empowerment of local communities. *Tourism Management, 20*, 245–249.

Selin, S. (1999). Developing a typology of sustainable tourism partnerships. *Journal of Sustainable Tourism, 7*(3), 260–273.

Selin, S., & Chavez, D. (1995). Developing a collaborative model for environmental planning and management. *Environmental Management, 19*(2), 189–195.

Smyth, H. (1994). *Marketing the city: The role of flagship developments in urban regeneration.* London: E & FN Spoon.

Spittler, R., & Haak, U. (2001). Quality analysis of European ecolabels. In: X. Font & R. C. Buckley (Eds.), *Tourism ecolabelling: Certification and promotion of sustainable management* (pp. 213–246). Wallingford, UK: CABI.

Sproule, K. W. (1996, April 12–14). *Community-based ecotourism development: Identifying partners in the process.* Paper presented at the Ecotourism Equation: Measuring the Impacts (ISTF) Conference, Yale School of Forestry and Environmental Studies, New Haven, Connecticut.

Stronza, A. (2008). Partnerships for tourism development. In: G. Moscardo (Ed.), *Building community capacity for tourism development* (pp. 101–115). Wallingford, UK: CABI.

The Tourism Company. (2011). *GSTC accreditation manual: A guide to the accreditation of sustainable tourism certification programmes.* Version 7.1. Ledbury, UK: Author.

Thwaites, R. (2007). The Australian EcoCertification Programme (NEAP): Blazing a trail for ecotourism certification, but keeping on track? In: R. Black & A. Crabtree (Eds.), *Quality assurance and certification in ecotourism* (pp. 65–80). Wallingford, UK: CABI.

Uhlik, K. S. (1995). Partnership step by step: A practical model of partnership formation. *Journal of Park and Recreation Administration, 13*(4), 13–24.

United Nations Environment Programme (UNEP). (1998). *Ecolabels in the tourism industry.* Paris, France: Author.

United Nations Environment Programme (UNEP). (2010). *The global partnership for sustainable tourism.* Paris, France: Author.

Wearing, S. (1995). Professionalism and accreditation in ecotourism. *Leisure and Recreation, 37*(4), 31–36.

Wearing, S., & Neil, J. (2009). *Ecotourism: Impacts, potentials and possibilities.* Oxford, UK: Butterworth-Heinemann.

Wood, D. J., & Gray, B. (1991). Toward a comprehensive theory of collaboration. *Journal of Applied Behavioral Science, 27*(2), 139–162.

World Commission on Environment and Development. (1987). *The Brundtland report.* Oxford, UK: Oxford University Press.

United Nations World Tourism Organization (UNWTO). (2002). *Co-operation and partnerships in tourism: A global perspective.* Madrid, Spain: Author.

World Wide Fund for Nature (WWF). (1998). *PAN Parks: Investing in Europe's future.* Zeist, Holland: Author.

The Global Sustainable Tourism Council

Erika Harms

LEARNING OBJECTIVES

- Underscore the impact of tourism on the Millennium Development Goals (MDGs)
- Introduce a framework for measuring and reporting on tourism's impact on the MDGs
- To understand the importance of a common language in sustainable tourism development
- To raise awareness of the Global Sustainable Tourism Council (GSTC) and its criteria

---

The tourism industry has been an undervalued player in helping to achieve the Millennium Development Goals (MDGs), a set of eight goals adopted by the countries of the world in 2000 to reduce extreme poverty by 2015. While a clear driver of job creation, issues such as gender equality and environmental conservation have been neglected. There are many important empirical reports on the positive or negative impact of tourism. However, to this date, no clear methodology or tools exist for this purpose. Reporting on the impact of tourism on the MDGs has been focused on case-based examples, and no clear measuring and reporting tool has been developed for this purpose.

The Global Sustainable Tourism Council (GSTC) was created in 2010 with the vision that tourism can be a driver of conservation, preserve destinations, and provide socioeconomic benefits for all stakeholders—owners, managers, employees, and host countries. Through the GSTC Criteria, the sector now has clear guidance on how to implement actions that will help attain sustainability and contribute to the MDGs. The GSTC will provide the mechanisms and tools to the private and public sectors with which to accomplish these goals. Its accreditation process will, for the first time, collect the necessary data to allow businesses to move towards a more sustainable direction, measure the concrete economic and social benefits of sustainability, and aggregate the data that will allow countries to report on the tourism sector's contribution to the MDGs.

Challenges and Opportunities

Tourism has the potential to support the accomplishment of the Millennium Development Goals. As the fastest growing industry in the world, it is an important contributor to economic activity, with a 5% contribution to world gross domestic product (GDP). In advanced and diversified economies, tourism is a comparatively small sector representing only 2% of GDP. In developing countries, however, tourism is an important pillar of the economy, representing over 10% of GDP, and even more in some least developed countries (LDCs).

The most visible contribution of tourism to a destination is the creation of jobs. Worldwide tourism is estimated to provide 6% to 7% of the overall number of direct and indirect jobs. According to the UN World Tourism Organization's (UNWTO) *Global Report on Women in Tourism 2010*, women have a higher uptake of jobs in tourism than in any other sector, and they average 50% of the tourism job force. Although the tourism industry is a staff-intensive activity, potentially employing a lot of people, it has some challenges in directly addressing poverty alleviation. It is very seasonal, particularly in areas that are activity and weather dependent like ski resorts, providing an unstable source of income for local workers. It also is conducive to immigration and displacement of local communities, particularly where wages are very low and labor is unskilled. Immigrant workers are drawn from other parts of the country or abroad, increasing pressure on the demand of goods and services. There also is inequality in the positions women occupy and the salaries they receive. A clear example cited at the launch of the report on March 11, 2011, is the case of Colombia, where 84% of the clerks and service workers are women; however, this percentage decreases to 45% in the professional jobs, according to Dr Louise Dr. Twining-Ward (UNWTO, 2010a).

The UN Environment Programme's (UNEP) Green Economy report (2011) suggests the world is moving towards a new economic paradigm that moves away from the current allocation of capital to one that considers the environmental risks, ecological scarcities, and social disparities. Such a model will automatically impact the MDGs. Although the UNEP report indicates small investments in sustainable practices will produce significant improvement in environmental and social indicators, until now there have been no global studies that support or refute these assumptions, yet data are fundamental to investment and policy decisions.

Tourism is growing at an accelerated annual rate; it is expected that by 2020, 1.6 billion people will travel and will have impacts on the tourist destinations. According to Myers et al. (2000), only 1.4% of our natural environment has more than 44% of all plants and 35% of mammals, birds, reptiles, and amphibians. These areas also house more than 1 billion people below the poverty line. Among the priority biodiversity hotspots are some of the most attractive and popular tourism destinations like the Caribbean, Mesoamerica, and the Mediterranean. How tourism develops in these regions will determine whether it is a threat to biodiversity and local communities or it facilitates conservation and poverty alleviation.

Although tourism presents an opportunity to achieve the MDGs, there are two distinct challenges (i.e., leakage and sustainability) that need to be addressed. As it is conducted today, tourism has not reached its full potential to influence poverty alleviation due mainly to leakage (i.e., the percentage of a tourist's expenditures that do not remain in the destination country). According to the UNEP (2010), only about 5% of the dollars spent by a tourist on vacation remain in the destination. For example, leakage represented 70% of tourist spending in Thailand, 80% in the Caribbean, and 40% in India. Leakage occurs because of the special requirements of travelers who are seeking to maintain an experience that would represent their own personal needs, encouraging food, equipment, and other product imports. Leakage also occurs because the capital is invested in tourism buildings and infrastructure. Particularly in developing countries, investment is sought at an international level, and when the investment is repaid it leaves the country. All-inclusive vacations are also an important source of leakage because they discourage travelers from consuming outside the hotel and supporting local economies. Sustainable tourism and the GSTC Criteria consider the actions that need to be undertaken to increase and improve the economic impact in the destination and the local communities.

Development in the tourism industry traditionally has not been sustainable, and consideration to ecosystems, biodiversity, and communities is a recent issue. Development was planned to suit increased visitation without taking into consideration its impact on a destination. In his address on World Wetlands Day (February 2, 2012), Ahmed Djoghlaf, executive director of the Convention on Biological Diversity, expressed that development has been a threat to the environment, but, if done correctly, it could bring great benefits. He had expressed tourism as the "devourer of landscapes," given the extensive impact on land use, local economies, and culture, but he now establishes a clear link to place and people to achieve the MDGs. The GSTC has recently launched the draft Global Sustainable Tourism Criteria for Destinations, which is geared to create the link between business and destinations.

The Global Sustainable Tourism Criteria and the MDGs

The GSTC Criteria are the minimum requirements that any tourism business should reach to protect and sustain the world's natural and cultural resources, while ensuring tourism meets its potential as a tool for conservation and poverty alleviation. The GSTC Criteria are part of the tourism community's response to the global challenges of the United Nations' MDGs. Poverty alleviation and environmental sustainability, including climate change, are the main cross-cutting issues that are addressed through the criteria.

The GSTC Criteria are the outcome of a global and multistakeholder initiative to achieve a common understanding of sustainable tourism. The GSTC Criteria are organized around four main themes: effective sustainability planning, maximizing social and economic benefits for the local community, enhancing cultural heritage, and reducing negative impacts to the environment. Although the criteria are intended to be used initially by the accommodation and tour operation sectors, they have applicability to the whole tourism industry.

The GSTC Criteria provide detailed, clear, and basic guidelines for tourism businesses of all sizes to become more sustainable, and help them choose sustainable tourism programs that fulfill these global criteria. The GSTC Criteria, particularly through sections B and D, enable businesses and governments to support MDG 1 to eradicate extreme poverty and hunger, and MDG 7 to ensure environmental sustainability. Furthermore, the GSTC Criteria will serve as guidance for travel agencies and consumers in choosing sustainable suppliers and sustainable tourism programs. Finally, the criteria provide a clear guideline for governments to establish national and regional policies based on the GSTC Criteria, recognize sustainable businesses, create procurement policies, and have guidelines for impact assessment of the tourism industry.

Supporting MDG 1: Eradicating Poverty

Several of the GSTC Criteria address different aspects of poverty eradication. Target 1A of this goal seeks to "halve the proportion of people whose income is less than $1 a day." With the tourism industry representing 6–7% of world employment, it can make a substantial contribution to meeting this goal. The GSTC Criteria address this target by considering direct employment through criterion B2, "employing local residents and providing them with training," as well as "ensuring adequate legal protection, including paying living wages," as stated in criterion B8.

Locally developed tourism builds on a wide resource base, allowing for a wide scope of productive activities to support the sector, ranging from basic goods like locally produced foods to services like tour guides. The GSTC Criteria promote indirect employment in local communities, incentivizing "purchase of local products and services" (criterion B3) and promoting "support of local entrepreneurs" (criterion B4). The tourism industry, through training and building capacity locally, can reduce migration and provide local communities with alternative sources of income to address seasonality.

According to the UNWTO (2011), there is a greater uptake of jobs by women, supporting Goal 1B, to "achieve full and productive employment and decent work for all including women and young people." The GSTC Criteria support this target through criterion B7 "ensuring the hiring of local minorities and women, including management positions." Given the trends of gender exploitation and abuse, from which this sector is not exempt, this criterion is complemented by criterion B8, "compliance with labor laws," and criterion B6, "addressing commercial exploitation of children and adolescents."

Supporting MDG 7: Ensuring Environmental Sustainability

The GSTC Criteria address environmental sustainability by establishing criteria to "maximize benefits to the environment and minimize negative impacts." MDG target 7A, "integrate the principles of sustainable development into country policies and programs and reverse the loss of environmental resources," has been integrated as one of the criteria's key pillars. The GSTC Criteria present actions for the industry, while the GSTC works with governments to adopt the criteria, develop policies, and support programs. GSTC criterion D1 addresses conserving resources through purchasing policies that favor environmentally friendly products and the measurement of goods, energy, and water consumption. Environmental resources can also be lost through environmental degradation; criterion D2 targets the reduction of pollution, particularly greenhouse gas emissions, waste water, solid waste, noise, light, and other sources of pollution.

The MDG goal of reducing biodiversity loss by 2010 has not been met. As stated previously, the impact of tourism on natural resources, landscapes, and biodiversity will depend on the type of tourism development. Construction has a direct impact on ecosystems, but long-term management and operations also impact the loss of biodiversity. On the other hand, tourism provides alternative sources of income to local communities that might otherwise poach or hunt in protected areas.

The GSTC criterion A1 addresses the impacts of design and construction of tourism buildings and infrastructure, demanding respect for natural and cultural areas while encouraging the use of appropriate local construction materials. Furthermore, through criterion A7, travelers are educated about their responsibilities and appropriate behavior in natural surroundings.

Biodiversity loss and conservation of ecosystems are addressed through GSTC criterion D3 from two perspectives: first, the use of biodiversity in tourism facilities, by discouraging captive wildlife and encouraging the use of native plant species, and second, supporting local conservation, particularly in protected areas.

Supporting MDG 8: Developing a Global Partnership for Development

The GSTC is a global membership council and serves as the international body for promoting the increased knowledge, understanding, and adoption of sustainable tourism practices. It is a global multistakeholder initiative with representation from diverse sectors of the tourism industry and multiple organizational types, with balanced geographical representation. Since its creation in 2011 over 100 members have joined the organization and over 2,000 actors have been actively involved in the process of creating and implementing the criteria. In the United States, 172 cities have endorsed the GSTC Criteria. In countries like India, Egypt, and Cambodia, the GSTC has supported multistakeholder national processes to integrate sustainability into tourism national policies.

Industry leaders recognize the potential of sustainable tourism to positively influence conservation and poverty alleviation. They realized that a strong, global, and multistakeholder partnership had to be built because one sector alone would not accomplish the sustainability mission. From the onset, the industry collaborated with academia, engaged governments to change policy, opened its doors to communities, and sought the support of nongovernmental organizations that could support the implementation of the sustainability mission. The recognition that sustainability, and with it the MDGs, could only be accomplished through public–private partnerships that involved civil society, has given GSTC its strength. Its open, inclusive, and consensus-building processes with wide stakeholder outreach have given it the credibility it requires to drive change.

Supporting the Industry

The GSTC can use the GSTC Criteria as the baseline to support the tourism sector to accomplish the MDGs by fostering increased knowledge and understanding of sustainable tourism practices, facilitating the adoption and promotion of universal sustainable tourism principles, building demand for sustainable travel and increasing market access opportunities, creating a knowledge sharing network on- and offline, and providing updated and relevant tools and information regarding sustainable tourism.

The GSTC has worked with many of its partners, including the International Ecotourism Society (TIES), Rainforest Alliance, Solimar International, and Adventure Travel Trade Association (ATTA), to develop tools that would aid tourism businesses to become more sustainable. Although a small percentage of hotels and tour operators have undergone the process of certification, the majority has not undertaken any sustainability program. The objective of the GSTC is to take businesses and walk them up the sustainability ladder by providing the necessary tools and rewarding them with recognition for their efforts. The process starts with a self-assessment tool that reviews the business's baseline, followed by an action plan. The business is supported by training materials and accompanied by an accreditation program that enables recognition of sustainable providers compliant with the GSTC.

Accreditation seeks to recognize standards and certification bodies that are credible, transparent, impartial, and aligned with the GSTC Criteria. In many other industries there is usually one certification program, whereas in tourism there are over 120, often creating confusion in the marketplace. This proliferation of certification programs is driven mainly by the local nature of tourism, with specific sector and regional needs. Although the GSTC provides an overarching language and a common understanding about sustainable tourism, the implementation of programs needs to be adjusted to local situations. The GSTC accreditation program will enable those local programs to exist and credible programs to be recognized, and will seek to promote the value of certification while reducing confusion in the marketplace, and still provide a common understanding through the GSTC Criteria.

The accreditation program will be supplemented by a market access program that enables the recognition of hotels and tour operators that meet both the accredited standards and the requirements of the GSTC. The information gathered through the accreditation program will feed into a mechanism that gathers and distributes information to distributors, retailers, media, and consumers that want to find or promote sustainable products. The value for an industry to work with GSTC lies in the opportunity to link retailers and consumers with sustainable travel choices through the common language established by the GSTC Criteria and through increased market awareness and incentives.

The Case of Fairmont Mayakoba

The Fairmont Mayakoba on the Yucatan Peninsula in Mexico is a tourist destination nestled in the heart of Riviera Maya. Working with the GSTC, the Fairmont Mayakoba has moved towards being fully sustainable while also protecting the surrounding habitat, flora, and fauna.

Sustainability was considered early in the planning of the project. The hotel was designed and built to protect the area's mangrove forests. During the hotel's construction more than 1,500 trees were relocated around the property's gardens. "One of the best things about joining the GSTC was how easy it was for our hotel's management to implement a sustainability program and measure progress toward our overall goals," said Lyn Santos, Ecology Manager at the Fairmont Mayakoba. "The GSTC also provided us with opportunities to get the word out about our sustainability programs, and gave our program legitimacy, to avoid the stigma of greenwashing."[1] Inside the hotel there has been significant progress on the natural restoration of the grounds, waste reduction, natural resource conservation, and sustainable food service.

The Case of Sabre Holdings

Sabre Holdings is a company that provides technology and management solutions to businesses and governments. Sabre provides a Global Distribution System and, as a company, has made a commitment to sustainability in tourism and travel that extends beyond reducing its own environmental footprint. It proactively promotes environmentally responsible and sustainable practices to the travel and tourism industry. Sabre is one of the founding members of the GSTC.

Sabre's commitment extends to the traveling public, showing leadership in promoting and educating customers about sustainable travel, encouraging its suppliers to engage in the programs and maintain rigorous standards to avoid greenwashing. Travelocity, Sabre's online portal, launched its Travelocity Green Hotel program based on the GSTC. This was launched before the GSTC accreditation program was established, and the directory works with second-and third-party verified hotels. The standards are selected according to their alignment with the GSTC Criteria and the ability to demonstrate verification. Today over 1,500 hotels participate in the program (CMI Green, 2010). The program will grow as other certifications align with GSTC.

Studies conducted by Sabre indicated that 59% of respondents seek more environmental choices (Latimer, 2011). However, in a different study conducted by PhoCusWright (2009), data suggested that consumers need to have information easily available, want standards they can trust, would follow a certification, and did not trust the brands. Certifications provide trust in brands, but in tourism the proliferation of certifications and labels and various levels of credibility create consumer confusion.

---

[1] Personal communication.

Supporting Governments

The Secretary General of the UN, Ban Ki-Moon, stated, "the MDGs are achievable when nationally owned development strategies, policies and programs are supported by international development partners" (Permanent Mission of the Republic of Suriname to the United Nations, 2010). The GSTC aims to engage with governments, and at the invitation of some host governments has worked in several countries to establish local processes that will lead to national policies on sustainable tourism based on the GSTC Criteria.

Governments have yet to take a stand on sustainable tourism. Although some national sustainable tourism development strategies and regulatory frameworks seek to incorporate sustainability, most of the efforts in this area occur at a state or provincial level. However, Europe, Australia, New Zealand, South Africa, and several other governments are showing active participation and leadership in this area. In the United States, 172 mayors led by those in San Francisco, Miami, and Baltimore adopted the GSTC Criteria in 2009. Building on the Roadmap for Recovery provided by the UNWTO (2010b), governments are asked to make tourism a priority in transforming the economy into a "green economy" by contributing to carbon-clean operations, energy efficiency, and generating sustainable jobs.

The GSTC Criteria have helped guide some countries such as Egypt in their efforts to establish regional or national sustainable tourism programs, drive certification providers to adhere to the criteria and become eligible for accreditation, allow distributors to recognize and promote sustainable services, and build the base for financial criteria that can guide financial institutions to invest in more sustainable project development.

Measuring Progress

In the future, the GSTC proposes collecting data from thousands of tourism businesses and eventually destinations through the use of voluntary initiatives and performance indicators. Collecting baseline data on key sustainability and economic indicators from certification programs and tourism businesses, before and after implementing the GSTC Criteria, will enable a permanent, ongoing impact assessment program and establish baseline data on greenhouse gas emissions, energy and water consumption, waste management, biodiversity conservation, and key socioeconomic factors. Subsets of the data should indicate return on investment (ROI) and internal rate of return on investments in infrastructure as well as corporate social responsibility (CSR).

The data will allow businesses and governments to establish adaptive management strategies for enhancing the positive and reducing the negative economic, social, and environmental impacts of tourism as well as to aggregate the data by country or region, report on impacts and changes, and demonstrate progress towards MDGs.

Most recently, the GSTC (2012) announced that Amadeus, Melia, Royal Caribbean Cruises, Sabre Holdings, and TUI Travel are among the first group of global travel and tourism corporations to publicly commit to promoting sustainable tourism products and services recognized by the GSTC. Each of these companies has committed to using the GSTC Criteria as the reference for sustainable travel.

The objective of the program is to recognize and reward genuine practitioners of sustainable tourism, which in turn builds confidence and credibility with consumers. The commitment from these organizations demonstrates their belief that sustainable tourism is an important component of their business practices and that the widespread adoption of sustainable tourism standards is relevant.

The GSTC also announced the first GSTC-Recognized standards:

- Bundesministerium für Land und Forstwirtschaft, Umwelt und Wasserwirtschaft (BMLFUW)'s, Austrian Ecolabel for Tourism (Österreichisches Umweltzeichen)
- Costa Rica Tourist Board (ICT)'s Certification for Sustainable Tourism (CST)
- Ecotourism Australia's Ecotourism Standard
- Ecotourism Australia's Advanced Ecotourism Standard
- Ecotourism Ireland's Ecotourism Ireland Label
- European Ecotourism Knowledge Network's European Ecotourism Labeling Standard (EETLS)
- Fair Trade in Tourism for South Africa (FTTSA)
- Instituto de Turismo Responsable's Biosphere Hotels
- Japan Ecolodge Association's Environmentally Sustainable Accommodations Standard
- Rainforest Alliance's Standard for Tourism Operations
- Sustainable Travel International's Sustainable Tourism Eco-Certification Program (STEP)

Each standard went through a rigorous review and authorization procedure and is considered equivalent to the GSTC Criteria.

This marks a significant milestone in the development of credible sustainable travel and tourism products. The GSTC-Recognized standards are the cornerstone and first step of a three-stage GSTC process. Stage 1 recognizes that a standard, which is a written statement that can be verified, is compatible with the GSTC Criteria. Stage 2, called GSTC-Approval, is the evaluation of the processes for certification to ensure they are transparent, impartial, and conducted by people with technical competence. The third and final stage is full accreditation (GSTC-Accredited) and will begin implementation in December 2014. To learn more about the GSTC Process, please visit the GSTC website (http://www.gstcouncil.org).

The GSTC will continue to work with standard owners around the world to provide GSTC recognition. An initial call for standard applications was successful, with almost 30 standards applying for recognition.

Conclusion

The tourism industry has a responsibility to assist in supporting and meeting the Millennium Development Goals. As the fastest growing industry and one that is represented in many countries, particularly in least developed countries where it is the main source of economic growth, tourism holds the key to poverty alleviation and conservation. However, the complexities of the industry, the diversity of actors involved, and the lack of understanding of more sustainable practices make achieving these goals difficult.

The Global Sustainable Tourism Council, mainly through the implementation of the Global Sustainable Tourism Criteria, can be the catalyst of change. The GSTC can provide guidance to those just beginning the journey to sustainability. It separates credible programs from greenwashing, it is developing the tools to support change, and it is creating market opportunities to recognize leaders in implementing sustainable practices. It also is working with governments at the local and national levels to establish and promote more sustainable practices.

The GSTC has proved to be an effective public–private partnership with global outreach and local impact. Adopted by some countries, implemented by industry, and recognized by the UN, the GSTC Criteria are clear guidelines to achieving the MDGs. Industry and governments should commit to the MDGs through the implementation of the GSTC Criteria and support of the Global Sustainable Tourism Council.

References

CMI Green. (2010). 2nd Annual Green Traveler Study 2010–2011. Retrieved May 1, 2012, from http://communitymarketinginc.com/cmigreen/docs/cmigreen2010_11.pdf

Global Sustainable Tourism Council (GSTC). (2012). The Global Sustainable Tourism Council. Retrieved December 10, 2011, from http://www.gstcouncil.org

Latimer, L. (2011, May 15). Presentation at the GSTC Annual Meeting, Barcelona, Spain.

PhoCusWright. (2009). *Going green: The business impact of environmental awareness on travel.* Sherman, CT: Author.

Myers, N., Mittermeier, R. A., Mittermeier, C. G., da Fonseca, G. A. B., & Kent, J. (2000). Biodiversity hotspots for conservation priorities. *Nature, 403*, 853–858.

Permanent Mission of the Republic of Suriname to the United Nations. (2010, Sept. 21). High level plenary meeting of the General Assembly on the Millennium Development Goals. Retrieved May 2, 2012, from http://www.un.int/wcm/content/site/suriname/cache/offonce/pid/22224;jsessionid=5A7F2400FD37F56D1EFF0141CDD42274

United Nations Environment Programme. (2010). *Towards a green economy: Pathways to sustainable development and poverty eradication.* Paris, France: Author.

United Nations Environment Programme. (2011). Economic impacts of tourism. Retrieved April 13, 2012, from http://www.uneptie.org/scp/tourism/sustain/impacts/economic/negative.htm

UN World Tourism Organization (UNWTO). (2010a). *Global report on women in tourism 2010.* Retrieved May 2, 2012, from http://ethics.unwto.org/en/content/global-report-women-tourism-2010

UN World Tourism Organization (UNWTO). (2010b). *Tourism and the Millennium Development Goals.* Madrid, Spain: Author.

UN World Tourism Organization (UNWTO). (2011). *UNWTO world tourism barometer*, 9(1).

The Protected Area Network of Parks: Monitoring the Balance Between Nature Conservation and Sustainable Tourism

Stuart Cottrell and Jana Raadik-Cottrell

LEARNING OBJECTIVES

- To understand the strengths and weaknesses of PAN Parks and the research network
- To understand the PAN Parks research process: Analysis of Perceptions and Attitudes (APA)
- To summarize key research findings on the benefits for the social, environmental, economic, and institutional contexts of nature conservation, tourism development, and the quality of life of locals
- To discuss lessons learned from the research process, and lessons for sustainable tourism development, park management, and PAN Parks

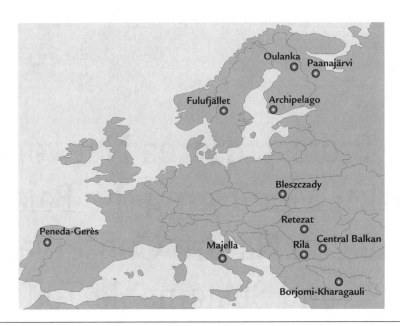

Figure 12.1 Certified PAN Parks in Europe.

Goal 7 of the Millennium Development Goals concentrates on ensuring environmental sustainability. In the spirit of this development goal, this case study illustrates a research process (Analysis of Perceptions and Attitudes) for enhancing parks and protected area management/conservation efforts via networks and standards of quality, with sustainable tourism playing a key role in that process. The Protected Area Network of Parks (PAN Parks) is a third-party certification system under the World Commission on Protected Areas (WCPA) Framework for Management Effectiveness. PAN Parks sets benchmarks for high standards in protected area management with the aim to protect European wilderness. PAN Parks (2010) defines wilderness as "an area of at least 10,000 hectares of land or sea, which together with its native plant and animal communities and their associated ecosystems, is in an essentially natural state." These areas represent lands least modified by humans, and represent the most intact and undisturbed expanses of remaining European natural landscapes (see **Figure 12.1**). As a network of 11 wilderness protected areas in Europe, PAN Parks provides examples of successful practices in wilderness management, working with local communities while offering unique wilderness experiences to visitors.

The PAN Parks project, started in 1997 by the World Wide Fund for Nature (WWF), was listed as one of the two most relevant management practices for Natura 2000 sites in Europe (DG Environment, 2001). PAN Parks was implemented as a means to encourage synergy between nature conservation and sustainable tourism in Europe's protected areas. The aim of PAN Parks is to change tourism from a threat to an opportunity by building partnerships with nature conservation organizations, travel agencies, the business community, and other groups on a local, national, and international level (Font & Brasser, 2002; PAN Parks, 2010).

To receive PAN Parks's verification (adopted in 2001), a park must meet five principles with the following specific criteria:

1. *Natural values:* PAN Parks are large protected areas, representative of Europe's natural heritage and of international importance for wildlife and ecosystems.
2. *Habitat management:* Design and management of the PAN Park aims to maintain and, if necessary, restore the area's natural ecological processes and its biodiversity.
3. *Visitor management:* Visitor management safeguards the natural values of the PAN Park and aims to provide visitors with a high-quality experience based on the appreciation of nature.
4. *Sustainable tourism development strategy (STDS):* The Protected Area Authority and its relevant partners in the PAN Parks region aim to achieve a synergy between nature conservation and sustainable tourism by developing and jointly implementing a sustainable tourism development strategy.
5. *Tourism business partners:* PAN Parks's tourism business partners are legal enterprises that are committed to the goals of certified PAN Parks and the PAN Parks Foundation, and actively cooperate with the local PAN Parks group to implement effectively the PAN Parks region's sustainable tourism development strategy.

The STDS (Principle 4), with its focus on nature conservation, is what makes PAN Parks unique compared to other sustainability certification schemes in Europe. The PAN Parks Analysis of Perceptions and Attitudes research has focused primarily on the impacts of Principle 4.

The PAN Parks Research Network

From its beginning in 1996, with the formulation of the principles and criteria, PAN Parks has cooperated with research institutes and universities. The successful integration of the theory and practice of sustainability is what distinguishes PAN Parks as an innovative concept. Following implementation in 2002, researchers from several institutions continued to commit themselves to PAN Parks's efforts and serve on the advisory council. Among them are representatives from Leeds Metropolitan University (United Kingdom), Glion Institute of Higher Education (Switzerland), the Professional University of Leisure Studies and Wageningen University for Life Sciences (the Netherlands), and Colorado State University (United States). In addition, graduate students from other universities have conducted research on behalf of the foundation at both verified and candidate parks. To ensure the quality of graduate research and the optimal contribution to problems faced during the implementation of the PAN Parks concept, a PAN Parks Research Network was created in 2003 to coordinate a research program. The research network was originally hosted at Wageningen University for Life Sciences.

This network consists of research institutes and universities in different countries in Europe and the United States. Most of the studies have been done on a volunteer basis by faculty in the research network, with the help of graduate and undergraduate students who for the most part pay their own costs to do the research. Thanks to this volunteer support, results in the form of reports, conference presentations, and journal articles have been useful to management and PAN Parks decision making.

The Research

An important part of the PAN Parks concept is cooperation with local stakeholders on implementation of sustainable tourism, in other words, the socioeconomic aspects in the context of ecological sustainability. These aspects have been examined by the PAN Parks research network since 2003, and several studies have been conducted. Some examples include the meaning of wilderness for Europeans, studies related to the verification process and the Sustainable Tourism Development Strategy, product development and financial mechanisms, collaboration, marketing, visitor management, and many others.

The PAN Parks Foundation argues that apart from improved protection and management practice, local businesses and communities benefit from PAN Parks status as well. Yet the socioeconomic benefits are less visible than those for conservation. After 10 years of implementation, the question became "Does PAN Parks certification provide the benefits promised?" The time had come for PAN Parks to monitor and document successful outcomes. Research efforts provide insight into the situational context (i.e., environmental, sociocultural, economic, and institutional) at several PAN Parks locations for comparison among the parks and to provide information for decision making and interventions useful to the foundation and park management authorities.

What Is the Analysis of Perceptions and Attitudes?

In 2005 the research network created a methodology to measure local perceptions of the economic, environmental, institutional, and sociocultural impacts of PAN Parks on the region around certified parks. This methodology is referred to as the Analysis of Perceptions and Attitudes (APA). A sustainability framework was adopted as the theoretical lens to guide the research process.

Prism of Sustainability

Figure 12.2 (adapted from Cottrell & Raadik, 2008a) shows those dimensions important to a holistic approach to sustainable tourism development (STD). STD is difficult to obtain without consideration of some aspects of the economic, social, environmental, and institutional dimensions of sustainability (Cottrell & Cutumisu, 2006; Eden et al., 2000; Spangenberg, Pfahl, & Deller, 2002). The *environmental dimension* emphasizes the need to reduce pressure on the physical environment (Mowforth & Munt, 2008; Spangenberg et al., 2002; Swarbrooke, 1999; Valentin & Spangenberg, 2000). The *economic dimension* considers human needs for material welfare (e.g., employment) in a framework that is competitive and stable (Roberts, 2002; Sirakaya, Jamal, & Choi, 2001). An economic system is

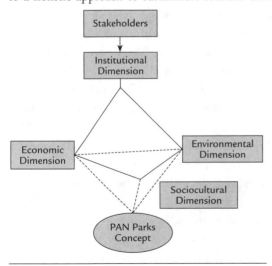

Figure 12.2 Prism of sustainability.

environmentally sustainable only as long as the amount of resources utilized to generate welfare is restricted to a size and quality that do not deplete its sources for future use. The *social dimension* refers to individuals' skills, dedication, experiences, and resulting behavior. Institutions (such as the PAN Parks network) represent organizations within a system of rules governing interaction among members (Choi & Sirakaya, 2005; Mitchell & Reid, 2001). The *institutional dimension* calls for strengthening people's participation in political governance (in this case the institution is PAN Parks, with STDS as the mechanism (Gunn & Var, 2002; Speck, 2002; Waldron & Williams, 2002). As acceptance of and identification with political decisions increase, public participation may be strengthened via empowerment and the ability to contribute to decision making.

As it pertains to PAN Parks, the starting point in the PAN Parks sustainable tourism concept is environmental sustainability, which links well with the environmental imperative found in the prism. Meanwhile, many nature conservation organizations understand that sociocultural and economic sustainability in a region with protected areas is important when it comes to nature preservation (Mowforth & Munt, 2008). Controlled tourism through planning and management can be an instrument for sustainable development and nature protection, providing nature with an economic value, and as such incentives for nature protection (Speck, 2002; Swarbrooke, 1999). Meanwhile, nature protection can lead to sustained environmental integrity, thereby providing sociocultural sustainability benefits (e.g., improving quality of life, maintaining natural/cultural heritage) (Waldron & Williams, 2002). In addition, careful planning, collective strategy formulation, and responsible management as part of the institutional mechanisms make it possible to minimize the negative impacts of tourism development while maximizing the positive impacts (PAN Parks, 2010; Shen, Cottrell, Morrison, & Hughey, 2009).

Valentin and Spangenberg (2000) suggest that the four dimensions can be linked to potential *indicators* (in this case, resident beliefs in the benefits of PAN Parks status). Sustainable tourism indicators developed in the context of the prism of sustainability over a range of studies (Choi & Sirakaya, 2005; Cottrell & Cutumisu, 2006; Cottrell, van der Duim, Ankersmid, & Kelder, 2004; Cottrell & Vaske, 2006; Shen et al., 2004; Sirakaya et al., 2001) have been applied in the APA studies.

Methods

The methodology is a process to gain insight into who the stakeholders are, in what way they are involved in (tourism) development in and around the national park, and in what way they perceive the four dimensions of sustainability (Cottrell & Raadik, 2008a). Several subquestions were included to measure general feelings about tourism development, and PAN Parks's benefit to local businesses, local communities, and sustainable development. In addition, questions addressed social change and perceptions of those changes, company involvement in the decision-making processes in the park region, and economic benefits for local entrepreneurs. Both PAN Parks's partners and nonpartners were included in the study, which consisted of two phases using a mixed methods approach (Creswell, 2009; Creswell & Plano Clark, 2007; Zeisel, 1997):

- *Quantitative phase:* Questionnaire with local residents
- *Qualitative phase:* Semi-structured interviews with different stakeholders

Quantitative Phase

The quantitative phase of the research sought information guided by the following eight secondary questions:

1. What is the profile of tourism stakeholders in the park region?
2. To what extent are tourism stakeholders familiar with the PAN Parks concept?
3. What are the benefits of PAN Parks status?
4. Who benefits most from PAN Parks status?
5. How important do stakeholders feel the institutional, economic, sociocultural, and environmental aspects of tourism are to the PAN Parks region?
6. To what extent are stakeholders satisfied with the institutional, economic, sociocultural, and environmental aspects of tourism to the PAN Parks region?
7. To what extent is local participation in sustainable tourism development evident?
8. Is there a relationship between PAN Parks status of the park and stakeholder satisfaction with tourism development?

Thirty-seven items representing the four dimensions of sustainability were used as indicators to assess beliefs about the benefits of tourism to the certified PAN Park. Both importance and performance scores were measured for each item for an importance-performance analysis to assess the gap between each aspect of sustainable tourism to the park. **Table 12.1** illustrates the average performance scores for those items used in studies at three PAN Parks locations in Poland (Bieszczady National Park, 2005; Cottrell & Raadik, 2008a, 2008b), Bulgaria (Central Bulkan National Park, 2006; Mateev, 2007), and Finland (Oulanka National Park, 2007; Cottrell, van der Donk, & Siikamäki, 2008; Puhakka, Sarkki, Cottrell, & Siikamäki, 2009, 2011). Ten items represent the economic dimension, and the social, environmental, and institutional dimensions include nine items each.

Importance–Performance Analysis

Martilla and James (1977) developed the Importance–Performance Analysis (IPA) method in the field of marketing to aid in determining ways to modify products and services to improve customer satisfaction. IPA has been used in numerous socioeconomic benefit studies as a means to monitor perceived benefits (Oh, 2000). Each item is measured for importance on a 5-point *not important* to *extremely important* scale and for performance via a 5-point Likert agreement scale from *strongly disagree* to *strongly agree*. Importance–performance action charts (see **Figure 12.3**) are then calculated per sustainability dimension as a means to visualize the gap between what's important to local residents and the perceived performance of each item. Interpretation of IPA is relatively simple, using four quadrants. Each quadrant is given a corresponding action strategy. The first quadrant (Keep Up Good Work) includes attributes stakeholders think are important and performing well. Quadrant two (Possible Overkill) includes attributes that are less important yet performing well; thus, management efforts toward these attributes can be reduced. Quadrant three (Low Priority) tells us that attributes falling in this quadrant both are low in importance and perform lower than average. For managers it means that little effort should be focused on actions influencing either

Table 12.1   Average Performance (Satisfaction) Scores for Aspects of Sustainable Tourism per National Park

Dimensions of Sustainability Statements[a]	Bieszczady $n = 43$ (average)	Central Bulkan $n = 92$ (average)	Oulanka $n = 315$ (average)
Economic			
Tourism to the park is a strong economic contributor to community.	4.03	3.61	3.56
Tourism to the park creates new markets for our local products.	4.00	3.89	3.48
Tourism to the park diversifies the local economy.	3.94	3.90	3.64
Tourism to the park brings new income to local communities.	3.94	3.79	3.57
Tourism to the park creates job opportunities for local people.	3.89	4.04	3.67
Tourism businesses should hire at least 50% of their employees from within the community.	3.77	4.36	3.64
The park contributes to increased value of local property.	3.53	–	–
Products and services have become better available in general from tourism to the park.	3.42	3.87	3.46
Thanks to the park, the region gained importance to the government, resulting in improvements to infrastructure (e.g., roads).	3.42	–	–
Prices of local products (food, medicine) and services increased from tourism to the park.	2.64	2.73	3.36
Institutional			
A long-term view is used when planning for tourism to the park.	3.81	4.24	3.54
Tour guides to the park are well trained.	3.78	3.58	3.57
Communities' residents have an opportunity to be involved in tourism decision making.	3.58	4.09	3.31
The park must monitor visitor satisfaction.	3.58	4.21	3.78
Participation in the development of tourism development plans is encouraged by local authorities due to the park.	3.28	3.30	–
Entrepreneurship in tourism to the park is encouraged by local government.	3.08	3.27	3.59
Tourism facilities are developed in cooperation with local businesses in the park region.	3.03	3.22	3.32
I can access the decision-making process to influence tourism development in the park area.	2.75	3.64	2.29
Good communication exists among parties involved in the policy/decision-making process of tourism to the park.	2.61	3.40	3.02

(continues)

Table 12.1 Average Performance (Satisfaction) Scores for Aspects of Sustainable Tourism per National Park (*continued*)

Dimensions of Sustainability Statements[a]	Bieszczady *n* = 43 (average)	Central Bulkan *n* = 92 (average)	Oulanka *n* = 315 (average)
Social			
My quality of life *improved* (deteriorated) because of tourism to park.	4.44	3.34	2.80
More people visit here because of the park.	4.42	3.78	4.23
Tourism to the park *decreases* (increases) criminal activity in the region around the park.	4.33	3.47	2.91
Visitors to the park are encouraged to learn about local cultures.	4.08	3.70	3.23
Local traditions become *more* (less) important because of tourism to the park.	4.03	3.57	3.52
Tourism to the park *positively* (negatively) influences norms and values in the area.	3.92	3.80	3.97
Quality of the environment in the community *increased* (deteriorated) because of tourism.	3.69	3.33	2.96
There are more educational opportunities for locals due to tourism to the park.	3.50	3.61	2.96
Women gain more economic freedom due to tourism to the park.	3.14	3.09	2.97
Environmental			
The diversity of nature at the park is valued and protected.	4.44	4.54	4.19
Good examples of environmental protection are shown at the park.	4.42	4.30	3.89
Tourism is developed in harmony with the natural and cultural environment.	4.39	3.90	3.73
As a result of the park, people's awareness of environmental protection has improved.	4.22	3.88	3.66
The park strengthens efforts for environmental conservation.	3.72	4.22	3.90
Tourism activity to the park is channeled into areas with suitable facilities.	3.58	4.00	3.84
Tourism to the park *does not* cause pollution of environment (water, soil, and air).	3.39	2.62	3.08
Increasing exhaustion of water and energy resources was *not* caused by tourist activities.	3.22	3.16	3.39
The number of visitors to the park results in *positive* (negative) impacts on plants and animals.	3.06	3.34	2.93

[a] Performance (satisfaction) measured 1 = strongly disagree; 2 = disagree; 3 = neutral; 4 = agree; and 5 = strongly agree.
Key: Items recoded to a positive direction as reflected by word added in *italic*; –, Item not included in the study.

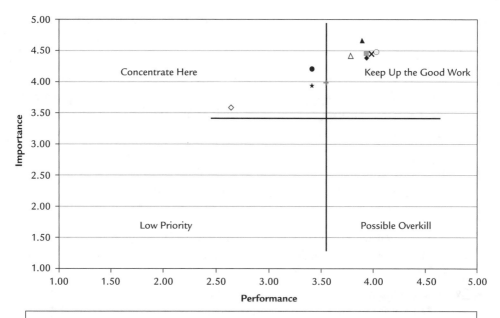

Figure 12.3 Sample importance–performance chart for the economic dimension.

the importance or the performance of the attributes in this quadrant because stakeholders have little concern for the items that fall here. Attributes that are very important to stakeholders, yet do not perform well, are found in quadrant four (Concentrate Here). Managers should focus on improving the performance of items falling within this quadrant.

Figure 12.3 is a sample IPA chart from the 2005 APA study at Bieszczady National Park. For interpretation of the economic aspects, three items fell in the "concentrate here" category. *Products and services have become better available in general from tourism to BNP* and *Thanks to BNP the region has gained importance for the government resulting in improvements to infrastructure (e.g., roads)* were important yet did not meet stakeholder expectations. Meanwhile, although the third item, *Price of local products (food) and services (educational) increased from tourism to BNP*, is in this category, apparently prices have not increased greatly; thus, this could actually be interpreted as a good aspect. Meanwhile, *BNP contributes to increased value of local property* is right on the borderline between "concentrate here" and "keep up good work."

The IPA analysis allows PAN Parks to determine which of the dimensions of sustainability are most important for each park as well as which dimension scores highest in performance (Cottrell, 2005). Such data allow the park to compare management actions against public perceptions about the park and to compare across the parks while taking the sociocultural context of the parks into consideration.

Qualitative Phase

The qualitative phase, which used semi-structured interviews, provides insight into the following topics (research questions are adapted as necessary for each study setting):

- What is your general opinion of tourism development in the region?
- Do you think that tourism development in your area is developed according to sustainable ideals?
- What do you think the role of businesses should be in promoting tourism to the PAN Park?
- Does the PAN Parks concept benefit businesses in the surrounding region?
- Does the PAN Parks concept contribute to local community development? In general and specifically?
- Does PAN Parks status contribute to open communication/cooperation between the PAN Park and local inhabitants? Please explain.
- What is the economic contribution of PAN Parks to your business or businesses in the PAN Park region?
- What is your opinion about the social-cultural contribution of the PAN Parks status to the local community?
- What is the environmental contribution of PAN Parks status to the local area?
- Are there any conflicts between the PAN Park and local people now?

The goal of the semi-structured interviews was to gain an in-depth understanding of the sociocultural and economic benefits of PAN Parks status for communities and tourism development in the PAN Parks region. The intention of the qualitative phase of the study was to link findings from actual semi-structured interviews from respondents who had completed the survey as well.

Development of the Research Tool

A mixed methodology, including a four-page questionnaire and a 15-question interview protocol, was developed and pilot tested at Bieszczady National Park (BNP), Poland, in 2005 with translations in Polish. Based on the pilot study, the questionnaire was simplified slightly and the interview questions reduced to 10. A PAN Parks methods manual was written as a guide to conducting similar studies in all certified PAN Parks (Cottrell, 2005). Baseline studies among all of the parks using a similar methodology allow the PAN Parks Foundation to compare data between parks and to learn from the different studies. The methodology will be repeated to measure changes in beliefs, opinions, attitudes, values, and impacts over time.

To date, the research has been carried out among residents and tourism-related stakeholders at BNP in Poland (as a pilot test in 2005; Cottrell, 2005), Retezat National Park in Romania in 2006 (van Hal, 2006), Central Balkan National Park in Bulgaria in 2006 (Mateev, 2007), and Oulanka National Park in Finland in 2007 (Cottrell et al., 2008).

Results

Providing detailed results from four studies is beyond the scope of this case study; thus, the most pertinent result highlights are provided.

Does PAN Parks Benefit Local Communities?

The answer is "to a slight degree for some people." PAN Parks status has some benefit (direct or indirect) for 25% of the sample based on beliefs concerning the more inherent values of PAN Parks status on quality of life and nature conservation issues (BNP in Poland). PAN Parks status is believed to enhance the quality of the tourist experience among those people who perceive direct or indirect benefit from PAN Parks status.

From the interviews in Poland, the park was seen as a major contributor to community development for the region. It creates jobs and attracts tourists to the area, thus it is considered the main attraction. One interviewee stated that,

> As I observe, the mentality of business owners is positively changing step by step. This is due to influence of Pan Parks in this area. Thus, "yes" you can say that Pan Parks has a positive influence in the region. More locals need to be aware of the PP concept and what it possibly brings to the park. More partnerships are developing and this is attributed to the last few years from STDS development and the work of the PAN Park contact person.

In Romania, interviewees clearly felt that PAN Parks contributed to environmental policy: "It is only through the criteria of PAN Parks that the environmental policies of the management plan are so well-thought-out and consequent" and "A management plan was set up in 2003; also because of the PAN Parks criteria we became very critical about conservation and environmental sustainability."

Meanwhile, for the sociocultural contributions, interviewees mentioned several examples such as education, funding, marketing, and guidance in management. They were especially enthusiastic about the educational programs and the guidance of the park employees in the management of the park. This was surprising because it seemed PAN Parks was not feasible; apparently PAN Parks is mostly known for its educational role in Romania. Interviewees mentioned that PAN Parks can play a major role in the success of Retezat National Park and that the foundation "cannot be missed anymore in the area."

The PAN Parks concept is not currently evident to all local residents due to awareness and visibility issues. Among the stakeholders, those most actively involved in tourism development were either PAN Parks partners, part of the local PAN Parks stakeholder group, or those who have participated in the STDS process. They see the potential of PAN Parks for Bieszczady NP in strengthening community development, especially if park administration follows the

Table 12.2 Beliefs in the Benefits of PAN Parks Status

PAN Parks Status Belief Statements	Poland 2005 (n = 43) % Stakeholders		Bulgaria 2006 (n = 92) % Residents/ Stakeholders		Finland 2007 (n = 315) % Residents/ Stakeholders	
	Disagree	Agree	Disagree	Agree	Disagree	Agree
PAN Parks status increases the value of the tourist experience.	19	48	4	70	9	67
PAN Parks increases the quality of life of the area for the local population.	29	50	12	56	24	28
PAN Parks status contributes to nature conservation.	6	85	3	80	5	75
PAN Parks status attracts more tourists.	13	56	7	62	6	75

PAN Parks principles. PAN Parks' visibility is an issue for all of the parks in this study. Overall, benefits of PAN Parks are still too early to assess in many countries researched thus far other than Finland; further visibility and extension of the sustainable tourism network is necessary.

What and Who Benefits from PAN Parks?

Several survey questions inquired about PAN Parks' status effect on the value of the tourist experience, quality of life in the area, contribution to nature conservation, and environmental values across four studies (see **Table 12.2**). Except for the Polish study, 67% or more of the respondents felt that PAN Parks status increased the value of the tourist experience. Meanwhile, 56% of the Bulgarian sample felt that PAN Parks status increased the local quality of life, followed by 50% in Poland and 28% in Finland. Seventy-five percent or more of the survey participants in all the studies felt that Pan Parks status contributes to nature conservation. Over half of the respondents (56% or greater), for all three studies, felt that the PAN Parks status attracts more tourists to the park because of the international reputation of PAN Parks.

Lessons Learned

Research Methods

The mixed methods applied in this study have thus far been adaptable to the different regions with lessons learned from each location.

Sampling Techniques

Sample methods include on-site self-administered surveys and mail surveys with follow-up mailings (e.g., postcard reminder). An email or online survey has not been trialed to date. An on-site self-administered survey was conducted in Poland and partially in Bulgaria and Finland, primarily directed towards PAN Parks partners and tourism stakeholders that also participated in the interviews. This approach was taken to corroborate findings between the questionnaire and stakeholder interviews. A mail survey with a postage-paid self-return envelope was carried out in Romania, Bulgaria, and Finland. An 80% response rate was gained from a convenience sample (n = 92) in the Central Balkan National Park region, Bulgaria. In Finland, a 31% response rate was achieved from a random sample of households in summer 2007. This is a moderate response considering the postcard reminder with its drawing for prizes; however, the modified mail survey approach (two mailings versus three or four) resulted in a response rate equivalent to other studies using a mail survey and postcard reminder only. In Romania, only a few returns were received; most of the surveys were completed on-site. The studies at both Retezat (Romania) and Central Balkan (Bulgaria) national parks were undertaken by master's students and can be considered as pilot studies with small samples. The study completed at Ou-lanka National Park, Finland, was the first study with a relatively robust sample and serves as a model approach for future APA studies. Researchers from the Oulanka Research Station, PAN Parks Foundation, and Colorado State University conducted the study as an interdisciplinary team, which represents the ideal approach for future studies.

What are some lessons learned? On-site surveys and mail surveys are costly, requiring trained researchers. Although a general methodology has been established, the expectation that park personnel will be able to conduct a similar study without technical assistance from the PAN Parks Foundation is unrealistic for a successful monitoring program.

Interviewing Techniques

In essence, the semi-structured interviews provided the most insightful information about the effectiveness of PAN Parks. Interview questions were modified according to the study site because of the type of interviewees, cultural context, and experience of the interviewer. Interviews were conducted in Romania and Poland using on-site native speakers as the interviewers with direct translation to English following the interview. In Bulgaria, the researcher was a Bulgarian; both Finnish and English speakers conducted the interviews in Finland. Interviews are meant to be voice recorded; however, in the case of Romania, interviewees were more open when the voice recorder was not used. Although a standard interview protocol is available, on-site conditions such as language, terminology, and interviewer experience must be considered to allow modifications.

Analysis

A larger sample provides more reliable results. However, several studies with small samples, such as Bieszczady National Park in Poland and Central Balkan National Park in Bulgaria, yielded valuable insights and recommendations for park management and the PAN Parks Foundation. Consistent results among studies allude to the value of the theoretical/analytical approach used to guide the research.

Data Collection

We found that the mail survey is the easiest way to collect information from larger samples. However, it is more expensive and is not applicable in all destinations. It is important that local people who have the confidence of the local population are involved in the study to create reliability and willingness for support, as was the case in Poland and Finland. Especially in villages and locations where people are very critical of outsiders or park representatives, a credible person with the trust of the locals has to help and/or conduct the interviews to gain reliable data.

Language

Surveys and interview questions must be translated into the local language and pilot tested to check for appropriate meaning. This means both the surveys and interviews should be conducted among local people to test for understanding, reliability, and validity. In Poland and Romania, for instance, a translator/interpreter was necessary because the researchers did not speak the local language. This is, of course, more time consuming and runs the risk of misrepresentation because of the translator's interpretation.

Timing

Study timing is crucial. Most tourism stakeholders are too busy in the high season, which varies among countries (i.e., winter is the low season in Poland but a high season in Finland). Site-specific activities such as berry picking, hunting season, or religious holidays also may influence resident willingness to participate in studies.

Interviewees

Background knowledge of the interviewees is essential because the semi-structured interview questions demand some background information. Interviewees are expected to understand the concept of sustainable tourism and to be informed about its benefits for business and tourism numbers.

Time and Costs

The total cost of a study with a mixed methodology is high. The number of person-hours increases quickly because of the time necessary to conduct interviews and transcribe the content of the interviews (a 1-hour interview = 3 hours transcribing on average) and entering survey data (5 to 10 surveys per hour) as well as analysis, interpretation, and report writing. Sample generation, labor, incentives, supplies and materials, travel, study duration, and other costs can be estimated based on the size of the sample population. The key to time and cost effectiveness and efficiency is local support and coordination. In Oulanka National Park, Finland, in 2007, for instance, 273 out of 908 surveys were returned and 40 semi-structured interviews were conducted, with an estimated cost of 20,000 Euros for volunteer labor, travel, materials, and sample generation.

The Researcher

An important point to consider is who will do the research. In some cases, interviews are best carried out by local researchers familiar with the culture and preferably with the local people. This approach avoids language barriers, and answers can be given on a confidence basis. When we worked in Romania with students who did not speak the local language we had the most difficulties.

In Bieszczady National Park, local stakeholders were pleased that a park staff member asked their opinions together with an international researcher. This approach provided opportunities for integration and greater exchange of information, which would not have happened otherwise. Data gained from the interviews have been very useful for the park staff. In addition, further information and local insights were shared between the interviewee and local researcher that were not specific to APA but provided an overall view of sustainable tourism development in the region. By conducting the research as foreigners representing PAN Parks or with third parties (i.e., students from foreign countries as volunteers) we risk losing valuable context-specific information because it remains with people not involved with the PAN Parks project on-site or with the national park itself.

Lessons for Sustainable Tourism Development

Is tourism marketing the park's responsibility for the region? People living around protected areas expect the park to serve as a magnet for tourists, and local expectations often are short term and too high. For instance, a study at Bieszczady National Park in 2003 (van den Berg, van Bree, & Cottrell, 2004) showed that local businesses expected an increase in domestic and international visitors to the park following its verification in 2002. Obviously unrealistic, such expectations led to local dissatisfaction and disillusion with PAN Parks.

Direct contact between local stakeholders and park management is necessary for an STDS to result in increased credibility of park management among locals. Local people may feel better informed about park-related matters and, in turn, be more committed to support management decisions.

Survey questions measuring the four dimensions of sustainability, in essence represent potential sustainable tourism indicators. *Indicators* are measurable manageable variables that reflect the essence or meaning of management objectives. Survey items have been consistent across research locations, supporting application of a sustainability framework to monitor resident beliefs in the value of PAN Parks, benefits derived, and feelings about sustainable tourism development. The next step in the research agenda is to create standards for the indicators. *Standards* are the minimum acceptable condition of each indicator variable. For example, what percentage of local residents need to be satisfied with each dimension to claim that PAN Parks has made a positive contribution to the local region? Development of indicator-specific standards is only possible with continued monitoring of tourism development.

Lessons for Park Management

The various studies described in this chapter provide insight into and understanding of the local situation among PAN Parks and provide data that may be useful for park management and tourism development in the region. Although most of the results are park or site specific, general findings show that local people feel it is important to be kept informed about issues and be involved in decision-making processes. Often opportunities exist for local participation, yet locals' awareness of or familiarity with those opportunities is limited. The need for improved communication from park managers with local communities has been a key recommendation in many of the studies.

Global trends suggest that people living close to protected areas tend to be dissatisfied with tourism development (Cottrell et al., 2008). The Oulanka National Park, Finland, study had similar findings in a location well noted for quality management, nature protection, and tourism development. This alludes to the importance of communication strategies and the goals of an STDS, which forces park agencies to look externally to the buffer zones and local regions.

Lessons for PAN Parks

The results show that local knowledge among residents about PAN Parks is very limited, as might be expected given the infancy of this initiative. Local people know about PAN Parks but not what the concept actually represents; disseminating this information will take time. However, in all the studies described in this chapter, local people's expectations are quite positive, especially regarding the environmental contribution of the PAN Parks certification, as well as sociocultural contributions. Although we do not claim cause effect, research (Cottrell et al., 2008; Cottrell & Raadik, 2008a, 2008b; Mateev, 2007; van Hal, 2006) consistently shows that when familiarity with PAN Parks increases, satisfaction and positive feelings among local people about tourism development in the region is higher than among those not familiar with PAN Parks. As beliefs in the benefits of PAN Park's increase, so do positive feelings about the various aspects of sustainable tourism in the PAN Parks region. We cannot claim that increases in satisfaction with tourism development and the various aspects of sustainability are only because of PAN Parks certification; however, study results allude to potential attitudinal changes that support the need for further research.

Local people have limited knowledge about PAN Parks Foundation activities to support their region. Improved communication and cooperation with the park agencies are key aspects of the foundation's criteria: the Sustainable Tourism Development Strategy (Principle 4) and working with local businesses (Principle 5). This type of work is done behind the scenes and will not be seen by local people as an outcome of the PAN Parks partnership. Although not important, this may deter local beliefs in the benefits or value of PAN Parks' contribution to local and/or regional development.

Conclusion

The APA process has only just begun, and the results encourage PAN Parks to seek more information such as: What is the situation in the other parks? How does the situation change in park locations over time? It will take time to determine whether PAN Parks benefits sustainable development in PAN Parks locations, and initial results provide benchmarks for further study. Based on the APA, valuable information is produced for potential investors, to satisfy board members, and to guide management of certified PAN Parks as well as defining focus areas and showing the strengths of the network.

Although cause effect of the PAN Parks concept cannot be claimed, perhaps those stakeholders familiar with the ideals supported by PAN Parks have a better understanding of what sustainable tourism involves; consequently, they tend to value the importance of the various aspects of sustainability more than those people not informed about PAN Parks. PAN Parks' primary benefit tends to be environmental sustainability, yet there is evidence that it also contributes to aspects of sociocultural sustainability. Institutional benefits accrue regarding the development of a sustainable tourism network via linking park policy and activities to local businesses and communities. Stakeholders value the PAN Parks concept, and this is likely to improve and spread to other stakeholders in the future.

Based on the qualitative interviews conducted among the various parks, PAN Parks certification contributes most to environmental protection and an improved community attitude about nature conservation. Sociocultural aspects for the community were noted as public outreach, environmental education, promotion of the arts, and sustainable development of the region. Open communication between the park and local communities received mixed reports, indicating a need for further awareness building by the parks among local residents. Based on the quantitative survey, stakeholders familiar with PAN Parks gave higher satisfaction scores for the cultural, economic, and environmental aspects of sustainability than those who did not know about it.

In a recent 3-year evaluation of PAN Parks, conversations with representatives of PAN Parks in Nordic countries, which might be expected to have the highest management standards and most well-resourced management teams of any wilderness protected areas in Europe, showed that even these sites have management issues that can be positively addressed by PAN Parks. In Fulufjället National Park, for example, there is no national/local verification of the high management standards required in Sweden. PAN Parks' verification provides that vital check as well as a potential lever for lobbying the County Administrative Board, which has significant responsibility for implementing management improvements under Sweden's devolved system (Jones, 2011). Results of Jones' online survey showed that the majority of respondents (91%) either strongly agreed (47%) or tended to agree (43.4%) with the statement:

> PAN Parks has a clear role and adds significant value to the work being done by others at national or European level to conserve wilderness areas in Europe.

One respondent to the online survey had this to say:

> PAN Parks is for me the only organization with visible results in its wilderness work. It delivered, and keeps the standard for wilderness work high. On top of this, it was able to collaborate with others involved in the area and greatly helped to develop EU wilderness policy and approach. (European Commission official)

PAN Parks, with its sustainable tourism development strategy process, is viewed as a driving force for sustainable development combining protected area concern for environmental protection with active involvement of tourism businesses. The PAN Parks Foundation continues to examine the benefits of PAN Park certification with studies at park locations in Bulgaria and Italy. Similar results found at Central Balkan National Park in Bulgaria and Retezat National

Park in Romania imply that PAN Parks status enhances resident involvement in tourism development, improved park management, and their belief in the value of nature conservation due to international recognition. Further and continual research is necessary, but funding is limited. Although depending on a predominantly volunteer research approach is not the ideal situation, the number of studies completed has been remarkable despite the absence of funding. However, to implement a successful monitoring program for PAN Parks, external funding for a more rigorous program of research is necessary.

References

Choi, H. S., & Sirakaya, E. (2005). Measuring residents' attitude toward sustainable tourism: Development of sustainable tourism attitude scale. *Journal of Travel Research, 43*, 380–394.

Cottrell, S. P. (November, 2005). *Report 1 of socio-economic analysis of PAN Parks: Bieszczady National Park, Poland* (PAN Parks Tech. Rep.). Fort Collins, CO: Colorado State University, Department of Human Dimensions of Natural Resources.

Cottrell, S., & Cutumisu, N. (2006). Sustainable tourism development strategy in WWF PAN Parks: Case of a Swedish and Romanian national park. *Scandinavian Journal of Hospitality and Tourism, 6*(2), 150–167.

Cottrell, S. P., & Raadik, J. (2008a). Benefits of protected area network status: Pilot study at Bieszscady National Park, Poland. *Journal of Tourism, 9*(2), 25–47.

Cottrell, S. P., & Raadik, J. (2008b). Research note: Socio-cultural benefits of PAN Parks at Bieszscady National Park, Poland. *Finnish Journal of Tourism Research (Matkailututkimus), 1*, 56–67.

Cottrell, S. P., van der Donk, M., & Siikamäki, P. (2008). *Results of questionnaire study 2007. Report 1 of Socio-Economic Analysis of PAN Parks: Oulanka National Park* (PAN Parks Tech. Rep.). Fort Collins, CO: Colorado State University, Department of Human Dimensions of Natural Resources.

Cottrell, S.P., van der Duim, R. E., Ankersmid, P., & Kelder, L. (2004). Measuring the sustainability of tourism in Manuel Antonio and Texel: a tourist perspective. *Journal of Sustainable Tourism, 12*(5), 409–431.

Cottrell, S. P., & Vaske, J. J. (2006). A framework for monitoring and modeling sustainable tourism. *e-Review of Tourism Research, 4*(4), 74–84.

Creswell, J. W. (2009). *Research design: Qualitative, quantitative, and mixed methods approaches* (3rd ed.). Los Angeles, CA: Sage.

Cresswell, J. W., & Plano Clark, V. L. (2007). *Designing and conducting mixed methods research*. Thousand Oaks, CA: Sage.

DG Environment. (2001). *Sustainable tourism and Natura 2000: Guidelines, initiatives and good practices in Europe*. Luxembourg: Office of Official Publications for the European Communities.

Eden, M., Falkheden, L., & Malbert, B. (2000). Interface. The built environment and sustainable development: Research meets practice in a Scandinavian context. *Planning Theory and Practice, 1*(2), 259–284.

Font, X., & Brasser, A. (2002). PAN Parks: WWF's sustainable tourism certification programme in Europe's national parks. In: R. Harris, T. Griffin, & P. Williams (Eds.), *Sustainable tourism: A global perspective* (pp. 103–120). Oxford: Butterworth-Heinemann.

Gunn, C. A., & Var, T. (2002). *Tourism planning: Basics, concepts and cases* (4th ed.). London: Routledge.

Jones, T. (2011). *PAN Parks 3-year evaluation: Final report* (PAN Parks Tech. Rep.). Györ, Hungary: PAN Parks Foundation.

Martilla, J. A., & James, J. C. (1977). Importance-performance analysis: An easily-applied technique for measuring attribute importance and performance can further the development of effective marketing programs. *Journal of Marketing, 41*(1), 77–79.

Mateev, P. (2007). Analysis of the benefits of PAN Parks: Central Balkan National Park, Bulgaria. Unpublished master's thesis, Wageningen University, The Netherlands.

Mitchell, R. E., & Reid, D. G. (2001). Community integration: Island tourism in Peru. *Annals of Tourism Research, 28*(1), 113–139.

Mowforth, M., & Munt, I. (2008). *Tourism and sustainability: Development and new tourism in the Third World* (2nd ed.). London: Routledge.

Oh, H. (2000). Revisiting importance-performance analysis. *Tourism Management, 22*, 617–627.

PAN Parks. (2010). Mission. Retrieved April 20, 2012, from http://www.panparks.org/what-we-do/mission

Puhakka, R., Sarkki, S., Cottrell, S. P., & Siikamäki, P. (2009). Local discourses and international initiatives: Socio-cultural sustainability of tourism in Oulanka National Park, Finland. *Journal of Sustainable Tourism, 17*(5), 1–22.

Puhakka, R., Sarkki, S., Cottrell, S. P., & Siikamäki, P. (2011). Socio-cultural sustainability of tourism development in Oulanka National Park, Finland. In: M. Nuttall, H. Strauss, & K. Tervo-Kankare (Eds.), *Society, environment and place in northern regions* (pp. 129–141). Oulu, Finland: University of Oulu, Thule Institute.

Roberts, L. (2002). Farm tourism: Its contribution to the economic sustainability of Europe's countryside. In: R. Harris, T. Griffin, & P. Williams (Eds.), *Sustainable tourism: A global perspective* (pp. 195–208). Oxford, England: Butterworth-Heinemann.

Shen, F., Cottrell, S. P., Morrison, K., & Hughey, K. (2009). Agritourism sustainability in mountain rural areas in China: A community perspective. *International Journal of Business and Globalization, 3*(2), 123–145.

Sirakaya, E., Jamal, T. B., & Choi, H. S. (2001). Developing indicators for destination sustainability. In: D. Weaver (Ed.), *The encyclopedia of ecotourism* (pp. 411–432). Oxford, England: CABI.

Spangenberg, J. H., Pfahl, S., & Deller, K. (2002). Towards indicators for institutional sustainability: Lessons from an analysis of Agenda 21. *Ecological Indicators, 42*, 1–17.

Speck, E. (2002). The Fairmont Chateau Whistler Resort: Moving towards sustainability. In: R. Harris, T. Griffin, & P. Williams (Eds.), *Sustainable tourism: A global perspective* (pp. 269–283). Oxford, England: Butterworth-Heinemann.

Swarbrooke, J. (1999). *Sustainable tourism management*. Wallingford, England: CABI.

Valentin, A., & Spangenberg, J. H. (2000). A guide to community sustainability indicators. *Environmental Impact Assessment Review, 20*, 381–392.

van den Berg, C., van Bree, F., & Cottrell, S. P. (2004, June 16–20). PAN Parks principles: Cross-cultural comparison—Bieszczady and Slovenski Raij national parks. In T. Sievänen, J. Erkkonen, J. Jokimäki, J. Saarinen, S. Tuulentie, & E. Virtanen (Eds.), *Policies, methods and tools for visitor management—Proceedings of the second International Conference on Monitoring and Management of Visitor Flows in Recreational and Protected Areas, Rovaniemi, Finland* (pp. 227–234). Retrieved April 13, 2012, from http://www.metla.fi/julkaisut/workingpapers/2004/mwp002-32.pdf

van Hal, M. (2006). *Results of semi-structured interviews: Retezat National Park, Romania* (PAN Parks Tech. Rep.). Wageningen, the Netherlands: Wageningen University, Department of Socio-Spatial Analysis.

Waldron, D., & Williams, P. W. (2002). Steps towards sustainability monitoring: The case of the resort municipality of Whistler. In: R. Harris, T. Griffin, & P. Williams (Eds.), *Sustainable tourism: A global perspective* (pp. 160–173). Oxford, England: Butterworth-Heinemann.

Zeisel, J. (1997). *Inquiry by design: Tools for environment-behaviour research*. Cambridge, UK: Cambridge University Press.

Conclusions

Ecotourism and Sustainable Tourism: Transitioning into the New Millennium with Future Opportunities and Challenges

Rosemary Black, Kelly S. Bricker, and Stuart Cottrell

This chapter brings together the key findings from the previous chapters and highlights the future challenges and opportunities for ecotourism and sustainable tourism's contribution to supporting and meeting the United Nations Millennium Development Goals (UN MDGs). All tourism stakeholders must be cognizant of these issues if ecotourism and sustainable tourism are to effectively and meaningfully assist in creating a sustainable tourism industry that addresses poverty alleviation, environmental sustainability, global partnerships, gender issues, primary education, and health. We also need to identify where information is needed to guide future research on the impact and effectiveness of ecotourism and sustainable tourism in contributing to the UN MDGs, to better inform policy, and to identify best practices. Lessons learned from specific case studies can be useful to identify best practices, which can be applied more widely, as well as poor practices. Future research needs are highlighted throughout this chapter.

Traditionally tourism has been regarded as a tool for regional and local economic growth and employment creation. However, in the past 10 years, its potential as a tool to address global-scale development challenges, such as sustainable development and poverty reduction, has been promoted by many international agencies, nongovernmental organizations (NGOs), national governments, and scholars. More specifically, these organizations and individuals have suggested that tourism has the potential to assist in contributing to the UN MDGs.

It is clear that tourism cannot address all the goals and targets of the UN MDGs, but it has the capacity and potential to be a tool or a partial solution to address many of the goals. In particular, tourism can play an important role in meeting the goals for poverty, environmental sustainability, developing a global partnership for development, and empowerment of marginalized groups and communities. The interrelated nature of the environment, the economy, and communities means tourism also has the capacity to contribute to meeting the other MDGs regarding child mortality, health, and education.

Many chapters in this text (Chapters 1, 2, and 3) suggest that ecotourism and sustainable tourism can be effective tools for conservation and sustainable community development; when correctly implemented they can provide tangible opportunities to promote and finance global goals of sustainable development, poverty alleviation, and environmental sustainability. Specifically, these tourism sectors have the capacity to provide positive benefits to conservation, environmental protection, research, and capacity building; provide direct financial benefits and empowerment of local people; and provide other tangible community benefits such as roads and potable water as well as intangible aspects such as preservation of culture and lifestyles. Although all of these benefits will assist in meeting the UN MDGs, we must seek to maximize the distribution of these benefits across communities. Ecotourism can also play an important role; increased community awareness about climate change, deforestation, and loss of natural areas means that more people are seeking tourism experiences that minimize their impacts and contribute to communities.

Poverty Alleviation

Tourism plays an important role in most developing, least developed, and small island states as the main and sometimes the only means of sustainable economic and social development, with effective linkages to other sectors such as agriculture and handicrafts. As a multifaceted industry that is comparatively labor intensive, it can play a key role in the economies of poor countries. The tourism industry is growing faster in developing countries than in developed countries, suggesting that it has the potential to meet the needs of the poor. Many policies, programs, and projects now focus on the role of tourism in development, and the benefits of tourism can be strengthened by deliberate policy intervention, validated by research.

Ecotourism and sustainable tourism have the potential to address UN MDG 1 related to poverty and hunger through direct financial benefits and employment, and via this goal can influence and contribute to other MDGs like health and education. Chapter 2 provides a good example of a private organization, Xel-Há in Mexico, contributing to a number of the UN MDGs including education, health, employment, and community development. However, the authors caution about the inclusion of social welfare within a business paradigm, suggesting tourism may not be an effective or appropriate tool to improve social welfare because it promotes dependency on private tourism organizations and may abrogate these responsibilities from government. The authors recommend more research on corporate social responsibility (CSR) in tourism, especially the barriers preventing companies from engaging in CSR.

Van de Mosselaer and van der Duim (Chapter 3) focus their discussions on the "fuzzy" nature of pro-poor tourism, which gives it its ideological power but also means the concept has been hijacked as a label for most socioeconomic interventions in tourism. They identify a number of fruitful avenues for future research, particularly the multidimensionality of post assessment of tourism's impacts on poor people's livelihoods, how and by whom pro-poor strategies are developed and translated into tourism practices, and what role research plays in these processes.

Some case studies have demonstrated that ecotourism and sustainable tourism can yield positive benefits to host communities but have expressed some caution. In Case Study 1 on tourism in Vanuatu, the author indicates that although it is unclear whether financial benefits are accruing from *naghol*-induced tourism, tourism still offers the best prospects for these host communities. Despite this optimism, a number of issues still need to be addressed, such as the need for proceeds to be equitably distributed, the need for the influence of cultural brokers to be curtailed, and community-based tourism (CBT) that respects traditional structures and at the same time maximizes equitable distribution of revenues. Although tourism can bring benefits to communities, it can be a paradox whereby it addresses poverty and marginalization but conversely promotes and strengthens traditionalism. Cheer recommends further research on the impacts of pro-poor tourism and on the processes of governance. Although Donohoe and Blangy (Case Study 2) suggest there is a "space of hope" for indigenous tourism, there are concerns that tourism may perpetuate economic dependency, cultural insensitivity, and social and environmental injustice and inequities, as well as disconnects between indigenous and nonindigenous values, experiences, and expectations.

Noakes and Carlsen (Case Study 3) explore the link between poverty alleviation and tiger conservation, indicating that one of the barriers to developing tiger-sensitive ecotourism policies is the lack of policy or mechanisms across the 13 countries involved in tiger conservation. Collaboration and cooperation (partnerships) are needed among the relevant countries to create a shared cross-cultural meaning of the concept of "tiger ecotourism" before any effective, achievable, and measurable policy can be applied to ensure positive benefits of ecotourism to communities and tiger conservation. Partnership opportunities exist between the private and public sectors to mobilize funding, ecotourism businesses, and local protected area management agencies (see also Case Study 8) to develop tourism infrastructure and experiences for ecotourists.

Many chapters in this text suggest that to avoid problems, careful planning is needed for implementing tourism projects in developing countries. Issues that need addressing include careful market research or business planning as part of the planning process, lack of access to finance, communication problems, corruption, and flight schedule limitations. Tourism should not be integrated into broad development plans as an add-on; there should be genuine involvement of local people in the destination areas because tourism may have an impact on the community's social and cultural fabric and on traditional activities such as hunting and the collection of firewood or water; the environmental impacts of tourism may threaten the long-term viability of tourism and people's livelihoods. Rather than a piecemeal approach to tourism developments to address poverty, a more strategic approach is needed by creating partnerships with the private sector; linking local people to opportunities in mainstream tourism, not just niche tourism; and assessing and addressing the main market blockages that limit participation of the local people.

Education, Empowerment, and Building Community Capacity

In Chapter 4, Spenceley and Snyman discuss the economic impacts of tourism in Africa, which include capital investment, increased yield per tourist, job creation, market linkages, commercial opportunities for small business, and diversification of markets. They identify a number of mechanisms to enhance the economic impacts of tourism, such as investing in marketing and promotion and promoting strong market linkages between the destination and source markets. Although tourism projects in Africa have sought to benefit communities, they have been unable to demonstrate success at any scale due to a number of problems such as developing tourism enterprises that do not have a market and failing to integrate pro-poor tourism into destination development. The authors suggest a more strategic approach to tourism that includes partnerships, value chain linkages, and capacity building. Partnerships are also important in Case Study 4, which describes how a private ecotourism operation based in Fiji has expanded its conservation efforts to include an educational community outreach program for schoolchildren focusing on the importance of conservation in supporting their communities and way of life.

A number of chapters and two case studies (Case Studies 5 and 6) in this text demonstrate that tourism can promote gender equality and empower women. These case studies demonstrate the tangible benefits of ecotourism to women in local communities. Moya's case study in Costa Rica shows how a small group of women acting as agents of change have gained empowerment and reduced poverty through a small-scale ecotourism project and have linked their project with other community producers, resulting in greater community benefit and empowerment. In Nepal, Chetri and Brewer Lama describe how a private women-owned-and-operated trekking company is breaking down gender barriers and opening up employment opportunities for rural Nepalese women as tour guides. They provide a useful list of strategies and mechanisms to ensure meaningful involvement of women in the tourism industry. However, more work is needed to ensure the involvement of women in the tourism industry using approaches that facilitate dialogue between development planners and tourism market representatives, create opportunities for partnerships between the private and public sectors to provide training and financial support for women to participate in tourism, reward and assist tour operators to promote the involvement of women in tourism, and increase the awareness among women tourism professionals and potential entrepreneurs.

Health, Welfare, and Well-Being

As previously mentioned, tourism has the capacity to address the health-related MDGs indirectly through MDG 1's poverty alleviation and other mechanisms. A number of chapters highlight that humans and tourism both depend on a healthy ecosystem. Loss of species and related ecosystems degrades the health and quality of life for local communities as well as the destination's tourism profile and potential. Using their ecological model of health promotion Schwab, Dustin, and Bricker (Chapter 5) demonstrate the complexity, interrelationships, and interdependence between humans and the natural environment that characterize health's symbiotic nature. Ironically, even though HIV/AIDS is a major global health issue, tourism professionals are reluctant to own up to the connection between HIV/AIDS and tourism because it might be bad for business. The tourism industry is therefore complicit in the spread of HIV/AIDS and opens itself up for criticism for not acting in an ethical or professional manner. The tourism industry has a moral obligation to protect tourists, staff, and host communities. In the case of vector-borne diseases like malaria, the combination of climate change and deforestation are exacerbating the spread of these diseases around the world. Although tourism is only one of many professional sectors that can address this obligation, the industry has an ethical obligation to assume a leadership role in mitigating the spread of these diseases. The tourism industry needs to work at an international level to collaborate and cooperate with other stakeholders to address these major health issues that will help meet the UN MDGs.

The tourism industry also needs to monitor and respond to the impact of tourism on the quality of life of host communities. In a number of Fijian villages, Bricker and Kerstetter (Chapter 6) found that although the communities were experiencing economic benefits from tourism, the local infrastructure was inadequate, creating environmental and social problems. However, using a quality of life indicator they found that at a relatively early stage of tourism development, the industry played a positive role in residents' perceived quality of life.

Environmental Sustainability

Tourism, especially ecotourism and sustainable tourism, rely on a destination's natural and cultural resources, which local communities also depend on for their livelihoods and quality of life. This is a critical issue in developing countries where communities are dependent on the natural resources for food, firewood, construction materials, water, and handicrafts. In addition, given the dependency of tourism on natural and cultural resources, it is essential that these resources are not depleted by tourism activities.

A number of chapters in this text highlight the important contribution of ecotourism and sustainable tourism in meeting the UN's MDG 7, environmental sustainability. Eagles's chapter (Chapter 7) focuses on the role of ecotourism in preserving natural areas and biodiversity. His chapter demonstrates that ecotourism plays a significant role in the conservation of natural areas in many parts of the world, and that the virtuous circle of ecotourism leads to a self-reinforcing activity of positive attitudes and site visitation. This visitation provides support for conservation in several ways—tourism spending can support local economies, and tourists may donate time or money to conservation projects and may lobby governments to support biodiversity conservation. However, key challenges to the link between ecotourism and biodiversity conservation are increasing energy prices, which will reduce travel, and the growing global population, which will put pressure on remaining natural areas.

Using the regional case study of the Great Barrier Reef Marine Park Authority, the chapter by Cater (Chapter 8) also reinforces the role of ecotourism and sustainable tourism in achieving environmental sustainability. This case study emphasizes the critical roles of engaging all stakeholders; having effective, adaptive management regimes, community support, and long-term vision; and the need to embed environmental sustainability in policies and programs.

Mehta's case study on sustainable tourism development on the small island of West Caicos (Case Study 8) highlights the value of sustainable master planning to meet MDG 7 by helping protect fragile ecosystems, support biological diversity, and contribute to local communities. This planning approach also can strengthen the protected area system and other off-park conservation areas. To assist in achieving environmentally sustainable tourism planning, development, and infrastructure requires partnerships between public and private sectors.

The potential of ecotourism to support species-specific conservation programs like sea turtle conservation is highlighted in Case Study 7. Although there have been limited successes, the full potential of ecotourism has yet to be harnessed on a wider scale. Ecotourism has been advocated in most international sea turtle conservation strategies and has the capacity to benefit local communities through revenue for conservation programs, alternative sources of income for local residents, increased community support for conservation, volunteer assistance, and raising tourists' awareness of conservation and sustainability. Data show that nonconsumptive use of sea turtles has greater economic, social, and environmental benefits than consumptive use. Partnerships between local groups and national and international organizations are an important component of these types of projects.

Climate change and its impact on tourism is an important issue raised in a number of chapters in this text (Chapters 4 through 9). Estimates suggest that tourism currently accounts for approximately 5% of global CO_2 emissions. If the current rates of CO_2 emissions are maintained, by 2035 emissions from tourism are projected to increase by 130%. Chapter 9, in particular, highlights that changing climate and weather patterns are already changing travel demand and tourist flows; this is impacting tourism businesses, host communities, and other related sectors such as agriculture, handicrafts, and construction. Ecotourism and sustainable tourism both are affected by and contribute to climate change. These nature-based tourism sectors are more exposed than other tourism sectors to the physical impacts of global warming, and also tend to be more energy intensive due to the remote destinations and more mobile travel patterns. These tourism sectors contribute significantly to climate change but also are vulnerable to rising energy and transportation costs. However, on the positive side, these niche tourists are generally environmentally aware and expect tour operators to be environmentally responsible.

Addressing issues of climate change has, to date, generally occurred at the local destination or operational level rather than at a global level—for example, transport between the destination and the source markets and altered travel patterns. However, a contradiction exists because although ecotourism may provide some positive benefits to the local community and environment, these benefits are offset by the sector's greenhouse gas emissions, which may adversely affect the local communities and environment. The example of Namibia in Chapter 9 demonstrates this conflict. Mitigation measures to address climate change are needed, such as carbon management as discussed in Strasdas's chapter (Chapter 9). Although climate change has been addressed through some environmental and tourism certification schemes and in the accommodation sector, these issues have not been considered more broadly across the ecotourism and sustainable tourism sectors. A strategy to address climate change in the tourism industry needs to consider a wide range of approaches such as technological and managerial measures, sustainable transport, and travelers' behavior mitigation. These types of strategies benefit global climate as well as tourism stakeholders through cost savings for companies, health benefits for consumers, and the environmental and social benefits for local communities. Collaboration and partnerships will be a key to the tourism sector driving a global response to climate change.

Developing Partnerships

A strong theme running throughout this text is the importance of collaboration, cooperation, and creating and supporting partnerships to address each of the MDGs. Partnerships, whether at a local, regional, national, or global level, have the capacity to assist in creating a more sustainable tourism industry that can help meet the UN MDGs. Partnerships can be between organizations at a range of levels, or provide a mechanism to create and enhance local partnerships such as the PAN Parks model discussed in Chapter 12 for research and monitoring. Partnerships have many benefits as well as challenges. The PAN Parks case study provides an example of a partnership approach between local tourism enterprises and protected area management agencies that contributes to environmental sustainability. Although the evaluation of this approach is encouraging, there is a need for more research and data to determine clearly whether partnerships such as PAN Parks benefit sustainable development in PAN Parks locations. Indeed, comparative data between PAN Parks also are needed. The data to date suggest there are institutional benefits such as the development of a sustainable tourism network linking park policy and activities to local businesses and communities, contribution to environmental protection, and an improved community attitude towards nature conservation.

As discussed in Chapter 10, volunteer tourism can contribute to developing global partnerships, and through on-the-ground project work can help meet the UN MDGs of environmental sustainability, health, and education. Volunteer tourism can help bridge the development gaps through involvement of multiscale, cross-sector partnerships at individual and interorganizational levels as well as local, regional, and global scales. In particular, it can facilitate learning among stakeholders that will break down barriers and foster more realistic project goals that will lead to more sustainably developed communities in developing countries and actively involve host communities in project planning and management. Partnerships through volunteer tourism have the capacity to promote sustainable use of natural resources and enhance ecosystem and cultural stability and resilience, and thus create sustainable communities.

The case study by Edwards, Galaski, and Dodds (Case Study 9) suggests that on-the-ground partnerships also play an important role in directly linking ecotourism operators with local communities, thereby providing tangible benefits to individuals and host communities by delivering a consistent volume of tourists to small businesses. Partnership opportunities exist through a number of mechanisms such as direct community-based tourism development, stimulating small business for long-term partners, and buying from community-based tourism organizations or local tour operators. However, the feasibility of a community-based tourism initiative needs to be evaluated using market-based data prior to funding and implementation, and partnerships must be established. Case Study 10 demonstrates how, through partnerships, the Global Sustainable Tourism Council (GSTC) can effectively address the UN MDGs. To date, Harms argues the tourism industry has been an undervalued player in helping to achieve the goals but suggests that the GSTC can provide the necessary mechanisms and tools, such as accreditation, to accomplish these goals. She cautions, however, that the complexities of the industry, the diversity of actors involved, and the lack of understanding of more sustainable practices make achieving this goal challenging.

Accreditation and certification programs are the focus of Black's chapter (Chapter 11), which explores how partnerships at a range of levels have been used to successfully develop, establish, and manage a variety of different ecotourism and sustainable tourism certification and accreditation programs. This collaborative approach can benefit such programs through cooperation, mergers, marketing and promoting of ecolabels, economies of scale, and covering wide geographic areas. Although a partnership approach among programs has the capacity and potential to assist in meeting and supporting UN MDG 8, issues such as equity, power, transparency, and involvement of all relevant stakeholders need to be resolved. Further research is needed to investigate the role, processes, benefits, and challenges of partnerships.

Some Final Words

Although many of the chapters in this text demonstrate that ecotourism and sustainable tourism currently are playing and have the capacity to play, a significant role in helping to meet the UN MDGs, one of the common themes throughout this text is the lack of sufficient and reliable data to accurately measure the impact and effectiveness of tourism in meeting and contributing to the MDGs. Demonstrating the impacts of tourism on the UN MDGs is challenging; however, there is a vital need for a critical analysis of the benefits, challenges, and impacts of tourism. Monitoring, assessment, and reporting of the impacts of tourism on the UN MDGs is a key research need so we can gain an understanding of the beneficiaries and their experiences, and have comparisons over time and space. In addition to more data, researchers also need to use consistent, reliable, and appropriate methodologies, collect longitudinal and baseline data, and undertake comparative studies. To improve the conceptual and methodological underpinnings of this research, the gap between different disciplines and between disciplinary research and the work of practitioners also needs to be bridged.

It appears that we are still a long way from being able to provide policy makers and funding agencies with the evidence for informed decision making showing that the benefits of tourism reach the poor; this is partially because policy makers and donor agencies have not accessed the data they need to inform better policy decisions. Until we have sound information based on comparative and longitudinal data, the question of whether tourism is helping to meet the UN MDGs remains largely rhetoric.

The literature suggests that tourism has not been given sufficient recognition by many governments and international development assistance agencies, despite its potential to generate economic, environmental, and social benefits and contribute to the UN MDGs. At a policy level, if tourism is to continue to be part of the economy of a nation, it must be integral to economic, sociocultural, and environmentally sustainable development and integrated into national development programs and poverty reduction strategies. At an operational level, partnerships and cooperation should be encouraged and supported between tourism stakeholders, especially in the public and private sectors, to ensure the necessary infrastructure to facilitate tourism development. There is a need to address leakages using appropriate methodologies to measure economic linkages, and programs must be established to reduce leakages and generate positive linkages with other economic activities in developing countries, such as agriculture, construction, manufacturing industries, or handicrafts production. There also is a need to support and implement capacity building at local destinations, including improved employment policies; expanded education and training opportunities at the general education, vocational, and professional levels; and dissemination of knowledge and good practices through enhanced knowledge management systems.

The tourism industry needs to acknowledge its contribution to climate change and take action to mitigate greenhouse gases, especially those generated from transport and accommodation activities. Tourism businesses and activities are adapting and can adapt to changing climate conditions by applying existing and future technologies to improve energy efficiency and gaining funds to support the tourism industry in regions and countries. International and national government policies need to integrate tourism into current and future actions regarding climate change. There is a need to facilitate and support funding for tourism development projects that contribute to biodiversity conservation and other environmental objectives. At an operational level, we need to promote to existing and future businesses how they can contribute to the UN MDGs. For example, to eradicate poverty, businesses can recruit locally, purchase local goods, support fair trade and poverty awareness campaigns, and provide in-kind funds and staff participation in humanitarian projects.

Ecotourism and sustainable tourism have the capacity to make a substantially greater contribution than they currently are to poverty alleviation, economic growth, sustainable development, environmental conservation, intercultural understanding, and peace among nations. However, an increased commitment by governments, tourism industry stakeholders, scholars, international agencies, and NGOs is required to monitor and evaluate the impacts and effectiveness of tourism in contributing to the UN MDGs. The push for economic, social, and environmental justice from community leaders, key national and international organizations, and others has inspired tourism stakeholders as well as a new generation of tourists who are demanding responsible tourism experiences, providing a solid and positive future for sustainable tourism to assist in meeting the UN MDGs. The tourism industry must continue to seek creative strategies to support the balance among the economy, the environment, and society. Meeting the UN MDGs is vital to a sustainable tourism industry, and all tourism stakeholders should take an active role in promoting and supporting the UN MDGs.

INDEX

PHOTO CREDITS

Title Page Courtesy of The International Ecotourism Society (2011) www.ecotourism.org;
Introduction, page xxi Courtesy of The International Ecotourism Society (2011)
www.ecotourism.org

Chapter 2
2.2 © Alfonso de Tomas/ShutterStock, Inc.

Case Study 1
CS 1.1 © Antenna International/ShutterStock, Inc.

Case Study 4
CS 4.3 Courtesy of Rivers Fiji; **CS 4.4** Courtesy of Rivers Fiji

Case Study 6
CS 6.2a © Viktorya170377/ShutterStock, Inc.; **CS 6.2b** © Volina/ShutterStock, Inc.

Chapter 5
5.1 © s-dmit/ShutterStock, Inc.

Chapter 6
6.1 © iStockphoto/Thinkstock; **6.2** © iStockphoto/Thinkstock

Chapter 8
8.1 Courtesy of Mahonia Na Dari (Guardians of the Sea) Conservation and Research Centre

Case Study 7
CS 7.1 © iStockphoto/Thinkstock

Case Study 8
CS 8.1 © Volina/ShutterStock, Inc.

Chapter 12
12.1 © miha de/ShutterStock, Inc.

Unless otherwise indicated, all photographs and illustrations are under copyright of Jones & Bartlett Learning.